D0773286

DISCARD

SHAKESPIRITUALISM

SHAKESPIRITUALISM

SHAKESPEARE AND THE OCCULT, 1850–1950

Jeffrey Kahan

SHAKESPIRITUALISM
Copyright © Jeffrey Kahan, 2013.

All rights reserved.

First published in 2008 by PALGRAVE MACMILLAN® in the United States—a
division of St. Martin's Press LLC, 175 Fifth Avenue, New York, NY 10010.

Where this book is distributed in the UK, Europe and the rest of the world, this is by
Palgrave Macmillan, a division of Macmillan Publishers Limited, registered in England,
company number 785998, of Houndmills, Basingstoke, Hampshire RG21 6XS.

Palgrave Macmillan is the global academic imprint of the above companies and has
companies and representatives throughout the world.

Palgrave® and Macmillan® are registered trademarks in the United States, the United
Kingdom, Europe and other countries.

ISBN-13: 978-1-137-28220-0

Library of Congress Cataloging-in-Publication Data
    Kahan, Jeffrey, 1964-
    Shakespiritualism : Shakespeare and the occult, 1850-1950 / by Jeffrey Kahan.
      p. cm.
    ISBN 978-1-137-28220-0
    1.   Shakespeare, William, 1564-1616—Criticism and interpretation. 2.   Literature
and spiritualism. 3.   Occultism in literature.   I. Title.

    PR2965.K34 2013
    822.3'3—dc23   2012034876

A catalogue record of the book is available from the British Library.

Design by Scribe Inc.

First edition: February 2013

10 9 8 7 6 5 4 3 2 1

Transferred to Digital Printing in 2013

To Estelle and Judy,

Whose Love is Beyond . . .

CONTENTS

Figures   ix

Acknowledgments   xi

Introduction   1

1   Shakespeare, Poet of the Impossible   17

2   Crypts and Crypto-Graphology   39

3   The Afterlives of the Authors   73

4   Furness and His Poetic "Spirit"   97

5   Knight Visions   123

6   Beyond the Academic Fields We Know . . .   149

Appendix A: Glossary of Spiritualist Terms and Techniques   163

Appendix B: A Note on the Spelling of *Spirit*   169

Notes   171

Works Cited   229

Index   253

FIGURES

2.1 Delia Bacon. By permission of the
Folger Shakespeare Library.   41

2.2 Ignatius Donnelly. Courtesy of the
American Antiquarian Society.   43

2.3 *Sonnet* title page, reinterpreted by Alfred Dodd
(Personal Collection).   63

4.1 "Dawning Light": The Spirits descending on the
Fox household, heralding the new age of Spiritualism.
Courtesy of American Antiquarian Society.   100

4.2 H. H. Furness. By permission of the
Folger Shakespeare Library.   105

5.1 G. Wilson Knight, Self-Portrait. By permission
of the Trinity College Archives,
Robin Harris fonds, P2996.   146

ACKNOWLEDGMENTS

My great and lasting thanks goes out to the following people and institutions: Maia Isabelle Woolner, Editorial Assistant, Palgrave Macmillan; Brittney Todd, Project Manager, Scribe Inc.; Brigitte Shull, Senior Editor, Palgrave Macmillan; Al Clark and the members of the Faculty Research Committee of the University of La Verne for selective course releases in 2010 and 2011 and for funds to purchase the Spiritualist images used in this book; Jackie Penny, Graphic Arts Assistant, Rights and Reproductions Coordinator, American Antiquarian Society; Sylvia Lassam, Archivist, and Robb Gilbert, Student Assistant Archivist, of Trinity College Archives, University of Toronto; Kate Welch, Information Assistant, Shakespeare Institute Library; Anne George, Project Archivist, Cadbury Research Library: Special Collections, Edgbaston, University of Birmingham; Georgianna Ziegler, Louis B. Thalheimer Head of Reference, Folger Shakespeare Library; Rebecca Oviedo, Image Request Coordinator, Folger Shakespeare Library; Kasia Drozdziak, Team Librarian (Services), Special Collections, Brotherton Library, Leeds; Sophie Kemp, Graduate Trainee, Special Collections, Brotherton Library, Leeds; Christine Faunch, Acting Head of Heritage Collections and Culture Services, Library and Research Support, Academic Services, Old Library, University of Exeter; Sue Inskip, Special Collections, University of Exeter; Nancy Shawcross, Curator of Manuscripts, Rare Book and Manuscript Library, University of Pennsylvania; Paula Brach, Senior Administrative Assistant, Cushwa Center for the Study of American Catholicism, University of Notre Dame; William Kevin Cawley, Archivist, University of Notre Dame; Helen Hargest, Archives and Imaging Coordinator, Collections Department, Shakespeare Birthplace Trust; Gene Melton, Editorial Assistant, *John Donne Journal*; Mrs. Olivia Anderson, former secretary to G. Wilson Knight, as well as her aids, Alex and Matt; Edward Pechter, Hannah Chapelle Wojciehowski, and Stan Stewart, for much-needed insight and friendship.

Shakespeare

"The 'true' name of a person, like that of any other object, is far more than a mere denotative designation, for men who think in categories of magic; it is the essence of the person, distilled from his real being, so that he is present in it once again."

—Martin Buber

Spiritualism

"The Science, Philosophy and Religion of continuous life, based upon the demonstrated fact of communication, by means of mediumship, with those who live in the Spirit World"

—National Spiritualist Association of Churches

INTRODUCTION

THE DATE IS APRIL 3, 1921. MIDTOWN Manhattan. John Armstrong Chaloner takes the stage of the popular Cort Theatre and reports to the audience that in the last month he has been "conjuring up spirits of the great departed." He claims that Shakespeare in his astral self appeared and presented him with a divine revision of *Hamlet*, in which "Ophelia will not [*sic*] longer be mad; there won't be any grave scene, Ophelia will drink poison when Hamlet and Laertes go about spitting each other on their swords, and the royal lovers will die happily together." Hamlet's last lines are now said while locking eyes with his soul mate:

> And now, my darling, may I turn to thee
> And bid thee farewell, ere we take our flight.
> Kiss me, my sweetheart, ere we leave the world[;]
> Alas. Too faint am I to salute thee.

The new dialogue continues:

> *Ophelia*—Now die I—happy—for—I—die with—thee.
> *Hamlet*—Together we ascend—to Realms—of—Bliss.
>   The rest is silence. [Dies.][1]

This revision stresses and expands upon Hamlet's intuition of an afterlife and confirms that, unlike his father, Hamlet will not suffer for his sins. Instead, he and Ophelia, despite his murders and her suicide, will now drift happily in "Realms of Bliss."

The new ending may simply express Chaloner's dissatisfaction with the original play, which he corrects with a *Romeo and Juliet*-like ending. Further, we might dismiss his report of Shakespeare's spiritual manifestation as the ravings of a lunatic. The troubled Chaloner had been involuntarily committed by his own family to a psychiatric hospital in New York in 1897—from which he then escaped. In 1899, he was tried *in absentia* by a New York court, which declared him insane and ruled that he should be institutionalized permanently. In 1909, Chaloner, still a fugitive, shot and killed a man, John Gillard, who had been beating Mrs. Gillard with a pair of iron tongs at the time.[2] After repeated petitions in several states, Chaloner was finally declared legally sane in December of 1919; 15 months later, he was talking to Shakespeare.[3] (Chaloner also boasted of communications with P. T. Barnum, Abraham Lincoln, and George Washington.) Certainly, the journalist reporting the events at the Cort Theatre did not take Chaloner very seriously. The sarcasm is sometimes sharp enough to slice cheese: "After Mr. Shakespeare's new [lines] had been read, Mr. Chaloner read a *threat* from him to have it produced."[4]

Yet reports that Shakespeare had returned from the dead in order to revise his plays along spiritual lines were not uncommon. In 1869, the Boston medium Lizzie Doten received Shakespeare's repudiation of Hamlet's famous, though spiritually hesitant, "To be or not to be":

> "To be, or not to be," is not "the question";
> There is no choice of Life. Ay, mark it well!—
> For Death is but another name for Change.
> The weary shuffle off their mortal coil,
> And think to slumber in eternal night.
> But, lo! The man, though dead, is living still.[5]

Doten's work became something of a sensation and went through 17 editions in its first year of publication. A decade later, Professor Henry Kiddle, the superintendent of New York City's school system, published *Spiritual Communications*, in which Shakespeare's ghost offers his apologies for not being spiritual enough on earth: "*how much* I might have done if my powers of talent had been directed by the beacon light of my soul's immortality."[6] Likewise, in Sarah Taylor Shatford's *Shakespeare's Revelations by Shakespeare's Spirit* (1919), Shakespeare states that he has returned from the Spirit Realm in order "to correct my work, which I long to do, and to pay for this service rendered by this medium [Shatford], by helping her with her work, which is to help others."[7] Similar Shakespeare sightings, as this book will catalogue, were reported in London, Paris, Melbourne, and Cape Town.

Moreover, Shakespeare's prosopopeial appearances were very serious and terrifically affirming news to practitioners of a new religious movement: Spiritualism. Adherents included political elites (Queen Victoria, Abraham Lincoln, Tsar Alexander III); famous authors (Sir Arthur Conan Doyle, Sir Edward Bulwer-Lytton, Victor Hugo); and academics too numerous to mention.[8] Their numbers were dwarfed by ordinary citizens—estimated at 100 million Spiritualists worldwide; 11 million in America alone—who practiced or believed in its tenets.[9] But, for the purposes of this study, the most important of all Spiritualists was not alive, at least not in the corporeal sense. He was William Shakespeare, who, in 1874, declared himself to be Spiritualism's (still-active) apostle:

> I am quite overjoyed to return to the earth to provide confirmation of the belief which was the chief consolation of my so troubled life. Yes, I was a spiritualist . . . The hope that my works might endow spiritualists with some moral support aroused my greatest delight. If you had summoned me before, I would have deemed it my duty to appear at your bidding, for every spiritualist is my brother.[10]

Over the last three decades or so, Spiritualism has become something of a hot topic to historians, but most Shakespeareans remain befuddled and, frankly, a bit embarrassed by the theological.[11] As an example, we may turn to Ewan Fernie, editor of the collection *Spiritual Shakespeares* (2005), who tongue-twistingly explains that "spirituality is (or purports to be) the experience or knowledge of what is other and is ultimate, and the sense of identity and 'mission' that may arise from or be vested in that experience."[12] It's difficult to conceive of a less religious definition of spirituality.

Fernie's linguistic discomfort is by no means uncommon. As Courtney Lehmann (2002) observes, a good deal of recent discourse in Shakespeare Studies centers on the paradox of killing "the Author without giving up the ghost."[13] Lehmann here invokes the French Aloeidai: Roland Barthes (1968)—who argued that the death of the author signals the ends of the "author-God" and the release of the text from its "single 'theological' meaning"—and Michel Foucault (1969)—who argued that the "author does not precede the works"; rather, the work is made from the "decomposition" of other works.[14] Yet declaring the death of the author in favor of the continuous (hence eternal) generation of textual meaning merely shifts the immortal component from author to text. Likewise, even if we were to accept that Foucault was being nonliteral, his declaration still strikes me as theistic: if the "author does not precede" his works, then, literally and logically speaking, the works must precede the author. The King James version of John 1:1 makes a similar claim: "In the beginning was the Word."

I am not here suggesting that Barthes and Foucault were closeted Spiritualists or even religious but merely that their treatments of authorship and influence often rely syncretically upon nonsecular discourse. This aspect of my argument has been anticipated, albeit in a scientific rather than humanistic form, by Paul Adrien Maurice Dirac, who, in *The Principles of Quantum Mechanics* (1930), asserted that reality is no more accessible in mathematical codes than it is in spoken languages: "[Nature's] fundamental laws do not govern the world as it appears in our mental picture in any very direct way, but instead they control a substratum of which we cannot form a mental picture without introducing irrelevancies."[15] If this is correct, then the intersection of literary criticism and Spiritualist faith is merely a case of "irrelevancies"—two languages speaking past each other.

However, the aforementioned borrowings suggest that Spiritualists used Shakespeare as a way of discussing the otherwise inexpressible; likewise, present-day Shakespeare scholars often use Spiritualist expressions for much the same ineffable purpose. Thus Margreta de Grazia and Peter Stallybrass (1993) argue that Shakespeare is "a problematic category, based on a metaphysics of origin and presence that poststructuralism has taught us to suspect" but, absent of any ideological misgivings, then refer to him as a "ghostly thing."[16] Michael D. Bristol (1996), while attempting to locate Shakespearean meaning in a variety of historical contexts, admits that Shakespeare has "neither linguistic boundaries nor temporal limitations."[17] Charles H. Frey (1999) writes that Shakespeare's art is "alive—shining before death"; Shakespeare, defying mortality, "drives ideas through time, abstractions through concretions, language through gesture, content through form, mind through body, spirit through sense."[18] Terence Hawkes (2002), troubled by the identical issue of Shakespeare's stubborn transhistoricity, likewise relies on language that might have come from any number of Spiritualist texts: "at their most compelling, literary works do seem able to break free of the past, to leap across the centuries and speak directly to us, face to face, about matters of universal moment. They do so, it is said, by virtue of their access to a sphere that manages somehow to float freely above and beyond the material dimensions of time and place."[19] The imaginative and miraculous likewise fuse in Stephen Greenblatt's (2004) description of Shakespeare's theatrical power: a "magical, virtually nonhuman element," which "[Shakespeare] associated with the power of the imagination to lift itself away from the constraints of reality."[20] Even Eric S. Mallin, author of *Godless Shakespeare* (2007), can't help but exalt his supposedly atheistic idol: in our experience of Shakespeare's tragedies, "religious faith . . . pours into theatrical experience," and "our choral psychopomp becomes the only true redeemer of the play, capable authorially of constructing redemption."[21]

As anyone engaged in the field knows, Shakespeare Studies is an extensive territory of sometimes invidious debate. Short quotations from a variety of Shakespeare scholars may give us an inaccurate impression, and some necessary modification and correlation will be provided in the following paragraph. In transit, we may note that in terms of the aforementioned narrative clippings, none of these Shakespeare scholars admits to a belief in an actual Shakespearean ghost or in the occult.[22] Furthermore, we can straightforwardly acknowledge that the tone and tenor of their writings are wholly different from, say, that of bestselling author and unabashed bardolater Harold Bloom, who relates Shakespeare's artistic creations to the poet's "authentic spirit or breath," which "transmutes matter into imagination."[23] Bloom also raises (lets slip?) the possibility that Shakespeare was aided by Spirits, when he discusses the etymology of *genius*, which includes, from the Latin, "an attendant spirit for each person or place."[24] Bloom's uncertainty here between creator and conduit is not a matter of impoverished prose or superficial thinking. A more eloquent or polemical critic can scarcely be imagined. Rather, the seemingly ineluctable drift to the transubstantial is itself symptomatic of a wider cultural issue affecting Shakespeare Studies: the ways in which scholars, in the absence of theater manuscripts, diaries, or other material evidence, discuss Shakespeare's artistic—or, as Spiritualists would have it, phantasmal—faculty.

Lumping Bloom, even provisionally, with De Grazia, Stallybrass, Bristol, Frey, Hawkes and Mallin may be an uncomfortable combination of fair-weather friends and eternally warring opposites, but we may here note that Shakespeare critics have already introduced a variety of terms to capture, formalize, and discipline large and (seemingly) mutually disruptive cultural processes into trim and controllable elements. Gary Taylor (1989), for example, has christened the appropriation of Shakespeare by commercial and institutional elites as "Shakesperotics"; Terence Hawkes (1992) has dubbed the uses of Shakespeare by the academic industry as "Bardbiz"; and Michael D. Bristol (1996), examining the habits of mass consumption, has coined the phrase "Big-time Shakespeare."[25] This study will confine itself to only a "Small-time," or rather "small-time," aspect of Shakespeare Studies, a marginalized discourse that does not fit easily under any of the aforementioned inquiries. It will concern itself with a now-forgotten religious group, Spiritualists, and how its ensuing discussions of Shakespeare's meaning, his writing practices, his possible collaborations, and the supposed purity and (possible) corruption of his texts anticipated, accompanied, or silhouetted similar debates in Shakespeare Studies. I call this shadowed and shadow-casting phenomenon "Shakespiritualism."

Because of the complexities involved, I have devoted the first three chapters to an overview of the origins, processes, and personalities of Shakespiritualism. Chapter 1, for example, surveys the interrelationship of Spiritualism and bardolatry. Much has already been written on the apotheosis of Shakespeare, but—returning to the "small-time" aspect

of Shakespiritualism—this study focuses on a minor detail of early bardolatry that has been hitherto overlooked: the curtailment or simple
omission of some of Shakespeare's most powerful occult scenes in live
performance—for example, the ghost in *Hamlet*, the witches in *Macbeth*,
the specters in *Richard III*.[26] While an embarrassment to the increasingly
pragmatic audiences of the nineteenth century, these and like scenes were
embraced by Spiritualists, who found within them substantiation of their
own dramatically infused religiosity.

Chapter 2 delves into the Spiritualists' fascination with (and solutions regarding) the Authorship Question. It wasn't just Shakespeare
who returned from the dead; the ghosts of Sir Francis Bacon and the
Earl of Oxford also returned, each claiming the authorship of the Stratford poet's works. Often their respective ghostly proofs were conveyed
in acrostics, anagrams, and Pythagorean codes. William F. Friedman
and Elizabeth S. Friedman (1957), in their detailed study of Baconian
ciphers, noted a distinct lack of "mathematic probability" or even "common sense" in these systems.[27] As yet another unsympathetic critic put it,
Baconians and Oxfordians have "a desperate gullibility which will accept
almost anything as proof; a total lack of self-criticism; and a cheerful
confidence in one's own ingenuity which will survive all the arguments
of others."[28] While many of these systems strike traditional Shakespeare
scholarship as wrongheaded, our investigation is not centered on conventional, materialist-based evidence but on its opposite, or rather its transcendence—a Spiritual Realm whereby traditional boundaries of logical
thinking play no definitive role.

Shakespiritualism depends on aesthetic immediacy; it is not an intellectual conception but a visceral practice. Shakespiritualism sets aside the
professional aspects of academic criticism (i.e., the narrow purpose of producing publishable academic work for academic reward) in favor of higher
contexts concerning the poetic and, as old-fashioned as it now sounds,
the universal. In keeping with this concept, Chapter 3 continues the
exploration of the anti-Strafordians, this time in reference to the Spiritualist belief in "writing groups." Since Spirits are themselves collaborative,
and since they watch us constantly and aid us in our daily endeavors, no
activity is entirely devoid of their observation and intercession.

The last three chapters serve as case studies of individual Spiritualist
authors and events. Chapter 4 explores Shakespearean and Shakespiri-
tualist accommodations in the unlikely friendship of H. H. Furness and
Spiritualist figurehead Margaret Fox. Furness used a famous Shakespearean crux—the word *Vlloxra*—to test the tenets of Spiritualism and, while
that process was initially undertaken with great skepticism, he nonetheless

came, in his dealings with Fox, to appreciate the theatrical bond between Shakespeare and the new faith. In the fifth chapter, I look at two unpublished, book-length manuscripts by perhaps the most important Shake-spiritualist of all: G. Wilson Knight. While his Spiritualist ideas may alienate some readers, Knight's faith in the power of poetry can also be heartening, especially to anyone holding a degree in English. In Knight's view, to ignore the sacred is to reject the function of inspired and inspiring literature: "It is the business of both Spiritualism and Poetry to assist our advance; together they might remove the obstructions at present barring our established schools from so many of the most fascinating mysteries which interpenetrate our life."[29] Knight argues that all great poetry aims at transcendence; it therefore follows that anyone who reads poetry is already an informal practitioner of Spiritualism; likewise formal practitioners of Spiritualism are quite naturally poetic: "To anyone of poetic training and sensitivity the beautiful and coherent metaphysic of Spiritualism carries its own credentials"; "Spiritualism introduces us to a *poetic world*."[30]

Relatedly, in Chapter 6 I explore whether traditional academic approaches adequately capture what Shakespeare has to offer. My purpose in this last chapter is not to dwell on the limitations of our present-day materialist literary-isms, which, in whole cloth, have served academia well, not only because they rely on institutional safeguards against outrageous claims and unsubstantiated statements, but also because an institutionalized body of knowledge encourages uniformity and standardization.[31] That said, scientific or evidentiary approaches to Shakespeare sometimes leave little room for admiration and wonder. Instead of dissecting the corpse, Shakespiritualism attempts to breathe life into the centuries-old text and, more radically, to communicate directly with its author.

While a richer understanding of Shakespiritualism will come with a sequential reading of the entire study, the practicalities of research are such that many readers may only consult this book for a chapter or two. While indexes are often instrumental in pinpointing areas of interest for readers, the esoteric terms and concepts of Spiritualism, explained early in the book, will present some difficulties for readers only interested in the specifics of later chapters. To aid these readers in navigating some of the unusual concepts and unfamiliar terms employed throughout, a glossary of Spiritualist terms and techniques is provided as Appendix A.

A comparison of Spiritualism and Shakespeare Studies may suggest to some that I am weighing them as intellectual equals. That is not the case. Because Spiritualism is at heart a belief system—and an often contradictory one at that—it remains stubbornly resistant to secular analyses, especially those that emphasize political, sexual, and social differences or that

foreground hitherto unsuspected "faultlines" (a cultural materialist term
that naturalizes division within social formation). The current interest in
difference is important. It delineates the limits of the discussion. This is
not that. But negation is only one kind of learning. How can we understand Shakespeare's works (or anything, for that matter) if we are only
willing to talk about how different they are from what we know or prefer;
how can we learn all there is to learn when we are interested only in what
is not, rather than what is? To quote John M. Ellis, "if we are determined
to take from literature only the attitudes [in this case, hostile differences]
that we bring to it, it ceases to have any point."[32] Ellis has the makings
of a Spiritualist. While the séance allowed for considerable chicanery, the
Spiritualist faithful were not interested in intellectual talk of difference,
oppression, inadequacy, or agency. So far as they were concerned, all elements stemmed from the element; all thoughts were part of one thought;
because Shakespiritualists felt no separation, no isolation, there was no
need to parse anything; in the mystical moment the devout intuited their
own form of the Trinity—Shakespeare in the past, present, and future.

Then again, Ellis, despite his disapproval of cultural materialism, might
also dismiss Spiritualism as yet more hokum. Most of us would probably
agree that religious insight requires a different kind of learning, more
emotional than intellectual, difficult to delineate or replicate, impossible
to measure or schematize, but the study of religious insight is not futile
merely because it requires that we make wholesale adjustments to our way
of processing and validating argument. As an example, we may note that
many (though not all) Spiritualists believed that Francis Bacon was the
true author of Shakespeare's plays; the aristocrat allegedly hid his identity
because, as the illegitimate son of Queen Elizabeth, he feared arrest and
execution by King James's state apparatus. At least initially, we have what
looks to be a typical new historicist argument of sovereign power, but,
because the evidence for Bacon's purported suppression of identity has no
material evidence and relies solely on the interrelations of mediums who
supposedly speak to Spirit Guides who supposedly speak to Bacon, we are
removed from conventional forms of argument, traditional evaluation,
and simple fact checking. Relatedly, Spiritualism routinely rejects earth-
bound influence. Thus, when discussing literary sources, a ghostly Francis
Bacon, visiting the earth in 1947, insisted that the plots of "Shakespeare's"
plays were not borrowed "from anything that existed before. This is not
to be questioned."[33] Shakespeareans demand the exactitudes of evidence;
Shakespiritualists claim the rigors of faith.

Shakespiritualism's dismissal of traditional knowledge-bases and of
conventional modes of evidence and of argument is, of course, a real

concern; yet new departures in virtually every field have almost invariably been voiced in critical pronouncements so novel that they are at once rejected but whose very erratics and inadequacies help refine the emerging paradigm. Then again, to read Shakespiritualism as a series of prophetic visions of present debates is merely to ask of the past a question that legitimates our interests or, worse, to see our predecessors as instinctively correct but intellectually ridiculous. It seems more sensible to see Shakespiritualism as submitting questions that are (often but not always) similar to those posed in academia but answering them by radically different means.

Those radically different means, I think, are clear—séances. In terms of questions or interests, Shakespiritualism is in some ways a forerunner of "Presentism," the inability of scholars to discuss anything but the present, even when—or especially when—dealing with the past. Thus, via the radio-like vibrations emanating from the Spiritual Realm, in 1916–17 Sarah Shatford listened to Shakespeare express his views on the ongoing First World War, his regard for American and British fighter pilots, and his respect for the Red Cross. Another spiritual broadcast concerned Shakespeare's admiration for the lyrics to "The Star Spangled Banner." Shakespeare also disclosed to Shatford that he enjoyed spiritual wanderings through the streets of New Orleans and New York.

According to R. S. White (2006), Shatford "missed a golden opportunity to write the first posthumous autobiography . . . when . . . she spoke to Shakespeare using the Ouija board."[34] White wants Shatford to have asked Shakespeare, among other things, about "why he left Anne Hathaway his second-best bed or what was *Love's Labour's Won*."[35] Whether White seriously believed Shatford's psychic abilities to be legitimate is a side issue: the point here is that the "golden opportunity" is lost only to Shakespeareans interested in such questions. Shatford's Shakespeare is of her era, and what that era wants to know reasonably concerns the First World War and the spiritual afterlife of the soldiers killed in it.[36] The Canadian medium Louis Benjamin (1919), likewise involved in the present and the local, reported that Shakespeare was engrossed by Canadian theater;[37] Daisy O. Roberts (1949), dissatisfied with Laurence Olivier's film *Hamlet*, asked Shakespeare for his opinion—he didn't like it either;[38] James Merrill (1982), worried by the Cold War, learned via the Ouija board that Shakespeare had possessed the body of a "teenage nuclear physicist" living somewhere on earth.[39]

Shakespiritualism not only anticipates aspects of what critics today refer to as "presentism" but also explores its uncanny opposite: "eternalism," which claims that the past, present, and future exist perpetually.

The theory seemingly springs from J. M. E. McTaggart's essay "The Unreality of Time" (1908), in which he argued that time is an illusion; McTaggart's work was later popularized by John William Dunne (1929), who similarly asserted that time was nonlinear.[40] Spiritualism's version of eternalism, however, was both more ancient and literary. Drawing chiefly from the Old and New Testaments, which make several references to heavenly books (Daniel 12:1; Revelation 13:8, 20:12, 21:27), Spiritualists believed that all texts exist(ed) in a Spiritual Library, or what the spirit of G. Wilson Knight's mother called the "Hall of Ancient Wisdom."[41] Thus all past, present, and future writings, including Shakespeare's, were not personal creations: in 1863, Shakespeare's ghost told Spiritualist Sullivan Dwight that he wrote not by perspiration but by divination.[42] In 1876, the American medium Charles Henry Foster received a variety of messages from Shakespeare, who informed him that the plays and poems had come from a "band of poetic spirits in the spheres who controlled him"; without them, Shakespeare "could not have written one stanza of his works."[43] In 1879, Shakespeare told Henry Kiddle that the plays were scripted "by *inspiration*."[44] In 1886, Gerald Massey, after repeated psychic contact, ascertained that Shakespeare had merely transcribed verse from the immortals, whom he, Shakespeare, had compelled to appear.[45] Twenty-three years later, the medium Mrs. Chenoweth, channeling the Spirits who know all, explained that Shakespeare "had been influenced by transcendental agencies."[46] In 1919, Shakespeare divulged to the Spiritualist Louis Benjamin that he was merely the "universe focussed [*sic*] to a point of personality"—that is, a psychic receptor of texts.[47] In 1926, Shakespeare confided to Benjamin De Casseres that he was "only a reporter" of the spirit plays ascribed to him.[48] In 1961, Shakespeare revealed to Daisy O. Roberts that he was "extremely psychic" and that he had received his dramatic scripts "automatically or through telepathic communications" from a group of Spirits, called the "Order of the Round Table," consisting of Homer, Plato, Plutarch, King Arthur, Sir Francis Bacon, and Sir Philip Sidney.[49] Roberts logically concluded that if the soul is immortal, then it is nonsensical to say that Shakespeare existed in just one temporal moment. Shakespeare, Sidney, Bacon, Homer, Plato, Plutarch, and King Arthur were and are one.

Shakespeare might have been in contact with Spirits of the past, but the immortality of the soul allowed for all kinds of temporal anomalies. In 1919, Shakespeare told Spiritualist Louis Benjamin that Christopher Marlowe, who died in 1593, was the actual author of *Pericles*, which was composed in 1607–8.[50] In 1943, the ghost of Francis Bacon explained to Alfred Dodd that as he, Bacon, wrote Shakespeare's plays on earth, the immortal part of himself, hovering in the Spirit Realm, was able "to SEE the writings that are part of my life as I was to write them."[51] Bacon also revealed that the Regency poet Percy Bysshe Shelley, through the same process of immortality, had a hand in writing "Shakespeare's" Renaissance plays.[52] In 1947, the ghost of Bacon revealed to Percy Allen that the immortal Spirits of Beaumont and Fletcher were "largely responsible" for two plays, *The Taming of the Shrew* and *Titus Andronicus*—this despite the fact that Fletcher was about 12 years old when these plays were composed and Beaumont was 7.[53]

We might infer that these Spiritualists were discussing canonicity metaphorically—that all great writers share immortality; thus, they are in some sense forever united by their merits. That seems to be the way, for example, an ectoplasmic Shakespeare defined his immortal status to William Bliss (1947): "I know Matthew Arnold . . . as I know all poets, and consort with them more perhaps than with others. We are all poets, in a sense, in Heaven, and poetry takes on another [read: immortal] meaning."[54] To know Arnold is no different than to read or to know any other canonical poet: literary immortality creates a sense of transhistorical universality.

Metaphorical readings of immortality are all well and good, but a variety of Spiritualist texts demand literalism. This is especially true for Shakespeare's oracular pronouncements, which discuss the ancient, the current, and, most important, the forthcoming. Thus Shakespeare told Charles Henry Foster (1876) that he and the Spirits would help guide "the progress of the future"; a Spirit Guide named "William" explained to former Columbia ethics professor James Hervey Hyslop (1913) that "He [Shakespeare] has lots to do yet. He is not half through. He is something like you, with something to do, you know it."[55] Shakespeare told Sarah Shatford (1916–17) that "at the close of the present war in Europe, there will be a spiritual awakening; spiritual manifestations will take place all over the earth; . . . mortals will be given spirit-sight and spirit-hearing . . . Christ will appear and the dead arise."[56] During the Second World War, the ardent Spiritualist G. Wilson Knight wrote that many of Shakespeare's plays were outright occult prophecies: *Macbeth* was "Shakespeare's comment on such forces as England is fighting to-day"; the "ghosts gather[ed] round" Richard III symbolize the "various *countries* Germany has temporarily enslaved."[57] Again, the focus is on the near future, the aftermath of Germany's transitory enslavement of Europe. Likewise, Francis Bacon (alias Shakespeare) announced to Alfred Dodd (1943) that the Spirits are "ushering in a New Age, the rebirth of civilization."[58]

On the face of it, the pairing of a new age and Shakespeare seems contradictory, even nonsensical. How can something be new and old

simultaneously? (A similar contrariety haunts the term *new historicism*.)
But many Spiritualists resolved the incongruity with a chiasmus: the new
epoch was only new insofar as the ancient had been erased, dislocated,
rejected, or forgotten by the modern. Not surprisingly, many of the Spiritualists who championed this argument were also devoted to a study of
the past: Harriet M. Shelton was fascinated by Abraham Lincoln, E. Lee
Howard by precolonial American Indians, Gerald Massey by Egyptology,
and Ignatius Donnelly by lost Atlantis.[59]

Moreover, because many of Shakespeare's plays dealt with foreign
lands, uncharted islands, or legendary kingdoms, Spiritualists linked
his esoteric settings and perceived spiritual messages to the great theologians of China, India, and the Levant. The spiritual (though undeclared
Spiritualist) Ralph Waldo Emerson (1886) connected Shakespeare to the
twelfth-century poet Saadi, arguing that, since both were timeless, both
were also perpetually ancient and contemporary: "Let the distance [of
geographies and eras] from East to West be as great as you please, yet the
wisdom of the one [immortal poet] is as the wisdom of the other."[60] The
Spiritualist magazine *Light* (1889) thought of Shakespeare, Jesus, and
Buddha as spiritual compeers.[61] According to Richard Maurice Bucke
(1894), Shakespeare offered a "cosmic consciousness" through which the
reader might register the wisdom of Buddha, Mohammad, and Jesus.[62]
Nine years later, William Stanley attended a Parisian séance in which he
learned that the Spirits of Christ, Brahma, Buddha, Moses, Solomon,
Confucius, Zoroaster, Plato, Mahomet, and Shakespeare were "guide-
memorials" sent back to earth "to direct us."[63]

The Shakespearean dimensions of this study should now be apparent,
but I have hitherto ignored a real difficulty. Many academics may feel
qualified to discuss Shakespeare, but when it comes to Spiritualism we
tend to know only its pop cultural trappings (Ouija boards, Spirit rappings, prayer healing, scrying, palmistry, and so forth) and ignore its complex origins and accretions. Spiritualism, as I explain in Chapter 1, was an
amalgam of faiths. Moreover, its practitioners and practices were surprisingly heterogeneous: some Spiritualist mediums were native, some foreign;
some performed in private, some in public; some did their Spiritualist
work in the daylight, though most preferred a crepuscular gloom.[64] Some
ventriloquized the dead, while others used an early form of Morse code.
Adapting to the science of the late-nineteenth and twentieth centuries, in
which explorers were cutting through the jungles of Africa or trudging
through arctic ice, in which men of science were peering into outer space
or exploring the inner workings of the atom, Spiritualist masters believed
that Shakespeare had teleported to an unseen "Spirit Realm" or to the

planets. The French novelist Victor Hugo (1853) received messages from "Tyatafia," a Latin-writing Spirit from Mercury, who informed him that Molière and Shakespeare "lived" on Jupiter.[65] In 1961, Daisy O. Roberts contacted Shakespeare via a psychic "dictaphone."[66] Other earthbound mediums explained that Shakespeare spoke to them by way of a mysterious "fourth dimension" or still more unquantifiable "nth dimension."[67]

There were tipping mediums, who overturned or levitated furniture; singing mediums, who performed ditties; patois mediums, who spoke in languages they claimed they did not know; lettering mediums, who wrote down, sometimes backward, what the Spirits told them, or who allowed the Spirits to take possession of a hand or limb. There were conjuring mediums, who could manifest the dead in ectoplasmic form, and mediums who could summon a familiar fragrance or taste, a chilling breeze, a musical melody, or a weird glow.[68] Other mediums specialized in clairvoyant healing. Some mediums claimed to have amnesia after spiritual possession; others retained full recollection. Most mediums were female, but some were male; most were adults, though some were children. Mediums came from all social classes, aristocratic to unarmigerous. There were professional mediums who charged for services or accepted gifts; other mediums were amateur and unpaid.[69] There were local mediums and traveling mediums. The latter not only conducted séances but also lectured to the curious and the converted on the "trance lecture circuit."[70] Some mediums were progressive and feminist; others were apolitical; others were just "sexy."[71] Some were natural entertainers; others were trained actors and actresses; still others were con artists.

The same multiplicity applied to Spiritualist believers. Undoubtedly, most of the people who frequented séances and Spiritualist gatherings or who supported Spiritualist newspapers and journals believed in Spirits, but it's unlikely that all Spiritualists believed in Spirit Realms on other planets; some, but not all, believed in the healing power of crystals; doubtless some attended Spiritualist meetings to talk to their dead friends or family members; still others might have attended Spiritualist events because, despite the quackadoodles of its rituals, Spiritualism's political and social concerns dovetailed with a wide variety of progressive platforms (women's rights, prison reform, and pacifism). Still others (likely nonmembers) might have gone to Spiritualist gatherings for dramatic amusement, in the same way that someone of the present generation might latch on to something theatrical, pleasurable, and trendy—a theological version of the role-playing game *Final Fantasy*.[72]

Some patrons may have attended Spiritualist meetings merely to roll their eyes. A case in point: Spiritualist descriptions of the afterworld. In

Judaism, the soul sleeps until the day of Revelation, whereupon it is to be reborn in the flesh; in Christianity, as viewed by St. Paul and St. Augustine, the soul lives out of time, but whether the personality is saved is open to question. Spiritualism created the best of all possible (after)worlds—immortality of the soul, with a retention of personality and, with that retention, a desire to intervene or to offer guidance to those left behind on earth. As one Spirit explains to John Worth Edmonds (1853): "We live in this world of spirits, but our duties are as much with you, and on your earth."[73] To pass the time between interventions, the eternal Spirits go for walks, ride chariots, and sail pleasure crafts; read novels, attend the theater, or travel through time; study in "wonderful Palaces of Learning," cultivate gardens, and visit "splendid golden cities"; eat fresh fruits and vegetables, smoke Cuban cigars, and drink whiskey sodas.[74] In Henry J. Triezenberg's *Spiritualism: Asking the Dead* (1939), a Spirit named "Claude" details the supernatural suburbia-to-come: "You want to know about our houses? Well, they are built by bricklayers and designed by architects as they are on earth . . . Yes, we wear clothes, anything we like: to express ourselves."[75]

Yet, even accepting the multiplicity of Spiritualism, and the silliness of some of its ideas and rituals, we might here note that many ancient religions are just as illogical. The Greeks believed that Zeus and his extended family lived in a palace gated by clouds and guarded by the Seasons; the Romans had a god for virtually everything, including Cardea, goddess of door hinges; the Norse believed that the planet Venus was formed from the frostbitten toe of Thor's friend Aurvandill; the ancient Celts worshipped Accasbel, a Partholan who is credited with opening the first pub in Ireland, and so on.

Lest we think ourselves superior, much of the founding science of the Modern Age is likewise marked by superstition. Johannes Kepler was a student not merely of mathematics but also of "sacred geometry," cosmology, astrology, harmonics, and music; he thought that each planet (he knew of only six of them) was housed in a metaphysically perfect and harmonious form, a *musica universalis*. Sir Isaac Newton discovered gravity and calculus, but he was also a firm believer in ethereal Spirits and dragons.[76] A good deal of our language, including the words for the days of the week, is rooted in the pagan: Sunday and Monday are named after the ancient Celtic worship of the sun and the moon; Tuesday, Wednesday, Thursday, and Friday are named after the Norse gods Tyr, Woden, Thor, and Freya; Saturday goes to the Greek god Saturn. In like manner, the Easter Bunny, the Christmas tree, and Halloween are each based on defunct pagan beliefs and practices.

Some or all of these pagan traces may be common knowledge, and it certainly does not follow that we practice Norse or Greco-Roman worship; it merely demonstrates our passing familiarity with and tolerance of religious myth. Perhaps because these pagan belief systems are both ancient and defunct, they are commonly cited without thought as to how they clash with each other ideologically. But when it came to a more recent phenomenon like Spiritualism, a religion that attracted millions of people from all walks of life, a cultural agent was needed, one that might patch up, if not fully resolve, its opposing dynamics and make it attractive to potential converts. Fortunately, Spiritualists did find a language and a figurehead that captured their interests in all things immortal. Wrote ghosthunter Elliot O'Donnell, "No Spiritualistic séance is complete without . . . Shakespeare."[77]

CHAPTER 1

SHAKESPEARE,
POET OF THE IMPOSSIBLE

THE YEAR IS 1876. MELBOURNE. A GROUP of Spiritualists flock to the home of Hugh Junor Browne, the wealthy owner of Australian Distillery Works. Soft music hovers in the air. The medium, dressed in black, enters. His name is Charles Henry Foster, a renowned American Spiritualist.[1] The faithful gather round. Foster removes his jacket and then rolls up his right sleeve. His forearm is pasty, but then he waves his exposed flesh before a flickering candle and mutters a magical incantation: "*Magna Mater! Magna Mater! . . . Atys . . . Dia ad aghaidh's ad aodann . . . agus bas dunach ort! Dhonas's dholas ort, agus leat-sa! . . . Ungl . . . ungl . . . rrrlh . . . chchch.*" Almost immediately, writing begins to appear on his naked arm.

A series of cards and envelops are then handed out. Foster asks everyone in the room to write a question to a particular dead friend or relative. They do so. The questions are sealed in separate envelopes. The envelopes are handed to Foster, who proceeds to touch the first envelope to his forehead and to issue an answer—"Yes, Fred watches you and your family; he worries about the farm, but says that all will be well." Foster then opens the envelope and reads aloud the written question: "My brother Fred died last year in a farming accident. Is he here? Is he fine?" Foster proceeds to the next sealed envelope. He touches it to his forehead: "Your mother is fine; she still gardens and takes great pride watching you from above." The envelope is opened; again, the answer corresponds to the question. Foster moves on to the next envelope: "Your boy Sam was killed in a mining accident. His legs were blown off, but he is able-bodied now and happy." The envelope is unsealed; yet again, Foster's answer is in uncanny accord.[2]

Now to serious business. The shades are drawn; all lights are extinguished, save a single, thick white candle. Flame and shadow dance on the medium's face. The participants sit round the table. They hold hands. They grow silent. There is a preliminary prayer:

> O Infinite Spirit, manifesting Thy love and tenderness from fragile flower to mightiest oak; impressing in many ways Thy Infinite care and wisdom, we turn to Thee this hour and would be blessed by a more complete understanding of life's obligations and opportunities. We would have a more perfect understanding of the laws which govern our being, a more perfect comprehension of our duties, and greater strength to perform them. We would learn more and more of that great world of spirits to which the vast multitudes which have peopled the earth have gone from time to time.[3]

Then, quoting *Hamlet* nearly word for word, the medium continues: "We would know more of that country toward which we are all travelling—more of its structure, more of its spheres, its conditions, its illuminations, its glories." This is followed by a hymn:

> I need Thy presence every passing hour.
> What but Thy grace can foil the tempter's power?
> Who, like Thyself, my guide and stay can be?
> Through cloud and sunshine, Lord, abide with me.
> I fear no foe, with Thee at hand to bless;
> Ills have no weight, and tears no bitterness.
> Where is death's sting? Where, grave, thy victory?
> I triumph still, if Thou abide with me.[4]

Before the first hymn is finished, the medium lapses into silence, his head gradually nodding. The other members of the séance continue to sing, but they too halt when a strange muttering begins to emanate from Foster. His head rolls slowly back then suddenly jerks forward. His eyes are now glittering with a strange new intelligence. A Spirit has possessed Foster's body.

The Spiritualists around the table are not alarmed. They know who it is. They can tell by looking at the calendar. On Monday evenings, Foster's body hosts the Spirits of two theologian-mystics, Emmanuel Swedenborg and Franz Anton Mesmer. On Tuesday and Friday nights, Foster is possessed by William Shakespeare, who happily elucidates the meaning of the universe to all present. It is Friday Night. Shakespeare's night. Shakespeare has not come to entertain the Spiritualists; no, he has come to remind them that death is but the beginning of a new phase of life. Shakespeare informs the Spiritualists seated around the table, "This world is but the seminary for the great university of the spheres, where all pupils, without exception, must graduate, where eternal fountains of everlasting light and beauty glow, showing to man that there is a higher state than his present being."[5] Still more occult language follows: Shakespeare goes on to explain that his soul floats on "magnetic fluid" and that he can speak through Foster because of the medium's immense "magnetic will," which allows him to see "magnetic life."[6]

To understand "Shakespeare's" statements, as well as why he, along with Swedenborg and Mesmer, formed a Spiritualist trinity, we will need to move through time and space, visiting a variety of salons, lecture halls, and public theaters in London, Stratford-upon-Avon, Vienna, and Indianapolis.

The year is 1744. London. Emmanuel Swedenborg—(failed) inventor of a flying machine, a submarine, an air gun, a slow-combustion stove, and a "perpetual motion" machine—awakes on a cloudless afternoon from a postprandial nap. He writes in his journal, "I . . . saw him face to face. It was a face of such holy mien and everything indescribable and smiling so that I believe this was how he looked when he was alive . . . I woke, trembling, and came again into the state where I was neither asleep nor awake but in thought as to what this might mean, was it Christ, the son of God, whom I saw?"[7] Later that same year, while eating in a London restaurant, Swedenborg has yet another vision: Christ appears before him and tells him that, henceforth, he will be communing with Spirits.[8]

Swedenborg then brags to any and all that God has "accorded to him the remarkable gift of communicating with departed souls at his pleasure."[9] As a consequence, no secret is safe from this self-styled mystic, who, with the aid of his swift and servile Spirits, sees all. One of the more famous exhibitions of his Spiritual powers is recorded by the philosopher Immanuel Kant: "Madame Herteville (Marteville), the widow of the Dutch Ambassador in Stockholm, some time after the death of her husband, was called upon by Croon, a goldsmith, to pay for a silver service which her husband had purchased from him. The widow was convinced that her late husband had been much too precise and orderly not to have paid this debt, yet she was unable to find this receipt. In her sorrow, and because the amount was considerable, she requested Mr. Swedenborg to call at her house." Swedenborg accepts the invitation. Upon his arrival, Madame Herteville apologizes for having troubled him, but she feels sure that "if, as all people say, he possesse[s] the extraordinary gift of conversing with the souls of the departed," he can save her from financial ruin. Perhaps he would "have the kindness to ask her husband" the whereabouts of the receipt for the silver service? Swedenborg does "not at all object." Three days later, Swedenborg returns with news that he has "conversed with her husband": "the debt had been paid several months before his decease, and the receipt was in a bureau in the room upstairs." The lady replies that the bureau has been searched but no receipt has been found. Swedenborg then inspects the desk and, after pulling out the left-hand drawer, pops a lever. A secret compartment is then disclosed, containing the receipt.[10]

More visions follow. When attending the funeral of Christopher Polhem, his former teacher, Swedenborg tells all in attendance that Polhem's seemingly undetectable Spirit is present; the mystic then converses with the unseen ghost while onlookers gawk.[11] Another so-called miracle occurs in 1759: a nearby town is on fire, but Swedenborg tells everyone not to worry. The fire will be put out around 8 p.m. His prediction proves to be accurate. Still another vision occurs in July of 1762, in which he sees in his mind's eye the murder of Tsar Peter III of Russia. Again, all of Swedenborg's details are corroborated.[12] Soon after, a curious King Adolphus Frederick of Sweden invites Swedenborg to his court. His wife Queen Ulrica is "but little disposed to believe in such seeming miracles" and, therefore, demands a demonstration of his powers. She tells Swedenborg that her brother, the Prince Royal of Prussia, once whispered something in her ear. She adds that what he had said could not have been repeated to anybody nor had it ever escaped her own lips. Swedenborg's test, therefore, is to commune with his Spirits and then to reveal the secret message. Some days later, Swedenborg returns with a request for a private audience. The queen, playing cards, refuses. What he has to say can be said before the company:

> but Swedenborg assured her he could not disclose his errand in the presence of witnesses: that in consequence of this intimation the queen became agitated, gave her cards to another lady, and requested M. de Schwerin (who also was present when she related the story to us,) to accompany her: that they accordingly went together into another apartment, where she posted M. de Schwerin at the door, and advanced towards the farthest extremity of it with Swedenborg; who said to her, "You took, madam, your last leave of the Prince of Prussia, your late august brother, at Charlottenburg, on such a day, and at such an hour of the afternoon; as you were passing afterwards through the long gallery, in the castle of Charlottenburg, you met him again; he then took you by the hand, and led you to such a window, where you could not be overheard, and then said to you these words:———." The queen did not repeat the words, but she protested to us they were the very same her brother had pronounced.[13]

With his reputation as a psychic now secure, people begin to ask Swedenborg all kinds of questions. Do the Spirits have internal organs? Yes, he replies, an obliging Spirit has color-coded its own brains, marrow, lungs, liver, stomach, intestines, and even genitals for Swedenborg to see.[14] Do Spirits speak Hebrew or Latin? No, Swedenborg explains, Spirits speak and write to each other in a language different from that which they use when speaking to mortals, though the Spirits themselves are unaware of this phenomenon.[15]

Other questions put to Swedenborg suggest a confusion between Heaven and heavenly bodies—that is, the planets. Swedenborg reveals that his astral essence has visited Mercury, a bucolic land of oxen, cows, stags, and hinds tended by Mercurian men and their beautiful and slender women. On the planet Venus, he discovers "two kinds of men, [each] of opposite character; the first mild and humane, the second savage and almost brutal." The Spirits of the moon are a skittish sort, afraid of their own belching or "eructation." The ultimate Sprits of the universe reside on Jupiter and are known for their "gentleness and sweetness, and tender care of their children."[16]

Chary astronomers questioned why they had never observed people on Mercury and Venus, but Swedenborg had a ready reply: these beings dwell on the spiritual plane of other planets and are thus unobservable to science. In some instances, the Spirits may not even be aware of the material world at all: "the earth or planet Jupiter itself does not actually appear to spirits and angels; for no material earth is visible to the inhabitants of the spiritual world, but only the spirits and angels who are from it."[17] Fine, then, did the dead somehow live on or within the Spiritual Realms, and, if so, what did they do for all eternity? Swedenborg explained that the souls of the dead did indeed pass into the "World of the Spirits,"[18] where they spend much of their time(lessness) improving themselves through college courses. (We might here recall that Shakespeare's Spirit told Charles Henry Foster that souls float in a "great university of the spheres.")

Swedenborg also related a series of dreams (or astral dreams) concerning these universal universities. During his first visit, Swedenborg attended a lecture. In another dream, he entered five Spirit schools specializing in grammatical instruction; another dream had him entering a Spirit school of philosophy, wherein he argued with the philosopher Spinoza—Swedenborg converted his misguided colleague to his view of things seen and unseen.[19] Swedenborg also visited a Spiritual Library, wherein his eternal self discovered that every book that has ever been and would ever be written exists in a "large Library, which was divided into Classes containing different Books according to the different Sciences." As a "further Confirmation in these Particulars, they [three disembodied mortals accompanied

Swedenborg in his visits to the Spiritual Realm] were conducted to the Houses of the Scribes, who transcribed the Copies of Writings written by the Wise Men of the City, and they inspected the Writings, and wondered to see them so neat and elegant."[20] (The importance of the Spiritual Library will be explained in subsequent chapters of this study.)

Soon enough, Swedenborg turned all these anecdotes into a cohesive system of spiritual and material interrelations. Drawing upon the ancient traditions of the Pythagoreans, who saw in man harmonic correspondences with the cosmos, and the Kabbalah, a Jewish mysticism that argues that every element of the universe is interconnected, Swedenborg preached that humans and angels, though apparently separated by full awareness of each other, are actually part of a single divine entity.[21] It therefore follows that human events (revolutions and assassinations, for example) have an effect on their Spirit Realm, just as the activities of the spirits have an effect on our world. That view, of course, dovetailed neatly with Shakespeare's various expressions of heavenly order or upset: Odysseus's speech of social and astral harmony in *Troilus and Cressida*, or its negation, the sudden riot of comets in *Julius Caesar* or storms in *King Lear*, and so on.

By the late 1700s, Swedenborgian churches began to appear at the geographical and cultural margins of European culture, especially in America and Australia, where they met with little opposition; but when the cult made headway in England, George Beaumont, an Anglican minister at Norwich, was prompted to pen *The Anti-Swedenborg; or, A Declaration of the Principal Errors Contained in the Theological Writings of E. Swedenborg* (1824). In this same work, he warned that Swedenborg's teachings misled and beguiled "many simple, unwary, and ill-informed souls."[22] Likewise, David George Goyder's *Swedenborg and His Mission* (1853) denounced Swedenborg and his followers as victims of "delusion . . . that . . . could only proceed from satan [*sic*]."[23] The allegedly satanic aspects of Swedenborgism would remanifest in a Viennese cult called "Mesmerism." But before we travel to Vienna, we need to visit a small town in England, where another cult of personality—some might even call it a cult of idolatry—was taking shape.

The year is 1769. Stratford-upon-Avon. David Garrick, the most famous Shakespeare actor of his generation, is about to start Stratford-upon-Avon's tourist industry. Despite the fact that Shakespeare's plays were never written for or staged in Stratford, Garrick creates something he calls the "Shakespeare's Jubilee"—a three-day (September 6–8) festivity of all things Shakespearean, staged at a cost of £50,000.[24] The event schedule was so jam-packed that the festival began at 5 a.m.[25] By its conclusion, "Shakespeare stopped being regarded as an increasingly popular and admirable dramatist, and became a god."[26]

Signs of apotheosis were all around. One of the musicians hired for the event spoke of the jubilee as "the celebration of the *resurrection* of Shakespeare." On the banks of the river Avon were paintings of "Time leading Shakespeare to Immortality"; in the church, the poet's bust was loaded with branches of bays so as to look like "the god Pan in an old picture." In addition, "[t]he five windows of the town hall were filled with paintings of transparent silk—*Lear, Falstaff, Pistol, Caliban,* and the Genius of Shakespeare—'in a good stile.' At one end hung Gainsborough's portrait of Garrick, at the other a very good picture of Shakespeare in the attitude of inspiration." Shakespeare's birthplace was covered with an "emblematical transparency, the subject being the sun struggling through clouds to enlighten the world."[27] David Garrick presided over the opening event holding a wooden cup fashioned from a mulberry tree that Shakespeare had allegedly planted. Taking up the cup and evoking a quasi-religiosity normally associated with Christian Communion, Garrick enjoined all present to do reverence:

> Behold this fair goblet, 'twas carv'd from the tree
> Which, O my sweet Shakspeare, was planted by thee;
> As a relic I kiss it, and bow at the shrine,
> What comes from thy hand must be ever divine!
> All shall yield to the mulberry-tree,
> Bend to thee,
> Blest mulberry:
> Matchless was he
> Who planted thee;
> And thou, like him, immortal be![28]

Perhaps odder still, Garrick was often seen waving a "wand"—also said to have been made from Shakespeare's mulberry tree. While we might see the waving wand as a sort of orchestral baton, many townsfolk thought of it as satanic. Thomas Davies recorded that "the lower and more ignorant class of the people entertained the most preposterous and absurd notions of the Jubilee; they viewed Mr. Garrick with some degree of apprehension and terror; they considered him as a magician, and dreaded the effects of his wand, as strongly as the deluded populace did formerly, in the darkest days of ignorance, the power of witchcraft."[29]

Aside from Garrick's speeches, there was to have been a parade of 170 characters from Shakespeare's works and from Greco-Roman mythology, but the event was rained out—a circumstance deemed by many locals to be a "judgment and vengeance of Heaven."[30] In the evening the rain let up long enough for a spectacle of fireworks—whose "flickering manifestations" were "weirdly frightening" to the townsfolk, who, again, saw the displays as a sign of a "magician's art."[31] Other scheduled entertainments included balls, assemblies, masquerades, and other common public diversions. The event culminated with Garrick reading a poem in which Shakespeare is referred to as a demigod: "'Tis he! 'tis he!—that demi-god! / Who Avon's flow'ry margin trod; / . . . 'Tis he!—'tis he! / The god of our idolatry!"[32]

The imaginative/mystical/magical aspects of the Jubilee were apparent to George Saville Carey, author of *Shakespeare's Jubilee, a Masque* (1769), in which Macbeth's witches join with the supernatural deities of Oberon and Puck and the other *A Midsummer's Night's Dream* fairies. Using their arts, Falstaff is then "charm-call'd from his quiet grave" to join Caliban and other characters on a journey to Stratford, there to worship at the feet of their iconic creator:

Ye spirits that reside in air,
Or in deep caverns dwell,
Such as boast intentions fair,
Or fiends from native hell,
Come hither now
Such sprites as owe
To his creative boundless muse,
Their existence, birth, and name,
Come and revel to his fame;
What mortal, sprite, or fairy can deny,
To sing their master's immortality.[33]

Even Thomas Davies, while scoffing at the superstitions of the Stratford yokels, had to admit that the apotheosis of Shakespeare was based on the poet-playwright's own mystical beliefs: "In this rude and uncivilized spot [i.e., Stratford] was Shakespeare born, where, in his infant years, he imbibed the elements of poetical rapture, and fed his young fancy with the awful dreams of magic and superstition. Here first he learned to prattle of elves and fairies, of wizards, witches, and enchantments, and of the unseen wonders of the lower and upper regions. Here too his mind was enriched with that beautiful imagery and enthusiastic vision which afterwards impelled him to create new worlds, and to people them with inhabitants of his own formation."[34]

Should all or any of this be read literally? There is, after all, exaggeration at any celebration; faults are often brushed aside, papered over, forgotten. In fact, we can read even in Garrick's jubilee the opposing tendency: not the staging of apotheosis but an appreciation of Shakespeare as a historically situated mortal.

THE APOTHEOSIS OF SHAKESPEARE

Throughout the eighteenth century, professional actors, editors, collectors, and enthusiasts had repeatedly descended upon Stratford to learn more about Shakespeare. Between 1663 and 1693, John Aubrey interviewed the Stratford townsfolk concerning Shakespeare's parentage ("a butcher's son"), appearance ("handsome, well shap't"), and intelligence ("a naturall wit"); moreover, according to Aubrey, Dogberry and, presumably, other Shakespeare characters had been drawn from people the playwright had met in Stratford and its environs.[35] His full account ran to about two and a half pages. The next biographical study of Shakespeare was by Nicholas Rowe (1709)—based on the research of Thomas Betterton, who had also visited Stratford—and amounted to just ten pages. Eighty-one years later, Rowe and Betterton's ten-page narrative had become, under the stewardship of the indefatigable Edmond Malone (1790), a three-volume work of 1,490 pages.

While Malone's biographical research gave a sense of solidity to the man, the pages were swelled with facts concerning the era, rather than details concerning Shakespeare himself. Consequently, this intimidating bulk of historical evidence concerning Shakespeare's material existence was often waved off as worthless. Wrote George Steevens, "As all that is known with any degree of certainty concerning Shakspeare, is—that he was born at Stratford upon Avon,—married . . . went to London, where he commenced [as an] actor, and wrote poems and plays—returned to Stratford, made his will, died, and was buried."[36] Not only was little known; some preferred it remain that way. Writing to William Sandys in 1847, Charles Dickens, who had just helped raise the funds to save the Shakespeare Birthplace—"save" is appropriate; P. T. Barnum, the circus impresario, wanted to buy it and cart it off to New York—opined, "It is a great comfort, to my thinking, that so little is known concerning the poet. It is a fine mystery; and I tremble every day lest something should come out."[37]

In the absence of material facts, Shakespeare was steadily transformed along the lines Ben Jonson had envisioned in his monody for the 1623 Folio, a living monument not just for our time but for all time. The bookish Joseph Ritson (1783) called Shakespeare "*the God of the writer[ ]s idolatry.*"[38]

Walter Scott (1828) referred to Shakespeare's grave as "the tomb of the mighty wizard."[39] In the sonnet "Shakespeare," poet Matthew Arnold (1849) described the playwright as an "immortal spirit" who had outlasted and transcended "All weakness . . . all griefs."[40] But Shakespeare's monumental timelessness also depended upon a heap of critics intent upon dismissing any aspect that connected him to human mortality and frailty. Thomas Bowdler (1807) carefully excised all vulgarity, irreverence, lustfulness, and brutality from Shakespeare's works. Almost immediately, readers adopted the carefully effaced text as the true and accurate version of Shakespeare. In reviewing Bowdler's version, Francis Jeffrey (1821) wrote, "[Shakespeare] is by far the purest [i.e., most moral] of the dramatists of his own or the succeeding age,—and has resisted, in a great degree, the corrupting example of his contemporaries."[41]

Bowdler had cleansed Shakespeare of human vanities and vices; others were intent on ridding Shakespeare of yet another aspect of his writing—his plots. As Edmond Malone (1790) and other historians of the stage had already ascertained, Shakespeare's storylines were not his own; most had come from Greek or Roman classics or from British histories. They were, thus, in the eyes of many, non-Shakespearean. William Dodd's *The Beauties of Shakespeare* (1796) dispensed with non-Shakespearean plot so that the "graver, and some very eminent members of the church" might recognize Shakespeare's true "sacred function."[42] Thomas Carlyle (1840) chimed in agreement. Shakespeare was not really a playwright; if anything, his genius had been obscured by the stage: "Alas, Shakspeare had to write for the Globe Playhouse: his great soul had to crush itself." Fortunately, Carlyle was able to decipher within all the blather, bunk, and jibber-jabber of the stage Shakespeare's true role, that of "Priest of Mankind": "he lasts forever with us"; "I feel that there is actually a kind of sacredness in the fact of such a man being sent into this Earth. Is he not an eye to us all; a blessed heaven-sent Bringer of Light?"[43] Shakespeare was no longer a writer of plays or even of pleasant poetry: he was now a "lay bible" or source for practical wisdom and daily reflection.[44] Although Shakespeare was never officially canonized or beatified by the Catholic, Protestant, or Anglican Churches, the clergyman Henry Ward Beecher (1887) reassured his readers that devotion to Shakespeare would somehow bring them closer to God:

> You may suppose that everything would so breathe of the matchless poet that I should be insensible to religious influences. But I was at a stage beyond that. The first effect, last night, of being here was to bring up suggestions of Shakespeare from everything . . . I was dissolved; my whole being seemed to me like an incense wafted gratefully toward God. The

Divine presence rose before me in wondrous majesty, but of ineffable gentleness and goodness, and I could not stay away from more familiar approach, but seemed irresistibly, yet gently, drawn toward God . . . Without any intent of my own, but because from my seat it was nearest, I knelt down at the altar with the dust of Shakespeare beneath my feet. I thought of it, as I thought of ten thousand things, without the least disturbance of devotion.[45]

The still-more bardolatrous William Burgess (1903) considered Shakespeare's (selected) writings to be the Christian Bible by any other name: "Shakspeare drank so deeply from the wells of Scripture that one may say, without any straining of the evidence, without the Bible Shakspeare could not be."[46] By the Victorian era, an outing to Stratford afforded far more than an opportunity to visit a rustic village; it is now a pilgrimage to "The Holy of Holies," the scene of Shakespeare's "nativity."[47] Other than visit the Birthplace, the visitor characteristically paid respects to Shakespeare's grave, where, according to contemporary writer James Walter (1890), Shakespeare's Spirit "hovers."[48]

DISPUTING SHAKESPEARE'S SPIRITUALITY

The unrestrained religiosity is indisputable. Still, a religious inclination, no matter how devoutly matched with what we might today call "fan" or celebrity worship, seems worlds away from summoning and interacting with Shakespeare's Hamlet Sr.–like ghost. Further, the widespread Victorian appreciation and deification of Shakespeare did not depend on a sanctification of everything he had written. (As noted, in order to achieve the desired cultural uplift, Shakespeare's plots and characters were often marginalized.) Given the radical differences in the ways Spiritualists and non-Spiritualists read Shakespeare, we might here ask ourselves whether his plays and poems offered enough internal evidence to support the Spiritualist proposition that Shakespeare was one of their own. From our own cultural vantage point, the evidence, most would agree, is fairly evenly divided: the gods may drop in to resolve the miseries of Pericles; fairies may inhabit the forests of Athens; Spirits may respond to Prospero; witches may hover past Macbeth; a ghost or demon may haunt Elsinore; the ghostly Caesar may terrorize Brutus; portents, intuitions, and prophecies seem all too real in the tragedies and in the histories; miraculous revivals and chance meetings are treated with little fanfare in the comedies; yet the cosmos does not acknowledge Lear's death nor those of Hamlet, Othello, Cordelia, Desdemona, or Juliet.

Another issue is that magic in Shakespeare is often pointedly theatrical and propositional. When Paulina comes back to life in *The Winter's Tale*, Leontes remarks, "If this be magic, let it be an art / Lawful as eating."[49] That "If" is important: this is magic of the theater, which Coleridge famously described as a "suspension of disbelief." It is what we might call "choice magic": if a member of the audience chooses to accept the magic of the theater, then everything happening on stage is real. That is so not only for audience members watching one of Shakespeare's plays but also for the characters within the plays: in the case of Bottom, the choice is to sleep or to dream; in the case of Macbeth, to see what is or what is not; in the case of Lear, to believe or to doubt that Cordelia lives; in the case of Leontes, to flounder in misery or to ascend to good fortune. By comparison, traditional forms of magical conjuring are only of minor importance. Even *The Tempest* turns more on the mystery of human behavior than it does on the magic of books and incantations. At the end of the play, Prospero will drown his books, which no longer serve any real purpose; they are useless and relatively powerless compared to the attraction of teenagers and the absolution of brothers. The real magic, it seems, is personal and emotional, rather than external and supernatural.

Spiritualists, however, were only interested in a narrow selection of Shakespeare's dramaturgy. Practicing their own form of textual expurgation, they pointed to and praised the ghosts in *Richard III*, the witches in *Macbeth*, the magical prowess of Prospero, and Hamlet's talk of more things in heaven and earth than are dreamt of in traditional philosophy but generally ignored any passages that might undermine that self-serving sampling—for example, Hotspur's famous devaluation of the occult in *1 Henry IV*, in which the Welsh warrior, magician, and rebel, Owen Glendower, full of superstition and brimming with self-importance, boasts that, at his nativity

> The front of heaven was full of fiery shapes
> Of burning cressets, and at my birth
> The frame and huge foundation of the earth
> Shak'd like a coward.

But Hotspur, while not disputing the meteorology, casts doubt on its significance:

> Why, so it would have done
> At the same season, if your mother's cat had
> But kitten'd, though yourself had never been born.

The exchange continues:

> *Glendower.* I say the earth did shake when I was born.
> *Hotspur.* And I say the earth was not of my mind,
> If you suppose as fearing you it shook.

Glendower persists, "I can call spirits from the vasty deep," to which
Hotspur replies, "Why, so can I, or so can any man, / But will they come
when you do call for them?"[50]

Cheap charlatanry soon follows: in the same scene, Glendower, with
a wave of his hand, has his Spirits play music, but Hotspur suspects that
there is nothing magical about the event—after all, how difficult is it to
hide a few lute players behind a curtain? The medical journal *The Lancet*
(1860) referred to this very scene as proof that Shakespeare was a proto-
Spiritualist skeptic: "The spirits that *Glendower* boasted he could call
from the vasty deep would not come when the skeptical *Hotspur* taunted
the mystic Welshman to produce them." The same journal then goes on
to make an intriguing connection—that the ghost in *Hamlet*, written a
year or two after *1Henry IV*, parodies Glendower's mystical faith: "The
cock crows—the ghost vanishes: the sceptic [like Hotspur] utters a pro-
fane question—the spirit refuses to leave the immaterial world. Really it
is too gross to be ludicrous."[51]

In large measure, *The Lancet* is reading against the grain of these
plays. True, in *1Henry IV*, Percy seems to be unimpressed with Glendower's hocus pocus, yet he can still recall crucial occult images and poetic
prognostications:

> the dreamer Merlin and his prophecies,
> And of a dragon and a finless fish,
> A clip-wing'd griffin and a moulten raven,
> A couching lion and a ramping cat,
> And such a deal of skimble-skamble stuff.[52]

Hotspur's speech does not signal to theatergoers that he believes (or
that we should believe) Glendower to be an actual wizard; nor does it
prove that Shakespeare believed in or practiced the occult, but it does
indicate that even a nonbeliever like Hotspur finds the rites of occult
practice to be indelible. As for *The Lancet*'s reading of *Hamlet*, the apparition, whether a demon or not, confirms the otherworldly, at least within
the confines of that play. Following on, it seems safe enough to say that
plays like *Richard III*, *The Tempest*, *Macbeth*, *Hamlet*, and even *1Henry
IV* are certainly enhanced if we, like Hotspur, are partially seduced by

the theatricality of such supernatural scenes. Such numinous readings of the tragedies are by no means unproblematic, and we certainly might participate in the psycho-therapeutic agency of catharsis without a firm belief in the afterlife. The purgation of sin does not fully entail the promulgation of Purgatory. Still, we can acknowledge that Shakespeare's use of the supernatural was part of his dramatic design and that his repeated use of supernatural motifs suggests that these same patterns had a wide and spontaneous, if not uniform, appeal.

Two hundred years on, however, the miraculous elements of Shakespeare's works were often disparaged, downplayed, or eliminated altogether. Charles Lamb (1810–11), for example, wrote of his disappointment with live Shakespeare, which all too often betrayed the material aspects of its own presentment. "instead of realizing an idea, we have only materialized and brought down a fine vision to the standard of flesh and blood." This was especially true for Shakespeare's supernatural plays: the sight of actors playing the witches in *Macbeth* "actually destroys the faith" that we might otherwise have in "the incantations of those terrible beings"; in productions of *King Lear*, "the contemptible machinery by which they mimic the storm" obscures our "sublime identification of his [Lear's] age with that of the heavens themselves"; "Spirits and fairies [in *The Tempest*] cannot be represented, they cannot even be painted,—they can only be believed."[53]

Lamb's critique centers on the failure of the mechanical to reproduce the transcendent, but for most of the eighteenth and nineteenth centuries aesthetics, not mechanics, were often the overriding issue. In Colley Cibber's version of *Richard III*, the prophetess and witch, Queen Margaret, was excised completely, as were the appearances of the ghosts of Rivers, Grey, Vaughan, Hastings, and Clarence. In *Macbeth*, the Weird Sisters, arguably the creepiest characters in all of Shakespeare, were farcically recast as "three jolly-faced fellows, whom we are accustomed to laugh at."[54] In *King Lear*, supernatural aspects (storming heavens, for example) were downsized and dismissed to make way for "secularized subjectivity."[55] *The Winter's Tale* and *Pericles* were each turned into playlets (*The Sheep-Shearing* and *Marina*) with minimal magical elements.[56] Likewise, the ghost in *Hamlet* became "an embarrassment, a figure to be mocked as absurd."[57] The magazine *Irish Playgoer* (1900) even suggested that producers of *The Tempest* rid the play of Ariel and Caliban, "for nothing is more difficult to conjure up on the stage than the atmosphere of the supernatural, or to make fairies appear anything else but lightly clad human beings."[58] In sum, Georgian, Regency, and Victorian values corrected and ultimately disembodied the superstitious aspects of Shakespeare's work in order to create a rational, meditative deity. Shakespeare's plays were (at least on stage) denied the transcendent power to break materialist bonds.[59] The question is, what became of all those discarded conjuring scenes, those magic words, those spellings of spells?

The year is 1775. Vienna. A doctor dressed as a magician enters the room waving a magic wand. The wizard-doctor is chubby, with a pallid, studious face. The son of a Swabian gamekeeper, he has been educated for the Jesuit priesthood at the University of Dillingen and Ingolstadt; he also holds a medical degree from the University of Vienna.[60] The theologically minded doctor's basic premise is that the universe is filled with a "mystical universal fluid," also known as "magnetic fluid" or a "universal fluid," which, if manipulated correctly, might promote the body to heal faster.[61] His name is Anton Mesmer.

The doctor's remedies are based on hypnosis (what he termed "Mesmerism") and the application of magnets. Mesmer, for example, instructs his patients to wear magnetized clothes, to eat off magnetized plates, and to bathe in tubs filled with magnetized iron pellets.[62] Aside from individual magnetic remedies, there are two typical group activities. The first concerns patients sitting in individual tubs, placed in a circle. A single, looping metallic rope attaches to the patients' thumbs and index fingers—the idea being that the "magnetic fluid" of the collective somehow resets and rebalances the health of the individual bathers.[63] The second concerns a more formal group session, which Mesmer calls a "séance": The curtains are drawn. A candle is lit. The patients sit at a round table holding hands. Music plays in the background. Mesmer himself wafts through the room touching his patients with his wand, resulting in startling changes of behavior: women faint, men convulse.[64] When returning to their normal state, many patients recount out-of-body experiences; some believe that they have traveled to the past; others state that they have been to the future.[65] No doubt encouraged by the doctor, patients then write to family and friends of their "prophetic sleep" and of their "mysterious contacts."[66]

In 1777, more miracles follow. Mesmer treats the blind pianist Maria Theresia, a student of Antonio Salieri. Mesmer, calling on the "intermediary bodies" for a cure, is able to restore her sight. Unfortunately, the cure proves to be a Faustian bargain. The poor girl can no longer play the piano. Her family complains, and Mesmer stops his treatment. Sure enough, the girl's blindness, and her talent, return.[67] A year later, Mesmer moves to Paris; his fame grows, so much so that by 1784 Louis XVI creates a commission, headed by Jean-Sylvain Bailly, an important French astronomer, to study Mesmer and his so-called cures. In his report, Bailly describes Mesmer as a charismatic cult leader and a menace to public safety: "[Mesmer] can act upon man, at any moment and almost at will, by striking the imagination."[68] Others link Mesmerism to Satanism, especially satanic possession.[69]

If that sounds similar to David George Goyder's aforementioned attack on Swedenborg and his followers, that is because by 1830 or so the terms *Swedenborgism* and *Mesmerism* were used interchangeably; the charge of Satanism likely spurred the fledgling movement to adopt a new name—"Spiritualism."[70] Yet, even newly titled, "Spiritualism" continued to face the old charges. The titles of the following works speak for themselves: William Ramsey and Horace Lorenzo Hastings, *Spiritualism, A Satanic Delusion, and a Sign of the Times* (1856); J. W. Daniels, *Spiritualism Versus Christianity: or, Spiritualism Thoroughly Exposed* (1856); Charles Cowan, *Thoughts on Satanic Influence; or, Modern Spiritualism Considered* (1861); A. B. Morrison, *Spiritualism and Necromancy* (1873); and Arthur Pridham, *The Spirits Tried; or, Spiritualism Self-Convicted* (1874).

Despite this opposition, the new faith soon spread to France—where Tardy de Montravel (1887) believed that magnetism allowed the Spirit to vacate a mortal body temporarily in order to travel, as Swedenborg had, to the Spiritual Realm and its outlying planets[71]—and to America—where George Bush, a distinguished professor of Hebrew at New York University, noted that mesmerized patients often spoke in their sleep. Some were already arguing that this "talk" was merely a dream state, but Bush, a Swedenborgian, believed them to be messages from the Spirit world.[72] Likewise, in 1870–71, Kate Fox—the youngest of three family mediums known as the "Fox Sisters"—often conjured and conversed with Benjamin Franklin, "the father of electricity and the discoverer of the spiritual telegraph between two worlds."[73] Franklin's ghost explained that poor reception between the "spheres"—a Swedenborgian term—was due to a lack of Mesmeric or magnetized vapor.[74] Recalling his own experiments with Spiritualism in the 1880s, the Shakespeare collector and editor H. H. Furness joked that "Spiritualists had become so saturated with magnetism, that a man could not hammer in the tack to put down the carpet."[75]

SPIRITUALISM AND THEATRICALISM

Furness here repeats the claims found in early anti-Swedenborg tracts, that converts to the new cult were ignorant, working-class, "simple, unwary, and ill-informed souls," but he fails to see the attraction of the new religion—its theatricality. This is an aspect often overlooked by modern-day academics. Robert Darnton (1968), for example, suspected that Mesmer was nothing more than a "charlatan" hiding within the trappings of religious robes and rituals.[76] Darnton sees theatricality as a form of falsehood—Mesmer is, in his view, a con man. But, in the doctor's defense, we might here note that most established religions are both sincere and theatrical. Consider the pageantry of the Catholic Church: the monks of many monastic orders in their pointed cowls and dapper cloaks, the monsignors in cassocks spruced with purple, the seminarians in red vestments, the cardinals and bishops in their white and scarlet silks, the pope in his splendid robes and mighty headdress of intricate orphrey. Consider the stagings within almost all Christian churches: the brilliant banners floating down from roof rafters; the delicate stained glass luminous in the clerestory windows; the church organ filling the air with heavenly vibrations; the golden thuribles wafting incense; the sacred chalice filled (supposedly) with the transmuted blood of Christ; the congregation's ritual readings and ritual replies; the kneeling, the singing of psalms; the general solemnity associated with baptisms or other related blessings, marriages, funerals, or just daily services.

The link between the theater and religion is, however, difficult to define emphatically. While Jane Goodall (2008) states matter-of-factly that classical forms of Western theater are concerned with metaphysical questions about the nature and scope of human existence, we might also wade in the countervailing current, as described by ancient Roman historian Marcus Terentius Varro, who argued that state-subsidized theology, while "especially adapted to the theatre," was useful only insofar as it moderated and regulated public behavior: "from [staged religious service] is to be known what god each one may suitably worship, what sacred rites and sacrifices each one may suitably perform."[77] Recent studies of English medieval theater have likewise linked the Catholic Church's mystery plays to other state-sponsored events, such as royal entries, city pageants, tournaments, and courtly dances, but there is little evidence to suggest that worshipers believed they were actually seeing pneumatophany—the summoning of the Holy Ghost—at each religious or civic ceremony.[78] In the Renaissance, religion, theater, and the state were closely aligned, often with much the same inert results: according to Stephen Greenblatt (1988), Shakespeare, while adopting much of the theatrics of the Catholic Church, "evacuated [their] rituals" and "drained [them] of their original meaning."[79]

While the time frames and cultural contexts of these examples differ wildly, all indicate that staged religion, while theatrically magnificent, often lacked religious transcendence. The Spiritualist séance overcame all such difficulties by embracing the theatrical elements on which its own liturgy depended. Whether sincere or fraudulent, Spiritual mediums were obviously expert in staging supernatural events.[80] The darkened room, the rapping sound effects, the disembodied voices, the holding of hands, the unseen Spirit Guide, the floating furniture, the crystal ball—all suggested the innate mystery and theatricality of the new faith. Special lighting was often required, and pyrotechnics were common: phosphorescence and colored lights "allowed spirits to appear and disappear in startling and dramatic ways."[81]

The Fox Sisters, the aforementioned American medium threesome, were in many ways typical: while they came to prominence because Spirits rapped violently upon their commands, later Fox tours included skin writing, a form of spiritual communication that required the partial undress of these three attractive women.[82] The group also perfected table turning, also known as table tilting or table tipping, in which the table would rise and fall a number of times to indicate yes, no, or maybe.[83] Private séances might also include lampadomancy, pyroscopy, scrying, or tasseography. The three sisters had individual talents as well: Kate, the youngest, was adept at mirror-scripting, or writing backward right to left; for greater theatrical effect, Kate performed this feat while blindfolded. Kate also learned how to make guitars seemingly play themselves and chairs, even with heavy occupants aboard, to move on their own.[84] Margaret, the middle child of this Spiritualist ternion, mastered pellet reading; the eldest sister, Leah, managed to acquire a "pianola," what we would call a player piano, which was "sweetly played upon by spirit fingers."[85] (Early models of player pianos were on display in England in 1847 but were yet unknown in America.) Their act also included floating lights, which "usually showed themselves first behind and between [sisters] Leah and Kate, near the floor. Then they rose; sometimes remaining near Leah's head, sometimes near her sister's. One of [the lights] was nearly as large as a human head."[86]

Spiritualist meetings often turned into musical theater: in Cape Town, South Africa, medium Mrs. Butters (1931), while under the possession of a Spirit, broke out into Italian song so often that her fellow Spiritualists made a gramophone of the performances.[87] E. Lee Howard (1935) recounts matter-of-factly that his local Spiritualist meetings included song and dance by the Spirits, who—at appropriate moments—would temporarily inhabit the bodies of the living. A Mrs. Wickland, for example, "yielded to a request that she go into a trance and let a Spanish dancer repeat a beautiful performance given through her at a public séance a few weeks before"; another Spirit, "Lucille Weston," sang a duet with a living person in the room, who took her arm in arm.[88]

Relatedly, Spiritualists often used theatrical spaces for their sacred rites. Harry Houdini's memoirs, *A Magician among the Spirits* (1924), cite several instances of Spiritualist mediums renting out theaters in Chicago (The Palace Theatre, 2,500 seats) and New York (The Morosco Theatre, 955 seats).[89] In England, spaces like the Egyptian Hall in Piccadilly Circus—described as an "apartment of great size"—were often rented for large Spiritualist assemblies.[90] Still more important, some Shakespeare actors were also performing mediums. Whether conjuring Shakespeare on stage or in the more intimate confines of a séance, the actor had to connect with Shakespeare, had to internalize and then vocalize the immortal words. As an example, we will need to relocate to the American Midwest and then to points beyond . . .

The year is 1900. Indianapolis. The feminist, educator, and psychic researcher, May Wright Sewall, is introduced to an actress—known only as "Miss G."—who carries with her a letter "from an actress long since dead." This letter is a Spiritual communication, "received through her own hand," directing Sewall to introduce Miss G. to the public. Sewall looked the letter over: "At first I could not recall the name signed to this strange epistle, but finally remembered having heard it in connection with an actress of Shakespearian rôles." Sewall then organized a gathering of about "two hundred guests chosen from my friends as those most interested in the dramatic art, most familiar with the theater and therefore best qualified to judge her work." Sewall observed that, just prior to the recital, Miss G. fell into a trance:

> A shiver passed through her frame . . . and instantly she arose and went through the Dagger Scene from *Macbeth* with a power and finish which I have never seen surpassed although I have seen it rendered many times by the world's most famous actors, including Edwin Booth, Sir Henry Irving and Salvini.
>
> Miss G. told me that, according to her conviction, she acts always under the direct inspiration of some great actor already on the next plane; that having begun as a child to commit to memory Shakespearian tragedies all of the instruction in regard to gesture, literary interpretation and the use of the instrument her voice which she has ever known has come to her from the same source.

With no stage accessories, this remarkable woman "recited successively the climaxes of five great dramas, producing upon her auditors an amazing effect." We should here note that Miss G. performed the dagger scene in *Macbeth*, not because she looked or sounded the part or because she could hope to be cast in that titular role. No matter how extensive Mrs. Sewall's contacts, it remained unlikely that a theater company in turn-of-the-century Indianapolis would cast a woman as Macbeth. The theatrical display was of another sort—a demonstration that within her lay the right theatrical and spiritual combination for mediumship. It seems only appropriate, therefore, that at the close of the week, Miss G. rewarded Sewall with a private séance of automatic writing. After some hours of frantic lettering, the medium collapsed. Sewall then went through the papers, discovering the signatures of playwrights and actors "covering the period since and including Shakespeare's time."[91]

If Miss G.'s performance was sincere, it would seem that Shakespeare, on rare occasion, was intent upon turning séances into theatrical recitals. Moreover, Miss G.'s use of Spiritualism was related to her era's common method of theatrical preparation. In an age in which actors and actresses were lauded for bringing dead characters to "life," Miss G. simply did within the séance room what she was encouraged to do on stage—that is, allow a character to take possession of her mind and body.[92] Employing the language of the stage, the medium Frances H. Green (1853) noted,

> As there is no programme of the performances [i.e., possessions], and therefore the spectators [i.e., worshipers and curiosity seekers] do not know what is coming till it is nearly or quite past, and at the same time the actors [i.e., mediums in a state of possession], themselves, do not remember any thing of what has happened, when they return to the normal state, these representations seem to go by with a kind of meteoric splendor, which arrests the attention, and thrills the heart for a little while; and then it is extremely difficult to give any thing of a definite idea of what has passed; and even if the scenes and language could be correctly remembered by the observers in their original form and spirit, no merely verbal description could present them to other minds so that they could obtain the faintest notion of the effect produced.

In the same passage, she referred to spiritual voicings and movements as "dramatic scenes."[93]

Spiritualist posters and advertisements also suggest an overlap of the thespian and the theologian. The West Coast medium Richard Zenor, for example, marketed himself as would any itinerant performer. On June 24, 1931, the *Spokane Daily Chronicle* advertised that "Richard Zenor[,] said to be a world renowned boy medium[,] Will be at the First

Spiritual Science church 340 nights beginning Sunday." The August 6, 1932, *San Jose News* stated that "Richard Zenor, psychic of Hollywood," has just "completed a very successful weeks' campaign in the interest of psychic science;" on 20 August 1932, the same paper announced, with the subtlety of a circus barker, that "By popular demand Roy [*sic*] Zenor, boy psychic of Hollywood, will return to the Harmony Church of Spiritualists for a two weeks' engagement;" on August 27, 1932, the *San Jose News* stated, "Richard Zenor, boy psychic" will lecture on "The Future of the Universe" at the Harmony Church of Spiritualists. On May 14, 1939, Zenor was advertised in the *Los Angeles Times* classified section as the "Famous trance psychic"; on February 1, 1941, he was listed in the same paper's classified section as "The Original Boy Wonder."[94] In 1943, Zenor established his own church, Agasha Temple of Wisdom, still in existence to this day. In 1957, Zenor published his spiritual pronouncements, one of which reads, "Death is easy, but birth is far more difficult," a variation on the showbiz truism, "Dying is easy, comedy is hard."[95]

The foregoing documents the theatrical link between Shakespeare and an upstart religion calling itself "Spiritualism." Shakespeare was the natural focal point of the new religion because he was both a poet of the impossible and an apotheosized man of the theater. To the theatrically and theologically minded alike, Spiritualism, with its Swedenborgian Spiritual Library and its Mesmeric trance states, offered an immediate, an intimate, and a visceral relationship with Shakespeare. It was one thing to talk knowingly about Shakespeare, or, rather, to talk the talk that was (and is) expected of professional Shakespearean scholars—that is, reference to living and dead critics; familiarity with the plays' print and performance histories; appreciation of Shakespeare's cultural influence; command of the key dates of Shakespeare's life, career, marriage, and death; and so forth. It was (and is) quite another experience to have Shakespeare manifest before you, to see and to talk to the soul of the author himself, to have him listen carefully to *you* and respond to each of *your* questions, and then to learn that *you* have been selected by Shakespeare himself to participate in a revelation of sacred meaning. A still more profound experience awaited the Spiritualist medium or faith-based Spiritualist actor: imagine more than just talking to Shakespeare's Spirit; imagine having his immortal thoughts manifesting themselves within you, without any fear or misgivings on your part. Imagine no distinction, no separation; no longer you *and* Shakespeare; absolute harmony manifesting itself instant by instant. It such Zen-like moments, there is no feigning, no hamming, no acting, only being.

All well and good for those who believed that they were communing with Shakespeare; yet, there were still other Spiritualists who whispered that Shakespeare was not the author of Shakespeare's plays. Perhaps Sir Francis Bacon was the true Shakespearean soul of his age? There was but one way to find out. Ask him . . .

CHAPTER 2

CRYPTS AND CRYPTO-GRAPHOLOGY

THE YEAR IS 1858. SPRING GROVE HOSPITAL, near Hartford, Maryland. A new patient is delivered to the psych ward: She is 47 years old, has a habit of cocking her head to one side, and exhibits paranoid—even bizarre—delusions, disorganized speech, and thinking. She once tried to dig up a grave. Diagnosis: *démence précoce*, or what we call paranoid schizophrenia. In an effort to calm her mind, physicians administer liberal doses of narcotics, stimulants, emetics, and purgatives, subject her to cold and hot baths, and, when she turns violent, confine her to a bed or a "holding chair" with mechanical restraints.[1] All this because of a belief that Shakespeare did not pen the plays and poems of Shakespeare. The patient's name is Delia Bacon.

Yet as her biographer, Mrs. Hon Farrar, explains, Delia Bacon's initial interest in Shakespeare stemmed not from a love or hatred of that writer but from a courtship gone awry with Reverend Alexander McWhorter: Delia Bacon thought she had found her soul mate but was crushed when she learned that he was "secretly holding her up to ridicule among his friends, and, when it was reported he was engaged to marry her, he indignantly declared his surprise that any one who knew him should think him such a fool."[2] After being jilted by McWhorter, Delia Bacon left for England, desperate to prove that her namesake, if not her direct ancestor, was the man whose works were attributed to Shakespeare.

Considering Delia Bacon's internment, one expects her book *The Philosophy of the Plays of Shakspere Unfolded* (1857) to be filled with unreasonable arguments or convoluted correspondences. On that score, the book does have some odd pronouncements. But chiefly, the book is *not* about authorship, a subject Delia Bacon actually downplays: "the question of the authorship of the great philosophic poems," she writes, "is an incidental question in this inquiry."[3] What really interests Delia Bacon is a "new magic" by which she might read the plays, something akin to "the miracles of Oriental dreams and fables."[4] Her dissatisfaction with traditional analysis and logical explanation stems from her notion that the works themselves and the mind behind them are not encompassed by traditional thinking; they remain "unreduced to order by his [the author's] philosophy, unreduced to melody by his verse."[5] Thus what is needed is a Shakespearean way of approaching Shakespeare.

The search for a "new magic" led Delia Bacon to the notion that all great literature is somehow connected by a secret theological component. Nathaniel Hawthorne, at the time serving as American council in Liverpool, recalled, "The only time I ever saw Miss Bacon was in London . . . I was ushered up two (and I rather believe three) pair of stairs into a parlour somewhat humbly furnished, and told that Miss Bacon would come soon. There were a number of books on the table, and, looking into them, I found that every one had some reference, more or less immediate, to her Shakespearian theory . . . To be sure, there was a pocket-Bible among the books . . . I have no doubt that she had established subtile connections between it [Shakespeare] and the Bible likewise."[6] "I can never forget," wrote another of her supporters, "how clear she made it to us that the world was only then made fit for the advent of Jesus . . . she often spoke like an oracle."[7] Talk of Shakespeare led to esotericism, talk of esotericism led to mysticism, talk of mysticism led to God.

And had she ended her book on that point alone—that is, that Shakespeare's works are esoteric—she might today be labeled as just another bardolater with Romantic or antimaterialistic tendencies, not far different in tone and tenor than Thomas Carlyle's argument (stated in the last chapter) that Shakespeare was not really a playwright at all but a "Priest of Mankind." But Delia Bacon goes on to make two more important statements. The first concerns her belief that secret messages in Shakespeare would in turn lead to the discovery of a new "will and other documents relating to the conclave [i.e., a secret order] of Elizabethan philosophers." The second odd statement concerns the resting place of those "other documents," which, she explained to Nathaniel Hawthorne, "were concealed (when and by whom she did not inform me) in a hollow space in the under surface of Shakespeare's gravestone."[8]

The idea that a "new magic" is buried *within* Shakespeare's work is here reflected in the notion that there is something buried *with* Shakespeare's body. That might sound a bit baffling but hardly worth locking someone up over. But what really took matters to a new pitch was when Delia Bacon decided to prove to the world that she was right and everyone else

Figure 2.1   Delia Bacon. By permission of the Folger Shakespeare Library.

was wrong. She therefore went to Holy Trinity Church, Stratford-upon-Avon, seeking permission to dig up Shakespeare. Initially, she met with refusal, but she then applied to the vicar, who consulted with a lawyer. Amazingly, the vicar relented. The search of the grave was to take place after nightfall. The vicar and clerk waited only for Delia Bacon's word in order to set about lifting the tombstone. Hawthorne sets the scene: "in this apparently prosperous state of things, her own convictions began to falter. A doubt stole into her mind whether she might not have mistaken the depository and mode of concealment of those historic treasures; and after once admitting the doubt, she was afraid to hazard the shock of uplifting the stone and finding nothing."[9] Complete madness soon seized her and she was carted off to an insane asylum in Henley-in-Arden, eight miles outside of Stratford. She was still confined there when her book, *The Philosophy of the Plays of Shakspere Unfolded*, was published in 1857. In 1858, she was moved to the Bloomingdale Asylum in New York, and finally to the asylum at Spring Grove in Maryland, where she died in 1859.[10]

A BRIEF HISTORY OF BACONIAN CODE
BREAKERS AND OCCULTISTS

Delia Bacon's story, or at least its tragic arc, repeats in the case of Ignatius Donnelly, an earnest congressman and Swedenborgian minister turned sibylline sleuth. In 1881, while flipping through one of his little son's new books, *Every Boy's Book: A Complete Encyclopædia of Sports and Amusements*, Donnelly became interested in what that book had to say about ciphers: "Most of the examples given will only enable one to decipher the most simple kinds, such as are generally found in magazines, &c.; for if that intricate cipher of Lord Bacon's were put in a book for boys, it would be a waste of paper, as we will venture to say that not one in a thousand would be able to find it out."[11] Intrigued by the challenge, Donnelly then applied the ciphers he found in the book to Shakespeare's texts. There was just one problem. No cipher seemed to work consistently:

> I tried in every possible way to establish some arithmetical relation between these significant words. It was all in vain. I tried all the words on page 53, on page 54, on page 55. I took every fifth word, every tenth word, every twentieth word, every fiftieth word, every hundredth word. But still the result was incoherent nonsense. I counted from the top of the pages down, from the bottom up, from the beginning of acts and scenes and from the ends of acts and scenes, across the pages, and hop, skip and jump in every direction; still, it produced nothing but dire nonsense.[12]

Eventually, Donnelly, like Delia Bacon before him, put logic aside. The plays were one great philosophic poem, part of a great "spiritual design" that only he could read.[13] One contemporary called his process of reading "an intricate arithmetical, multi-literal cryptogram . . . of which the man in the street can make neither head nor tail."[14]

Donnelly published his opus, *The Great Cryptogram* (1887), in the aftermath of a disastrous political campaign, during which he had been ousted by his own party; the same period was marked by the declining health of his wife, Kate.[15] Despite, or perhaps in part because of, his sad

Figure 2.2   Ignatius Donnelly. Courtesy of American Antiquarian Society.

circumstances, the former congressman became something of a walking punch line:

> Mr. Donnelly began by elaborating his hypothesis and expounding and elucidating his cryptogram. A Colonel Wintersmith listened with the courteous attention but, as the story lengthened and the argument thickened, he could stand it no longer: "Mr. Donnelly," he said, "I cannot allow you to go any further on this line, because I know, as a matter of fact, that William Shakespeare, of Stratford-on-Avon, wrote those plays,—every one of them." Donnelly, startled, said: "How could you know that, Colonel Wintersmith?" Without a moment's hesitation, but with an air of finality, the Colonel replied: "Because I was there, sir, and I saw him write them." Though knocked almost speechless, Donnelly found voice to murmur, "Why, Colonel Wintersmith, it was three hundred years ago," and, turning placidly to Mr. Blackburn, the Colonel said, as if exchanging a pleasantry, "Joe, how time passes!"[16]

Now dismissed as "the prince of cranks," depressed by the downward spiral of his political and literary career, distraught over the failing health of his wife, Donnelly wrote, "I am nigh weary of life. My wretched fate pursued me . . . I cursed the evil spirits that are pursuing me and swore at the damnable subtlety of Francis Bacon which had sent Delia Bacon to the mad-house and covered me with ignominy."[17]

That sounds gloomy, but, in keeping with his studies, the line has to be read in code. Twelve years after the publication of *The Great Cryptogram*, Donnelly issued yet another study, *The Cipher in the Plays and on the Tombstone* (1899), in which he discussed the phrase "I am nigh weary of life." It is nearly a direct quotation from *Macbeth*: "I gin to be a-weary of the sun."[18] According to Donnelly, these same words were written by Bacon to signify a deeper, "true" knowledge, a knowledge protected by Delia Bacon's aforementioned "conclave," which he renamed the "Rosicrucian Society," a group of philosophers guarding the "*secresy, traditions,* and *publication*" of the works of Bacon/Shakespeare.[19]

There is, too, in *The Cipher in the Plays and on the Tombstone*, a growing certainty of the paranormal. Donnelly's wife Kate had died in 1894; her decline had been hastened by a major stroke the year before, which left her in a wheelchair. In May 1897, Donnelly attended a variety of séances to contact her.[20] Once contact with her Spirit was established, Donnelly had an epiphany: if his wife was not really dead, then graves were not graves. Perhaps the great code applied to more than just the works of "Shakespeare"; there were other texts to consider.[21] Donnelly then thought of Delia Bacon . . . yes! . . . of course! "Shakespeare's" tomb!

Delia Bacon had had the answer before her all along. It was found in the dire warning on the original grave slab:

> Good frend for Iesus sake forbeare,
> To digg the dust encloased heare.
> Blese be yᵉ man yᵉ spares thes stones,
> And curst be he yᵉ moves my bones.

Applying his complicated cipher to the tombstone epitaph revealed a hitherto hidden message: "There is something hidden here, that was not to be revealed until after a certain number of years had passed."[22]

In Chapter 6 of this study, I will argue that Spiritualists rely on nonlogic or free-form association. Donnelly offers us a preview of that argument: to decipher was to decrypt. Decrypt—crypt—corpse—corpus—literary corpus. The grave was not a grave at all but a secret library wherein Bacon's "original books and manuscripts [were] to be preserved until that day has arrived when they could be safely published."[23] Delia Bacon had similarly believed that the grave held a new "will and other documents," but she had stopped short of exhuming "Shakespeare's" grave. Was she right? Did the truth need to remain hidden, at least for now? Donnelly did not know. Perhaps it was best that the authorial secret remain shrouded, as Francis Bacon and the Rosicrucians had wished. Let the world fall away; Bacon would still be concealed, outlasting the chaos of mankind: "Bacon . . . postponed the revelation of his great secret until such time as the age would give it fair treatment and an impartial hearing. Is not that age here now? Will anything be gained by deferring it a few years, or a century or two, longer?"[24]

Armed with this "great secret," Donnelly felt an odd serenity. Bacon himself had been marginalized, cheated of his due; if so with the master, why not so with the disciple? Donnelly's book, *The Great Cryptogram*, would, like Delia Bacon's prior study, offer the world an alternative way of reading Shakespeare, one that was at odds with the "soulless, callous, materialistic development" of traditional criticism. It would stand against not only materially obvious reading but also the material realm, the fallen order of the flesh that had destroyed his wife and ruined his career.[25] Donnelly saw himself part of a Baconian "inner circle, of great and faithful men," a high priest crowned with a "halo of poetic splendor."[26]

As noted, Donnelly had already contacted the Spirit of his wife via séance; others had attempted to contact Bacon through the same means. In keeping with the premise that there was a deeper code within "Shakespeare's" plays and poems, Bacon's Spirit often replied in cipher. For example, during a séance in 1890, a Mr. J. Henderson received a message from a Spirit written in a "double cryptogram, which would supply his [true] name." Henderson promised he would set to work cracking the code, but the Spirit's anxiety was so intense that it could not wait; it, therefore, deciphered the *first* sequence of the double cryptogram for Henderson. The first decryption revealed a simple acrostic, WILLIAM SHAKSPEAR:

> **W**hen on the earth, my life was full of woe,
> **I**llness, and misery; but now that *I*
> **L**ive as a spirit, I as a spirit *l*ove.
> **L**ist to my tale, and mark me well; and lest
> **I**magination wanders, write it down; indeed,
> **A**ssured I have your interest at aim;
> **M**aking all things sure of who I am. So mark,
> **S**ee you not plainly how I toil and strive,
> **H**aving your welfare in my heart,
> **A**nd to show you how to answer those, who like the stupid ass,
> **K**now such things are, and yet they will not know?
> **S**ceptics at heart, they laugh, and jeer, and scoff,
> **P**riding themselves upon their wit, perhaps.
> **E**ven though they taunt, when dewy eve
> **A**rrives they tremble. They feel a certain awe
> **R**ise in their souls, to them 'tis real.

But what of the *second* cryptogram, which would reveal the "true" name? Here, the Spirit was more circumspect: it "whispered in my [Henderson's] ear instructions which I was on no account to repeat to any person, as my so doing might frustrate his intention. These instructions, he [the Spirit] assured me, if carried out faithfully and carefully, would not only relieve him of a great trouble, but would be an immense proof of the truth of Spiritualism."[27] While the second code was never cracked, the fact that there was yet another puzzle to solve confirmed that Shakespeare was not an identity marker but merely the first clue to a far deeper mystery.

In 1893, Orville W. Owen of Detroit, a short, thickset man with a heavy mustache and gold-rimmed spectacles, claimed, as Henderson had three years before, that Bacon's ghost had told him that there was indeed a secret code but that Donnelly had not fully solved its complexities. Bacon then shared the code with Owen, who constructed a "great wheel." By turning Shakespeare's text through this deciphering wheel, a slew of hitherto unknown and fully shocking histories were revealed: Queen Elizabeth, previously thought to have been a virgin, had married Robert Dudley, but Dudley had already married Ayme Robsart. The love-stricken Queen Elizabeth, therefore, sanctioned the murder of her rival. Further adventures detailed the banishment of Francis Bacon to France.[28] The sensational revelation as to why Bacon bothered to put his story down in code at all was still to come: he, Bacon, was the son of Queen Elizabeth! Were King James to learn the truth—that Bacon was the true king of England—his life would not be worth a jot:

> The man to whom I have referred within
> The circle of these narratives would
> Not only reveal them to King James,
> But would himself labour to give me
> A crown of martyrdom.
> He is held in great estimation by the king,
> Who is extremely jealous of me, and
> Is afraid the day will come that I
> Will fall between his titles and
> Take the throne; therefore, to save myself,
> I have observed these differing unities
> In manner of a mask.[29]

Owen then did what Donnelly had done: apply the cipher code to any and all texts related to "Shakespeare." He struck gold when deciphering one particular line from the poem opposite Shakespeare's woodcut in the First Folio: "It was for gentle Shakespeare cut," which he somehow decoded to read "Seek, sir, a true angle at Chepstow—F[rancis]." Owen did some checking. Chepstow Castle is a town in Monmouthshire, Wales; Bacon's father-in-law lived in nearby Beachly. Further decipherment indicated that there was a box buried in a "Bed of brace beams under the Roman Road." Owen then organized an archeological dig on a Roman road leading to Chepstow. One assumes that Owen expected to find Bacon's Shakespearean manuscripts, but press reports confirm that he hoped to find something else entirely: Owen told one reporter that it was likely that Shakespeare, a mere talking head for Bacon, had "quarreled with his patron" about money. Furious with Shakespeare, Bacon "drew his sword and ran Shakespeare through the heart." Sir Francis then "cut [Shakespeare's] head off, and buried it among the manuscripts."[30] The Roman road was more than a repository for Bacon's manuscripts; it was also a crime scene. Owen began digging in 1909 and kept at it, on and off, for the next 15 years.

To help fund his project, Owen tried to sell his discoveries to the *Daily Mail* for £5,000.[31] While the paper declined to pay for the exclusive, a reporter did interview him. Owen told him that the code would reveal still greater mysteries, among them an occult power that allowed Bacon to fly an airplane-like device several hundred years before the Wright brothers did. The secret device was capable of moving "so fast that its body will have to be covered with asbestos to prevent it catching fire and blazing up like a meteor." So why hadn't Bacon shown his airship to King James? Owen explained that he had, but the science had been branded as witchcraft, necessitating that Bacon not only hide his plans but also fake his own death—according to Owen, Bacon died in 1642, not in 1626 as his biographies state.[32] The full plans of the airship could not be revealed, but Owen confirmed that he had already built a prototype capable of lifting 22 tons. He planned to patent Bacon's discovery and to seek investors. But, since Owen liked the reporter so much, he was willing to sell him a "few shares at a hundred dollars each." Warming to his subject, Owen exclaimed, "Just think! . . . Ships out of date; trains out of date; motor-cars out of date. No part of the world that can't be reached in a few hours. It's the greatest opportunity in history."[33] The *Daily Mail* reporter remained unimpressed but hung around a few days as Owen continued to dig. When he found nothing, the unshakeable Owen told the reporter that either Bacon had "changed their [the manuscripts'] hiding place, or someone has been here before me and taken them away" or his deciphering wheel had been affected by a shift in the magnetic poles.

All this talk of airships and investors sounds like a con, a desperate attempt to raise money by any means.[34] But we should not lose sight of the mystical here: Owen was only able to crack the code because Bacon's ghost had given him the secret for the "great wheel." Further, Bacon's code revealed an occult, floating power, and if his calculations were off, it was only because Owen had not yet deciphered another, possibly related, occult mystery: Mesmer's magnetism (discussed in Chapter 1).

In 1899, Orville W. Owen's former assistant, the blond and bifocaled Elizabeth Wells Gallup, came up with her own deciphering method, which again revealed that Shakespeare's plays were by Bacon, as were some (though not all) of the plays of Ben Jonson, some (though not all) of the works of Robert Greene, some (though not all) of the works of Marlowe, and some (though not all) of the works of Spenser; Bacon had also scripted hitherto-thought anonymous plays, such as *Sir John Oldcastle* and *Yorkshire Tragedy*.[35] Similar to Owen, Gallup found within these texts Bacon's secret: Bacon was the child of Queen Elizabeth and the Earl of Essex and, "therefore, being the first borne sonne of this union should sit upon the throne, ruling the people over whom the Supreame Soveraigne doth shew my right, as hath beene said, whilst suff'ring others to keepe the royall power."[36]

Bacon, ever thinking of posterity, understood that deciphering the works would be difficult and time consuming, so he left a gift: a series of new poems and plays written in cipher and tucked near-invisibly *within* the published plays. These included abridged versions of the *Iliad* and *Odyssey* and three entirely unknown plays: *The Tragedy of Anne Boleyn, The Tragical Historie of Our Late Brother, Robert, Earl of Essex,* and *The Historical Tragedy of Mary, Queen of Scots.*[37] These hidden works, Bacon assumed, would be worth a fortune to anyone dedicated enough to find them: "The whole shall be the reward of my decypherer and will repay most generouslie his entire devotion to this labour."[38] As to why he decided to write plays within the plays, Bacon explained, in cipher, that he wrote in this manner: "In good hope of saving th' same from olde Father Time's ravages."[39] Why a play written in cipher would, in and of itself, help in its preservation remains unanswered. Gallup then discovered yet another secret, which she published in 1910: the whereabouts of Bacon's manuscripts. Bacon's plan, at least initially, had been to spread them out among the graves of his aliases, which included Robert Greene, Christopher Marlowe, George Peele, Edmund Spenser, Robert Burton, and, of course, William Shakespeare.[40]

Like Delia Bacon and Orville Owen before her, Gallup then traveled to England so that she could inspect the graves of these writers. Unfortunately, Robert Greene's grave lies "beneath the network of the Liverpool St. railway terminus; that of Christopher Marlowe fifteen feet below the tower of St. Nicholas Church, Deptford, while of George Peele's resting place there seems to be no trace."[41] She had better luck with Burton, whose memorial she found in the cathedral of Christ Church, Oxford. Applying her cipher to what seemed to be an unremarkable Latin passage revealed a clue: "Take heed; In a box is MS. Fr. B."[42] Still more deciphering told her that the key to all Baconian revelation would be found on "the stone of the Stratford Tablet."[43] Or at least that was the plan, but after Bacon's death, the papers were moved by Burton and William Rawley—the latter served as Bacon's personal secretary and chaplain—who left a note, in cipher, of course, which read, "No box is in so odd a place as that having th' MSS. that added so much to th' name of Will S., supposed in his time to write."[44] The manuscripts, the newly decrypted message revealed, were actually hidden in Canonbury: "*Certain old panels in the double work of Canonbury Tower, and at our Countrie Manor, Gorha'bury, alone sav'd most valu'd MSS. Thus co'cceal'd, more closely watched, more suited to escape sublest inquiry, you shall find th' dramas hee wisht to hide in th' stone he proposed should bee sett up in the Ch. of Stratford.*"[45] But the Renaissance portions of the Canonbury Tower had been largely reconstructed. Were the manuscripts therefore lost? Not necessarily! Rawley had the foresight to leave still more manuscripts in Gorhambury Manor, but, alas, that structure too had been ruined by time.[46] Nonetheless, a search ensued. No manuscripts, nor any other clues, were found. Gallup was eventually dismissed as a nutcase or a forger, perhaps both.[47] But if we adopt a more mystical or metaphysical approach, we can understand why Gallup was taken seriously by other Baconians: Gallup's cryptography negotiates the space between the materially false and the metaphysically real; she reinforces the notion that the eternal outlasts the material.

On first pass, our next Baconian investigator, Walter Conrad Arensberg, did not suffer the slings and arrows of outrageous fortune. He was Harvard educated and took pride in mentioning that he had worked as an "assistant in [that prominent] English Department."[48] He was a millionaire (his wife was an heiress) and had amassed one of the most substantial and important French art collections in the country—the Arensberg Collection is now part of the Philadelphia Museum of Art's holdings. Arensberg himself served as a board member of the Los Angeles Art Association (1937), Los Angeles County Museum (1938–39), and the Southwest Museum (1944–54). In addition, he was a founding board member of the short-lived American Arts in Action (1943) and the Modern Institute of Art, Beverly Hills (1947–49). His extant and hitherto unpublished letters reveal his friendships with an unlikely mix of respected authors, among them Shakespeare biographer Bernard Grebanier and prize-winning poet (and declared Stratfordian) William Carlos Williams. Oddly, Arensberg never discussed the authorship debate with either writer.[49] Grebanier's single extant correspondence with Arensberg is dated August 5, 1947, but the same letter intimates the frequent exchange of poems and a promise to visit Arensberg in California; two letters from William Carlos Williams, dated April 4, 1944, and October 8, 1950, are innocuous in nature. Arensberg's friendships suggest a man willing to accept differences of opinion. The novelist Christopher Isherwood, however, adds some important details to our portrait:

> Arensberg remained a charming enthusiastic sane host until you got on the subject of Bacon; then he became wild-eyed and rather incoherent, with ruffled hair and gestures of frenzied excitement . . . [he speaks like] a madman as he reveals to you the existence of international conspiracies and speaks with the smiling scorn of the enemies who are trying to outwit him. Arensberg's enemies were all those scholars and other members of the Establishment who were concealing from the world the truth about Bacon. And what was the truth? That Bacon was a reincarnation of Jesus Christ. (I don't think I can be making this up.)[50]

Arensberg had a huge collection of Baconiana—more than 16,000 volumes—which, along with his correspondence, is now housed at the Huntington Library in Los Angeles, California. But his personal research library was small—a mere 76 books. Aside from standard editions of Bacon and Shakespeare, the research library includes (alphabetically by author) Franz Hartmann, *Cosmology, or, Universal Science, Cabala, Alchemy: Containing the Mysteries of the Universe* (1888); William James, *The Varieties of Religious Experience* (1920); Sir Oliver Lodge, *Science and Human Progress* (1927); S. L. MacGregor, *Kabbala Denudata: The Kabbalah Unveiled, Containing the Following Books of the Zohar* (1926); Jacques Maritain, *The Situation of Poetry: Four Essays on the Relations Between Poetry, Mysticism, Magic, and Knowledge* (ca. 1955); Rodolphe Louis Mégroz, *Francis Thompson: The Poet of Earth in Heaven: A Study in Poetic Mysticism* (1927); Rudolf Otto, *The Idea of the Holy: An Inquiry into the Non-Rational Factor in the Idea of the Divine* (1950); Herbert Silberer, *Problems of Mysticism and Its Symbolism* (1917); Walter Terence Stace, *Time and Eternity: An Essay in the Philosophy of Religion* (1952); Thomas Taylor, *The Eleusinian and Bacchic Mysteries* (1891); Evelyn Underhill, *Mysticism: A Study in the Nature and Development of Man's Spiritual Consciousness* (1911); and Edwin Eliott Willoughby, *The Bible Cryptogram Book* (ca. 1949). Many of these same works contain his notes, underlinings, and circlings. For example, when reading Herbert Silberer's *Problems of Mysticism and Its Symbols*, Arensberg circled the following, presumably because it confirmed that Shakespeare's (or Bacon's) true message went beyond the constraints of logic: "Understanding and feeling go in different directions, the simpleton waits meekly by the door that leads to the interior of the great mother."[51] Likewise, in his reading of S. L. MacGregor Mathers's *The Kabbalah Unveiled*, Arensberg was particularly taken with one passage, which he emphasized with double underlining and referred to again in his notes, found on the back cover's inside flap: "The hidden sense of this somewhat obscure passage is, that the brightness arises from the skull, *which it conceals*, which latter is therefore the emblem of the Concealed One. The thirteen parts are three tetragrammatic forms, which give twelve letters, and symbolize thus the Trinity of the Tetragram; and the one supernal part is the unity."[52] Arensberg's esoteric readings were keys to his unlocking of the Bacon mystery; the secret of Shakespeare's works would only be revealed to a seeker who was at last ready to "question the assumptions of traditional logic."[53] Thus, much like other alternative-author seekers before him, Arensberg used word association to solve a problem that was seemingly beyond logic's ken. In *The Secret Grave of Francis Bacon at Lichfield* (1923), for example, he

notes that "IAMON" is the Spanish word for "BACON" and the "pho-
netic equivalent of HAMMON, the name of an Egyptian god who reap-
pears in Roman mythology as Jupiter Hammon." And, since "IAMON"
is an anagram of "OMNIA," which Arensberg translates as "the relation
of God to the universe," and is nearly identical to the "secret designation
for Bacon in the anonymous letter to Malvolio, in which the obvious
cryptogram M.O.A.I. is intended as an anagram for IAMO, a form of
IAMON," it likewise follows that Bacon's secret code within Shakespeare
reveals "the mystery of redemption" and the "Pythagorean doctrine of
transmigration."[54] In his later book, *The Shakespearean Mystery* (1927), he
offers another word game explaining why Bacon chose Shakespeare as a
pseudonym: "SHAKESPEARE = CUT SPEARE = CUT SHAFT = CUT
STAFF = TRUNCHEON = BATON = BACON."[55]

Arensberg also applied his deciphering system to the texts found on
a variety of literary monuments, including Shakespeare's statue in Westminster Abbey—installed in 1740.[56] But Shakespeare had died in 1616.
Why would a 1740 monument at Westminster Abbey have a ciphered
text? There must be, Arensberg posited, a secret order that protected (*and
continued to protect*) the code and the grave sites. Of course! Delia Bacon's
"conclave," also known as the "Rosicrucians," whose members were and
are "not permitted to make public acknowledgement of their status,
[thus] I believe that the society had, or has, no direct connection with the
self-acknowledged Rosicrucians of the present time."[57]

If I understand this correctly, there are two Rosicrucian orders, one
secret, one public. That must be kind of confusing when one member of
a secret order attempts to recruit a new member. Imagine two friends, Jeffrey and Robert, having a conversation: "Jeffrey, I am a Rosicrucian. We
would like you to join our order?" Jeffrey replies, "I'm already a Rosicrucian." Robert responds, "Are you a member of the regular Rosicrucians or
the *secret* Rosicrucians?" Jeffrey replies, "Umm, there is a *secret* Rosicrucian order?" Robert replies, "I have said too much."

It's not just the name of the secret fellowship that presents a challenge:
the function of the secret Rosicrucian Order seems to be to pretend that
it doesn't exist and to share a secret that no one is allowed to know. But
having members in on a secret is surely the worst way to preserve a secret.
Why not simply destroy all evidence and disband the group?[58]

Undaunted by logic and in pursuit of their sacred mission, the furtive
Rosicrucians had infiltrated still other fraternal organizations, such as
the Freemasons, whose members were in "either complete or partial
ignorance of the Baconian secrets."[59] Why, asks Arensberg, had Delia
Bacon been locked up, Donnelly ruined, Owen discredited, and Gallup

dismissed? It was because the cloak-and-dagger Rosicrucians, in their attempts to guard the "true secret" of Bacon's manuscripts, would stop at nothing! Arensberg trusted no one. The Rosicrucians were everywhere: "it is my belief that the society may still be in existence and that a small group of its members may still have knowledge of the secret grave and of the nature of its contents . . . I have discovered that the power of the society derived from sources high in the Church and in the State, and . . . in places as guarded as the church at Stratford, in connection with the Shakespeare tomb, and in Westminster Abbey, in connection with the Shakespeare monument."[60]

This was not mere conjecture. Arensberg had two sets of unassailable proofs: the first consisted of printed material and monuments that confirmed that he had solved the riddle of "Shakespeare's" First Folio. We have already discussed Shakespeare's statue in Westminster Abbey. Arensberg further informed his readers that he had also located secret messages in the English translation of Bacon's *Advancement of Learning* (1640) and in a variety of texts, both old and recent. Arensberg even found coded messages on ephemera such as the admission tickets tourists purchased to enter Holy Trinity Church—proof that the Rosicrucians were operating to this very day in Stratford.[61] Still more suspiciously, Arensberg found the same code in the *Hand Guide to Lichfield Cathedral* (1923) and in a tourist book concerning that cathedral's Chapter House. He therefore assumed that Bacon's body was not interned at St. Michael's Church in St. Albans but was secretly placed within one of the walls of the Lichfield Chapter House.[62] Well, perhaps not the entire body: following up on Owen's idea that Bacon had decapitated Shakespeare, Arensberg speculated that "Bacon may have intended . . . that his body should be buried first in St. Michael's and then secretly removed, either entire or perhaps no more than the head to Litchfield."[63]

The second set of unassailable proof was more difficult to present to the public because the secret order of Rosicrucians refused to allow anyone access to it: "evidence is still in existence, in the place where it was originally deposited"—that is, Bacon's secret grave.[64] Arensberg, therefore, applied to the dean of the cathedral, the Rev. H. E. Savage, to inspect the walls of Chapter House.[65] He was denied. Arensberg assumed that the Reverend's snub was yet further proof: clearly, the Rev. Savage would not allow him to rip up the medieval walls of Chapter House because he, the reverend, was in on the conspiracy. Arensberg, therefore, demanded in print that Savage and his secret brethren "now make a public acknowledgment of all that they know, and all that they have hitherto concealed" concerning Bacon's secret Litchfield tomb.[66] The Reverend either denied or simply ignored this bizarre accusation, prompting Arensberg to dig a tunnel to Bacon's undisclosed burial place. Not surprisingly, Arensberg was caught and thereafter barred from the property.[67]

Last in our brief overview of the Baconian Spiritualists is Alfred Dodd, who began his quest for the "true" author of Shakespeare's plays after a visit to Stratford-upon-Avon in the summer of 1929. Dodd could not understand how such a genius had come from such "humble" means. He immediately thought of Francis Bacon, and the very next day, a friend, Alex Hay, gave him a copy of Donnelly's *Cryptogram*. He then began a feverous study of all things Shakespearean and moved to Stratford to get still closer to the mystery. One night, either in a dream or on a visit to the "astral plane"—Dodd himself was unsure—he met the ghost of Shakespeare, who said, cryptically, "*There is no number one. We will find it . . . The Key is in F.*" F stood for Francis Bacon. As for the number 1, Dodd took that to be a clue that he was to reorder the *Sonnets*, and, if necessary, the lines in them, and still further, the very spellings of those same lines.[68] Dodd was then psychically drawn to lines 3 and 4 of Sonnet 74:

> My life hath in this line some interest,
> Which for memorial still with thee shall stay.

Miraculously, the text began to change before his eyes. There seemed to rise out of the lines a series of bright letters:

My life h**A**th in thi**S** line s**O**me i**N**terest, = MASON

Those letters then faded and another pattern appeared:

My life h**A**th in thi**S** line some in**TER**est, = MASTER[.] [69]

Bacon was a Master Mason! That made sense. Dodd had already read the works of Arensberg, who had argued that Bacon was both a Mason and the founder of the supersecret Rosicrucians, and Dodd's own research had uncovered what he thought was a pertinent detail: the Freemasons had conducted a ceremonial rite at the founding of the 1932 Shakespeare Memorial Theatre. He took this as proof that Arensberg had been right. There was a "direct connection between Shakespeare and Freemasonry."[70] It was now somehow obvious to him that "Francis Bacon was the creator of the secret Rosicrosse Literary Society, the Rosicrucian Manifestoes, and Modern Freemasonry."[71] He became convinced or, more properly, convinced himself that the sonnet Quarto of 1609 "reeks with Rosicrosse Signals and Masonic Signs."[72]

In an effort to learn their secrets, Dodd joined the Freemasons.[73] But they too seemed to be genuinely ignorant of the Rosicrucians. Seemed to be . . . maybe everyone was lying! Dodd began to notice how canny the Freemasons were: "The subtle [i.e., hidden] manner in which Masonry is mentioned is particularly worthy of notice."[74] It was "worthy of notice" because it was not immediately apparent—hence, proof that something must be hidden. Dodd likewise argued that many of the Shakespeare critics of past ages were in on the secret: he labeled the poet laureate, dramatist, and early-eighteenth-century Shakespeare editor, Nicholas Rowe, as well as his contemporary, the play-adaptor Charles Gildon, as ringleaders of the conspiratorial "Rosicrosse Brethren."[75] The proof of their secrecy was that they had never mentioned the secret.

Now sure that the upper echelons of the Freemasons (i.e., the "Rosicrosse Brethren") were spying on him, Dodd took solace, as had all the Baconians before him, in his outsider status. He was "maligned and abused," just like Francis Bacon.[76] And as a true Baconian, he was now ready to free himself from "*the worship of Dungara the God of Things as they are*— . . . irrespective of what the academics have taught in the past . . . If you, my reader, have arrived at this stage of mental and spiritual development, happy indeed are you."[77]

The reference to "Dungara" is significant. While this sounds like a deity of some sort, the name is actually from a Kipling story, "The Peculiar Embarrassment of Justus Krenk" (1888), thereafter sometimes published as "The Judgment of Dungara." In the tale, Justus Krenk and his wife, both German missionaries, have established themselves among the Buria Kol, a community of pagans that worships a god called "Dungara." The Krenks hope to convert the Buria Kol to Christianity; they are opposed by Athon Dazé, the priest of the Temple of Dungara. Athon Dazé offers the converts ceremonial robes, the fibers of which turn out to be poisonous. As a result, all the converts die. Filled with spiritual certitude, Justus Krenk irrationally accepts this mass murder as proof that the work of conversion and enlightenment must be undertaken multigenerationally: "the Lord has willed that some other man shall the work take—in good time—in His own good time."[78] Dodd, then, was admitting that conversion to Baconianism was costly, socially, if not physically, but the payoff, echoing those fictional martyrs who died at Buria Kol, would be the knowledge that they had embraced a great spiritual truth.

JUST HOW CRAZY IS THE IDEA OF A CIPHERED TEXT?

Alfred Dodd will return in the next chapter. For the here and now, we
might ask ourselves whether the details of these eccentric and often-tragic
lives are obscuring the central mission: an investigation of hidden meanings in the works we deem to be by Shakespeare. Of course, we recognize
that crazy people have some crazy ideas, and Donnelly, Owen, Arensberg,
and the rest do seem crazy, but we shouldn't dismiss the value of an idea
solely on the basis of an author or authors' personal characteristics. Albert
Einstein's hair is ridiculous; his theory of relativity is not. When dealing with hidden meanings or enciphered messages, we have to at least
acknowledge their rich history. The ancient Mesopotamians, for example,
used codes to protect the secret of how to make pottery. Later, Phoenician
alphabets, the forerunners of our writing systems, were used for similar
purposes. In ancient Egypt, traditional pictorial writings were sometimes
altered to increase the mystery of religious texts.[79] The mathematician
Pythagoras also created a cipher in which numbers and shapes were used
interchangeably. The most perfect shape in the system was a pyramid,
or, as he termed it, a "Holy Tetractys" by which, mysteriously, 4 digits
equaled 10.

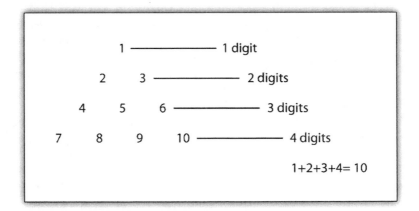

According to Plutarch, Apuleius, Iamblichus, and Apollonius of
Tyana, the function of the Holy Tetractys was to turn a horizontal
sequence into a linear equation capable of stacking and resequencing
time—that is, divination and time travel. They further stated that the
system was based on a secret tradition that had been passed down by
Orpheus, the musician who descended into the afterworld. Likewise,
in his *From Magic to Science*, Charles Singer notes that a ninth-century
manuscript by an English hand makes mention of a mathematical cipher,

a "sphere of Pythagoras," that was used as a magical device.[80] Still later, the Renaissance mathematician Johannes Kepler used Pythagoras's Holy Tetractys to determine the distances between planets, which, he said, somehow aligned with a variety of geometrical shapes. The harmony of these forms created a "music of the spheres"—later heard by Pericles, the titular hero of Shakespeare's play.[81]

Aside from Pythagoras's mystical code, the ancient Greeks created a cypher they called *gematria*, which assigns to each letter a numerical value and a linguistic significance:

Greek Cipher

	1	2	3	4	5
1	A	B	C	D	E
2	F	G	H	I/J	K
3	L	M	N	O	P
4	Q	R	S	T	U
5	V	W	X	Y	Z

In this system, a series of numbers might hide a message; for example, "Pythagoras" might be written as 5443124213.

In Roman times, Julius Caesar often used a similar cipher to convey important military and political messages to his troops and allies. This system, known as *temura*, relies on the substitution of letters. Caesar's version is today known as the "Caesar Shift." The code is rudimentary; the fourth letter of the alphabet is exchanged with the first, and so on:

Caesar Shift

PLAIN: a b c d e f g h i j k l m n o p q r s t u v w x y z

CIPHER: d e f g h i j k l m n o p q r s t u v w x y z a b c

Both Greeks and Romans also experimented with coded messages inserted into documents that looked to be, in all other regards, prosaic. This form of encryption is known as *steganography*.

By the second century A. D., steganography was a focal point for biblical interpretation. The Christian philosopher Origen wrote that God and the prophets concealed "from the multitude the deep meaning . . . the mystical meaning."[82] The Holy Scriptures, he wrote, "are like large houses with many, many rooms, and outside each door lies a key; but it is not the right one. To find the right keys that will open the doors—that is the great and arduous task."[83] In medieval times, the theologian philosopher Maimonides similarly posited that the Old and New Testaments had been written in code: "*Every time that you find in our books a tale of reality which seems impossible, a story which is repugnant to both reason and common sense, then be sure that the tale contains a profound allegory veiling a deeply mysterious truth; and the greater absurdity of the letter, the deeper the wisdom of the spirit.*"[84] This code, in turn, became the basis of Kabalistic study, a form of Jewish mysticism symbolized by the "Tree of Life," from which everything springs.[85]

Medieval and Renaissance cryptographers reworked the aforementioned ancient and esoteric systems. Temura, for example, was used by the author of *The Equatorie of the Planetis*, a work sometime attributed to Geoffrey Chaucer.[86] The same author also used other kinds of substitution. For example, *and* was represented as *2*; *King of England* as *&.*, and so on. In terms of political messages, Mary Queen of Scots (1583) used substitution ciphers in her correspondence with Gilbert Gifford.[87] In 1601, Shakespeare and his fellow players were accused of a similar sort of substitution when staging a revival of *Richard II*. Queen Elizabeth decoded the staging as a critique on her reign, commenting, "I am Richard II know ye not that?"[88]

In an effort to establish hidden messages in Shakespeare's texts, Baconians are keen to point out that Bacon was an expert cryptographer. In *The Advancement of Learning* (1605), Bacon states that "there be also Diuersities of METHODES vulgar and receued: as that of *Resolution*, or *Analysis*, of *Constitution*, or *Systasis*, of *Concealment*, or, *Cryptique*, *etc*, which I doe allowe well of; though I haue stood vpon those which are least handle and obserued."[89] Bacon also demonstrated one form of encoding, a bilateral cipher, in his *De Augmentis Scientiarum* (1624), in which five letters represent a single letter. For example, the word *Bacon* might be written thus:

B	A	C	O	N
aaaab	aaaaa	aaaba	abbab	abbaa

The *a*s and *b*s are then swapped out with other letters; let us say, for the sake of this example, *a* = *s*/*c* and *b* = *i*/*j*.

B	A	C	O	N
ssssi	sssss	sssis	siisi	siiss

Those letters are wrapped into words. The following is my example, not Bacon's. Nonetheless, if we are to understand the Baconian mind-set, we must be willing to explore their word games:

B = assass*i*nation
A = *consequence surcease*
C = *success* th*i*s
O = th*i*s shoal t*i*me, *j*ump l*i*fe
N = *i*n these cases st*i*ll

To further embed the secret message, a variety of null letters and words must now be added. Thus the word *Bacon* might, conceivably, be found in the following:

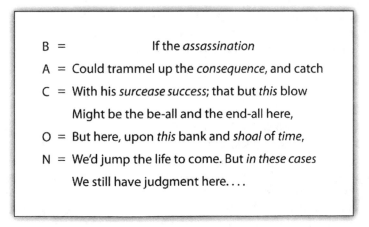

B =   If the *assassination*
A = Could trammel up the *consequence,* and catch
C = With his *surcease success;* that but *this* blow
         Might be the be-all and the end-all here,
O = But here, upon *this* bank and *shoal* of *time,*
N = We'd jump the life to come. But *in these cases*
         We still have judgment here. . . .

As the reader can see, a few extra, unwanted bilateral letters can be generated from the surrounding nulls. The example was, frankly, the best I could come up with, though I need not worry too much, since the Baconians acknowledge that the bilateral cipher is imperfect or, rather, purposefully imperfect because Bacon had already given the world his bilateral answer key and he would, thus, never so easily reveal the solution to his First Folio brainteaser.

In fact, the cryptographic code allegedly used in Shakespeare's plays is so complex that no one has been able to crack it. Writes Arensberg, the First Folio contains "a continuous cryptographic spelling which I have not yet been able to decipher . . . But it is chiefly in the form of the flexible structures that the clues to the inflexible structure of the Magic Ring are first discoverable."[91] In sum, the code must be there, hence fixed, but the code has been installed in an unfixed or flexible manner.

Not only is the bilateral code installed flexibly, it is also purposefully crowded amid still other codes. In *The Cryptography of Shakespeare* (1922), Arensberg argues that Bacon used a system similar to one developed by Dante—Arensberg's first book was *The Cryptography of Dante* (1921). That system sometimes relies on anagrams (letters that can be reshuffled to make new words), sometimes on acrostics (the first letter of each line of poetry or prose), sometimes on a combination thereof, or what he calls the "anagrammatic acrostic."[92] In essence, Arensberg takes a bunch of letters and recombines them to find the message that proves his thesis. And, since Bacon apparently also used the system flexibly, Arensberg is free to pick and choose which lines have or do not have the code.[93] Thus Arensberg takes the following line from *Doctor Faustus*—Bacon apparently wrote Marlowe's plays as well!—to prove Bacon's authorship:

Bloud conieales and I.

Consider in these words the following acrostic letters:

b. con. a. I
or, I, BACON.[94]

Likewise, in *The Baconian Keys* (1928), Arensberg combines the bilateral code with the Greek system of substituting numbers for letters. (For example, *A* no longer equals *aaaaa* but is now represented as *11111*; *B* is now *11112*, and so on.) He also created numerical values for punctuation, diphthongs, ampersands, and other literary devices. The result is what he terms "parabolical meaning," a phrase that suggests some connection to the aforementioned Pythagorean theorem that numbers relate to the occult mysteries.[95] Sure enough, in Arensberg's *The Magic Ring of Francis Bacon* (1930), we now learn that that aforementioned "parabolical meaning" symbolizes the "mysteries of antiquity": "expressed both in his secret grave and in the secret form of his writings, Bacon intended to express the expectation that he would be reborn. In his expression of this expectation he represents himself and his mother as the divine heads of a religious and philosophical mystery, analogous to the religious mysteries of antiquity, both pagan and Christian."[96] At other points in the same study, Arensberg presents evidence that Bacon's Shakespeare texts used Kabbalistic codings, including the "Sephirotic Tree" and the "Tree of Time."[97]

Still other Baconians have abandoned the bilateral cipher altogether. Employing temura, the aforementioned system of word substitution, Charles Alexander Montgomery (1927) decrypts Shakespeare's grave epitaph thus:

Encrypted Original Version	Decrypted Version
Good frend for Iesus sake forbeare,	Dig Honest Man dost THEE forbeare
To digg the dust encloased heare.	I SHAKES-SPEARE England's Tvdor Hire
Blese be ye man ye spares thes stones,	Graved below these mystic Stones
And curst be he ye moves my bones.	The mystery codes yet gab of bones.

Margaret Barsi-Greene (1973), on the other hand, suggests that only names are of value; all other words are merely nulls. As an example, she offers the following reading of a section from Jonson's "To My Beloved":

> My Shakespeare, rise, I will not lodge thee by
> Chaucer, or Spenser, or bid Beaumont lye . . .
> And tell, his farre thou didst our Lilly out-shine,
> Or sporting Kyd, or Marlowe's mighty line.

She comments, "Surely this was a clue" that Marlowe, Spenser, Kyd, Greene, and Shakespeare were all the same—all guises for Bacon. As for Chaucer, Spenser was often influenced by him, and Spenser was really Bacon; John Lyly wrote *Euphues*; Robert Greene employed the same deity in one of his works; thus, Greene was really Bacon; Kyd wrote the original *Hamlet*, so he must have been Bacon as well; and so on.[98]

To many readers, all this seems ridiculous. Yet these ciphered readings depend on their own rules of critical engagement. Further, it's not difficult to imagine that mathematically minded people and lovers of crosswords and other word games might even prefer Pythagorean numbers or sequence riddles to traditional literary strategies.

TEXTUAL ISSUES

To make any decoding system work, the given text, no matter how error filled, has to be treated as perfect, pellucid, and "brilliantly sane."[99] Indeed, since any acknowledgment of printing error might bring into question the possibility of recovering the hidden meaning, one of the chief forms of code hunting is to *spot something that looks like an error and treat it as if it were a carefully placed signpost of the enciphered text.* Thus the aforementioned Alfred Dodd believes that "every alleged . . . printing-error" associated with Shakespeare's texts can be "explained." His take, for example, on the dedication page of the *Sonnets* is typical: "Note the full stops after each word. What do they indicate? Were they so placed for mere fun? . . . Had they a serious intention? Of course they had!"[100] Dodd also asserts that the original arrangement forms two *T* shapes, one crowning the other. This is followed by the initials "T. T." Dodd states that the double *T*s are the "Two Pillars of masonry" and that the double *T*s can be rearranged to form one giant *T*.[101] This, he observes, proves that the true author of *The Sonnets* was somehow engaged in a number of "Secret Societies."[102] As to why Francis Bacon's name is absent from Shakespeare's plays and poems, Dodd—borrowing perhaps from Arensberg—argues that Bacon's authorial absence is confirmation that Bacon and his cohorts "deliberately altered [the text] to prove the Author's identity."[103] Writes Dodd, "It does not require a literary Sherlock Holmes to detect the very open clue that the author has left, so that you can trail him down."[104]

Likewise, Edward D. Johnson (1932), in his study of the seemingly haphazard pagination of the First Folio, sees no evidence of print house haste or the late insertion of materials. Instead, he sees a series of carefully placed clues: "the false paging is *intentional* and *not accidental*" because the same sort of mispagination is found in Bacon's *Proficiency and Advancement in Learning* (1605).[105] What follows is a bizarre mathematical sequence in which (supposedly) misnumbered pages get renumbered. The "evidence" relies on a numerological (hence, Pythagorean) code:

> It is rather extraordinary to find that page 47 in the Histories is numbered 49—a difference of 2—and that page 50 in the Comedies is numbered 58—a difference of 8—and that page 59 in the Comedies is numbered 51—a difference of 8; also that the true page 101 in the Tragedies is numbered 109—a difference of 8—so that all the pages in the Tragedies from 109 to 156 are numbered 8 more than they should be—and that all the pages after 57 in the Tragedies are numbered 2 less counting forward for the page numbered 80 in *Troillas and Cressida*.[106]

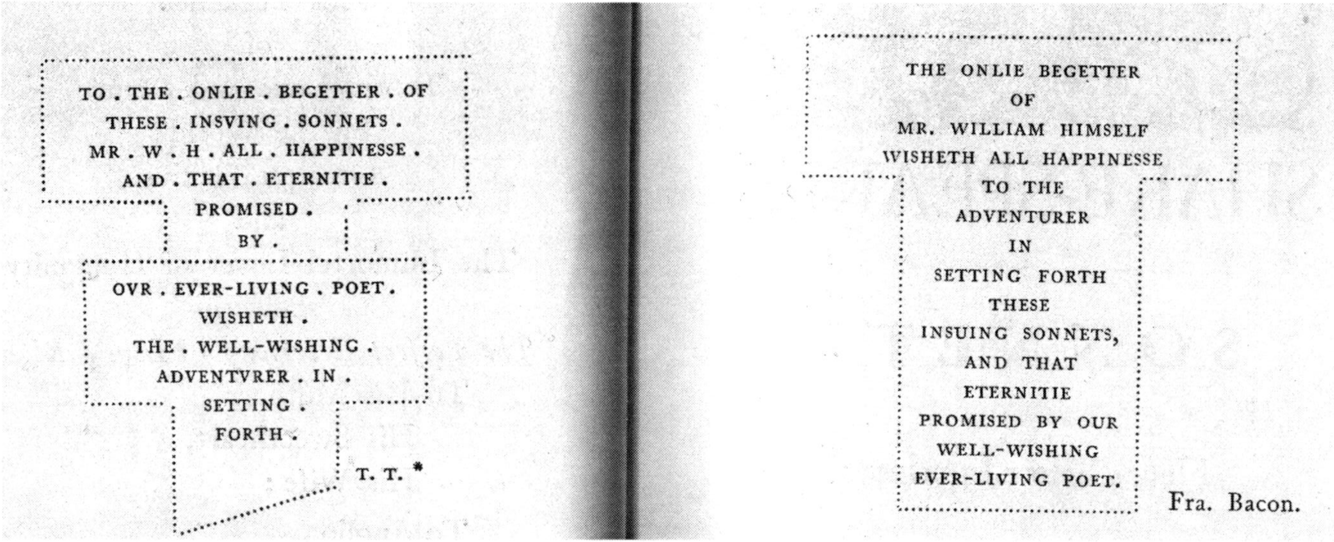

TO . THE . ONLIE . BEGETTER . OF
THESE . INSVING . SONNETS .
MR . W . H . ALL . HAPPINESSE .
AND . THAT . ETERNITIE .
PROMISED .
BY .
OVR . EVER-LIVING . POET .
WISHETH .
THE . WELL-WISHING .
ADVENTVRER . IN .
SETTING .
FORTH .

T. T. *

THE ONLIE BEGETTER
OF
MR. WILLIAM HIMSELF
WISHETH ALL HAPPINESSE
TO THE
ADVENTURER
IN
SETTING FORTH
THESE
INSUING SONNETS,
AND THAT
ETERNITIE
PROMISED BY OUR
WELL-WISHING
EVER-LIVING POET.

Fra. Bacon.

Figure 2.3 *Sonnet* title page, reinterpreted by Alfred Dodd (Personal Collection).

From Alfred Dodd's *The Secret History of Francis Bacon* (1931): (left image) The original double *T* formation of the initials "T. T.," allegedly standing for the double pillars of Freemasonry; (right image) the single *T* signifying a secret society behind Freemasonry. In this version, Dodd has employed a temura cipher to justify the swapping of "T. T." with "Fra. Bacon."

And why are multiples of two so important? Because the numbers "prove" that the book must be read in a mathematically double or even octuple sense. A similar system is employed by W. B. Venton (1968), who, following the ancient Pythagorean school of number and letter equivalents, notes that "EDWARD VI. + FRAN: BACON + WILLIAM SHAKESPEARE," somehow equal the number 822; the same number was arrived at by adding the numerical sums of "SON OF HENRY VIII." and, from the dedication page of Shakespeare's *Sonnets*, the phrase "THE ONLIE BEGETTER."[107] Never mind that in the first "proof" Francis has to be abbreviated or that, in the second example, history has to be doubly rewritten—Baconians consider Bacon to be the son of Queen Elizabeth, not Henry VIII. Even accepting all these flaws, squeezing them as *Twelfth Night*'s Malvolio does to find his name within an imperfect set of letters, we might ask, what is the significance of 822? Again, the solution is about mathematical multiples and multiplied, hidden readings: $2 \times 2 = 4$; $4 \times 2 = 8$. The same logic is employed by Jane W. Beckett in *The Secret of Shakespeare's Doublet* (1977) and by David Ovason in *Shakespeare's Secret Booke* (2010).[108] Beckett notes that the woodcut in the First Folio of 1623 depicts Shakespeare the actor in a doublet or double-it; Ovason uses numerological codes to refine a variety of lines in Shakespeare down to the number 33, the age of Christ at his death, and, moreover, the numerological equivalent of

B	A	C	O	N
2	1	3	14	13 = 33 or 3, 3.

As Benedick would say, "There's a double meaning in that!"[109]

WORD GAMES AND CRITICISM

For now, we might set aside these mathematical maneuvers in favor of larger cultural factors. As Jeffrey Kaplan and Heléne Lööw explain, fringe groups and their ideas collectively function as a "zone in which proscribed and/or forbidden knowledge" can be "exchanged" with or "modified" by the accepted center, but, for the good of both periphery and center, the modification must remain limited, the exchange unacknowledged.[110] Roger A. Stritmatter, a supporter of alternative authorship, and Michael Dobson, director of the Shakespeare Institute, sum up the extremes of both positions. Stritmatter derives his legitimacy by rejecting academia: "I think we prefer at this point in time to put our energies into less traditional venues."[111] In contrast, Dobson refuses to listen to any argument that does not fit within traditional norms: "fully explaining the authorship controversy isn't a job for a Shakespearean scholar: It's a job for a pathologist."[112] Both parties seem satisfied with the status quo. To Baconians, the dismissal of Delia Bacon and other anti-Stratfordians as (variously) penurious grave robbers, midnight cryptographers, and crazed prophets howling their truths into the wind validates their premise that traditional Shakespeare scholars will not entertain alternative ways of reading. On this point, the Baconians are doubtless correct: outright rejection of Baconian concepts allows traditional Shakespeareans to continue to see themselves as engaged in serious and rational (i.e., nonpoetic and nonplayful) discussions of the poems and plays. The reality, however, is otherwise. Shakespeareans love codes. They just believe in a different set of codes and ways of deciphering them.

Let me preface this phase of my argument by pointing out that all reading, especially literary reading, relies on code breaking. From our earliest literary experiences onward, we learn that letters can be combined in seemingly infinite combinations to form words and sentences, which, in turn, reveal hitherto unsuspected meanings.[113] As we master letter and word forms, we are taught how to look within a story for its often unstated theme or meaning; we are encouraged to reread stories in search of symbols or of allegories. Our sophistication grows with our ability to identify genre codes: comedy, tragedy, fables, parables, satires, parodies. We are taught the language games of irony, simile, metaphor, and puns and of simple, deep, or ironic comparison. We learn, too, the art of the riddle. In *Pericles*, for example, Shakespeare (and possible collaborators) presents us with a simple enough word puzzle:

> I am no viper, yet I feed
> On mother's flesh which did me breed.
> I sought a husband, in which labor
> I found that kindness in a father.
> He's father, son, and husband mild;
> I mother, wife—and yet his child.
> How they may be, and yet in two,
> As you will live, resolve it you.[114]

Yet the solution (incest) is so simple that we might suspect that there is something else going on here. We may further note that whether any of the suitors solve the riddle or not, the outcome is the same—execution.

Thus the initial solution to the riddle (incest) leads to another significance concerning the inevitability of death. In *The Merchant of Venice*,
Portia's suitors are made to choose among three caskets, each made of a
different metal. The three caskets—composed of gold, silver, and lead—
are each accompanied by a riddle. One of Portia's suitors, the Prince of
Morocco, helpfully reads them for us:

> The first, of gold, who this inscription bears,
> "Who chooseth me shall gain what many men desire;"
> The second, silver, which this promise carries,
> "Who chooseth me shall get as much as he deserves;"
> This third, dull lead, with warning all as blunt,
> "Who chooseth me must give and hazard all he hath."[115]

The Prince then asks, "How shall I know if I do choose the right?" Here,
the riddles are more complex, but the audience (likely) has already pro-
cessed the necessary clues, which we can breakdown into two distinct
layers: the first is a literal reading of gold as a valuable metal; the second is
nonliteral—that Portia herself is a precious metal that must be valued for
more than its superficial glister.

Other word-code games in Shakespeare may involve seemingly innocuous phrases. For example, in *Meaning by Shakespeare* (1992), Terence
Hawkes discusses how Hamlet and Ophelia interact in the mousetrap
scene. In asking "What *means* this my lord?" the character Ophelia speaks
in a concrete language; Hamlet, however, responds "from a slightly different ground." In the process, Hamlet introduces a new meaning for
the word "means": "It means mischief." As Hawkes notes, "there [is] no
direct engagement with 'meaning' on the level Ophelia intends. Far from
it. A tricky phrase in a different language quickly mocks and deflects her
reply."[116] Of course, Shakespeare has not created this "tricky phrase" so
that we cannot solve it. There are, to be sure, multiple levels of meaning at
play: Shakespeare wants us to think of Hamlet as sarcastic, difficult, and
mocking, but his character's puzzle must not be too difficult to decode.
Hamlet, no matter how unintelligible he may be to other characters in the
play, must be (generally speaking) intelligible to us.

Reading meaning into seemingly innocuous words has its uses. It can
also lead to abuses. As the always-rewarding James Shapiro (2010) points
out, most biographies of Shakespeare rely on the technique of Edmond
Malone (1790), who spent much of his early research setting the chronology of the plays and poems. Once satisfied with his arrangement, he looked
for key passages that corresponded to the historical record—for example,
the death of Shakespeare's child Hamnet in 1596. Malone then assumed

that any passage dealing with the death of a child written in that year or soon after drew upon that life experience.[117] The same logic was used by later writers to discern Shakespeare's thoughts concerning love, marriage, and even his dislike of dogs and candy.[118] If, as Shapiro suggests, Malone and others created and legitimated this process, the Baconians take it a country mile further: as the Baconians see it, their secretive author drew upon personal knowledge, which was then cryptically hidden in a series of plays and poems. To further shroud the secret, an alias ("William Shakespeare") was adopted. All this leaves me to wonder, why Bacon left so many clues to a secret he allegedly wanted hidden; alternatively, if Bacon really wanted us to learn the "truth," why not arrange for an autobiography to be published posthumously in, say, France or Spain?

REEXAMINING THE RULES OF OUR WORD GAMES

The limits of Baconian logic acknowledged, might looking at Baconian practices make us more aware of the limitations of our critical approaches? I think it might. After all, as Ludwig Wittgenstein (ca.1950) reminds us, the people who create a theory have to do some hard thinking, while practitioners of a theory have only to follow its rules: "We got to know the *nature* of calculating by learning to calculate . . . If you demand a rule from which it follows that there can't have been a miscalculation here," then you can never be wrong about what you are doing so long as there are enough people doing exactly the same thing in exactly the same way.[119]

A game does not preclude a depth well beyond the scope of a game's creator. Whoever invented chess was certainly brilliant, but even the creator could not have possibly envisioned every permutation of the modern-day grand masters. Just as the Kasparovs of the chess world work out one line of attack or defense and then rework a seemingly endless series of variations, so too one Baconian creates a method to locate and decode hidden meanings, which is then replicated and refined by another Baconian. No matter the approach, one player of the authorship game attempts a solution, then another has a go, and so on. Generations pass, warehouses of paper are consumed. We look on incredulously and say, "What a waste of time!"

Are academic games so different? Not according to Normal Rabkin (1981), who argues that once the game of criticism is set up and a number of participants agree to its rules, it is all but impossible not to join in "the institutional rules of the academic game [that] insure its proliferation."[120] And if our games are a waste of time, that is perfectly fine with Alan Sinfield (1994), who finds nothing very extraordinary about asking questions that have no solutions: "There is nothing mysterious about this.

Authors and readers want writing to be interesting, and these unresolved issues are the most promising for that."[121]

Further, like the Baconians already cited in this study, many of our traditional critical pastimes are concerned with locating and explaining concealed meaning. In his preface to *Alternative Shakespeares 2*, Terence Hawkes writes that texts are only worth studying if they "*conceal* significant difference . . . The effect is to make us ponder the culture we have inherited; to see it, perhaps for the first time, as an intricate continuing construction."[122] Catherine Belsey agrees: "the task of ideology is to *conceal* its own role in reproducing the conditions of the capitalist mode of production" In her view, the "solution, then, must be not only a new mode of writing but also a new critical practice . . . A form of criticism . . . [that] works to foreground [i.e., reveal] its contradictions."[123] Belsey apparently believes that the "solution" is not to answer the hitherto concealed problem. Rather, the "solution" is a "new critical practice," or a "form of criticism" that generates the problem.[124] This is a game wherein the concealed is foregrounded, and the foreground is backgrounded in a continuing topsy-turvy of contradictory and confused meanings. Oddly, game players of literary criticism don't have to clarify or elucidate; indeed, a master rule of the critical game is often quite the opposite. The "solution" *is* the problem, or, put another way, the "solution" is to problematize.

Coming still closer to Baconian word games and their approaches, in the 1980s Annabel Patterson offered academia her theory of "functional ambiguity," by which Shakespeare employed language that was carefully crafted to convey one assenting message while subversively suggesting another; in the 1990s, Louis Montrose argued that plays have unstated or hidden topical meanings, independent of their form and subject matter.[125] Interest in the (possibly) seditious politics of Shakespeare's plays has waxed and waned, yet the search for the personality of the author of the plays and poems remains—so argues Richard Wilson (2004): the "challenge to . . . interpreters [is] to reveal the identity of the mystery figure [i.e. the playwright-poet] who precedes the words."[126] Wilson is not an anti-Stratfordian; rather, he believes—pace Patterson and Montrose—that Shakespeare's resistance to religious extremism is implicit in his plays' linguistic indeterminacy. The critic's task is to "decrypt" the implicit.[127] The academic logic is nearly as baffling as any found in the aforementioned Baconian texts: how can something be implicit (i.e., understood) and indeterminable (i.e., unknowable)? Coming still closer to the Baconians, Clare Asquith, in her book *Shadowplay: The Hidden Beliefs and Coded Politics of William Shakespeare* (2005), premises that Shakespeare wrote in "coded terms" that have to be read like "cryptic crosswords." She somehow knows that "many more coded terms remain undiscovered," though, since they are undiscovered, it is difficult to understand how she knows this.[128]

The essentials of Baconian word games are likewise present in the textual scholarship of Leah Marcus, who, in her wonderfully playful book *Puzzling Shakespeare* (1988), suggests that Shakespeare's *Cymbeline* is informed by "Cryptonymy." In her view, the play is carefully constructed by Shakespeare to mean one thing and, on closer inspection, another, neither of which can be traced back to the author: "By interweaving the play's 'authorized reading' with a subtle critique of ideas about textual authority, Shakespeare gave the play back to the institution of the theater, [and thereby] created a potential for multiplicity and diversity in performance."[129] The occultism of the phrase is, I think, apparent. The play somehow existed before Shakespeare wrote it, or else how could he give it back? At the same time, the meanings of *Cymbeline* are diversified in performance. Whatever its origins, the play's meanings consist of "surface turbulence" and "deep structure," both of which, we infer, are recoverable, since Marcus can write so knowingly of their respective presences.[130]

In the epilogue of the same study, she adds that poststructuralist criticism is premised on its ability to "unsettle" traditional readings.[131] Continuing the topsy-turvy games favored by Hawkes and Belsey, she states that in order to preserve the text, it must be defaced: "Poststructuralist iconoclasm *preserves* the icon, if only as a continuing ground for its own energies of *defacement* and dispersal."[132] We can let that last paradox (preservation through defilement) pass. We have a more important issue to discuss: Marcus states that her intent is to localize Shakespearean meaning: "the idea of a Shakespeare who can be localized—attached to a particular place, institution, or ideology—has . . . , almost from the beginning, been resisted." Marcus then states that her approach will somehow allow her to gain "access to areas of a text which are culturally alien."[133] She concludes by arguing that the resulting poststructuralist topsy-turvydom is impermanent. A resistant "universe, or pieces of it, continue [*sic*] to exist 'under erasure' as the defining ground against which the critic's strategies are directed but by which they are also constituted."[134]

If I understand this properly, and I am not at all sure that I do, the local is a piece of the universal, but the local is "alien" to the universal. If this strikes the reader as illogical, then you are in good company. Immanuel Kant, in his *Critique of Pure Reason* (1781), noted that totality and division are logically interrelated: a foot might not connect directly to a hand, but "all parts are contained in the intuition of the whole."[135] No matter, writes Marcus, who, in her later study *Unediting the Renaissance*

(1996), urges us to stop thinking—or as she terms it "grousing"—about pure reason and just join in the fun of "puzzling" or problem making: "If we do not feel that our standard editions satisfactorily transmit the cultural imbeddedness and malleability we find in literary materials of the Renaissance or of any other era, we would do well to stop grousing about the shortcomings of past editors and become editors ourselves."[136]

We shouldn't get too distressed by such critical engagements. After all, some questions have no solution—for example, "What is the meaning of life?" Such problems must remain subject to further inquiry, or what some might call "a waste of time." Perhaps all philosophy is a waste of time, perhaps games like chess are a waste of time, or perhaps they are not. Philistines aside, I think many critics would join me in admitting that, whether useful or not, there is something pleasurable about participating in scholarly games, but, given the lax way key phrases are bandied about, or how critical "grousing" is papered over, we might wonder whether we have forgotten, pace Wittgenstein, that rule makers are thinkers and that followers are merely practitioners of rules. Sometimes it seems like the critical game generates mere nonsense—well-played nonsense, but nonsense nonetheless. Even a consummate critic like Graham Bradshaw (1993) is sometimes spellbound by such sophistry (in this case, his own!): "In the *Sonnets* these endemic tonal ambiguities also generate an interpretative uncertainty in the reader which is also too close to that of the Poet."[137] Here, the text creates "uncertainty" in the reader and the poet. Yet, if the text creates uncertainty in the reader, then how can he know with certainty that the poet was uncertain? How was the reader (presumably Bradshaw himself) able to break away from the universally uncertain response, a response so strong that it affected even the poet himself?

Likewise, the normally pellucid H. R. Coursen (1999) is sometimes possessed—and here I use the verb ironically—by glossolalia, a literary version of speaking in tongues or speech-like syllables that lack any readily comprehended meaning: "The way lies *through* the script, the generator of meaning, the energy that insists on being interpreted and reinterpreted with each decade, perhaps with each year as history itself seems to become subject to a rhythm in which the sine waves clench in upon themselves."[138] What exactly is within or "through" the text; how does energy "insist" on anything; and how, exactly, do sine waves—a mathematical function that describes a smooth, repetitive oscillation— "clench"? From the outside looking in, this kind of language looks less like jargon than it does jabberwocky—or it might, were it stated with more playfulness. Instead, the critic presents us with an air of indisputability.

To assert one's position, utterly positive of one's positioning, signifies critical acuity, a mastery of the rhetorical word game.

If a question like "What is the meaning of life?" is part of a larger philosophical game, then most, I think, would agree that the game is an important one. Some might ask whether literary questions, or, rather the ways in which timeless literary questions are engaged currently within academia, are equally significant. The mental elasticity needed for this sort of writing is considerable but not necessarily meaningful to more than a smattering of intellectuals. Then again, many powerful minds have occupied themselves with questions that have since retreated in significance. How many angels dance on the head of a pin was once a question worthy of serious debate. If we are going to pretend that a rhetorical game is other than a game, so be it, but let's not fool ourselves into thinking that what we deem to be important will, in the whirligig of time, remain so. In time, our own puzzles may be dismissed as silly, unworthy, or simply wrongheaded.

Given this possibility, it seems odd that both camps agree on the value of literary puzzles yet show little respect for each other's efforts. Most Shakespeareans see the Baconians as playing an elaborate version of the board game *Clue*, and the answer is, invariably, Sir Francis Bacon, in the study, with a quill; most Baconians, on the other hand, see Shakespeareans as obsessed with a "game of building up the house of cards."[139] Which is the more valuable game? To Shakespeareans, the Baconian obsession with authorship seems to render the plays and poems meaningless, a point most Baconians would, to some extent agree with, with one proviso—that the plays collectively reveal a story of clear moral interest. Cunningham writes, "Why [should we] allow the wonderful secret story of Bacon's life that has been hidden for 300 years to remain hidden ever? I think not; and I think that the careful study and unraveling of this bilateral cipher should be undertaken and followed up by all who admire and reverence Bacon's life and work, and by those who desire to see justice done."[140] Likewise, in *The Martyrdom of Francis Bacon* (1945?), Alfred Dodd writes, "It is not the elucidation of a literary problem, or the interpretation of his philosophy that matters. It is something far more important. It is a moral issue . . . a grievous wrong to be righted."[141]

To my mind, unraveling the secret moral history of Sir Francis Bacon doesn't seem worth the time and effort: the comedies, tragedies, histories, and philosophies of Shakespeare must give way to an amalgam of low and extremely recent literary forms—a whodunit/political potboiler. (Here, we might recall Owen's criminal investigation of Shakespeare's murder or Dodd's reference to a "literary Sherlock Holmes."[142]) But I am likely being too harsh. Charles Alexander Montgomery (1927) suggests that the various codes are themselves metaphorical "mystic stones," carefully placed to guide us to a still higher, greater mystery; Walter Conrad Arensberg (1930) likewise asks us to join him on a "cryptographic journey" or a "theogamy"—he means, I'm guessing, "theogony," a revelation of divine origin; Wallace McCook Cunningham (1940) suggests that we are not yet ready for a solution to the Bacon mystery: "discovery of the code is of much more vital and far-reaching importance than can *now* be realized."[143] It would seem that, even with the help of Bacon's Spirit, decoding must always remain, like so many academic games, open-ended, a work in progress.

CHAPTER 3

THE AFTERLIVES
OF THE AUTHORS

THE YEAR IS 1913. EDINBURGH. WE ARE at the deathbed of Edward Dowden, author of *Shakspere: A Critical Study of His Mind and Art* (1875), *Shakespeare Primer* (1877), and a study of *The Sonnets* (1881). It should have been a moment of Shakespearean serenity and supinity. As Gordon McMullan's recent *Shakespeare and the Idea of Late Writing* (2010) documents, throughout much of the nineteenth century, critics and biographers generally linked Shakespeare's work to his life and invariably did so with one aim in mind: to demonstrate that Shakespeare himself progressed morally and spiritually, that he was a "genius standing at the brink of heaven."[1] What was so of Shakespeare was equally true, at least in theory, of those who spent a lifetime studying his works. It certainly should have been true of Dowden, who so often claimed a penetrative understanding of Shakespeare's artistic and spiritual coalescence. In *Shakspere: A Critical Study of His Mind and Art* (1875) he famously conflated the wizard Prospero with Shakespeare: "we identify Prospero in some measure with Shakspere himself . . . If I were to allow my fancy to run out in play after such an attempted interpretation, I should describe Prospero [i.e., Shakespeare] as the man of genius, the great artist, lacking at first in practical gifts which lead to material success, and set adrift on the perilous sea of life in which he finds his enchanted island, where he may achieve his works of wonder."[2] In *Shakespeare Primer* (1877), Dowden added that Shakespeare's metrical art was not merely magical (i.e., poetical), it was supernatural: "In these 'Romances,' and in the 'Fragments,' a supernatural element is present; man does not strive with circumstance and with his own passions in darkness; the gods preside over our human lives and fortunes, they communicate with us by vision, by oracles, through the elemental powers of nature. Shakspere's faith seems to have been that there is something without and around our human lives, of which we know little,

yet which we know to be beneficent and divine."[3] To Dowden, Shakespeare's spirituality, especially in his last plays, allowed the mystic poet to
see "through [the material world] to deeper and larger things beyond."[4]

While the end certainly crowned all, in point of fact, Dowden read
virtually all the plays as a biographical record of four key phases of
the playwright's life. The first phase, which Dowden called "In the
Work Shop," dealt with Shakespeare's rapid intellectual development,
reflected in his literary experimentation with sonnets, long poems, and
plays. The second period, called "In the World," dealt with his business life, through which "he came to understand the world and the
men in it."[5] The third period, "Out of the Depths," was marked by
sorrow: Shakespeare's son Hamnet was dead, as was the playwright's
father. Under the weight of this grief, the poet "inquire[d] into the
darkest and saddest parts of human life."[6] In the last phase, "On the
Heights," Shakespeare, sensing his own mortality, found solace in spirituality: a man who peers upon his life from the vantage of a "high sunlit
resting-place."[7] Coming still closer to the Spiritualist aesthetic, Dowden
argued—in his 1896 collection—that critics were like mediums: "The
happiest moment in a critic's hours of study is when seemingly by some
divination . . . he lights upon the central motive of a great work"; in an
"instant his vision becomes clearer, and new meanings disclose themselves in what has been lifeless and unilluminated."[8]

Given the spiritual bent of Dowden's criticism, we might be tempted to
ask whether Dowden was a Spiritualist. The answer is no, and his hostility
to that new religion was doubtless increased by its connection to alternative authorship. In 1910, Dowden surveyed and summarily dismissed
anyone who thought that Francis Bacon or anyone else other than Shakespeare wrote the plays. These theories, he believed, would not impress
"serious students."[9] All that the Baconians had uncovered was "common
knowledge or common error of the time." As for the notion that one or
more Spirits had been dictating plays and poems to Shakespeare, Dowden
was magisterial: Shakespeare might have been filled with a spiritual sense
of forgiveness, and he was doubtless kind and wise, even Christlike, but
he was not a shaman or a creature of superstition.[10]

Dowden's irritation with alternative authorship was evident to his
daughter Hester, who nursed him in his final years.[11] She later recalled,
"It cost my father a fortune in research and books. He spent his lifetime
in the study."[12] Likewise, mediums who were interested in the authorship
question were hostile to Dowden's views. The irony, of course, was that
Dowden and the Spiritualists had much in common. Both agreed that the
works were more than they seemed; that they were in some ways covert,

cryptic, or mystical; that they were essentially autobiographical; and that the critic's task was to decode the personal messages within.

I have thus far concentrated on the anti-Stratfordian investigators who sought answers from Spiritualist mediums. But what of the mediums themselves? The query is especially pertinent in that the most important psychic of her generation was Hester Dowden, daughter of the aforementioned Edward Dowden. How this child became the greatest threat to her father's legacy forms but a part of this bizarre history of alternative Shakespearean scholarship. The more significant aspect of Hester Dowden's contribution to Shakespiritualism concerns not just the erasure of her father's authorial legacy but also the erasure of her own.

THE MAKING OF A MEDIUM

At age 4, Hester Dowden was an omnivorous reader of English and German texts. (Her favorite book was Goethe's *Faust*, in which a poodle transforms into the Devil.) By the age of 23, she was a music student of Fanny Davies, whose skills in playing Beethoven, Schumann, and Brahms were widely celebrated, but the death of her mother in 1892 prompted Hester to quit her music studies and to tend to her father and younger sisters.[13] In 1893, William Watson, a well-regarded poet who had already published nine books of verse and was (many thought) in line to be the next poet laureate, asked Edward Dowden for his daughter's hand in marriage. Dowden refused him. E. C. Bentley, Hester Dowden's biographer, argues that Watson was rejected due to a disparity of ages, but Watson was 34, only ten years older than Hester. More likely it was Watson's recent opposition to the Boer War that set Edward Dowden against him—Dowden had recently praised Kipling for his support of the British Empire.[14] In 1895, two years after refusing his daughter the right to marry, Edward Dowden remarried. His new wife, the poetess Elizabeth Dickinson West, was promptly addressed as "Mrs. Edward Dowden."

Well, widowers sometimes marry, and if Edward thought marriage better for him than for his daughter, we can accept, if not agree, with his logic. His daughter, in the meantime, had quit the piano and now had dreams of becoming a great critic, like her father. Edward Dowden was unsupportive. In an 1896 essay, he dismissed all female writers as a "crew of disorderly persons" who had "lost . . . all sense of shame."[15] Edward Dowden's misogyny must have shocked Hester. Whatever their growing differences, her father had always shared his love of literature with her. His letter of April 6, 1876, filled with discussion of lectures, poetry, and art, is typical. He begins by relating the "Conversazione" he had at the Royal Society, with all the "great *savans* in London"; the next day, he inspected the manuscript of Sir Isaac Newton's *Principia* and Newton's death mask. That afternoon, he visited one of the editors of the *Oxford English Dictionary*, James Frederick Furnivall. The following morning, he toured Saint Paul's Cathedral and then Westminster Abbey, where "most of the great poets and writers are buried." He also found time to inspect a variety of William Blake's drawings: "When I go home I shall perhaps try to tell you something about the pictures by William Blake I have seen. There are some even more beautiful, and some more terrible, than in 'The Grave' or Young's 'Night Thoughts.'" He then signed off with "Love to mother"—that is, Hester's mother, Dowden's first and now-forgotten wife.[16]

On her father's say-so, in 1896 Hester married Dr. Richard Travers-Smith. The good doctor was far less romantically inclined than had been her former poet-lover: Richard Travers-Smith was a dermatologist who had once lectured on the case history of a woman with eczema on her left nipple; his other research interests included varicose veins and the effects bacteria had on tobacco.[17] Hester stayed with Travers-Smith until her father's death in 1913.

And then the decisive revelation: upon the death of her father, Dowden's second wife published a variety of letters the two had written to each other. The letters reached back to 1867, decades before the death of Hester's own mother. The dates of those first letters must have shocked Hester, who was born in 1868. Her father had been carrying on a clandestine correspondence with this woman stretching back to 1867, the very year Hester was conceived. She continued reading the letters, all detailing an "intimate correspondence" and an "intellectual love affair."[18] Hester was no fool. She knew these letters were the sanitized version of the truth. Her father had, doubtless, been carrying on for years with this woman. His life had been a lie.

And that extended to his work, which argued that men, as they aged, amended their lives and found forgiveness in God. But Edward Dowden had not been "Out of the Depths" when his wife died; instead, he had simply replaced her with a new Mrs. Dowden. Her father had argued that Shakespeare's life was discernible in his work, but Dowden's own writing proved nothing of the sort. He was a liar, an unfaithful husband, a fraud who sent his "love" to his wife while writing faithfully to his mistress. And then there was the matter of her father's misogyny. Women writers were a fraud, a joke. But he had married a poetess.

Hester Dowden now dedicated herself to undoing her father's legacy. In 1914, she divorced her husband, again took the name Dowden, and set up shop as a psychic.[19] Hester's first Spiritual Guide was someone/something calling itself "Eyen," the archaic form of "eye"—a truth seer—but she soon made contact with another Spirit, "Johannes," who stated that he was connected with Hester's father, Edward, "in a long line of ancestry."[20] An experiment was then made using photographic plates—based on the idea that the images of Spirits could be captured by photography. The picture, she swore, was the very likeness of her father.

With this new, agreeable image of her father now working on her behalf, Hester soon established herself as one of the preeminent psychics of the day and counted among her clients many of her father's friends, including the Oscar Wilde family, the Henry James family, and William Butler Yeats. Her client list grew to include the novelist Thomas Clayton Wolfe, and the Prime Minister of Canada, William Lyon MacKenzie King. Our main focus, however, concerns Hester Dowden's dealings with Alfred Dodd and Percy Allen.[21]

ALFRED DODD AND HESTER DOWDEN

As we might recall from Chapter 2, Alfred Dodd was first visited by Shakespeare's ghost in a dream. He thereafter became convinced that the "Rosicrucians" were guarding a grand secret concerning Bacon's authoring of the plays and poems attributed to Shakespeare. In an effort to gain access to the Rosicrucians, Dodd then joined a Masonic lodge, which he believed operated as a functional arm of the secret sect. Dodd, however, discovered nothing. That lack of proof was in turn proof of a cover-up and thus served as evidence that he was on the right track. In 1936, after seven years of these dream-visions and Rosicrucian investigations, Alfred Dodd visited Hester Dowden, then residing in Chelsea. She began by asking Dodd a variety of questions. She then explained the psychic process to him:

"Do you know anything respecting automatic writing?" she asked.

"Just a little," he replied.

Dowden attempted to clarify matters: "Please understand I am not a clairvoyant. I have a guide named Johannes. He uses my hand to write—sometimes of its own volition without conscious thought on my part. Usually, a few sentences are written. The purport of which I do not know until I read them to you. You can talk to me as I write. You can ask any question, or anything arising out of the writing."

"Right," said Dodd, "I understand."[22]

The first name Hester Dowden spelled out was *HELEN*, the name of Dodd's former lover, now departed. Johannes had made immediate contact with her. The next name was *FRANCIS*. Helen and Johannes then explained that this Francis was the son of Queen Elizabeth.

Dodd replied, "Yes, I know. It IS Francis Bacon."[23]

After this encounter, Dodd reread Bacon/Shakespeare's works in the light of "the poet's psychic and psychological knowledge."[24] What he found convinced him that Bacon was not only the author of Shakespeare; he was, moreover, a "Supreme Ethical Teacher, the Prince of Poets, the most Illustrious of Philosophers, . . . [who] also sits in the Chair of Apollo as the Father of Modern Science" and, more enigmatically, served as "our earthly English god," a "Teacher of Open Truth and Secret Truth," a man who had gained the "knowledge of the Unseen Worlds," a "Psychic and a Mystic" who had a "thorough grip of the Ancient Wisdom, The Mysteries, the Hermetic Lore of the Ages."[25] Bacon, Dodd somehow intuited, had an "uncanny knowledge" of "Secret-Wisdom," "Theosophic philosophy," "Physic Phenomena," "Occultism," something called "Divine Fire," and the mysterious "Thirty-Three Degrees of Modern Freemasonry."[26] Bacon saw "visions of the other world. He knew there were no dead [sic]."[27] These occult secrets were encoded in the plays, which, to the carefully instructed, reveal a "Higher Truth"; likewise, the Sonnets "not only show that he [Bacon] was familiar with the wonderful powers of the mind but that he, himself, had a developed Sixth Sense which brought him en rapport with the unseen worlds beyond our normal senses. He indicates that he had a knowledge of telepathy, clairvoyance, the human etheric body which often traversed the astral plane at night-time."[28]

While occult language is used in many of Alfred Dodd's works, his most focused application is in The Immortal Master (1943), which records his use of mediums to contact the ghost of Sir Francis Bacon. According to Dodd, Spiritualism was the natural choice for this sort of inquiry because Bacon was and is a "psychic." In terms of authorship, Dodd's Spiritualist investigations confirmed his own hypothesis, that the works we traditionally deem to be solely by Shakespeare were done in Spiritualist piecemeal by a writing group calling itself the "Shadow of the Throne." Sir Walter Raleigh contrived the theatrics and the plots; Shakespeare, another "psychic," may have had a hand; Bacon then turned the story into verse and, more important, added, in code, his secret history—that he was the child of Queen Elizabeth and, thus, heir to the throne.[29] As for the lost manuscripts, Bacon reported that they were yet safe, stored in a tin box at Gorhambury—just as Gallup had said![30] Another medium, Helen Duncan, promised Dodd that Bacon would manifest in the ectoplasmic flesh, but the séance was a failure. Bacon apparently "could not slow down his vibrations," which pulsated with an unseen white light.[31]

At still other séances, Dodd was told that he was a reincarnated Elizabethan.[32] Another medium told him he was a "Stuart."[33] Dodd also conversed with his dead ex-girlfriend, Helen, who explained to him that they had been lovers in another incarnation and "so belonged to each other from the Past." She further explained that Dodd himself was a reincarnated spiritual envoy: "You DID live in the Elizabethan Era. Never mind who you were. It doesn't matter. I will tell you again. You injured Francis [Bacon] by upsetting his vast plans; and because of this injury you volunteered, to help bring his Diary to the Light."[34] But it was Hester Dowden who offered still greater gifts: the cipher to at last unlock the true meaning of Bacon/ Shakespeare's plays; the location of the lost manuscripts; and proof that Bacon was the founder of Freemasonry. Hester relayed to Dodd the following: "I [Bacon] shall give you a clue, which may be called A KEY. And perhaps then the World would know that I WAS THE FIRST TO FOUND THE ORDER. *This is my Work.* I have told you before I was to show the Manuscripts which will show my connection with Masonry as well."[35]

Bacon was so careful with these secrets that he refused to share them even with Hester Dowden present. All Bacon would say to Hester was, "Ask him [Alfred] to try to get in touch with me alone. I have a very Special . . . MESSAGE to give him." Dodd was at a loss: how was he to contact Bacon without the aid of a medium? Bacon replied, "Inspirationally."[36] This sort of message is a vital part of the medium's trade, because it reinforces the belief that the medium is only initially necessary. Once properly trained, the client can reestablish contact for himself or herself. This Spiritualist idea that no one in particular owns an authorial voice anticipates some celebrated postmodernist ideas—a point to which we will soon turn.

For now, we can, I hope, appreciate the glamour of the situation: Dodd, yearning for a lost love, is told that all his unhappiness is an illusion. Just as Bacon had an unhappy life but found solace in the construction of an authorial other, so too Alfred Dodd, through Spiritualist practice, comes to realize that he is *not* Alfred Dodd; he is something far greater, a hero of his own life, a participant in a great and immortal adventure. It dawns upon him that Bacon himself "believed he had been reborn on earth according to a divine Plan" and that he, Dodd, now able to contact Bacon directly, has a role to play: "I can see there is no such thing as CHANCE: that I had to follow a plan which I never suspected until a prolonged illness brought me to a standstill from further psychic inquiry."[37] In this regard, what he writes of Bacon seems applicable to himself: "We stand on the threshold of a great Mystery. The Mystery of a Personality that is bound up [i.e., confined, hidden] in the Mystery of the Folio [i.e., the mystery of identity]."[38]

PERCY ALLEN AND HESTER DOWDEN

As for Percy Allen, he is described by Roger Nyle Parisious as a "ruined man," ripe for Spiritualist conversion. Allen had suffered disastrous financial losses; he had recently gone blind in one eye; he had been physically assaulted by thieves; he had been separated from his family; his twin brother had recently died.[39] Not surprisingly, his sanity and his scholarship had suffered. Allen had once been a Shakespeare scholar of merit. From 1928 to 1934, Allen had published no less than seven books and two pamphlets on the subject. His early work, *Shakespeare, Jonson, and Wilkins as Borrowers* (1928), argued that Shakespeare was a professional and busy writer, who spent much of his time talking shop with other professional and busy writers. Inevitably, one busy writer borrowed from another: "Compelled often to work in haste—they would turn readily to the common fund, and borrow freely therefrom such stuff as might best serve the moment's need . . . [Thus] it has become almost impossible to determine accurately the individual share of a particular writer."[40] If no individual share was traceable, then it was nonsensical to discuss any play as reflective of an individual writer's emotional, intellectual, or spiritual growth.

In outline, Allen's early work anticipates our own postmodern paradigm—namely, that Shakespeare's texts are the result of "multiple impulses and operations, only some of which originate with the author or are even assessable to his (or, belatedly, her) own control"; his plays are "provisional scripts," shaped by and worked on by social, material, and, most pointedly in this case, political conditions of the era (i.e., governmental and self-censorship). These new modes of textual study de-center Shakespeare and scatter him "in the necessary collaborations of play and book production."[41] So far, Allen looks pretty good in our eyes. However, the closing chapter of *Shakespeare, Jonson, and Wilkins as Borrowers* speaks to a growing madness. Allen argued that George Wilkins, when writing *Pericles*, pinched passages from a variety of Shakespeare plays in order "to convey a general impression that Shakespeare was substantially the author."[42] Wilkins was not simply borrowing from Shakespeare but creating Shakespeare, forging Shakespeare's authorial identity in order to attribute *Pericles* to him. Why Wilkins propped up Shakespeare's reputation is unstated, nor does Allen explain how Wilkins thought to pass off his forgery to the King's Men, given that Shakespeare was very much alive in 1609 and active in that very company. The plot thickens in Allen's *The Oxford-Shakespeare Case Corroborated* (1931): Wilkins was acting "under orders" of some mysterious superior, perhaps de Vere, perhaps Sir Francis Bacon.[43] In his follow-up study, *The Life Story of Edward de Vere as William Shakespeare* (1932), the scheme becomes a full-blown conspiracy: Shakespeare's comedies, for example, were written by a group "under Oxford's leadership," including "Marlowe, Kyd, Greene, Lyly, Munday, Lodge, and Nashe."[44] If only there were some way of proving all this. And so, like Dodd before him, Percy Allen paid a visit to Hester Dowden.

BACON AND DE VERE RETURN FROM THE DEAD

In their first séance together, Hester introduced Allen to her guiding Spirit, "Johannes," who informed him that "Bill Shakspere had a lot to do with the gist of [the plays], but did no finished work"; the real writing was done by Edward de Vere, the Earl of Oxford, aided by a variety of writers, including Francis Bacon.[45] As Allen told Dowden more about his life, she had Johannes make contact with Allen's dead twin brother Ernest, who thereafter often served as an alternate Spirit Guide. Ernest was not only happy to speak to his brother, he also brought startling news: he could substantiate Johannes's claim.[46] No, he had not spoken to Shakespeare directly; he had no access to the "great men of Elizabeth's day." However, "he *can* obtain access to documents which are the works of the discarnate spirits."[47] He was referring here to the "Spiritual Library," a concept that sprang, as we discussed in Chapter 1, from Swedenborg. Ernest had been to the Spiritual Library and had seen the original manuscripts of Shakespeare's works, and he was sure that there were many hands involved in their writing—proof that Shakespeare's plays and poems were collaborative.[48]

Once Ernest disclosed the truth, the Spirit of de Vere came forward, along with the spiritual essences of his colleagues, Bacon, Shakespeare, Beaumont and Fletcher, George Peele, and George Chapman.[49] The Spirits themselves admitted that much of what had been revealed seemed strange and unverifiable, but they knew of a simple enough way to prove it all: Allen was free to consult the earthly versions of the manuscripts, all of which had been buried with Shakespeare. (Why the manuscripts were buried with Shakespeare, rather than with Beaumont and Fletcher, both of whom outlived him, was not explained.) Speaking through Johannes, recorded on the Ouija board by the medium, and transcribed by the assistant, Shakespeare instructed Allen to go to his grave at Holy Trinity Church, Stratford-upon-Avon, and there to "stretch out your hands towards the head and feet" of the grave. Shakespeare further prepared Allen for the encounter with a ghoulish warning—your "flesh will creep."[50] Allen took the command seriously and set off to Holy Trinity, where, indeed, as anticipated, Allen's flesh did creep. In a subsequent séance, Allen was told that the Spirit of Shakespeare had been beside him at Stratford, along with the Spirit of the Earl of Oxford. Through Hester Dowden, the Earl sent the following message: "We [he and Shakespeare] gazed at the manuscript of *Hamlet*," which still resides on the corpse's breast.[51]

But Allen remained a bit suspicious. After all, Alfred Dodd's aforementioned *The Immortal Master* (1943) had reported that Bacon was the leader of the Spiritual Writing Group. If so, then why did Oxford now claim to be the principal writer? Further, Dodd had also used Hester Dowden. Might it be that the medium was simply telling her clients what they wanted to hear? Bacon assured him that the medium was not to blame: "I was acting through a deputy [a Spirit Guide] in the case of Dodd—a deputy who has never been personally in touch with me."[52] Samuel Schoenbaum, in reviewing this conversation in his eminently readable *Shakespeare's Lives* (1993), remarks, "Some spooks, it seems, are unreliable."[53] But, so far as Allen was concerned, the Spirits, while differing in specifics, agreed in both instances that "Shakespeare" was merely a cover for a group of authors.[54] Whether Bacon or Oxford led this group was perhaps of minor importance. After all, what's in a name? To answer that query, we have to break away from Hester Dowden and her clients and explore the writings of two seminal social theorists: Michel Foucault and Roland Barthes.

SPIRITUALISM AND THE POSTMODERN

In the Introduction, we noted, albeit briefly, that Michel Foucault's and Roland Barthes's famous pronouncements concerning the nature and even death of the author have theological overtones, in that such assertions presume that literary works somehow predate their authors and are, thus, immortal. Not surprisingly, Barthes and Foucault—while sometimes hostile to traditional Christianity—were not necessarily hostile to theology: Barthes was buried in a Catholic cemetery, while Foucault had a traditional Catholic Mass and funeral.[55] Of the two, Barthes's writings more closely fit the Spiritualist paradigm, even adopting some of its occult terminology. In "The Death of the Author," Barthes notes that in other cultures the "responsibility for a narrative is never assumed by a person but by a mediator, shaman or relator."[56] Coming still closer to Spiritualism, Barthes argues for a form of criticism that circumvents the biography of the writer; he speculates, however, that this will only be possible through an alternative form of writing—one already practiced by Spiritualists: "the Author [should be] entrusting the hand with the task of writing as quickly as possible what the head itself is unaware of (automatic writing)."[57] *Automatic writing* is the very phrase used by Spiritualists to describe their direct reception of messages from the Spirits. The related mechanics of the séance will be revealed later in this chapter.

As for Foucault, that critic readily admitted that his archaeologies of knowledge and sexuality examined only the "conditions of possibility" underlying the assorted structures of knowledge of which science is merely a branch.[58] Foucault himself differentiated between his analysis of Christianity and the "teaching of God."[59] Further, interviews with

Foucault reveal that his own uses of the term *God* vacillated from an easy, slang-filled secularism—"*God knows how much* it is spread throughout our entire culture"—to a more formal, if personal, expression of faith— "And *if God grants me life*, after madness, illness, crime, sexuality, the last thing that I would like to study would be the problem of war."[60]

The task of connecting his essay "What is an Author?" to the basic tenets of Spiritualism is undemanding, if sometimes broadly spectrumed. To begin with the widest lens possible: both Spiritualism and Foucault are at odds with the phenomenology of Edmund Husserl and Maurice Merleau-Ponty, who collectively argue that, through a meticulous examination of ordinary experiences, we can discover the truth about ourselves as human beings and the "meaning" of the world. Phenomenology is premised on the value of science: if only we observe a sufficient number of people objectively and examine dispassionately their experiences within their natural settings, we can discover the truth about how humans live and act in the world. Both Spiritualism and Foucault disagree, each arguing that an unseen presence—what the former calls "spirit" and what the latter calls "power"—is pervasive yet unobservable.

The latter descriptives are qualities traditional Judeo-Christian theologians often associate with God. Noting the connection, J. Joyce Schuld (2003) argues that Foucault's writings are "not so much un-Christian or anti-Christian as they are colorful fragments [that pose] . . . no threat to Christian discourses and practices."[61] She further argues that Foucault's theory of an omnipresence of "power" is compatible with the writing of St. Augustine and that both critic and saint recognize that power is an inescapable component of human relationships, which become so "familiar that they are effectively hidden from view."[62]

There are, of course, tremendous differences between these writers. Augustine sees all power relationships as tying into a harmonious and loving relationship with God. Foucault, on the other hand, examines hierarchy (knowledge, punishment, sexuality, etc.) as a cellmate might inspect an inescapable prison—inescapable because it is created and reinforced by a variety of moveable social contradistinctions: normality in relation to abnormality; sexuality in relation to perversion; and so forth.[63] The result is a process of endless scarring, cutting, breaking, and pounding: power, Foucault believes, produces "*cleavages* in a society that shift about, *fracturing* unities and effecting regroupings, *furrowing* across individuals themselves, *cutting* them up and *remolding* them, *marking off* irreducible regions in them, in their bodies and minds."[64]

While Foucault imagines power as an ongoing, painful, and scarring process, we may also note that this same cutting and cleaving allows for a small, temporary (and perhaps illusionary) victory: "The main interest in life and work is to become *someone else that you were not in the beginning*."[65] To become "someone else" through self-interest is to exert the will knowingly in the face of opposition. This explains, in part, Foucault's hostility toward conventional ideas of authorship, which he sees as violating the basic tenets of alterity; Foucault, in essence, sees traditional forms of authorship as fixed. Authorship, he writes, "impedes the free circulation, the free manipulation, the free composition, decomposition, and recomposition of fiction."[66] The brutality of cutting and cleaving is no longer present, yet Foucault's descriptors suggest that he sees traditional authorship as power focused to such a degree that it obstructs alternative formations: "the author provides the basis for explaining not only the presence of certain events in a work, but also their transformations, distortions, and diverse modifications (through his biography, the determination of his individual perspective, the analysis of his social position, and the revelation of his basic design). The author is also the principle of a certain unity of writing—all differences having to be resolved, at least in part, by the principles of evolution, maturation, or influence."[67]

All this seems rather remote and hypertheoretical. What, if anything, had he to say about Shakespeare? As it happens, in his famous essay "What is an Author?" (1969), Foucault singles out Shakespeare, or at least the ways critics of his era read Shakespeare, as a prime example of the dangers of author-centric criticism:

> If I discover that Shakespeare was not born in the house we visit today, this is a modification which, obviously, will not alter the functioning of the author's name. But if we proved that Shakespeare did not write those sonnets which pass for his, that would constitute a significant change and affect the manner in which the author's name functions. If we proved that Shakespeare wrote Bacon's *Organon* by showing that the same author wrote both the works of Bacon and those of Shakespeare, that would be a third type of change which would entirely modify the functioning of the author's name. The author's name is not, therefore, just a proper name like the rest.[68]

Accepting that Shakespeare's name carries more cultural weight than others, what, then, might authorship without the author look like? As with Barthes, Foucault here falls back into a language that Spiritualists might employ. In the first paragraph of "The Order of Discourse" (1971), he imagines what it would be like to be possessed by a Spirit: "I would have liked to slip surreptitiously into the talk that I am about to give today and into those that I will perhaps give here in years to come. Rather than launching into speech I would have wanted to be enveloped by it, and to be carried far beyond all possible beginnings. As the moment of speech, I would have liked to perceive that *a nameless voice had long preceded me.* It would then have been enough for me to connect to and pursue its phrasing . . . *I would have been at the mercy* of its unfolding."[69]

In retrospect, it is clear that Foucault's essay embraced aspects of new criticism, which tends to exclude all biographical references; likewise, his concept of power is fundamental to political readings that seek to make visible the contexts of a literary work. There is, nonetheless, some tension between the two arguments. How can one embrace context but exclude biography? If everything is in flux, then why is the concept of traditional authorship to be avoided so fixedly? We might resolve some of these tensions by noting that Foucault's notion of ever-shifting power pretty much guarantees that his views on anything are subject to flux. (To be fair, the same remains true for any critic: no one is bound to hold a consistent view throughout a long academic career.) Less kindly, we may note that this social theorist has a fairly limited understanding of literary criticism, at least as it pertains to author-centered analysis. Foucault believes that biographical criticism is a "neutralization" that maintains the author's privileged position.[70] But, as Jack Stillinger (1991) points out, the history of these forms of criticism is one of continuous innovation, open possibility, and debate. Author-centric criticism includes the critical deployment of journals, diaries, and conversations; details that may be traced to the author's life experiences; links to similar ideas and images in other works by the same author or by his or her contemporaries; tensions between the author and the era, which may spawn caricatures, parodies, or censorships of one kind or another, and so on.[71]

The point here is not to rescue Foucault from what seems to be an open absurdity concerning the allegedly fixed power of author-centric criticism but to suggest that Spiritualism anticipates Foucault's ideal of unmoored authorship. Unlike Foucault, however, Spiritualism does not value the anonymous text one way or the other. Alterity, whether natural or supernatural, is inescapable and thus neither positive nor negative. It simply is. In the Spirit Realm there are no names, no identities, no distinctions. And while it is true that Spiritualist group work often takes the name of a famous leader (i.e., a Shakespeare group or a Bacon group), the group itself does not work to sustain the earthly identity of the leader, nor does the leader impose a strict code or aesthetic upon the work. Rather, the writing group works harmoniously; there is, then, no obstruction but only Foucauldian free exchange and fluidity; no success or failure, only mystical cooperation.

That cooperation can create various indigenous iterations of the divine. To use the Christian Bible as a pertinent example: Daniel is not the author of the Book of Daniel, nor is Isaiah the author of the Book of Isaiah. No matter their sectarian differences, Catholics, Lutherans, Methodists, Adventists, and so forth all agree that each book of the Bible is inspired and inerrant. That is to say, God is the actual author and Daniel, Isaiah, and so forth are scribes. However, the biblical authors are not merely amanuenses of the Judeo-Christian God; rather, this same God utilizes the personality and style of each writer, and since God must know what He or She is doing in selecting each scribe, all human aspects of the writing are a necessary part of the divine plan. Thus the scribes' texts are perfect in their shared divinity and mortality. In such an instance, Daniel is both medium and coauthor.

Mediumship or Authorship?

The biblical prophets certainly seem sincere in their belief, but it is doubtful whether the same can be said of a medium like Hester Dowden, who, as we have seen, used Spiritualism as an ax to hew down her father's legacy. When it comes to Spiritualism, the collaborative ownership of the work is, depending on how one interprets the legitimacy of the process, either falsely concocted and theatrically presented or divinely dictated and devoutly received. While I think it is likely that Hester Dowden was a fraud, she still had to create the impression that she was not the author of the messages created for her clients. In this, she was highly successful. For example, the aforementioned Percy Allen published Hester Dowden's spiritual communiqués in a book titled *Talks with Elizabethans* (1947), yet she was not given any authorial credit for this work.

We will return to *Talks with Elizabethans* and the complexities of its authorship. For the moment, we might first state that Allen had already enjoyed an extensive career as a travel writer—*Songs of Old France* (1908), *Burgundy: Impressions of Provence* (1910), *The Splendid Duchy Studies and Sketches in South Burgundy* (1912), *Berry: The Heart of France* (1923), and *Roman and Mediaeval France* (n.d.)—a theatrical biographer—*The Stage Life of Mrs. Stirling* (1922)—and a playwright—*The Life That's Free: A Play in One Act* (1925), *Tradition and the Torch: A Play in Three Acts* (1925), *The Seekers: A Play in Four Acts* (1925), and *Comers Down the Wind: A Play in One Act* (1925).

Percy Allen's play *Tradition and the Torch* (1925) is perhaps his most interesting fictional work in terms of the present subject, insofar as it is a play about putting on a Shakespeare play. Rosaline, auditioning for the part of Juliet, performs opposite the elder and more seasoned actress, Mrs. Beatrice Morrowdale. The Shakespearean resonates, since everybody who has read or seen *Romeo and Juliet* knows that Rosaline is the name of

Romeo's first love; likewise, most Shakespeare readers and playgoers know that Beatrice is the lead character in Shakespeare's *Much Ado About Nothing*. While the issue of Shakespeare's authorship is never raised, and while *Tradition and the Torch* does not pretend that Shakespeare's words were written by someone other than Shakespeare, Allen's play turns Shakespeare's play into a part of Allen's play. So in a real sense, Allen makes Shakespeare speak for Allen.

That, too, was the case in the séance communications Allen received through Hester Dowden. Having spent a considerable part of his career arguing that Shakespeare was a stand-in for a variety of authors (principally Oxford working with others, including, in a minor capacity, Shakespeare), Allen now received proof of his theory, since Shakespeare himself informed Allen that "we two [Shakespeare, by name, and Oxford, by authorship] are Shakespeare."[72] More accurately, Shakespeare should have said, "Our group—including Oxford, Bacon, Shakespeare, Beaumont and Fletcher, George Peele, and George Chapman and still others—are one." One of those also-rans is Allen himself, who is told, "My dear sir, you surely know you were one of us, though not conscious of it in this incarnation."[73] Allen, then, is the reincarnated essence of the Shakespeare Writing Group. Indeed, the group has had a hand in writing all of Allen's academic books: "As for the statement that I am not the only writer of the book, I have long felt this to be true of *all* my writings on Elizabethan subjects, granted that they were not dictated to me directly from the beyond. I have stated frequently . . . that I have continuously felt, during the progress of these writings, the effective urge of some higher power working through me."[74]

But what of Hester Dowden's contribution? As the title suggests, in *Talks with Elizabethans* Allen wants to give his readers the impression of direct engagement, a talk, as Hamlet had with the Spirit of his father. The title effectively erases the medium from the process. That notion is confirmed when Bacon explains to Allen that "She, the woman"—Hester Dowden plays such a minor role in Allen's version that she does not deserve identification—"acts as a link between you and me."[75] Hester Dowden was merely a vessel or servant, a "gifted amanuensis," not the coauthor or ghostwriter of *Talk with Elizabethans*.[76] Was Allen being ungenerous and, considering that his subject matter was authorial attribution, hypocritical? That is certainly possible. But it is equally conceivable that Allen really did think that Hester Dowden had not composed anything. In part, that is because mediumship deliberately veils the medium's contribution in the writing process.

THE MECHANICS OF DIVINE
SPIRITUALIST COLLABORATION

When critics talk about collaboration they, like Foucault and Barthes, often adopt Spiritualist language. Michael Schrage (1994), for example, describes the editorial activities of F. Scott Fitzgerald's editor Maxwell Perkins thus: "Like a medium, Perkins became a vehicle for his writers [Fitzgerald among them] to refine, reshape, and reinvent their thoughts."[77] Likewise, Jill R. Ehnenn (2008)—discussing the collaboration of Katharine Bradley and Edith Cooper, who were jointly inspired by the poetess Sappho—also lapses into the same theological language: "For them, Sappho is not dead; she is only sleeping. They see, feel her presence, her verses scattered like leaves around her bed. Together, they invest her with new breath; and whispering back to them in a voice both new and old, she comes to their text, as they had come to hers."[78]

In a crucial sense, these critics are wrong: a medium differs from a traditional literary collaborator insofar as the former claims to be receiving a *single* text from the Spiritual Realm but receives it in a *fractured* condition, which, to become intelligible, must be reassembled collaboratively. As the aforementioned Percy Allen understood the spiritual process, the collaborative activity of writing follows this schematic:

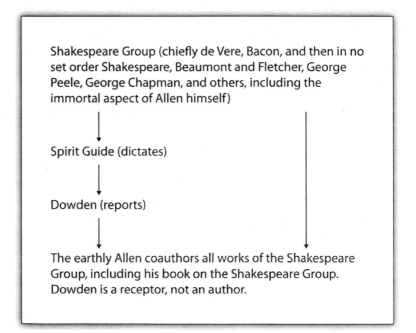

Shakespeare Group (chiefly de Vere, Bacon, and then in no set order Shakespeare, Beaumont and Fletcher, George Peele, George Chapman, and others, including the immortal aspect of Allen himself)

Spirit Guide (dictates)

Dowden (reports)

The earthly Allen coauthors all works of the Shakespeare Group, including his book on the Shakespeare Group. Dowden is a receptor, not an author.

But the actual practice of Spiritualist writing was far more complicated. To understand the process fully, we need to consult four of Dowden's assistants—Geraldine Cummins, S. G. Soal, Frederick Bligh Bond, and Peter Fripp—all of whom left detailed specifics on Dowden's careful veiling of authorship.

Let's begin with Geraldine Cummins, who befriended Hester Dowden in part because of a Shakespearean connection: an early devotee to Shakespeare, Cummins spent much of her childhood searching for Shakespeare's ghosts and fairies in the cellar and garden of her family home.[79] As a child, she loved reading *Macbeth* and *Hamlet* and would often dress up in a white sheet to play Hamlet's father. She practiced the scene with her brother Harry and soon added to her repertoire Clarence's dream of watery death in *Richard III*—"I never forgot it, and even at my present ripe age can recite it word for word"[80]—and Mark Antony's funeral oration from *Julius Caesar*. It was, in fact, the occult aspects of Shakespeare that later drew her to Spiritualism.[81]

In 1921, Dowden, now assisted by Cummins, was hired by Oscar Wilde's family to make spiritual contact with the dead author. Dowden then summoned her Spirit Guide Johannes, who contacted Wilde. Assisted by Cummins, Dowden recorded, via the Ouija board, Johannes's messages from the Irish rake, including the following: "It may surprise you to learn . . . I have dipped into the works of some of your modern novelists." Hester then asked her Spirit Guide Johannes to ask Wilde if he had read James Joyce's *Ulysses*. Wilde responded that he had skimmed it—apparently eternity is not long enough to read *Ulysses* cover to cover: "Yes, I have smeared my fingers with that vast work . . . I gathered that if I hoped to retain my reputation as an intelligent shade, open to new ideas, I must peruse this volume."[82]

Dowden then asked Johannes to ask Wilde about that season's fashions. Wilde was not impressed: "The world of London looks as if it had cast off all its beautiful clothing and adopted the grimy garments of the artisan. That is how it strikes me . . . There was no illusion nor any glamour thrown out from the audience to the stage."[83] The stage? Had Wilde been to the theater? Yes, he had seen some recent plays by George Bernard Shaw but didn't think him very funny: "He is ever ready to call upon his audience to admire his work; and his audience admires it from sheer sympathy with his delight."[84] London was, that very season, reviving Wilde's *The Importance of Being Ernest*. In celebration thereof, Dowden, Johannes, and Wilde decided to go on perhaps the weirdest date in history: Dowden went to the theater and put herself into a trance. Meanwhile, Johannes brought Wilde's Spirit to the theater. Wilde then inhabited Dowden's body. Later, the three compared notes. Wilde reported that the play was "absolutely without life"—which, coming from the undead, might not be a complete putdown—but the rest of his critique left little doubt as to his disappointment: "it fails to amuse me," a "complete misapprehension of my Play."[85]

A frustrated Wilde then decided to write a new comedy, which he called "Is It a Forgery?"[86] Dowden received each letter of each word via the Ouija board. The letters were recorded by Geraldine Cummins, who then read the completed sentences aloud to Wilde, who, if unhappy with a passage, moved Hester's hand around the Ouija board. The assistant then recorded the revisions and inserted them where the Spirit directed. Wrote Hester, "While I had my hand on the traveller of the Ouija board . . . Wilde would say 'Stop' when these 'pearls' were to be dropped in, and he dictated them."[87]

It would seem that Dowden herself was taking the role of secretary, merely receiving what Wilde purportedly dictated to Johannes. If we assume the transmissions to be actual psychic experiences, then it was Cummins who had more of a literary role, since her function was not only to write down what Dowden spelled aloud but also to punctuate and, more important, to read the script aloud. Why is that so important? Because it was Cummins who gave first voice and first life to the play; thus, it was she who first tested "Wilde's" new verse and dialogue on the ear. Dowden also admitted, in her dealings with the Spirit of Oscar Wilde, to "correcting" and even "improving the dialogue," but only in scattered instances.[88]

Dowden found still other ways to veil her authorial signature. Hester Dowden sometimes had one of her assistants hold her pencil (see "automatic writing" in Glossary of Spiritualist Terms and Techniques), which she directed: "Mr. V. [actually S. G. Soal, who later became a "noted psychic researcher"[89]] was given pen and paper and told to relax." The medium then gently guided his wrist:

> At first [Mr. V.'s] pencil tapped repeatedly on the paper, then it began to move more rapidly than at our last meeting. He wrote the name of his deceased friend again; the message concerned his daughter Lily. "I want my daughter Lily, my little Lily," it began . . . He seemed only half conscious, his eyes were closed. His pencil was so firmly controlled that I found it very difficult to move it from the end of one line to the beginning of the next. I lifted my hand from his; the pencil stopped instantly; it merely tapped impatiently on the paper.[90]

In still other sessions, Dowden, using the Ouija board, dictated the Spirit's message as Mr. V. watched and recorded each letter, which then formed words and sentences.[91]

Sorting through this system is difficult but not impossible. The Spirit sends a message, which may have originated with a group or perhaps from the Spiritual Library; the message is received by the Spirit Guide, who then repeats it to the medium, who can only receive the message a single letter at a time. Unable to know which words are forming, she calls out each letter, which is recorded by the assistant, who then turns the text into proper words and sentences, adds punctuation, and, in the case of plays, presumably stage directions. The assistant reads the work back to the Spirit, who sends corrections to the medium. In addition, the medium and the assistant may also on occasion receive direct communications from the authoring group. The following stemma may provide some clarification:

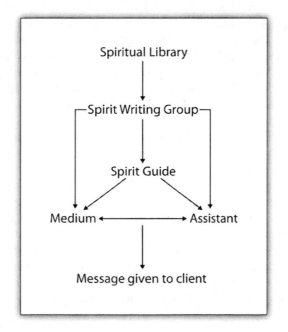

We have here a literary shell game, in which authorship is shuffled about until the client is utterly baffled. The difference is that, in a shell game, the client (or "mark") understands *who* is doing the shuffling. In the case of a séance *no one* seems to be the creative center. We might here further note that the obscurity of authorship is vital to its Spiritualist authentication. The multiple hands recording the Spirits creates the impression that the creative center is not *physically present.*[92]

There is some irony here, of course: just as Dodd and Allen were attempting to reveal the "true" author of Shakespeare's works, the medium who wrote the messages was intent on effacing her authorial contribution. There was pragmatism in such self-effacement: Hester Dowden's reputation as a psychic relied on mystification, and she was well paid for her communications. Likewise, she could hardly undermine her father's reputation if it were clear that she, not the Spirits, wrote the scripts she presented to her customers. While revenge, not money, was, I argue, Hester Dowden's primary motivation, her carefully constructed façade was tested, not by atheists or by scientists, but by the law courts . . .

The year is 1924. London. Geraldine Cummins had, by now, left Hester Dowden's employ and had set up her own shop as a medium. Now working the planchette herself, she hired an assistant: Frederick Bligh Bond.[93] A year later, Bond published Cummins's conversations with the Spirits.[94] As a result, Cummins took Bond to court for stealing "her" work.[95] In defense, Bond argued that since Cummins was only a medium, she was not the "author" of anything and thus was not entitled to all or any publishing royalties. (It did not occur to Bond that, if his argument were validated, then he too would have to forfeit book royalties, since he was not the author either!)

As part of the court case, Cummins demonstrated her automatic writing technique: "The plaintiff covered her eyes with her left hand, took a pencil in her right hand and rested it on a wad of foolscap paper. After a while she passed into a sort of dream state, and her hand commenced to write very rapidly, sometimes over 2000 words in an hour and a half without any pause."[96] Bond was then asked what role he played in the compositional process. He replied that, for each of Cummins's Spiritual communiqués, he "transcribed it, punctuated it, and arranged it in paragraphs, and returned a copy of it so arranged to the plaintiff." He further stated, and Cummins did not contradict his statement, that he, Bond, "annotated the script, and added historical and explanatory notes."

That sounds as if Bond did far more than transcribe Cummins's writing. He edited, arranged, revised, and annotated the work. We might say he turned a plot outline into a real story. Nonetheless, the court sided with Cummins. The judge ruled,

> I am not impugning the honesty of persons who believe, and of the parties to this action who say that they believe, that this long departed being is the true source from which the contents of these documents emanate; but . . . the communications are written to indicate that they could not have reached us in this form without the active co-operation of some agent competent to translate them from the language in which they were communicated to her into something more intelligible to persons of the present

day. The plaintiff claims to be this agent and to possess, and the defendant admits that she does possess, some qualification enabling her, when in a more or less unconscious condition, to reproduce in language understandable by those who have the time and inclination to read it, information supplied to her from the source referred to in language with which the plaintiff has no acquaintance when fully awake.

The manuscript, then, was a posthumous collaboration. Cummins had acted as a translator, and, in the judge's view, that was enough to deem her and her Spirit Guide to be the "joint authors and owners of the copyright." However, since her Spirit Guide was already dead, only the plaintiff was entitled to the royalties.[97]

Even after the 1927 court ruling, the copyright of mediumistic writings was subject to debate. Just prior to Hester Dowden's work with Allen, another of her assistants, Peter Fripp, not only went out on his own but also took the Spirit Guide Johannes with him, publishing in 1941 *The Book of Johannes*.[98] Similar to Bond's court testimonial, Fripp described his duties as "clerical."[99] But Fripp also thought of himself as an author. According to Fripp, at some points in composition he and Hester Dowden traded off in "an infinity of combinations": Hester Dowden was Johannes's "amanuensis, and I his interlocutor."[100] At still other points in their "three-cornered collaboration," Fripp, rather than Johannes, served as the creative author and Johannes acted as editor: "Johannes is indeed wise, for he has simplified *my* work."[101]

If these variations bring into question the exact role of authoring, writing, and copying, Fripp remains unruffled. Anticipating Foucault's question "What is an Author?" Fripp asks serenely and rhetorically, "Who is the author?"[102] While never fully explaining the added difficulties imposed by the Spiritual Library—for example, which came first, the Spiritual book or the authors?—Spiritualist dictation did prove that no one is ever truly alone and, thus, can never really write alone. This is so even in the Spirit Realm, for we later learn that even Johannes himself is merely the name of yet another group of Spirits: "Johannes is the name of my group, for we all—we who work with you from a higher sphere must have a group or Brotherhood to which we belong, and with whom we work in harmony."[103]

ANONYMOUS AUTHORSHIPS

A similar inability to claim writing as a solitary activity is apparent in Hester Dowden's later mediumistic activities with "Heather," the departed Spirit of the daughter of one of her clients:

> This lady [Mrs. Gwendolen Vivian] made a regular weekly appointment each Monday, and during the sitting her daughter would write to her mother through Hester's hand. "Heather" (Joyce Vivian) died when she was eighteen, but during the last year of her earthly life she had managed to write a remarkable children's story which has become a minor classic of its time. Her mother published this book, which Joyce had called *Riding with Reka* [London: Eyre & Spottiswoode, 1937] and had used the nom-de-plume of "Heather."[104]

In the coming years, Hester would continue to receive messages from "Heather."

As a result, Heather, although dead, continued to write. Her first comeback book was *Hero: A Story for Dog Lovers of All Ages* (1943); another "Heather" book followed: *Yoyo, by "Heather" Written from Another World* (1945).[105] Thereafter, Hester attempted to exert greater and greater claim to "Heather." The next book in the series is titled *Fiddlededee. by "Heather" Written from Another World* (1950), but it also has the following addition to its authorial attribution: "Stated to have been written through the mediumship of Mrs. H. Dowden." The last Heather book is not a children's book, nor is it published with a children's press. It is, rather, an eight-volume work on Spiritualism, published, appropriately, by the Psychic Press. It is titled *The Curtain Drawn, By "Heather"* [i.e., J. M. Vivian] . . . *Written from Another World. Through the Psychic Help of Mrs. Hester Dowden* (1949). Ultimately, Hester Dowden's claim over these works failed. WorldCat.org and libraries around the world attribute the "Heather" books to Mrs. Gwendolen Vivian, not to Hester Dowden.

In the case of *Talks with Elizabethans*, Allen might have claimed that Bacon himself did not consider Hester Dowden to be an author; she was merely a "link." Yet Hester Dowden had her revenge. As Allen sheepishly admits, the ultimate proof—Allen called it the "interlocking proof after proof"—that the collaborative writings emanating from the Spirit Realm were genuine rested on the reception of three *new* sonnets, which, in his view, matched "in poetic quality, the very best Shakespearean sonnets which we possess."[106] Regrettably, the poems were transcribed by his "link" when Allen was absent: "Mrs. Dowden . . . wrote them at short intervals, in my absence, and without my knowledge."[107]

When "receiving" a particularly artistic message, Mrs. Dowden often preferred to work alone. On her play with Oscar Wilde, for example, Dowden later confessed that "more than half this script came to me when I was sitting *alone* at the Ouija board . . . I prefer it to automatic writing because of the speed with which I can get messages in this way."[108] It was during one of her solitary sessions that these three poems had come to her. Moreover, one of these poems heralds Dowden's place as one of many true authors of the Shakespeare group:

> Deep in thy soul she hides herself and me.
> Here is no fear of time, of age no trace;
> Forever of restraining fetters free—
> So we enjoy the glory of the sun,
> In sure affinity—for we are one.[109]

Allen refused to believe that Hester Dowden could have written these lines. It was he, not she, who was part of the "one." Hester Dowden was only an "amanuensis" who had "thus patiently, and correctly, recorded" the writing group's verse.[110]

In February 1949, Hester Dowden died. In June 1949, Percy Allen published an article in the Spiritualist rag *Light* titled "Was It Hester Dowden?" According to Allen, he had been in contact with Johannes, who told him that "He [Allen] is to continue his work." At a later séance, Joyce Vivian, otherwise known as "Heather"—Hester Dowden's nom de plume for her children's books—spoke to Allen: "I have a message for you from Mrs. Dowden. You must finish your book." (Note that once again it is fully Allen's book.) Allen replied, "I suppose you mean the sequel to *Talks with Elizabethans?*" Vivian answered, "Yes, I do. Mrs. Dowden wants you to promise her that you will finish it." Allen promised.[111] He soon after appeared at Hester Dowden's home with an offer to purchase the medium's planchette, by which he believed he could reestablish contact with the Shakespeare group. (Again, the inference was that Hester Dowden was not an actual author; the planchette had done the real work.) Her daughter, Mrs. Lennox Robinson, informed him that the desired instrument had been burnt with her mother's body.[112] The sequel was never completed.

CHAPTER 4

FURNESS AND HIS
POETIC "SPIRIT"

THE YEAR IS 1884. PHILADELPHIA. A LONE woman, dressed in black, leaves the house of Shakespeare scholar H. H. Furness. In her bag is a train ticket to New York. She has little else in the world. She is 51 years old, destitute, single, childless, nearly friendless, and longing for a drink. She is Margaret Fox, the high priestess of American Spiritualism.

Fox's initiation into Spiritualism was accidental. It began with a practical joke, perpetrated when she and her sister Kate were children. In 1844, the Fox family moved to a drafty house in Hydesville, New York. Imagining the house to be haunted, Margaret Fox, then age eleven, and her sister, Kate, six and a half, hid under their bedsheets, convincing themselves and their parents that they had heard something odd. A series of loud "raps" coming from their bed followed. The girls then crawled into the bed of their parents, but the rappings followed them, some so intense that the bed began to shake. The next day and for days following, the raps seemed to follow the two girls as they moved about the house.[1]

Kate then told her parents that the raps came from a Spirit, a Native American named Mr. Splitfoot, haunting the house. Attempting to prove his existence to her parents, she set up a demonstration. "Mr. Splitfoot, do as I do," she said, clapping her hands.[2] Her claps were instantly followed by the same number of raps from the mysterious presence in the house. When Kate stopped clapping, the sound ceased for a short time. "[Margaret] said, in sport, 'Now, do just as I do. Count one, two, three, four,' striking one hand against the other at the same time; and the raps came as before."[3] Seeing that her parents were taking it all a bit seriously, Margaret added, "Oh, mother, I know what it is. To-morrow is April-fool day, and it's somebody trying to fool us."[4] But the mother, who was super-stitious, then

> asked the noise to rap my different children's ages, successively. Instantly, each one of my children's ages was given correctly, pausing between them sufficiently long to individualize them . . . and then three more emphatic raps were given, corresponding to the age of the little one that died, which was my youngest child.
>
> I then asked: "Is this a human being that answers my questions so correctly?" There was no rap. I asked: "Is it a spirit? If it is, make two raps." Two sounds were given as soon as the request was made. I then said: "If it was an injured spirit, make two raps," which were instantly made, causing the house to tremble. I asked: "Were you injured in this house?" The answer was given as before. "Is the person living that injured you?" Answered by raps in the same manner. I ascertained by the same method that it was a man . . . [and] that he had been murdered in this house, and his remains were buried in the cellar; that his family consisted of a wife and five children, two sons and three daughters, all living at the time of his death, but that his wife had since died. I asked: "Will you continue to rap if I call my neighbours that they may hear it too?" The raps were loud in the affirmative.[5]

The next day, April Fools' Day, several neighbors came to the house to question the Spirit. One asked, "Were you murdered?" Raps affirmative. "Can your murderer be brought to justice?" No sound. "Can he be pun-ished by the law?" No answer. The neighbor then said, "If your murderer cannot be punished by the law, manifest it by raps." The raps were made clearly and distinctly.[6]

Using this method, Mr. and Mrs. Fox learned that Splitfoot had been murdered in the east bedroom about five years before, on a Tuesday night at 12 o'clock; that he was murdered by having his throat cut with a butcher knife; that his body was taken down to the cellar; and that it was not buried until the next night. It was also ascertained that he was murdered for his money: "'How much was it—one hundred?' No rap. 'Was it two hundred?' etc., and when he mentioned five hundred the raps replied in the affirmative."[7]

The reader will note that there were only two girls involved in the initial hoax: Margaret and Kate. But a third sister would now join. Her name was Leah Fox, age 31. Leah did not live in the same house or even the same town. Since the age of 14, she had been living with a Mr. Bowman Fish, in the city of Rochester, about 25 miles away. But Bowman Fish had just abandoned Leah for the comfort of a rich widow.[8] Leah now eked out a meager living by giving piano and voice lessons. After the rappings in Hydesville, Kate was sent to live with Leah, but the rappings followed Kate to Rochester and continued to follow Margaret, who remained in Hydesville. After a brief time—time enough for Kate to show Leah how the rappings were done—the same spiritual knockings began to follow the eldest Fox sister, too. The locals then decided that it was not the house that was haunted. Rather, all three sisters were psychic.[9]

People began to fixate on the otherworldly qualities of the sisters, all of whom had long, dark hair, dark eyes, and, above all, "transparent paleness, such as we have observed in persons highly susceptible to mesmeric influences."[10] Leah was the one who turned their prank into a "new religion"; it was she who tried to convince her sisters that the Spirits were real even while she coached them in the fraud, this according to Margaret Fox, who in the 1880s recalled, "Our sister, Leah, used us in her exhibitions, and we made money for her"; "in all of our séances, while we were under her charge, we knew just when to rap 'yes'; and when to rap 'no' by signals that she gave us, and which were unknown to any one but ourselves."[11] It was Leah who managed the group, booking them for private sittings, then into small halls, then larger assemblies; it was she who turned the night-time rappings into a daytime, supernatural spectacle. She even began to tell people that she had received messages from her own sisters before they were born, promising that "they were destined to do great things."[12] As for their brother, David, a successful peppermint farmer in his late twenties, whether a believer in Spirits or not, he is often accredited with devising what soon became a key component of the act.[13] Asking a Spirit a variety of "yes" or "no" questions was tedious. David suggested that his sisters ask a question and then quickly run through the alphabet.[14] The Spirit would then knock when the right letter was called out. With some practice, the girls could now quickly receive words and phrases.[15]

Performances soon followed. At first, their fees were nominal—just 25 cents per person—but the crowds were heavy: 1,200 people paid to see them over three days in November of 1849.[16] The Fox sisters caught the attention of theatrical impresario P. T. Barnum, who put them up at his posh New York City hotel for three months and introduced them as a magical/Spiritualist act.[17] They were suddenly national celebrities. Just as New York's distinguished scientific and literary community called on them, so too did the cranks: one caller presented Leah with poisoned flowers, and the toxins nearly killed her.[18] At the height of their popularity, the sisters went international, taking their show to Europe, where they dazzled audiences. In a daylight demonstration at The Hague, Netherlands, Margaret conjured stupendous "rappings" that literally followed her wherever she went: "They came from the floor, from cupboards, from

Figure 4.1   "Dawning Light": The Spirits descending on the Fox household, heralding
the new age of Spiritualism. Courtesy of American Antiquarian Society.

doors, &c. They were very different in force, often as strong as hammer-
blows . . . They answered Questions by the alphabet, very quickly; they came
sometimes in showers, and made the effect, as if you were placed in the midst
of a carpenter's workplace where heavy woodwork was in preparation."[19]

The act seemed to be going well, but the sisters were already going their
separate ways. The eldest sister, Leah Fox, married Daniel Underhill, the
wealthy president of the New York Insurance Company, and continued
to host séances in their New York house, but she did not charge for these
social gatherings.[20] Nonetheless, Leah still continued to hone her art. On
October 21, 1860, she unveiled a new shtick that would soon become the
gold standard for séances: ectoplasmic manifestation. Robert Dale Owen
recalled sitting with Leah and several others in a darkened room, holding
hands. All the doors were locked, the windows sealed. But then he felt

a cool breeze blowing on my cheek . . . After a few minutes I perceived a
light, apparently of a phosphorescent character, on my left, near the floor. It
was, at first, of a rectangular form, with the edges rounded . . . After a time
it changed its appearance and increased in brightness. It then resembled

an opaque oval substance, about the size of a child's head, muffled up in the folds of some very white and shining material, like fine linen, only brighter. As it moved about, I began to hear, at first imperfectly, afterward somewhat more distinctly, the rustling as of a silk dress, or of other light article of female apparel . . . Thereupon it moved slowly around to my left side. This time the folds appeared to have dropped, and what seemed a face (still covered, however, with a luminous veil) came bending down within five or six inches of my own face, as I turned toward it. As it approached, I plainly distinguished the semi-luminous outline of an entire figure of the usual female stature. I saw, very distinctly, the arms moving.[21]

Leah never profited by the trick, but her sister Kate did. Between 1861 and 1866 she was engaged exclusively by Charles F. Livermore, a rich widower who missed his wife. During the almost four hundred séances she performed for him, Kate used ectoplasmic manifestation (she likely learned the technique from her sister Leah) to reunite Livermore with his dead wife.[22] Kate also used live electricity and magnets—claptrap associated with Mesmerism—in her séances.[23] After five years of paying her for such visits, Livermore threw in a bonus: full expenses for Kate and a companion to travel throughout Europe.[24]

Between 1869 and 1871, Kate lived rent free at the home of George Taylor, a doctor, who had recently lost his two children: Frankie, who died at age three of tubercular meningitis, and his still younger sister, Leila, who died of scarlet fever.[25] Using a set of Spirit Guides, among them Benjamin Franklin, Kate relayed messages to and from Taylor's dead children.[26] In 1871, Kate left for England, where she met a lawyer and Spiritualist, Henry Jencken. They married a year later. Two children followed. Kate's husband died in 1882; the widow, with children in tow, returned to America. By May 1886, we read of Kate in a "miserable saloon, drunk"; in August of the same year, she was locked up by the police for public intoxication.[27] The *New York Times* for May 5, 1888, reported,

One of the once-noted Fox sisters, Mrs. Kate Fox Jencken, was arrested yesterday, charged with neglecting her two boys, Purdy and Henry, aged 13 and 12 Years respectively . . . An agent of the Society for the Prevention of Cruelty to Children visited the house yesterday and found the woman drunk and the children suffering from neglect. She has held spiritual séances in her apartments for the last two months, but from the fact that during her sober hours she has done other work in order to make a Livelihood, it is supposed that the spiritual business proved very unremunerative . . . she was held for trial on $300 bail, and the children were sent to the Juvenile Asylum.

As for Margaret, in 1852 she met the famed arctic explorer Elisha Kent Kane, the dashing, if slightly built, eldest son of prominent parents (his father was a federal judge in Philadelphia). She claimed they married in secret, but the evidence for this is nonexistent.[28] What has been documented concerns Elisha Kent Kane's disapproval of Margaret's Spiritual activities. He also censured his own self-promotional tours. He wrote to Margaret Fox, "When I think of you, dear darling, wasting your time and youth and conscience [on Spiritualist activities] for a few paltry dollars, and think of the crowds who come nightly to hear of the wild stories of the frozen north, I sometimes feel that we are not so far removed after all."[29] In the words of Dennis Drabelle, "the lovers were kindred spirits": Fox was, to many, a fraud, and "Kane was a faker, too—a weakling passing himself off as a swashbuckler."[30] Nonetheless, while he continued to do theatrical readings, he forced Margaret to give up her career. She complied and "had nothing to do with spiritualism; her hatred to that, and her aversion to its votaries, increased every day."[31]

In the summer of 1855, Kane, now captain of the ship *Advance*, attempted to reach the North Pole, but his ship became locked in ice floes. He and his men attempted, on foot, to reach the nearest settlement, only 31 miles away, but the various detours resulted in an actual trek of over 300 miles. Along the way, many died of scurvy and exposure.

On October 11, 1855, the forts of New York City fired cannons to welcome back Kane and his crew. The long-suffering Maggie Fox, in town on a visit, expected her man to pay a call that evening. She waited up for him till midnight, but in vain. He stopped by the next day, only to drop a bombshell. His family was adamant: he could never marry her. He asked her to sign a statement denying their secret arrangement, which she did. A few days later, he found the courage to return, handed the paper over, and watched as Fox tore it up.[32]

Kane then left for England and, later, still recovering from his arctic ordeal, warmed himself in Cuba. Margaret remained in Philadelphia. On February 16, 1857, Kane died. The city of Philadelphia put on a splendid memorial display: a "multi-city funeral procession, by boat and barge and train and carriage, with the route lined by mourners"; no one, however, seemed to have taken much notice of Margaret Fox. Kane bequeathed to her $5,000, but his family refused to pay.[33] Margaret was still just 24 years old and might have reinvented herself; but, with no education, no friends, no savings, and no other source of income, she returned to the new faith, hosting séances or appearing for a fee at Spiritualist gatherings. Unlike her sisters, Margaret never updated her act. She continued to rely on Spirit raps, while other mediums, including her sisters, had perfected ectoplasmic manifestations.

Still, she had a powerful patron, Henry Seybert of Philadelphia. Seybert's interest in Spiritualism stemmed from personal tragedy. The son of a prominent chemist and politician—his father served three terms in the House of Representatives—Henry Seybert was born in 1801. His mother died in giving him birth. In time, Seybert pursued scientific studies but, upon his father's death in 1825, Seybert, now only 24, inherited a sizeable fortune, which he continued to invest wisely. He also put his money to use in a variety of philanthropic projects; he is perhaps best remembered for his 1876 donation of the bell and clock that grace the tower of historic Independence Hall in Philadelphia. But Seybert's personal passion was Spiritualism. He collected books, manuscripts, crystal balls, anything connected to the new faith. His house became something of a joke, known to all as the "Spiritualist Mansion." Margaret Fox was part of the collection, hired as Seybert's medium-in-residence. Margaret conjured for her employer and his friends "nearly every martyr and saint in the Protestant calendar, and . . . the famous sages and rulers of old."[34]

The arrangement did not last long. Fox chaffed at her virtual imprisonment and Seybert's "fanaticism."[35] By the mid-1870s, she had moved to New York. She was now addicted to spirits of a more earthly sort—gin and laudanum.[36] By 1884, she was 51 years old and destitute. According to Isaac Funk, "for five dollars she [Margaret] would have denied her mother, [agreed] to anything," including being interviewed by the famous Shakespeare scholar H. H. Furness.[37]

ENTER THE MILLIONAIRE SHAKESPEAREAN

H. H. Furness seems to have led a charmed life. The son of a Unitarian minister with an interest in Shakespeare, Furness graduated from Harvard in 1854, studied in Germany, then was admitted to the Philadelphia Bar in 1859.[38] In 1860, he joined the Shakspere Society of Philadelphia, and there—amid the cigars, the cozy fires, the "superabundant oysters and lobster salad"—might Furness have passed an unremarkable life.[39] But, as luck would have it, his father-in-law, the iron-monger millionaire Evan Rogers, died, leaving Furness and his wife a trust fund valued at more than three-quarters of a million dollars, plus real estate holdings consisting of five mansions in Philadelphia and more properties besides in St. Louis and New Orleans.[40]

The money and its attendant freedoms were welcome, but Furness's mind was disciplined and orderly. He needed something to do. His fortune now secure, Furness, like Seybert, began to collect. But Furness was not interested in Spiritualism; rather, his passion was Shakespeare and the teeming mass of clarification and interpretation generated by scholars worldwide.[41] Furness realized that this embarrassment of riches often made for a comedy of errors. In his own dealings with the local Shakspere Society: "it constantly happened that we spent a whole evening over a difficult passage (and as we were all members of the Bar they were battles royal) only to find that the whole question had been discussed and settled by learned men elsewhere. Hence it dawned on us that if we were to pursue our studies with any of the ardor of original research we should exactly know all that had been said or suggested by our predecessors."[42] Furness, therefore, planned to collect, catalogue, and summarize all known Shakespeare commentaries, which he hoped would prove to be "fascinating to the scholar and suggestive to even the ordinary student."[43] Today, we call these bulky editions the "Furness Variorum." By 1880, Furness had completed four plays: *Romeo and Juliet* (1871), *Macbeth* (1873), two volumes of *Hamlet* (1877), and *King Lear* (1880). These works alone made him a towering figure in Shakespeare Studies.[44] But the work was time-consuming. It is, therefore, a surprise to learn that in 1883 Furness put aside his work on Shakespeare to chair the Seybert Commission, a scientific inquiry into Spiritualism funded entirely from a bequest by Henry Seybert, the same man who had made Margaret his medium-in-residence at the Spiritualist Mansion.[45]

Did Furness just need a break from the tedium of his variorum project, or was there something more to his interest in Spiritualism? As we will see, Shakespeare appeared to Furness several times around the séance tables. While he was initially hostile, over time Furness came to understand Spiritualism's odd practices and some of its fantastic and phantasmal attractions.

THE STATE OF THE PROFESSION

Furness's career dovetails with a remarkable shift in Shakespeare Studies, summed up in a letter Furness received from the British critic Walter Raleigh: "It occurred to me the other day that Samuel Johnson was nearer to Shakespeare in time than a man of fifty now is to Johnson. And perhaps Johnson's England was more like Shakespeares [*sic*] than ours is like Johnson's. We are drifting (or steaming) very fast, and losing the old marks. So the commentators deserve a kind of Encomium which is seldom given them."[46] As Michael D. Bristol (1990) shrewdly observes, "this letter represents in some detail the pattern of shared feeling in circulation among private scholars and professional academics at [the] time"—that is, that, culturally speaking, Shakespeare was a kind of Latin, a dead language, and that, consequently, it was Furness's thankless task to explain words and ideas that had since lapsed into the dustpan of history.[47] The

Figure 4.2   H. H. Furness. By permission of the Folger Shakespeare Library.

study of the English language's greatest playwright had somehow been reduced to clerical work. Gary Taylor, for example, describes Furness as engaging in "simplified data retrieval."[48]

Despite the difficulties of Shakespeare's language, this shift from living to dead author was far from natural or inevitable. Early eighteenth-century editions by Nicholas Rowe (a playwright) and Alexander Pope (a poet) treated Shakespeare as a living author. That approach was overtaken by archival methodology, typified by Edmond Malone's late-eighteenth-century scholarship, which, as Colin Franklin points out, relied upon "multiplication of instances to prove meaning."[49] Malone's system was, basically, odd-man-out: if two readings differed, similar examples were gathered from contemporaneous documents until a preponderance of readings suggested a solution. But this often meant that math (two valid documents are better than one) had replaced principles of taste. Not everyone was in agreement with this method. Thomas Warton (1782), for example, rejected archival evidence outright: "It is not from the complexion of ink or of parchment, from the information of cotemporaries [sic], the tales of relations, the recollection of apprentices, and the prejudices of friends, nor even from doomsday-book, pedigrees in the herald's office, armorial bearings, parliamentary rolls, inquisitions, indentures, episcopal registers, epitaphs, tomb-stones, and brass-plates, that this controversy is to be finally and effectually adjusted. Our arguments should be drawn from principles of taste, from analogical experiment, from a familiarity with antient poetry, and from the gradations of composition."[50] Nonetheless, in the coming century the new evidentiary approach—Malone was a lawyer—would be codified into a strict set of editorial principles and embraced by Shakespeare scholars virtually the world round. Obviously, to Furness—also trained as a lawyer—this evidentiary system made impeccable sense. There was, however, a hitch: Malone's system turned living Shakespeare into an artifact. Shakespeare was now a museum piece; the editor was a curator, who examined the texts and laid out the facts in a dispassionate, scientific manner.

Shakespiritualists believed that their task was the exact opposite: Shakespeare was spiritually alive and available, ready to speak directly to us (sometimes literally through us) and, more often than not, in the modern vernacular. That Furness dabbled in Spiritualism suggests his growing attentiveness to the problem of a dead or culturally irrelevant Shakespeare. His interaction with Margaret Fox and, indeed, his sudden interest in Spiritualism is a curious moment in the history of Shakespeare scholarship. While Furness was firmly in Malone's materialist camp, his interaction with Fox suggests that he came to understand the limitations of his scholarly approach. In short, he had what we might term a scholarly midlife crisis.

THE RIDDLE OF *VLLORXA*

As part of his initial investigations, Furness attended séances—some thirty in all. Initially, he seemed not just startled but genuinely puzzled by the behavior of many of the clients who sat round the table:

> Again and again men have led round the circles the materialized spirits of their wives and introduced them to each visitor in turn; fathers have taken round their daughters, and I have seen widows sob in the arms of their dead husbands. Testimony such as this staggers me. Have I been smitten with color-blindness? Before me, as far as I can detect, stands the very medium herself, in shape, size, form, and feature true to a line, and yet one

after another, honest men and women at my side, within ten minutes of each other, assert that she is the absolute counterpart of their nearest and dearest friend; nay, that she *is* that friend.[51]

How, he wondered, could they be so gullible? Sensing his cynicism, Spiritualists pulled out all the stops. On a variety of occasions—Furness uses the word "invariably"—Shakespeare himself appeared in what we would today recognize as a "Magic Box."[52] When confronted with the ghost of his idol, Furness remained unimpressed: "I venture most humbly to ask him what the misprint, 'Vllorxa' in *Timon of Athens* stands for."[53] Furness reported that never once did Shakespeare submit a reply. The Bard, however, did exhibit some anger: Furness reported that "he [Shakespeare] always slams the curtains in my face." On Shakespeare's silent but aggressive retort, Furness added, "I meekly own that perhaps he [or it] is justified."[54]

Indeed, he or it was. Furness not only presented the "ghost" with a pointedly academic question, he went so far as to offer a question that even he, Furness, could not answer. True, Furness called *Vlloxra* a "misprint," but a misprint of what? The compositors of the Second Folio recognized a problem with the word but, finding no solution, simply cut it. George Steevens (1773) suspected a printer's error—he compared the printer's skill here to dog poop—but, unable to explain Shakespeare's meaning, left it as is; Edmond Malone (1790) retained the Folio's *Vllorxa* in his text but changed the spelling to *Ullorxa*—hardly what we might deem a clarification; J. P. Collier (1842) proposed "all, look sir"; Nicolaus Delius (1854) suggested "O, my lord!"; Thomas Keightley (1864) argued for "all on 'em"; F. G. Fleay (1867) emended to "all luxors"; Howard Staunton (1873, 1874), admitting to the oddly "amorphous" and "unintelligible" nature of the word, still preferred his reading of "All rogues."[55]

As for Furness's own commentary on the word, he writes, "it must be confessed that sometimes no sense whatever can be made . . . emendation is hopeless . . . we may guess till doomsday but shall never know." We might here speculate that Furness's invocation of doomsday places *Vlloxra* in some sort of synecdoche with the afterworld. But no. According to Furness, this single word should just be passed over in silence, since its impenetrability does not "eclipse a single beauty of the play." Moreover, Furness urged that readers and editors alike stop obsessing over Shakespeare's oddball words:

> I have wasted the time to count roughly all the lines which go to make up the comedies. There are over thirty-two thousand. Now, how many are the lines in this number where through some error or other, or printer's blunder, the sense is perverted? In view of the outcry which is made over

the obscurity and the corruption of Shakespeare's text, I really think you would be justified in making the very moderate guess of five hundred. Surely there ought to be five hundred out of thirty thousand to justify the clamoring and hammering editors. But no, you are far astray. Then halve the five hundred. Still far, far wide. As a matter of fact, out of the thirty-two thousand one hundred and fifty-seven lines in the comedies, the lines that are beyond the power of assured healing are just nineteen. In mathematics, as you know, infinitely small quantities may be neglected, and, really, I think, we might without offence apply this mathematical rule to the hopeless obscurities of Shakespeare's text . . . the proportion of these hopelessly obscure lines has been greatly exaggerated.[56]

Furness, however, is not being entirely accurate, and given his knowledge of all things Shakespearean, I am inclined to say that he is not entirely forthcoming. As he knew, there are far more than 19 impenetrable cruxes in Shakespeare: The playwright and poet invented about 1,700 words, or the equivalent of almost one-fourth of the words in the Bible. A scattered sampling of these words might include *affined, attasked, cadent, bubukles, congreeing, crants, dispunge, enactures, fracted, immoment, incorpsed, intrenchant, mered, mirable, mistempered, operant, oppugnancy, plantage, propugnation, relume,* or *Vllorxa.*

Certainly, some of these words might be accidentals, the result not of Shakespeare's seemingly boundless imagination but of print house errors. Even so, it seems unlikely that errors alone can account for 1,700 or so unique or bizarre words. Even if the compositors had miscast these words, why wouldn't they have miscast them as words they themselves could understand? No, the function of these words, at least as the compositors understood them, was as mysterious to them as it was to Furness and is to us.

On the other hand, it's also possible that Furness used a nonsense word in a nonsense question because he considered the séance to be nonsense. He had every right to do so; after all, he had dedicated a large portion of his life to Shakespeare Studies. He was not going to abandon that disciplined effort because some yahoo dipped in pancake mix pretended to be Shakespeare. While some might see the séance as fun and games, to Furness these appearances of Shakespeare were an affront to his scholarly practice.

That being said, it does seem a bit odd that a man who had dedicated his life to the study of the greatest playwright in the English language was unable or unwilling to see that a séance, like any form of theater, depended upon a suspension of disbelief. In Chapter 1, we discussed the similarities between live theater and Spiritualism séances. I would here add that Furness's cynicism points to a serious flaw in his ability to interact with the Shakespearean text or its live theatrical component. Theater actors will often tell you that an audience is not a passive agent but an integral part of the show. The audience's reactions may shift from night to night due to any number of factors: ticket sales—a full theater has a different energy than an empty theater; demographics—a theater filled with children is nothing like one filled with university professors; weather conditions—a cold, wet night often makes for miserable theater; and so on. But chiefly, a good audience is composed of spectators who come with a horizon of expectations. Those expectations may range from a knowledge of the play to a predisposed emotional range—for example, to laugh or cry a lot. In all instances, the audience must be a willing participant in the event.

That Furness would not play along with the theatrical rules of the séance is, I think, pretty clear. Likewise, Furness's scholarship seems to have been at odds with the theatrical aspect of Shakespeare's art. As informative as Furness's bulky editions are—no one writing on Shakespeare's reception in the nineteenth-century can afford to avoid them—they are also poetically and dramaturgically inert. The arrangement of text and commentary silently impels the reader to scan one line of text and then to plunge down to the corresponding paragraph, paragraphs, or pages of commentary. This constant skimming and scanning destroys any sense of dramatic tension or lively character engagement. While the Malones of the world thought this was quite proper, it must have left (and likely still leaves) common readers cold. What Furness's scholarship lacked was a sense of Shakespeare's poetic "Spirit."

THE MILLIONAIRE AND THE MEDIUM

Living in a New York flophouse, Margaret Fox received a letter from Furness, dated October 22, 1884, which read,

> I wrote to you some ten days ago, but, since I have not heard from you, fear that my letter has miscarried, and will therefore repeat it.
>
> I am anxious, very anxious, that the "Seybert Commission," of which I am the chairman, should have an opportunity of investigating the "Rappings." Will you, therefore, appoint some day and hour, at your earliest convenience, when I can visit you in New York and make arrangements with you personally?
>
> I sincerely trust that your summer has been healthful and peaceful, and beg to subscribe myself
>
> Yours respectfully,
> Horace Howard Furness.[57]

On November 1, 1884, Margaret replied, accepting his invitation, with certain cash and date stipulations:

> Dear Sir,
>
> Pardon me for writing you on a subject that is very disagreeable to me.
>
> It is not my custom to attend Spiritual gatherings except occasionally on the 31st of March, the Anniversary of Spiritualism, when I am professionally engaged, and then, it is my rule to receive some money in advance. Would it be convenient for you to forward me whatever amount you may see fit to send, so that it may reach me before Wednesday the 5th the day on which I expect to leave Philadelphia. Should this meet with your sanction, please send what portion you may think right by P. O. money order. Care of Mr. Daniel Underhill, 232 W. 34th St.
>
> Very truly yours,
Margaret Fox Kane.

Furness agreed to all terms. A day later, Furness wrote happily to his sons that the famous medium would be staying with them "for a few days. I hope the spirits will cut up no high jinks while she is in this house."[58] Taking the Pennsylvania Railroad train, or the "Pennsy," from New York, Margaret Fox made her way to Philadelphia. She traveled alone, and no one recognized her. Her celebrity, which had peaked some thirty years before, was at an end. Upon her arrival, Furness introduced her to the members of the Seybert Commission—11 male academics, joined by Mrs. Pepper, wife of one of the commission members, and Miss Logan, who recorded all events for the commission members' later study and discussion. As for Margaret Fox, Furness found her to be attractive and completely demoralized: "She is a small gentle little woman, with a ready and sympathetic smile, which greatly illuminates an otherwise plain face. There is so little self-assertion about her that she rather wins your favour at first sight. She has a timid air, and a little bashful catch in her breath when talking, so that it seems as though a very harsh, bluff manner would make her acknowledge that black was white."[59] As she had done in America and Europe to great fanfare, Margaret first demonstrated some Spirit rappings, but the committee members thought that she was producing them fraudulently and asked if there was any way to prove that the rappings were actually disembodied. Margaret replied that she could stand on four glasses of water, and direct the Spirits to make the rapping come from the floor. Sure enough, "faint and partially distinct" rappings were heard to emanate from the floor and the vicinity of a nearby table. Using the system of one rap for "No!," two raps for "Doubtful!," and three raps for "Yes!," Furness's colleague, a Mr. Sellers, then asked if a Spirit was with them. Three raps. He then asked if it was the recently deceased Henry Seybert, the man in whose name they had gathered. Again, three raps. Will he communicate with others at a séance? Three raps.

The next night, the commission met with Fox yet again. A sober and suitably somber Margaret faced the commission. Furness seated himself next to Fox. The curtains were drawn. The candles were lit. The rappings commenced. Furness, with Margaret's permission, then got down on his knees and placed his hands upon one of her feet. More rappings followed. Furness then addressed Margaret: "This is the most wonderful thing of all, Mrs. Kane; *I distinctly feel them* [the rappings] *in your foot* . . . there is an absolute pulsation."[60] They then tried a variety of other tests, standing on a couch, then upon a cushioned chair, next upon a step-ladder, but no rappings were heard. Margaret then suggested she try her hand at automatic writing.

The offer marked a new phase in terms of performance dynamics. Whereas Furness and the commission had previously held hands with Margaret Fox in a dark room or had observed her feet as she stood on glasses of water, automatic writing was a far more frenzied, even sexy, activity in which female mediums gave over to a "sinister element of irregularity and uncontrol." If Margaret's automatic writing was anything like that performed by other female mediums of the period, Furness and his colleagues watched as she bucked feverously, erotically, her hair unbraided, tossed about, her hand grappling with the pencil, which moved violently across the page in a "wild scrawl."[61] The message read, "You must not expect that I can satisfy you beyond all doubt in so short a time as you have yet had. I want to give you all in my power, and will do so if you will give me a chance. You must commence right in the first place or you shall all be disappointed for a much longer time. *Princiipis Obsta Sereo Medicina Paratum*. Henry Seybert." The Latin translated to "Mend the fault in time or we will all be puzzled." One of the committee members, George S. Pepper, who had known Seybert for many years, pointed out that his friend did not know a word of Latin.[62] An awkward pause ensued. Furness later related in a letter to his uncle, George S. Fullerton,

> I told [Margaret] that the Commission had now had two séances with her, and that the conclusion to which they had come is that the so-called raps are confined wholly to her person, whether produced by her voluntarily or involuntarily they had not attempted to decide; furthermore, that although thus satisfied in their own minds they were anxious to treat her with all possible deference and consideration, and accordingly had desired

me to say to her that if she thought another séance with her would or
might modify or reverse their conclusion, they held themselves ready to
meet her again this evening and renew the investigations; at the same time
I felt it my duty to add that in that case the examination would necessarily
be of the most searching description.[63]

"Searching description" is a euphemism for a strip search, a common practice for scientists when examining mediums, who were often
thought to be hiding fake ectoplasm in their shoes or even vaginas. But
what Furness hoped to find in this particular instance is difficult to say,
since Margaret Fox never specialized in ectoplasmic manifestations. Perhaps he wanted to see her feet to ascertain whether or not the rapping
sounds came from her toes. But a strip search sounds extreme. Why not
simply ask her to remove her shoes?

MEDIUMS AND MADAMES

As odd and as indelicate as this sounds, Furness might have been asking whether Margaret Fox was a prostitute.[64] The medium Florence
Cook, a former school teacher, presents us with a famous but far from
extraordinary instance of sex and séancery. In 1871, Cook, then a pretty
15-year-old girl from East London, held séances in her parent's kitchen.
Guests would sit at the kitchen table, while Cook would enter a cupboard
area to gather psychic strength. This same cupboard had a head-sized hole
cut in the wall, through which appeared a series of girlish Spirit Faces,
each of whom would gaze at and sometimes speak with the guests gathered in the kitchen. One of the Spirits claimed an outrageous identity—
"Katie King," the daughter of a pirate and, in her own right, an adulterer
and murderer. We can follow the free association here: Florence Cook—
Captain Cook—Pirate—Cook—servant—king's servant—Katie King—
school teacher negated—whore—caregiver negated—murderer.

A year later, now taking her act to Europe, Florence Cook manifested
full materializations of Katie King, who in time grew still bolder with her
clients. She would walk freely among them, talk to them, even allow them
to touch her. One sitter, Cromwell Varley, reported that Katie's hand was
very cold and clammy. Sometimes the Spirit moved among her sitters for
over 30 minutes. Not everyone was convinced. Perhaps Florence Cook
was simply dressing up as Katie and then dipping her hands in icy water
to achieve the desired clammy chill? So Florence agreed to be tied to a
chair or roped to a cot of some sort. Even when Florence was supposedly bound in the cupboard, Katie King soon exited and roamed the
room all the same.[65] Spectators were not permitted to inspect the cabinet

or cupboard area while Katie was present, but the sitters could plainly hear female sobs and moans coming from within, suggesting Florence's discomfort or, possibly, pleasure.[66] On December 9, 1873, an obnoxious doubter, William Volckman, grabbed the so-called Katie King Spirit by her hand, but other men came to her defense. Katie King then made a hasty retreat to the cupboard. Within a year, all pretensions of modesty were dropped. Edward Elgie Corner, Florence Cook's husband, gave clients "permission to experiment to heart's content with his wife" in the Magic Box/cupboard. One punter happily recalled that he fondled the moaning Florence Cook and did "not despair of getting a full form"— that is, an erection.[67]

While we cannot assume that Margaret Fox allowed clients to grope her, we might here note that, by Margaret Fox's own admission, séances staged exclusively for men often included projections of nude women— pornography—and the most private séances for wealthy clients sometimes turned into backroom orgies: "there are other seances where none but the most tried and trusted are admitted, and where there are shameless goings on that vie with the secret Saturnalia of the Romans. I could not describe these things to you, because I would not."[68] There is also evidence that Margaret sometimes slept with her clients. In an 1870 session of automatic writing, Kate Fox's Spirit Guide wrote, "Curses follow the people [who had Margaret for a private séance]! To give her drink and keep her overnight!"[69]

Given the risqué nature of séances, the Seybert Commission (with only one exception) maintained decorum by inviting a number of women to be present for interviews with female mediums. When interviewing a Mrs. Lord, for example, Furness assembled a team of women he called the "Women Searchers"—the term suggests they were present specifically to undertake strip searches on behalf of the all-male committee.[70] At Margaret Fox's first séance with the Seybert Commission, there were two women present; but at the second séance—the one in which Furness suggested a strip search of Margaret Fox—no female witnesses were present.[71]

Agreed, it's difficult not to read sexuality into this. But to read this situation only in sexual terms is a mistake. Furness not only requested a stripping of clothing but also, less titillatingly, wanted, like William Volckman, to take hold of the truth. The impossible had to be exposed, defined, delineated, rationally explained. Still, even if Furness meant only to undertake a clinical examination, the solicitation seems particularly aggressive in light of Margaret's polite and nervous behavior. Recall Furness's first description of Margaret Fox: "She has a timid air, and a little bashful catch in her breath when talking, so that it seems as though a very harsh, bluff manner would make her acknowledge that black was white."[72] Perhaps that was the point—to bully her. Citing her "present state of health," she tactfully excused herself from any more activities with or on behalf of the commission.[73] Margaret Fox soon left Furness's house, but Furness and Margaret Fox would meet again. In fact, they had already formed an unlikely familiarity.

A PAIR OF STAR-CROSS'D LOVERS?

Furness's encounter with Margaret in Philadelphia had not been their first. They had already met in New York:

> November 2, 1884
>
> Last Monday, I went to New York to engage Mrs. Margaret Fox Kane to come here and give some seances for the Seybert Com. She agreed and is to be our guest, next Wednesday, for a few days.[74]

The significance of this date will become clear in due course. Margaret is not mentioned again in this letter. Instead, Furness discusses yet another medium he visited, Henry Slade:

> I had a séance with him [Slade], in the broad daylight, and certainly the phenomena were extraordinary, not to say uncanny. Strong, vigorous writing appeared at once on the closed slates, and the slate was at one time taken from Slade's hand under the table, and poked up above the table at the side behind Slade (who sat sideways at the table that his feet might not be underneath) and farthest from him. Three good blows were delivered on my leg, on the side away from Slade, and my chair with myself in it was pulled a foot away from the table! I felt creepy.[75]

Perhaps embarrassed by his "creepy" experience, days later Furness repeated the account, though now in a far more comical tone, in another letter to his sons. This time, Fox is not mentioned at all:

> I went to New York, got a bite of dinner, and then to Slade's, the "mejum's." His family is not large certainly, consisting only of his niece, a stylish-looking girl of some twenty "summers," but very deaf, almost as deaf as I am, and his amanuensis, a Miss Hall, quite cultivated and bright. They were expecting me & received me with much cordiality, and Slade too beamed upon me with a sort of malicious twinkle in his eye, as though spotting a victim . . . It was the same old story, of which I am growing tired. Spirits in white emerged a few inches & retired, &c, &c. At the close I was summoned into the Cabinet where the medium was seated,

pretending by her talk that she was an Indian Squaw: after she had clasped both my hands so that I couldn't feel around in the pitch dark, spirits punched me in various regions of the body; from the location and feel of the punch I was convinced that it was done by the medium's foot or knee.[76]

These narratives, however, do not correspond to what we know of Henry Slade, a polished and well-heeled psychic who would certainly not have pronounced *medium* as "mejum." It was, in fact, Slade's refined demeanor that had already sprung him from jail: an American by birth, Slade was a magician who saw Spiritualism as an opportunity to rake in some easy money. In July 1876, Slade crossed the Atlantic and set himself up in London as a medium. According to Harry Houdini, Slade was quite a showman and easily "bamboozled the credulous of his day."[77] John Nevil Maskeyne, English magician and inventor of the pay toilet, attended one of Slade's shows: "Crowds of people rushed to witness the phenomena . . . , paying one guinea each for a sitting lasting but a few minutes. You would think they were giving gold guineas away. The 'Doctor' [Slade] must have netted some hundreds of pounds weekly."[78]

The authorities soon tired of Slade, who, on October 1, 1875, was arrested and eventually convicted under the Witchcraft Act of 1735 (also known as the British Vagrancy Act), which classified all manner of magical practitioners (i.e., fortunetellers and tarot card readers) as vagrants and con artists.[79] The English judge, while stating that he full well understood that Spiritualism was "a kind of new religion" and that he did not wish to offend sincere believers, sentenced Slade to three months' hard labor in the House of Corrections.[80] The sentence was overturned on appeal, on the argument that Slade was an educated truth seeker, one capable of making heavy objects hover like feathers. New charges under the old Witchcraft Act were readied, but before Slade could be arrested yet again, he fled England, intending to settle in Paris, but the French authorities had been tipped off to his coming.[81] Slade instead went to Germany, where he mixed easily with the educated elite. The distinguished physicist Johann Zöllner of the University of Leipzig examined Slade and concluded that the medium's powers derived from his mysterious access to the "fourth dimension."[82] Zöllner even denominated a new branch of science to explain the phenomena: "Transcendental Physics."[83] By the 1880s, Slade was living in New York and apparently using the same polished (or slick) shtick.

Slade was, in fact, so well-mannered that, on February 4, 1885, he sent Furness and the rest of the Seybert Commission a polite thank-you note, the language and tone of which hardly suggest the lower-class image Furness conjures in his letters:

Dear Mr. Furness:—I take this opportunity to express to you, and through you to the other members of the Seybert Commission, my hearty approval of the course pursued by them in their investigation of phenomena occurring in my presence. Fully realizing that I am only the instrument or channel through which these manifestations are produced, it would be presumption on my part to undertake to lay down a line to be followed by the unseen intelligences, whose servant I am. Hence, I did say their conditions must be acceded to or *I would return to New York*. That they did so, is evident to my mind from the results obtained, which I regard as a necessary preliminary to a continuation, when other experiments may be introduced with better prospects of success. It may be well not to insist on following the exact course pursued by Professor Zoellner, but leave it open to original or impromptu suggestions that may be adopted without previous consideration, which, if successful, would be of equal value as evidence of its genuineness, at the same time give greater breadth to the experiments. In conclusion, allow me to say that in the event of the Committee desiring to continue these experiments through another series of sittings with me, it will give me pleasure to enter into arrangements for that purpose.

Very truly yours,
Henry Slade.[84]

It's not just Slade's vocabulary and education that seem off. Slade writes that he would *return to New York* because the meeting had gone badly. But Furness said that the meeting was *in New York*. Why had Furness lied to his sons about his trip to New York? There is another detail that strikes me as odd: in his letters to his sons, Furness does not mention other members of the Seybert Commission having gone with him; yet Slade is clear that he was interviewed by not just Furness but by other members of the commission as well. Another detail: Furness states that Slade and Hill performed in pitch darkness. But that would not fit Slade's common practice, which was always to perform in broad daylight.[85] Then there is Furness's mention of a "pretty woman," and the tickling of his leg—that is, sexual arousal.

It is here that we can at last discuss the date of Furness's aforementioned letter to his sons: November 2, 1884. Why is that date so odd? Because Furness had already made contact with Margaret Fox in October and she had stated, in the previously cited letter dated November 1, her reluctance to visit Furness in Philadelphia. Yet, in his letter of November 2, Furness writes, "*Last Monday*, I went to New York to engage Mrs. Margaret Fox Kane to come here and give some séances." The second of November was Sunday, so by the phrase "Last Monday" Furness is here referring to October 26, 1884. That is odd, however, since Fox never mentions meeting him or confirms her intent to travel to Philadelphia. Readers can plainly see for themselves that her letter of November 1 raises a series of preconditions: Margaret will not perform on March 31; she will not perform without payment; she must receive said payment in advance; the payment must be by money order. And then there is the date of the Slade letter to the commission, dated February 4, 1885. While we can accept that Slade's gentlemanly letter was not penned the moment Furness and his cohorts left the room, it seems incredible to believe that Slade waited until February to thank Furness for a meeting that had happened (at least according to Furness's letters to his sons) three months earlier. The inescapable conclusion is that many of the facts and dates concerning Furness's first meeting with Margaret Fox do not align.[86]

That Furness was hiding something concerning his relationship with Margaret Fox seems to be a long way from a discussion of Shakespeare or even of Spiritualism. But that is, perhaps, the very issue. Furness and Fox could have not been more different. He was educated, rich, married, and disciplined; she was unschooled, poor, unmarried, and ruined by drink. He studied the literary texts of the immortals; she communicated with them by way of a Spirit Guide. He believed in cause and effect; she argued for the unseen and the unexplained. Faced with a spiritual practice and a woman so opposite to himself and his way of thinking, Furness might have continued to attack Fox and her beliefs; he might have exposed her as a fraud. Instead, the two began an exchange of belief systems.

While initially doubtful of and even hostile to her, Furness soon entered into a prolonged correspondence with the medium whom he had once threatened with a strip search. An early letter—dated October 23, 1884—details Margaret Fox's reduced circumstances and her continuing changes of address. Furness replies by promising to visit her in New York. Margaret Fox wrote again on November 22, complaining of neuralgia—a euphemism for drinking too much.[87] On December 30, 1884, she wrote to Furness again, informing him that she had pawned her only remaining valuables, a diamond ring and bracelet, valued at $450—gifts from her former lover, Mr. Kane. She had "fought hard through many years to save" these possessions but she now had had no choice but to pawn them. She could redeem them if he would just send her $125; if not, then she would be "crushed by the terrific interest required by pawn brokers. The repose of mind would contribute greatly to my ability to earn money." She also hopes that he will fulfill his promise to visit her in New York "in the first week of January."[88]

This certainly sounds like Margaret Fox was bilking Furness. Four months later, on April 15, 1885, she was happy to report that her health was on the mend, and, and, better yet, she had her diamond ring and brace-let again. Furness, it seems, paid her. Perhaps to allay any doubts that Furness might have had, she assured him that "I met with success [i.e., found the money] even before your letter reached me." She also wrote that she had moved yet again, this time to 41 Greenwich Avenue, New York, which sounds upscale and trendy, but—circa 1870–1920—the area was home to new waves of near-penniless immigrants and quite a few drunks.

PLAY-ACTING

Furness, meanwhile, continued his investigations of Spiritualism. But a change in direction is marked. Hitherto, he had merely visited mediums looking for fraud, but after forming a relationship with Fox, he began to explore Spiritualism with a different frame of mind. As Margaret Fox had counseled him, "You must commence right in the first place [i.e., enter the séance in the right frame of mind] or you shall all be disappointed for a much longer time." While in New York on yet another trip, Furness met with the medium Joseph Caffray, who stated that Furness possessed "extraordinary Spiritual capabilities." Emboldened, Furness decided to develop his own psychic gifts. Furness thus bought two slates from Caffray and carefully followed his directions:

> The instructions which I received from Caffray were to keep those slates carefully in the dark, and every evening at about the same hour to sit in total darkness, with my hands resting on them for about a half or three quarters of an hour; to maintain a calm, equable, passive state of mind, even to think of any indifferent subject rather than to concentrate my thoughts too intently on the slate-writing. There could be no question of the result. A Medium of my unusual and excessive power would find, at the end of three weeks, faint zig-zag scratches within the closed slates, and these scratches would gradually assume shape, until at last messages would be legible, probably at the end of six weeks, or of three months at the very farthest.[89]

The tone here in undeniably comical, but Furness kept up the routine for six months, even bringing the slate with him on vacation—all to no effect.[90]

He then moved on to pellet writing (see Glossary of Spiritualist Terms and Techniques). As with his query about *Vllorxa*, this test also had an element of the Shakespearean: Furness placed an envelope under a skull that he had obtained from a friend. The skull was that of the Shakespeare actor George Frederick Cooke. Next, Furness wrote the identity of the skull on a piece of paper and sealed the answer in the envelope. A series of mediums were then asked to hold the envelope and identify the skull psychically. One replied that it was the remains of a black woman of about forty years old. Another, calling herself Marie St. Clair, returned the envelope with a poem that sounds Shakespearean: "From the brightest stars, / And viewless air / Sweet Spirit, if they home be there, / Answer me.—Answer me." If these lines were meant to fool Furness into thinking that he had found a genuine medium, one apparently capable not only of contacting Shakespeare but also of recording new lines by the Bard, Furness was not so easily taken in. The lines were, in fact, copied from Felicia Dorothea Browne Hemans's collection *Songs of the Affections with Other Poems*, published in 1830.[91]

Furness then experimented with magnetic paper. This new-fangled form of Spirit communication derived from the experiments of a Scandinavian nobleman, Baron Ludwig de Güldenstubbé, who noted that the Bible had two instances of direct Spirit writing—the first being God writing the Ten Commandments on two tablets for Moses, and the second being a mysterious sentence on the wall of King Belshazzar's dining room: "mene mene tekel upharsin," which defied all attempts at interpretation. (Later studies suggest the writing on the wall was in a "supernatural cipher."[92] Ciphers played a role in Chapter 2, but, here, the impenetrability of the text links nicely to Furness's pet crux, *Vllorxa*.)

Inspired by biblical precedent, the good Baron, aided by his sister, locked a pad and paper in a box and waited several days for the Spirits to write him a message. At first, no marks appeared. Then a few scratchings were seen. The Baron kept at it. One day, he received a message in Estonian. More followed. The Baron was soon receiving messages from Mary Stuart, Plato, and Julius Caesar—in English, Greek, and Latin, respectively.

Perhaps there were Spirits writing to him, but how could the Baron be sure that these Spirits were who they claimed to be? Perhaps he was the victim of some prank? Güldenstubbé then hit upon a test: he would leave his pencil and pad at the stone monuments of the dead. If the Spirits of the departed identified themselves properly, he would know the messages to be genuine. (It does not seem to have occurred to the Baron that a mischievous Spirit might simply read the gravestone and then impersonate the departed, nor did the Baron allow that someone might simply follow him, wait for him to leave, and then write something on the pad.) In any case, the credulous Baron Ludwig de Güldenstubbé published his results in *Pneumatologie Positive et Expérimentale. La réalité des Esprits et le Phénomène Merveilleux de Leur Écriture Directe* (1857; *Spirits Positive and Experimental: The Reality of Spirits and the Marvellous Phenomenon of Their Direct Writing).*[93]

Some thirty years later, Güldenstubbé's practice of pad and pencil was modified. The newest technique included magnetic paper— Mesmerism yet again—and instead of a monument or tomb, the paper was placed nearest to a spiritual receptor—that is, the brain. So, at considerable expense, Furness bought and wore magnetized blotting paper: "I must wear, night and day, a piece of magnetized paper, about six inches square, a fresh piece every night and morning; its magnetism was exhausted in about twelve hours." His results: "Not a zig, nor a zag."[94] Furness's last bit of Spiritualist research was conducted in April of 1886; he was in Boston, investigating a medium who claimed that the Spirits materialized fresh flowers for her once a week.[95] Why had Furness suddenly favored mediums in Boston over those in New York? It may only be a coincidence, but Margaret Fox had moved to Boston.[96]

In 1887, Furness published his report on Spiritualism: *Preliminary Report of the Commission Appointed by the University of Pennsylvania to Investigate Modern Spiritualism in Accordance with the Request of the Late Henry Seybert.* Furness was careful to stress that Spiritualism might be real, but that the mediums he examined were all frauds. He therefore hoped that "wherever fraud in Spiritualism be found, that it is, and not whatever of truth there may be therein, which is denounced, and all Spiritualists who love the truth will join with us in condemnation of it."[97] This also explains his subsequent notation in his edition of *The Tempest* (1892): "I beg leave to say, parenthetically, that personally I have mistrusted all lesser Spiritualist influences in the elucidation of Shakespeare's texts." Note "all *lesser* Spiritualist influences": even if Furness's Spiritualist experiences had been marked by fraud, he allowed that greater (i.e., possibly genuine) Spiritualists might really be having conversations with Shakespeare.[98]

MINDS TRANSFIGURED TO SOMETHING OF GREAT CONSTANCY

If that seems like an odd opinion coming from the hitherto skeptical Furness, we might here note a similar volte-face for Margaret Fox. This is not to say that she was suddenly reformed. On March 22, 1888, she set sail for England; on May 14, 1888, she wrote to the *New York Herald* (published May 27, 1888) that she, along with other mediums, had defrauded the faithful from "all their worldly possessions." So far as she was concerned, these people had invited her to take their money: "I have found that fanatics are as plentiful among 'inferior men and women' as they are among the more learned. They are all alike. They cannot hold their fanaticism in check, and it increases as their years increase. All they will ever achieve for their foolish fanaticism will be the loss of money, softening of the brain and a lingering death."[99] Despite her unrepentant tone, Fox had here admitted to fraud. Three months later, she agreed to an interview with the *Herald.* The reported asked point-blank, "It is all a trick?" Margaret Fox replied, "Absolutely."[100]

On October 21, 1888, a year after Furness's negative report on Spiritualism, Margaret and her sister Kate appeared before a crowd at the New York Academy of Music and admitted that all their psychic encounters, which they had perpetrated for decades, had been fraudulent. The two sisters then revealed their "Spirit rapping" trick—a simple popping of the joints.[101] Leah, noticeably absent, continued to state that she had been a legitimate medium.

On November 12, 1888, Margaret wrote to Furness yet again. She and Kate had already been paid $1,500 for the live confession delivered at the New York Academy of Music. Perhaps Philadelphians would be interested in a repeat performance?

> Dear Sir,
>
> If I could find an honest man who would engage a place in Philadelphia and who would be able to give a short lecture, I would come on and give an exhibition and, show upon what ground the word "Spiritualism" has its origin. I would share half the profits [presumably net profit] with a man who would act honorably. I have had a manager and a lecturer here in Boston but I don't believe they have acted honestly with me.
>
> I should think the committee with whom I met at your request would be interested in this exposure.
>
> I enclose you one of my cards and [hope to] show you that I never admitted that the dead had any thing to do with the manifestations or what the fanatic has called "Spiritualism."

The affixed calling card read, "Mrs. Kane does not claim any spirit power; but people must judge for themselves."[102] In a postscript to her letter, she added,"You must bear [*sic*] in mind that the simple trick, from which millions have become 'Spiritualists' began when Katie and I were little children [Leah is not mentioned] and with our minds unformed we were not able to designate right from wrong." I have found no record of Furness's reply, nor any engagement booked for Margaret Fox. In any case, the confessions did little to undermine the bedrock belief of many Spiritualists, who later claimed that Kate and Margaret had sided against their sister Leah not out of any newfound devotion to the truth but because the telling of lies was now the easiest way to keep the money rolling in.[103]

Yet this counterclaim by Spiritualists made little sense. Shows were commonly reported in newspapers; we can hardly assume that crowds in multiple cities would pay to see how a trick was done, especially after the mechanics of the trick had been reported by the press. True, money was important to Margaret Fox, but her continued correspondence with Furness suggests something more than a quick-cash grab. As he accommodated to her religious beliefs, she moved closer to his materialist position. Perhaps she sought to earn more than money; perhaps she sought to earn his respect.

And yet it would be too much to say that Fox or Furness changed; at best we can say that both enjoyed a flirtation. Fox, after confessing the truth, did not give up drinking and soon found herself broke. Her "friends" in Spiritualism offered her an easy way out—all she had to do was recant and say that she had been temporarily possessed by the Devil. She did so and went back to hosting séances; though, with her having once confessed to fraud, the general public remained leery. Halls that were once packed with hundreds of believers now stood nearly empty.[104] Margaret Fox never saw Furness again and died destitute on March 8, 1895. Furness, while wearing magnetic paper hats and adding a Spiritualist reference or two to his *Variorum* project, never abandoned his palatial lifestyle or the materialist rationale that underwrote it—his rich father-in-law, we recall, was an industrialist.

While Margaret Fox and H. H. Furness were very different people when they met, they grew to be more like each other by the time they parted: Whether Margaret Fox was or was not seeing Furness romantically, she was at least exploring what it was like to adopt Furness's worldview. (It must have been quite an adjustment for Margaret Fox, who had been peddling Spiritualism since the age of 11.) As for Furness, the editor's devotion to psychic rituals and enactments suggests that he at last understood the draw of Spiritualism. Wearing his magnetic paper hat, he was, in effect, fantasizing.

Chapter 5

Knight Visions

THE YEAR IS 1950. A GRAVEYARD IN Exeter. G. Wilson Knight and his brother, the classical scholar Jackson Knight, bury their mother, Caroline. She had been a difficult woman who had suffered from a variety of phobias. If she overheard news that she considered distressing—such as references to prisons and executions, which held formalized and punitive implications—she had to give away all the clothes she wore while hearing it.[1] Trying to ignore the problem only made matters worse, spreading the evil, and she would end by discarding all the clothes that she had worn during her period of denial.[2] Caroline Knight's condition worsened with time. After one visit to the theater, she discovered that it was near a police station and from then on that particular theater was, for her, taboo.[3] No social gathering was really safe unless she could either direct its course or escape at will.[4] She was also a pyromaniac and burned down two of the rest homes that had agreed to take her in. She went to a London psychiatrist but returned with the conviction that psychiatry did not understand her trouble whatsoever.

G. Wilson Knight confessed that there were moments when he recognized that his mother was mentally ill: "Her small room, so cluttered with paper wrappings of all sorts, worried me, not only through fears of fire but more from the pain I suffered from her neurosis, which forced her into irrationalities. It seemed to hit me as with a desecrating ugliness. I would try hard not to see, or if that was impossible, to stifle consciousness of it."[5] More often, however, both brothers were convinced that Caroline's erratic behavior—they never seem to have called her "mother" until after her physical death—had something to do with her Spiritual knowledge. Even the phobias were a sign of her innate psychic powers. She was, according to G. Wilson Knight, "rather like a psychometrist reading the radiations of an object, and sensing its past history and present influences."[6]

Both brothers paid close attention to her as her illnesses progressed, sure that she might reveal some important fact about life after death.

They were (at least initially) to be disappointed. Her deathbed description of the afterlife was that the Spirits looked "rather like hens."[7] She died of cancer on July 8, 1950. At the funeral, G. Wilson Knight could not help but think of her as Shakespearean: "like Shakespeare's Love in *Venus and Adonis*, 'a spirit all compact of fire', she had for long, in the manner of Cleopatra's dying words, 'I am fire and air', looked forward to cremation. Thinking of it, she would say, 'At last I shall be warm.'"[8] Knight added, "When I wrote on the spiritualised gaiety of Cleopatra, I had Caroline in mind."[9] Knight is here referring to his essay "The Poet and Immortality" (1928), in which he writes, "That which inspires love cannot die, although it seems to die; the beautiful thing which is lost, is not lost but is in safe keeping and will be restored. Hermione and Thaisa thus wake from seeming death to the sound of music, and are restored to Leontes and Pericles . . . We must cease to assert that Shakespeare throws no light on these eternal facts and that the final plays are inartistically 'unreal.'"[10] Soon after her death, first Jackson and then G. Wilson began to talk to the Spirit of their mother and to her new friends, among them Shakespeare.

It is fair to say that G. Wilson Knight occupies a unique position in Shakespeare Studies. On the face of it, his career is orderly, even enviable. After earning a master's degree from Oxford, G. Wilson Knight taught at the Dean Close School in Cheltenham, then accepted a job as a lecturer of World Drama at the University of Toronto. He returned to England during the Second World War and put on a variety of Shakespeare plays, which he hoped would bolster the war effort; from 1941–45, he taught at Stowe School before landing, in 1946, a more appropriate academic position as a reader at Leeds. Knight gained professor rank in 1956; he retired in 1962.[11] In 1968, he was made a commander of the Order of the British Empire.[12] His publishing output to 1950—the year of his mother's death—is astonishing: 17 books, including the classics *The Wheel of Fire: Interpretations of Shakespearian Tragedy* (1930), *The Imperial Theme* (1931), and *The Starlit Dome: Studies in the Poetry of Vision* (1941). By the time of his death in 1985, Knight would produce another 23 books.

Yet, despite a multigenerational audience, professorial Shakespeareans often dismiss Knight's work as "arbitrary,"[13] "nonanalytical,"[14] "absurd,"[15] "laughable,"[16] "perverse and unacceptable";[17] filled with "vanity,"[18] "tangible eccentricity,"[19] "appalling insensitivity,"[20] "well-known hyperbole,"[21] and "boldly preposterous proposition;"[22] marked by a "failure to comprehend"[23] and likely to "annoy those Shakespeare critics who characteristically eschew what cannot be demonstrated rigorously";[24] the ravings of "revivalist preacher"[25] and an "imbecile."[26] Northrop Frye, then a new member of the faculty at the University of Toronto, remembers Knight as a bardolatrous bumpkin: "he was completely possessed by Shakespeare, and gave the impression of not knowing a Quarto from a Folio text, certainly of caring even less." Frye continues, "He showed me once his main instrument of scholarship—a Globe Shakespeare with a mass of pencilled annotations"—another dig, since the Globe Shakespeare was generally considered to be vastly inferior to the Arden and other scholarly editions.[27]

Hostility toward Knight often centers, however, not on his supposed ignorance of codicology—a common enough deficiency among many Shakespeareans—but on his spiritualized writings and practices, which many traditional academics deem to be inappropriate or taboo.[28] William K. Wimsatt (1954) seems to have Knight or someone very much like him in mind when discussing the term "Intentional Fallacy"—specifically, the idea that a definitive meaning can be derived by asking the ghost of the author what he meant: "Critical inquiries are not settled by consulting the oracle."[29] Wimsatt's certainty is echoed by Terence Hawkes (1996): "Shakespeare can still engage modern audiences . . . without [their] needing to locate a phantom quality of 'transcendency' in the plays, or to construct ghostly entities vaguely promoted by the plays themselves."[30] However, many scholars continue to circumvent Wimsatt and Hawkes. We regularly read that "the text problematizes" or that the text "gives voice to"—coded and pleasant familiarities that imply critical neutrality. The seemingly inanimate text speaks for itself; the critic is not interpreting, he is merely listening and recording what the text somehow magically imparts. Isn't that the very definition of oracular?

The difference is one of frankness and perhaps even of perspicacity. New criticism, like later forms of new historicism (e.g., Stephen Greenblatt's stylish "self-fashioning"), participates in a rhetorical gambit by which meaning somehow naturally coalesces moment by moment and subject by subject. Fair enough, but we are still (however unknowingly) overlapping with G. Wilson Knight's Spiritualist paradigm, which rejects any distinction between Shakespeare's or anyone else's meaning: all souls are linked; all writing is collective and collaborative. To Knight and other Spiritualists, the endless reincarnation of Shakespearean meaning is itself the proof of its eternalism.

A SPIRITUALIST INTERPRETER OF SHAKESPEARE

Just when did Knight become a Spiritualist? One of Knight's few sympathetic readers, Helen Sword, argues that Knight's religious faith was a "logical extension of his atemporal, spatializing critical mode."[31] The grammar suggests that Spiritualism came late to the process. That thinking needs to be reversed. As Knight himself insisted, Spiritualism had always been at the heart of his interpretative process.[32] We have already glanced at "The Poet and Immortality" (1928), but any number of his works confirm his Spiritualist faith. In *Myth and Miracles* (1929), Knight refers to *The Tempest* as a "crystal act of mystic vision" and to *Pericles* as a "mystic apprehension of a life that conquerors death."[33] In his essay "Mystic Symbolism" (1931), Knight argues that Shakespeare's late plays should be considered "essentially as mystical resolutions" to the human condition.[34] In *The Shakespearian Tempest* (1932), Knight argues that Shakespeare's plays were "divinely inspired" and, "having attributed the true origin [of Shakespeare's plays] to Divinity, we shall not be surprised to find profound meanings in the result."[35] The point is reiterated in *The Burning Oracle* (1939): "the greatest poets are as receiving-stations for invisible messages across the ages."[36] In *Starlit Dome* (1941), he opines that "the business of great literature may be defined as the interweaving of human affairs with spiritualistic appearances, phantasms of the dead, portents, resurrections and visitations."[37] In *Shakespeare and Religion* (1967), he states that *The Tempest* prophetically explores "the esoteric movements of our time, and especially the greatest of them, Spiritualism, [which] must be faced and incorporated within our seats of learning and councils of state before we can attain to mastery."[38] In his unpublished "Caroline: Life after Death" (started circa 1952; last revised 1985), we read that his aim had always been to link his "experiences of Spiritualism to the work of imaginative interpretation"; likewise, in *Shakespearian Dimensions* (1984), Knight writes that "other-dimensional intuition" was at the core of his work "from the first."[39]

Knight's Spiritualist beliefs were no doubt informed and reinforced by his daily Spiritual activities. Knight was a member of the Harry Edwards Spiritual Healing Sanctuary, the Psychic Research Society in Leeds, the Spiritualist Association of Great Britain, and the local National Spiritualist Church in Exeter. Knight's secretary Olivia Anderson (née Mordue) recently informed me that both G. Wilson and Jackson Knight preached regularly to the Spiritualist faithful: "The Exeter Spiritualist Church in York Road was an old Army mission hut. Later, thanks to many donations from the congregation, including the Knights and other sources, a real church was built a few yards away on the opposite side of the road near the main road of Sidwell Street. Both men preached for 15–20 mins during formal services on several occasions. For 'absent healing' they took down names to pray for the sick and were in touch with The Harry Edwards Healing Sanctuary in South-East England."[40]

Like Swedenborg, Knight believed that Spirits passed the time by attending Spiritual Universities ("halls of learning"); like many twentieth-century Spiritualists, he thought that Spirits lived in "great cities" and worried over us ("Spirits cannot interfere too directly. They can, to some extent warn").[41] Like Mesmer, he believed that the Spirits might heal the sick; like Sarah Shatford, he believed that Spirits were radio waves; thus, one might tune in to the "frequency of the vibrations of the[ir] forces of life."[42] He elsewhere refers to the ability to talk to Spirits by "turn[ing] on the switch" of the mind's psychic radio; he likewise believes in the existence of a "poetic x-ray" and that flying saucers and aliens "function as a necessary . . . link" between our world and the Spirit Realm—all echoes of Spiritualist nomenclature discussed in the introduction and Chapter 1 of this study.[43]

Knight's Spiritualist pronouncements can be baffling, and his writing style can be irksome. He can be, on occasion, maddeningly imprecise, often preferring metaphor to explanation: "poetry of any worth is a rounded solidity which drops shadows only on the flat surfaces of philosophical statement." Timon, he says, is "like some majestic liner . . . bosomed on the swell and heave of ocean, by the lode-star of a titanic love."[44] At other points, he can be overly determinative. When looking at the Romantics, for example, he has no qualms about seeing poetry as a decipherable code, not far in (il)logic from the Baconians discussed in Chapter 2: "river" symbolizes "life"; bubbles are "Poetic imaginations"; boat journeys are "psychic conflicts."[45] Sometimes Knight chooses a symbol but leaves its meaning undeclared. The bird in Coleridge's *The Ancient Mariner*, for example, "*seems to suggest* some redeeming Christ-like" reading, or maybe it's "a nature-force"; on this particular point, Knight shrugs and muscles through: "Anyway, the central crime is the slaying of it"[46]

Knight is, mercifully, crystal clear on one key point: his readers must keep in mind that he is not, by his own definition, a scholar or a critic; rather, he is an interpreter. In *The Wheel of Fire* (1930), Knight describes his method as a "translation from one order of consciousness to another"; a reexpression of the poet's "experience in its [or Knight's] own terms."[47] In his 1952 book *Lord Byron: Christian Virtues*, he argues that "artist genius"—and by that term we may include his own interpretative method—involves selecting symbols, or images that might serve as symbols, without regard to context or to the author's original intent: "materials [must be] wrenched boldly from their habitual association . . . often with little or no emphasis on the temporal succession from which they have been removed."[48] In his 1958 book *The Sovereign Flower*, he explains that "criticism aspires to a judgement, a valuing," whereas "interpretation aspires to an understanding of it. Criticism brings its own ethical or aesthetic standards to the judgement of literature; interpretation goes to literature to discover standards for use elsewhere."[49] In his unpublished "Caroline: Life after Death," he writes unapologetically of his exegetical approach: "My present book is constructed more on imaginative lines . . . That does not mean that it is less in touch with reality, with personal experience; indeed, the exact reverse is true; it is because it concentrates on personal experience that it holds an imaginative validity."[50]

Knight's readings are deeply personalized; they are shaped not merely by reading Shakespeare but by all his experiences, from which Shakespeare cannot be isolated. Thus he sees no reason to keep his Spiritualist beliefs separate from his poetic evaluations and daily interests. The works of Shakespeare and Byron are, therefore, legitimate places to discuss "'astral travelling' or 'astral projection'" or the "emphases in contemporary Spiritualism on vibratory speed as characterizing higher states of consciousness."[51] Likewise, Knight is as apt to cite Spiritualist rags (*Two Worlds* and *The Psychic News*[52]), Spiritualists books (*The Psychic Life of Jesus, The Bible as Psychic History, The Study and Practice of Astral Projection, Spirit Teachings, Yoga Made Easy*, and *The Sacred Mushroom*), and Spiritualist authors (William Stantain Moses, Geraldine Cummins, and J. W. Dunne) as he is to cite more traditional literary journals (*Shakespeare Quarterly, PMLA*, and *TLS*) or mainstream Shakespeare critics (A. C. Bradley, T. W. Baldwin, and E. K. Chambers).[53] Knight has no misgivings in stating that Macbeth suffers from "spirit possession," a supernaturalism inexplicably confirmed by "flowers, which are said to be impregnated by the souls of the dead"; that Lady Macbeth has mediumistic powers, or that Banquo's ghost reveals "the truths of spiritualism";[54] that the so-called curse on *Macbeth* is real, the revenge of "inimical spirit-powers";[55] that Emilia is "hypnotised" by Othello's magical handkerchief;[56] that plays like *Pericles* and *All's Well That Ends Well* explore "spirit-healing" and "faith-healing";[57] or that *The Winter's Tale* is a psychic tale with "Paulina acting as medium. Materialisation is formed by a kind of ectoplasm drawn from the medium and moulded, by a kind of artistry, by spirit-powers; it is sometimes compared with sculpture."[58]

KEY CONCEPTS

Despite the oddities of specific statements, in the main Knight's interpretation of Shakespeare differs from traditional Shakespeare criticism in four important ways. The first issue stems from Knight's rejection of the temporal: "in life or a Shakespearian play, we have sense of a time-sequence, we also have sense of an emotional field, what I have elsewhere called the spatial quality. This spatial quality may be regarded as vertical and the whole life thought of as lifted, generating a spatial area as it moves upward or downward, at right angles to the horizontal time-stream."[59] This vertical line "is creative in time as well as in eternity. The prophet at every moment feels life sinking its shaft to the rich centres below, and mines vertically before creating horizontally."[60] In effect, Knight argues that plays have almost nothing to do with their temporal plots; they are best understood by their vertical (i.e., symbolic) meanings. He takes the same view concerning Shakespeare's entire oeuvre. It makes no difference in what order the plays were written, nor their genres. They are all united symbolically or thematically. Thus the comedies *Taming of the Shrew*, *Much Ado About Nothing*, and *Twelfth Night* are listed matter-of-factly against a tragedy (*King Lear*), two Roman plays (*Antony and Cleopatra*, *Coriolanus*), a romance (*The Winter's Tale*), and a history (*Henry VIII*);[61] the early history *2Henry VI* is matched with the mature tragedy *Macbeth*; the midcareer comedy *Much Ado About Nothing* is paired with the last history *Henry VIII*; the early tragedy *Romeo and Juliet* with the late Roman *Coriolanus*.[62] Plot and context are dispensable: *Hamlet* and *Macbeth* are united as "powerful, death visions and immortality myths"; *King Lear* and *Timon of Athens* are "purgatorial"; *Pericles* and *The Winter's Tale* are "myths of creation."[63] As for *The Tempest*, it alone is treated chronologically; it "sums up the Shakespearian universe. The contemplative peace and philosophic forgiveness."[64]

To make these sorts of arguments, Knight must see Shakespeare himself as an island impervious to the stream of time, untarnished by the conventions of the playhouse, unaware or, at any rate, unaffected by the activities of rival writers. Collaboration is certainly out of the question. Thus, in *The Shakespearian Tempest*, Knight argues that *Henry VIII* and *Pericles* cannot be collaborative works; to see them as such would invite "intellectual chaos": "once we feel the massive unity of Shakespeare, we shall begin to understand the separate plays as contributing to this single harmony; and, understanding, we shall be less and less inclined to raise questions of authorship. Many doubtful passages will be seen to have been doubtful only because not understood."[65]

For historically minded readers, his rejection of temporal concerns is an intractable flaw. Linking images and themes in early and late plays or comedies with tragedies is only possible if Shakespeare used the same set of symbols and themes to mean exactly (or nearly exactly) the same thing throughout his career. In effect, Shakespeare would have to have had all his symbols worked out in his head before he ever wrote a single play. Another problem: for *The Tempest* to "sum up" the themes of the entire corpus, Shakespeare would have had to consider that play to be his farewell to playwrighting. Knight probably lifted the idea from Dowden, but, whatever its origin, the premise is badly blemished by the historical fact that both *Henry VIII* and *Two Noble Kinsmen* come after *The Tempest*.[66] And, since Shakespeare's plays are, in his view, noncollaborative (at least in the secular sense), he cannot adopt the fallback position that *The Tempest*, while not the last play Shakespeare had a hand in, was, at any rate, Shakespeare's last *full* play. But Knight is not to be ensnared by objections based on chronology and genre, or, as he terms them, "false associations and illegitimate logic."[67] Chronology and the related concept of plot mean nothing to someone sure of a timeless Spirit Realm. So far as Knight was concerned, if non-Spiritualists did not understand the nature of the perpetual, it did not follow that Shakespeare was just as ignorant: "Most of us [i.e., not Shakespeare] live only on the surface. All such vision, revealing the true life at one point in the time-stream, inevitably affects that stream itself. Sight of the eternal world includes past, present and future."[68]

Knight's total faith in the survival of the soul after physical death leads us to another of his challenging opinions: his total rejection of Shakespeare's tragedies as tragedies. Once the so-called tragic facts are put in their true place, suffering and loss disappear. The protagonist might perish, but he is not defeated; in Knight's view, he triumphs.[69] Thus Lear does not die howling in anger or seduced by delusion; rather, in death, he recovers "semi-transcendental meaning. Nothing can destroy its beauty, its power, and its serenity."[70] The latter reading is unlikely to raise many eyebrows, but more controversially, Knight states that Othello's love and murder of his wife are a "tragic synthesis and triumph, a pinnacle of near superhuman experience, his finest hour."[71] Likewise, *Timon of Athens* is not a tragedy of despair but an "archetypal love-play" touching that "eternal otherness" to which the titular character aspires.[72] Macbeth's end is not one of nihilism and senseless violence but a "state-of-being beyond, or above, time; and the rest is unknown, or undefined"; Macbeth "is spiritually intact."[73] Likewise, Hamlet is not a man of flesh and blood ruled by passions but a "spirit of penetrating intellect," whose survival in the afterlife "holds the deeper assurance for humanity."[74] In Cleopatra's suicide, we receive an "immediate immortality intuition beyond the ordinary tragic acceptance."[75] Knight's elemental and spiritualistic intuitions and experiences open manifold possibilities; and if, as he thinks, we are wiser to think more of multiple and coordinated realms of spiritual existence than of a single accidental universe, then, following his logic, the probability and promise of spiritual survival are only multiplied: death "is but a sorry caricature, lacking the *one dimension of reality*."[76] Like Percy Allen's mediumistic encounters with Oxford, Bacon, and Shakespeare, Knight is sure he is right because he feels his experiences to be true. No direct textual evidence is necessary.

Another (related) revision of Shakespeare concerns the poet's presumed bisexuality. To discuss Shakespeare's sexuality seems to pull us away from Knight's spiritual interpretation. Yet in Knight's sacred construal, bisexuality is not a matter of gender confusion; it is, rather, a matter of spiritual integration. Since differentiation implies limitation, Knight supposes that "the more fully integrated and inclusive man will be the less in need of a sexual partner."[77] In *As You Like It*, Rosalind consequently exhibits a "bisexual dimension" with "all that is sexually limited, or lustful, being left out";[78] in *The Merchant of Venice*, the cross-dressing Portia merges both sexual allure with a masculine "Christian aura";[79] in *Twelfth Night*, the cross-dressing "Viola finally wins from him [Orsino] a devotion deeper than his flashy [i.e., sexual] infatuation with Olivia."[80] In the *Sonnets*, the Dark Lady stands for "sexual duality."[81] In *Much Ado About Nothing*, "bisexuality" is expressed "not by creating a central figure in disguise but by showing each partner drawing towards such a state to meet the other."[82] Even the overtly heterosexual attraction of Romeo to Juliet is, by this logic, bisexual as soon as lust turns to love: "Perfect love and normal sexuality are, paradoxically, opposed"; "the state of being in love *is* the bisexual state."[83]

We might say that the error here is in swapping sexual longing with spiritual intuition and in turning Shakespeare into something greater than a playwright.[84] Knight counters that Shakespeare's plays merely express his own personal readings, and—while he hopes that his Spiritualist interpretations will catch fire with his reader's imagination—he recognizes that his readings do not and will not "exert the appalling authority over our daily life and deepest *being* that characterizes religion."[85]

We now turn to a last, crucial distinction: science and faith. Often in Spiritualist writings, we seem to be presented with a choice between science and séance. Knight is more accommodating. In his view, Spiritualism and science are not mutually exclusive belief systems. In *Hiroshima: On Prophecy and the Sun-Bomb* (1946), Knight expressed his hope that "Religion and science could make common cause in terms of the 'spiritual' basis of matter."[86] What Knight meant by *science*, however, may not fit everyone's definition. Rather than cite Einstein or Newton, Knight often invokes dubious researchers and institutions. For example, in *Starlit Dome* (1941), Knight argues that Spiritualism is a legitimate field of scientific study. He applauds the work undertaken by the Marylebone Spiritual Association and the College of Psychic Science in London. He further cites the distinguished and ongoing work of Professor Rhine of Duke University.[87]

Let's begin with a quick look at the Marylebone Spiritualist Association, founded in 1872; in 1955, it petitioned the Board of Trade for modification of its name to The Spiritualist Association of Great Britain (SAGB). The following is from its (now online) charter: "It must be [clear] to many non-Spiritualists that until March [1844] psychic phenomena and mediumistic powers were unheard of, and that by some magic, psychic powers were suddenly given to certain individuals after the Hydesville outbreak." But, as we noted in Chapter 4, two of the three Fox Sisters responsible for the so-called Hydesville outbreak admitted to fraud in 1888.[88] That the SAGB bases its formation on events of admitted fraud hardly instills confidence. The same can be said of the British College of Psychic Science, whose own honorary principal, Rose Champion De Crespigny, warned its members not to be too stringent in examining psychic phenomena: "we are spiking our own guns, and inhibiting production of the phenomenon." This was said as part of a keynote address at one of the college's annual dinners.[89]

As for Professor Rhine, Knight is here referring to the work of Joseph Banks (usually known as J. B. Rhine), a botanist who founded the parapsychology lab at Duke University, the *Journal of Parapsychology*, the Foundation for Research on the Nature of Man, and the Parapsychological Association. He coined the term *ESP*. Yet, as Martine Gardner (1999) has recently noted, most of Rhine's findings were never verified, and many of his star pupils and assistants were caught cheating on experiments.[90]

If Knight should have known better, and he should have—why believe in a movement whose founders admit it is all a fraud?—he was not alone: Spiritualists were not interested in the details or in their verification—a point to which I will return in the conclusion of this work. Spiritualists, Knight included, felt that there is something beyond, something eternal. That intuition might be confirmed by Spiritualism or, in Knight's case, with poetry. Thus, in his essay "Jesus and Shakespeare"(1934), he writes that great poetry is "intrinsically prophetic."[91] Seven years later, in *Starlit Dome*, he adds, "Literature reveals a spiritualized universe, and the close study of its implications, which is only beginning, introduces us directly to those realities which are the stock-in-trade of modern Spiritualism."[92]

AS FOR G. WILSON KNIGHT'S BROTHER JACKSON . . .

G. Wilson Knight, we recall, had to work in Canada and at a variety of boys' schools, which—relative to Oxbridge—were educational backwaters; it wasn't until 1947, 16 years after the publication of his seminal *The*

Wheel of Fire, that he landed a university job in the United Kingdom. At least Knight was gainfully employed. His brother was not so lucky: Jackson Knight never taught full time, eking out a living as a part-time lecturer at St. Andrews and then as a part-timer at Exeter.[93] In 1951, he was teaching, temporarily, in South Africa. While underemployed, Jackson Knight was, nonetheless, a classical scholar of some merit. He served as secretary for the Virgil Society—Jackson Knight objected to the spelling, preferring "Vergil"—and authored several books: *Vergil's Troy* (1932), *Cumaean Gates* (1936), *Accentual Symmetry in Vergil* (1939), *Roman Vergil* (1944), *Vergil's Latin* (1958), *Ovid's Metre and Rhythm* (1958), and, most famously, a prose translation of *The Aeneid* for Penguin (1956).

We might ask, why did Jackson fail to gain full-time employment? Some might argue that his career was blocked by his sexuality. Jackson was almost assuredly gay.[94] However, we may here note that Cambridge and other topflight British universities were known refuges for homosexuality.[95] No, to answer why Jackson, an active and published scholar, never succeeded in academia, we must look elsewhere. The answer lies both in his personal habits—he inherited some of his mother's "extreme neurosis"[96]—and in his religious interest in Spiritualism. As G. Wilson Knight admits, his brother was an unusual scholar: "The core of his scholarly and poetic investigations had been from the start a trust planted in the mysteries . . . He [was] at every point aware of both the claims of current scholarship and the truths of modern Spiritualism."[97]

While it is true that many of G. Wilson Knight's essays often contained explicit Spiritualist references, those same essays usually found safe harbor in secular outlets—much of Knight's most celebrated work was published by Oxford University Press. Jackson Knight's scholarship, on the other hand, was far more radical. In his book *Poetic Inspiration* (1946), Jackson Knight argued that Vergil's poetry was akin to "negro magic" and that the poet himself composed much like an "African witchdoctor."[98] In 1950, he compared Vergil's timeless metrics to "waves" similar to "wireless telegraphy"—a common Spiritualist way of describing communication with the dead.[99] Jackson Knight also wrote articles on Spiritualism. These included "My Conviction of the Truth," published in *Two Worlds* (December 13 and 20, 1952), and "The After-Life in Greek and Roman Antiquity," published in *Folklore* magazine (1958). While the latter article sounds suitably stuffy, it cited two Spiritualist books, Maurice Elliott's *The Psychic Life of Jesus* (1938) and Alan Howgrave-Graham's *The Dead Companions* (1950).[100] Jackson Knight was an active member of the Church of the Spiritualist National Union in Exeter and served as chairman of that church's Fellowship for Psychical and Spiritual Studies; he also joined a faith-healing prayer group.[101]

Given the intensity of Jackson Knight's faith in Spiritualism, it is not entirely surprising to learn that when he edited *The Aeneid* for Penguin, he often turned to a medium, Mrs. Margaret Lloyd of Cape Town, South Africa, for help on difficult textual problems.[102] Initially, Jackson did not meet Mrs. Lloyd face-to-face. His point of contact was yet another Vergil scholar and Spiritualist, T. J. Haarhoff.[103] Jackson Knight was a sluggish author, but these psychic consultations were an added drag on his production. Jackson Knight would write his questions to Haarhoff, who, upon receiving this letter from half a world away, then had to meet with Mrs. Lloyd—she would only meet on a Tuesday; no reason was ever given for this specific day. Mrs. Lloyd would then summon her Spirit Guide, who then spoke to Vergil and thereafter relayed the replies to Lloyd, who then told Haarhoff, who then wrote to Jackson, who awaited the return letter in England. In his later years, Haarhoff was asked whether he simply pretended to be Vergil when answering Jackson Knight's queries, but he insisted that it was in fact Vergil who replied: "Vergil came to me regularly every Tuesday evening and during JK's translation of the *Aeneid* I put before him questions raised by JK . . . This is quite genuine. Then V. would write replies to JK's questions in Latin. JK himself told me that on comparing V.'s interpretation with that of the scholars, he generally found it the simplest and the best."[104]

In all, Haarhoff and Jackson Knight exchanged over 140 letters, written over 27 years, all concerning Spiritualist contact with Vergil.[105] The number would have been substantially higher, but, with the death of his mother in 1950, Jackson moved to Cape Town to be closer to Haarhoff and his powerful medium, Mrs. Lloyd. Studying with both Haarhoff and Lloyd, Jackson soon developed his own psychic ability, which allowed him direct access to Vergil. Part of that study included an increased devotion to Spiritualism: thrice daily, he prayed at the Cape Town Spiritualist Church, and, upon his return to Exeter, his faith was rewarded. In 1955, Jackson Knight reported that "Vergil sends many messages and now some reach me directly at Exeter, where he's told me to go slow and be extra careful."[106] Jackson Knight's Penguin editors were not happy when they learned of Knight's method, but he carefully omitted any reference to Spiritualism in his edition. Still, Jackson Knight worried that Penguin might pull the project and wrote of his fears to Haarhoff, who then consulted Vergil, who told him all would end well: "When JK [Jackson Knight] had difficulties with the Penguin people, V[ergil] said—let him give in on minor points—in the end he will triumph. And so it came about."[107]

G. WILSON KNIGHT TALKS TO SHAKESPEARE

Jackson's abiding faith and bold results with Vergil had already convinced his brother to consult a variety of local mediums. Surprisingly, G. Wilson Knight didn't want to talk to Shakespeare, or at least he didn't think he wanted to talk to Shakespeare. Instead, he wanted to reach out to his mother. The following comes from *Jackson Knight* (1975)—G. Wilson Knight's biography of his brother—and two of Knight's unpublished manuscripts, both at the University of Exeter: "Spirit-Writing" (1950–71) and "Caroline: Life after Death" (1954, revised 1985).

November 8, 1950. A psychic, a Mrs. Louie Hill of London, tells Knight that he and his dead mother remain intertwined not only emotionally but also spiritually. Mrs. Louie Hill asked for an object—remember Furness's experiments with an actor's skull, discussed in Chapter 4: "I offered a wallet which she pressed against her forehead. Starting with some general remarks concerning my life and work, she soon—I may have prompted it—turned to my mother." She said, "Were you not rather more than mother and son: I think you were twin souls."[108] Mrs. Hill also related that his mother told her to tell him to consult the psychic Frank Spence of Manchester.[109]

December 14, 1950. Knight consulted Frank Spenser in Manchester, whose Spirit Guide, the African Ugandi, told him that "there is a child here" trying to contact Knight; "his spirit-name is Progress."[110]

December 15, 1950. Knight sat with psychic Mrs. Elsie Hardwick of the Marylebone Spiritualist Association and spoke to his mother through her Spirit Guide, Starbeam, an African girl. Knight told her that his research—he was writing a book on his mother—was "stuck," but his mother told Starbeam that her son was on the right path: "Your mother is saying that it is correct . . . They [the Spirits] will lead you." On the same date, Starbeam put Knight in touch with his deceased father, George: "You are not to grieve; I am your father. You are not alone. Both [mother and father] are with you." Starbeam then related a message from his mother: "She [Caroline] wants you to know [that] Daddie and she are both very proud of your progress."[111] Starbeam then added that the Spirit of his mother watched over him while he slept.[112] Turning from the Spirits to Knight himself, Starbeam told the famed Shakespeare interpreter that he had "plenty of psychic power" and should not need a medium. Starbeam therefore instructed Knight to try automatic writing to see whether Caroline could write through him. "She'll enjoy it. She will impress you. She will enjoy working with you, and using your mind."[113] (This seems to be a common way of enticing the client to accept more counseling and training; we might here recall that H. H. Furness and Alfred Dodd were told the same thing.) The session ended with Starbeam mentioning someone or something named "Cjon."[114]

December 20, 1950. Knight slipped on his mother's wedding ring, put into his hand a pencil and pad, and awaited her message. At first the writing was gibberish: "Gveyhlhlglllghtghltlight . . . ghlght." But within a few lines Knight seemed to find the right frequency: "God Bless you my Dickie God Bless you Dickie my own Give my love to Jack." Later in the same message, Caroline mentioned "Johnne"—a link perhaps to Starbeam's "Cjon"?[115] For five days following he continued to receive the same message. Knight felt himself to be somehow blocked. Days later, Knight experimented with Spirit Photography. He did not, however, attempt to photograph disembodied Spirits but tried instead to capture his own Spirit on camera by posing naked in Shakespearean poses.[116] At the time, he did not understand why he felt compelled to take these photos, but his activities prefigured his later theatrical work.

January 3, 1951. Knight's father sent a message: "you will be successful and will be successful you will be successful and you will be successful good night my Dickie my own."[117] Later that same year, Jackson, accompanied by Haarhoff, consulted Lloyd.[118] Her Spirit Guide was a woman calling herself "Tutu." Tutu informed Jackson that their mother would bring G. Wilson Knight spiritual roses on his upcoming birthday.[119] Sure enough, on her next communication Mrs. Lloyd reported that Caroline had in fact given Knight a "deep pink rose" and kissed him on his forehead.[120]

When Knight wrote back, complaining that he had no such rose, his brother replied, "she *gives* you flowers, but such are your limitations that *you* can't see them, and you only get the sense-advantage if you provide on your level roses you can apprehend."[121] Knight then bought himself roses and put them in a vase. Tutu then confirmed that the "spirit-roses" had been put in his room and that he should, thus, place the physical roses there.[122]

February 28, 1951. During a trance address of Ugandi, Frank Spencer introduced a new character, a "lively and humourous Irishman named Michael," who told Knight something that excited him greatly: "I find that Scotland comes continually in messages."[123] A connection to *Macbeth*?

On March 25, 1951, his automatic writing also revealed that he had a Spanish ancestor.[124] The rest of the secret, however, would have to come from someone else. As the Spirit Guide Sunshine explained, "Someone in Africa is trying to help."[125] Sunshine then told him he would receive still more help from a "black man."[126]

March 2, 1951. Tutu reported that "Johnne is helping your work . . . you will be guided."[127] This message was repeated on June 28, 1951. Was Johnne *Don Juan*—that is, Byron? Knight was, at the time, working on the index for his new book, *Lord Byron: Christian Virtues* (published 1952). The work was exhausting; his mother, ever watchful from the Spirit Realm, complained, "Must you make such a large Index to Byron?"[128]

March 10, 1951. The Spirits told Knight, "We are helping." On April 15, 1951, another medium, Mrs. Nella Taylor of Derby, worked with Knight. She told him that a man had appeared to her "holding out towards me a roll of parchment." Knight thought perhaps this might be a legal "Will."[129] Knight was slowly coming to the realization that his biography on his mother was actually the Spirits demanding that he trace his family tree. It had something to do with Scotland . . .

April 27, 1951. Only a handful of days after Shakespeare's birthday, Haarhoff reported that Tutu had told him that "Bob" and "Johnne" were "fixed in my mind."[130] But Haarhoff had no idea what their manifestation signified. Might Bob or Bill be a diminutive of Will? Might Cjon be John, or Don Juan?

November 10, 1951. Mrs. Lloyd was in London and brought her Spirits along with her. Tutu reported that Bob "comes from a higher sphere." Then Tutu and Bob became one: "I know you well from heaven, for I so often come close when you are depressed or weary to lend you strength. Remember I will also be a brother."[131] And, Tutu reported, there were still other Spirits helping Knight, including his mother: "Now she's here working this side [of existence] to help."[132]

November 15, 1951. Knight, through automatic writing, asked his mother whether Tutu was "a very important spirit?" "Yes," came the reply, "*she* is very highly developed in spiritual things, but that shouldn't mean that she can take messages to you any better than another. It is very difficult indeed."[133]

January 3, 1952. Yet another psychic, Dorothy Perkins at Exeter, reported that her Spirit Guide, Sunshine, had a message: "Your father sends his love. He is helping also."[134]

April 4, 1952. Another of Ms. Perkins's Spirit Guides, this one named "Fifi," reported, "Your father is very close to you at times."[135]

April 15, 1952. Knight met with yet another clairvoyant, Mrs. Gwen Jones of Exeter. He told her he was thinking about either going to California, where he was offered a "permanent post," or going to South Africa to visit his brother. (South Africa held another attraction: he would be closer to Mrs. Lloyd and her Spirit Guide, Tutu.) Jones consulted the Spirits, who said Knight should go to South Africa immediately.[136] That night he consulted his mother through automatic writing, but she vacillated.[137] He then consulted Dorothy Perkins, who had her Spirit Guide Fifi speak to his mother. The answer now was clear: "I want you to go . . . I want you to go . . . To Africa . . . *Not* to America."[138] To Africa, to Tutu in South Africa. The mystery was becoming clear. Cjon . . . pronounced with the French "je." Johnne. *Johannesburg!* But who was Bob?

July 1952. Knight left for South Africa. Upon arrival, he consulted with Mrs. Lloyd and her Spirit Guide, Tutu.[139] Tutu explained that all the other messages from Starbeam and Sunshine were merely "partially controlled"—that is, inaccurate or garbled messages.[140] Tutu then told Knight that all his communications with the other mediums had been false messages. Knight recalled that this information "rather staggered me."[141] (We have seen this before—Sir Francis Bacon told Allen that prior communications with him had been faulty or fraudulent.) But Tutu would set all to right; after all, look what the Spirits had done for his brother and his Vergil project! Knight then asked Mrs. Lloyd whether Tutu could "speak" through or on behalf of other agents (the very same issue the courts ruled on in *Cummins v. Fripp*, discussed in Chapter 3).[142] Tutu explained that there is no singular Spirit but rather a community or "group-knowledge": "I would like you to understand that when a spirit or medium gives forth spiritual teaching, it is often the teaching of a group and not an individual soul. But for purposes of transferring it, one individual and one name is used. If it is any very spiritual teaching, it is usually a group-knowledge that comes through."[143]

Professor Haarhoff was present on this occasion and pressed the issue. Fine, there was a group mind, but Tutu was also the spokeswoman of the group. Might she describe herself? Tutu then corrected Haarhoff. Tutu was now male. Knight became agitated. Of course, Tutu was both male *and* female; bisexual, just like Shakespeare! Tutu then described himself. He had "broad shoulders," a "black beard and moustache," and "high cheek-bones"; "He had a cloak." And Tutu had another name, a spirit-name: "Arabia."

Knight then asked, "What sort of cloak? An opera cloak?" "No," replied Tutu, "not an *opera* cloak." Mrs. Lloyd emphasized "opera," as though suggesting some sort of innuendo. Haarhoff made an inspired guess. Not opera, but theater: "Elizabethan?" asked Haarhoff. No reply. Haarhoff pressed. "Was he English?" Tutu admitted it. "A poet?" asked Haarhoff. Again, Tutu agreed, but added, "I mustn't say more, or I shall get into trouble."[144] Haarhoff then asked whether Tutu was in fact the man Knight had devoted his life to—whether Tutu was Shakespeare. Tutu replied that Knight was "quite sure" of the truth. Indeed, Knight was. After all, why Arabia? Had it something to do with the line "all the perfumes of Arabia"?—Macbeth; a descendant of Malcolm; the demand that he find the answer in Africa—all, all had led him to this discovery.[145] Just as Percy Allen had concluded that Shakespeare was Bacon and a ghostly host of others, just as Daisy O. Roberts had concluded that Shakespeare was Homer, Knight had divined that Shakespeare was Tutu, a bisexual African Spirit hovering over Cape Town.

September 4, 1952. Knight, now back in England, received a letter from Mrs. Lloyd in South Africa. Tutu, via Mrs. Lloyd, informed Knight that he has a lost brother. No, not someone named John but someone named "Robert"—or "Bob." (Bob had never been born; the pregnancy was miscarried. In the Spirit Realm, Bob is an adult nonetheless.) Tutu told Knight that Bob looks "very like you, but a bit thinner. He wants you to send him a thought whenever you have spiritual difficulty, and he will help."[146]

KNIGHT COLLABORATES WITH THE SPIRITS

While still in England, Knight attended a meeting of the Leeds Psychic Research Society (November 12, 1952) and was given a Spirit clue via Frank Spencer, which urged the Spiritualist-academic to investigate his obscure Scotch ancestry.[147] Knight then found evidence that he was in fact related to Scottish nobility—another link to *Macbeth*.[148] This connected to Tutu's Arabia reference and, thus, to South Africa. Knight took this to be an example of "collaboration" with the Spirits, who were guiding him to a discovery.[149] But why had the Spirits revealed these truths though poetic word association or insinuation? Why not simply come right out with a clear, intelligible message, and why not just tell Knight where he might immediately lay his hands on corroborative historical facts? Knight suggested that "Spirit-messages are rarely good at exact names and dates, except with certain types of highly-trained clairaudience," though they "appear to be behind, watching, and perhaps inspiring, the research."[150]

Still working on his biography of his mother, Knight went to her family home in Jamaica to find more information. Caroline Knight was the daughter of a minor plantation owner on the island, but the family had ruined the business and then moved to England with very little means. All this was known to Knight before his trip. His real breakthrough came in a new flood of psychic messages, many of them concerning Shakespeare. Caroline told him that her first exposure to Shakespeare was a performance of *Macbeth*, starring Henry Irving.[151] Again the reference to Macbeth . . . Was there yet another message hinted at? Perhaps this message concerned the witches who council, perhaps even control, Macbeth? Was that the meaning? That he was being controlled by his mother and other Spirits?

We now skip the entries for 1953 and their pages of Spiritualist messages of love and support to the next key communiqué. On January 22, 1954, Caroline told Knight that all publishing ideas came from the "Hall of Ancient Wisdom, which is the place where you get your thoughts for your books."[152] Knight's books were not his own.

We have already seen (in Chapter 3) that Percy Allen thought of himself as collaborating with Bacon, Oxford, and Shakespeare. Knight found himself interrogating the very same issue of authorship, specifically whether Knight was the author or merely the agent of a Spiritualist group that included Shakespeare, his mother, his father, a still-born brother, and some sort of Spiritual Library. Knight often worried that he was merely a scribe for his mother and other Spirits. The Spirit of his mother knew of this anxiety and sought to reassure him that while she and others were helping him, "all the best bits [of your writing] *are* you."[153] On April 1, 1955, Caroline hinted that everything written was "all part of a [divine] plan which you will one day understand, and it will be wonderful."[154]

Still, the idea that his writing was not his own continued to haunt Knight. One of Knight's many mediums counseled acceptance. After all, while Knight was not an author in the modern sense of the word, the same was true for any form of mediumship: "The messages are not being sent to me; they are being sent directly to you. I merely intercept them, and clarify them for you."[155] Another of his Spirit Guides, Ugandi, urged him to accept collaboration as a sign of spiritual growth: "Slip the anchor of the 'I'" and "become the 'we', and then you'll begin to live."[156] As we noted early in this chapter, Knight also believed that Shakespeare, while in mortal form, received his plays from a divine source, so he was, at least, in good company. Eventually, Knight came to embrace the concept. In *The Poetry of Pope: Laureate of Peace* (1955), he writes, "Poetic symbolism [the study of which he was the acknowledged master] . . . correspond[s] closely to reports received by trance-communication purporting to come from higher planes"—that is, the Spirit Realm.[157] In *Neglected Powers* (1971), Knight explained to his readers that "you do not make thoughts. You receive thoughts and send them on their way. The thoughts you receive are determined by the kind of apparatus that you are."[158]

Even putting the more outlandish possibility of a Spiritualist collaboration aside for the moment, we might easily claim that much of Knight's writing was, in fact, a family affair. While living, his mother Caroline had acted "as counsellor, even sometimes as agent, in many of its practical aspects."[159] It was she who urged Jackson to specialize in Vergil.[160] When Knight was offered a post at the University of Toronto, it was Caroline who urged her son to take it, and then, to ensure that he concentrate on his teaching and writing, invited herself along to serve as his helpmate and companion. It was she who reminded him of Cleopatra, she who inspired his writings. Indeed, Knight later confessed that all his writing had, in one way or another, been circumscribed by his fascination with his mother: "She herself *was* literature . . . In her was Medea, Lady Macbeth, and Hedda Gabler . . . the sparkle of Shakespeare's witty heroines, Rosalind, Beatrice and Portia; and, crowning all, Cleopatra."[161] More than that, he considered her to be his sounding board, his collaborator, and his editor. As death approached, one of the last promises she made to him was that "she would still see the continuance of the campaign, our work."[162] Sure enough, Tutu/Shakespeare told him that "she [Caroline] often listens to your talks, your lectures, and tries to help you."[163] Nearly four years after her death, on March 5, 1954, his mother told him that she and he were one: "You are not to think that I am *without*, for I am *within* you, and it is the only way to think of me, for I am in your thoughts always, so you can be sure of that . . . I understand so much more than I ever understood before."[164] On June 18, 1954, Caroline revealed still other Spiritual agents were "helping you and Jack in your work."[165] In addition to receiving messages concerning his own academic projects, Jackson sometimes sensed Spiritualist communications meant for his brother. In 1963, G. Wilson Knight began to write on the poet and playwright Powys, who had died in June of that year; in December, Jackson reported to his brother that "Powys wants to give some evidential cross-reference."[166]

JACKSON KNIGHT'S POSTHUMOUS COLLABORATIONS

Jackson Knight's death was slow and painful. In the late 1950s he began to complain of stomach ailments, which, by 1961, forced him to retire from part-time teaching. He began to visit traditional doctors, who subjected him to a variety of tests, none of which revealed a physical problem.[167] He then consulted homeopathic herbalists. He continued to complain of pain but held out hope that further Spiritualist prayer would set him right: "My pain's nearly gone. The doctor [on the other hand] says he has a cold (Spirits always put us on to Earth Doctors when necessary)."[168] By 1964, psychiatrists were consulted for Jackson's erratic behavior. They diagnosed him as suffering from growing hysteria; the psychiatrists referred him to a neurosurgeon.[169]

Not trusting to medicine alone, G. Wilson Knight sought Spiritualist help for his ailing brother. The medium Gwen Jones had a Spirit Guide, Dr. Karl, who gave instructions for a concoction of honey and onions.[170] Jackson swallowed the noxious brew, but it had no positive effect. G. Wilson Knight was then comforted by the Spirit of his mother, who, on September 24, 1964, explained that Jack "is getting much better. There is nothing much wrong but he is very tired because he uses so much psychic energy."[171] In November 1964, a cancerous tumor was found in Jackson's bowel; a secondary tumor was found in his brain. On December 4, 1964, he died.[172] That same day, Knight also conferred with the Spirit of his mother, who told him that Jack was already nicely settled in the afterworld: he will "be a great influence on the young, Jack [will be] at the universities and that is what he always wanted to be and there will be more opportunity now."[173]

Going through Jackson's papers, Knight found two unfinished manuscripts—one on Vergil, the other on Homer. Knight wanted them completed and published as a lasting tribute to his brother. Then on April Fools' Day 1965—a significant day in Spiritualism, as explained in Chapter 4—G. Wilson Knight began to receive messages from Jackson. Knight asked him whether he had seen Caroline and George. "Of course. Mother and Dad are well. Mother has done very well. I can see her whenever I wish. She is working in a spirit sphere beyond." Had he met Vergil? "Yes, in a sense I have met him. I was not quite awake. There will be more to come. I was not fully conscious." He discussed his adjustment to the Spirit Realm: "I was so excited at first. I wanted to show myself to everybody that I knew. It's a wonderful experience, Dick. They let me have a go, and then I had to rest." What was his life like now? "Not a lot different, except that things are more beautiful than perhaps they were. Flowers, trees, animal life. Very lovely. And there's no pain. No ugliness.

If I wish I can see the dark places. I'm not quite ready yet. I would be interested . . . All that we were told is absolutely true."

Messages also poured in from various mediums. Three days after Jackson died, G. Wilson received a letter from Dorothy Perkins in Exeter: "I sensed your brother very excited and saying, 'Tell Dick I'm alright and give him my love' . . . He seemed very bright and excited. I got nothing more; maybe he was just allowed to make this contact to let you know all was well with him." On December 8, Miss Iris Yeoman of Cullompton wrote, "I had imagined, quite wrongly, that he [Jackson Knight] would have a rest before taking up an active new life, but yesterday at intervals from 7 a. m. until the late evening I was aware of his presence, vitally alive as he must have been when very young. He has been again today and wants me to write this letter. With great emphasis he writes, 'Tell him Mother met me. What a reunion. It seems as if she had never left us. Don't grieve for me, I have life more abundant now, I'll be around when you need me.'"[174] On December 17, 1964, there was another communication from Fifi, who allowed Jackson to speak through her:

Do thank my brother so much. Sorry I left things a bit muddled, but I do not think they were too bad. Thank him for answering all the letters.

I tried to draw my brother's attention one night by pulling his quilt. This is all such fun. I just wanted to see if I could do all these things, and make myself known. Thank you all so much.

My great love to my brother. I am so sorry that my illness was such a worry to him at the last. It was so much work for him, and all those letters, but I thank him. Ask him to go on with everything as we had arranged.

I have not experienced a lot yet because I wanted to make these experiments and prove I could come back, but shortly I will be going on and seeing all there is to see. It is not usual for people to hang around so, or to stay so close to earth after they have passed, but I expressed the wish that I should visit friends before I went on further, and it has been granted. I do not feel tired now, I have seen my nearest relations, and others who welcomed me . . . I have seen my mother and father, and that was delightful. Tell Dick I hope to talk to him soon, I must go now. Thank you for letting me come. I hope Miss Dorothy Perkins will let me use her.[175]

With communication between the brothers now reestablished, G. Wilson Knight began to collaborate with Jackson on those two unfinished manuscripts. One series of communications concerned the poet Homer. The project was published in 1968 under the title *Many-Minded Homer*. The title page makes no mention of G. Wilson Knight. Instead, Jackson is listed as the author with J. D. Christie acting as editor. The truth, however, is that the authorship of *Many-Minded Homer* was many minded. Let's deal first with Jackson's contribution: as with his edition of Vergil, Jackson had made use of mediums when writing the initial draft. Christie had been aware of Jackson's unusual method of collaboration and actually encouraged Jackson to do the same with his Homer project. On October 18, 1955, he wrote to Jackson, "If your Spiritualist friends would contact Homer, that *would* be something!"[176] G. Wilson Knight applied the same principles by contacting his brother Jackson for advice. In one automatic writing session, the Spirit of Jackson Knight was unsure exactly who was writing what. Perhaps his earthly brother was writing on his own; perhaps Jackson was inspiring him: "Dickie, you are doing *on your own as I would like* and it could not be better."[177]

Knight likewise set to work on yet another of Jackson's unfinished book projects, a manuscript titled *Elysion*.[178] Knight had a harder go with this one and sought advice from Jackson Knight's Spiritualist circle. He shared sections of the manuscript with Haarhoff, who, on January 23, 1965, shared them with Mrs. Lloyd, who shared them with Tutu, who shared them with Vergil, who had some comments. Other additions were made by Christie and by Hugh Stubbs, the latter an Exeter lecturer of history apparently known for his excruciatingly dull lectures; other additions were made by the classical scholar Raymond J. Clark.[179] As for G. Wilson Knight's own embellishments, he writes that "wherever adjustments have been needed, I have done what I could to preserve the tone and wavelength [a Spiritualist term—see Introduction and Glossary of Spiritualist Terms and Techniques] of my brother's style."[180] In *Neglected Powers* (1971), not surprisingly, he cites the published *Elysion* (1970) as a work composed entirely by his brother.[181] What we have here is not an example of false modesty but of pious certainty.

CANDID FAITH

Knight's book *Symbol of Man: On Body-Soul for Stage and Studio* (1979) was perhaps his most spiritual and, to many traditional academics, his most embarrassing—it included near-naked self-portraits of Knight posing as his favorite Shakespeare characters: Hamlet, King Lear, and Timon of Athens. The university and private academic publishers rejected it. The book was eventually published by the Regency Press, a specialist in Spiritualist books. (The press's other offerings include Diana Adair, *A Moonlight Witch* [1970]; Arthur Shuttlewood, *UFOs, Key to the New Age* [1971]; Margaret Claire Mitchell, *A Message to Mankind* [1975]; Joy Cooke, *"Guardian Angels Around My Bed": The Psychic Life of Medium Sally Jane Danter* [1991]; Larry Kingston, *An Experiment*

With Alien Intelligence [1991]; and Karl Nowotny, *Messages From a Doctor in the Fourth Dimension* [1990]. The company stopped printing new books in 1995.)

While *Symbol of Man* mentions Spiritualism often, the book is, in the main, about Knight's nude photos, which he snapped back in December 1950. Knight felt so strongly about these photos that he, upon their publication in 1979, decided to self-finance a dramatic tour promoting the book.[182] He would lecture, then dramatize his interpretations. In the performance portion of the evening, Knight wore only a loincloth and a G-string; in performances of *Timon*, however, he stripped off completely for his reading of Act V.[183]

As noted, Knight read virtually every Shakespeare play exegetically. But of all of Shakespeare's plays, it does seem odd that he was so attached to *Timon*, a play that, on the face of it, concerns a man who dies bitter and alone. Frank Kermode is typically saturnine in stating that the "language of Timon's tirades against society and the universe in general is truly spectacular," but those pyrotechnics concern "just complaint."[184] Knight provides a far more upbeat assessment: in *Wheel of Fire* (1930) Knight suggested that the play reveals an "implicit philosophy, exposing its peculiar universality, and the stark contrast of the partial and imperfect nature of humanity and the world of the senses with the strong aspiration toward infinity and perfection."[185] The protagonist moves "beyond the mysterious nothing of dissolution, [and into] a new dimension congruous with the power and the passion which have forced him toward death."[186] Fifty-four years later, in *Shakespearian Dimensions*, Knight argues that the play "draws close to Indian teachings and in especial Buddhism"; Timon, in Knight's view, becomes a "magical personage"—not at all like Prospero. who, while able to manipulate weather patterns and enslave Spirits, remains for much of *The Tempest*, an angry and by turns bitter person, but someone more like the Buddha himself, someone who, by abjuring the material, embraces the spiritual. As Knight was so fond of pointing out, the key to the play is found in Timon's line "nothing brings me all things." Whereas many might have read the phrase acerbically, Knight interpreted the line as a renunciation of the material in favor of "all things" spiritual.[187]

Citing W. H. Mackintosh of the *Psychic News*, Knight emphasized that his public nudity was not a sexually provocative act—he was 82 years old when he performed Timon in the buff—but a sign of his spiritual purity: "clothes are worn here [on earth] either to protect the body or to adorn it. Neither reason seems applicable to the spirit world."[188] I do not entirely dismiss that reading, but Knight had long been something of a nudist. When applying for a job at the public school at Stowe (1941),

Figure 5.1 G. Wilson Knight, Self-Portrait. By permission of the Trinity College Archives, Robin Harris fonds, P2996.

G. Wilson Knight allegedly "spiced" his application form with a photograph of himself almost naked as Timon of Athens. (They hired him anyway.)[189] Still, the disrobing, the acting out, the freeing of oneself from gender-specific clothing suggests something of a coming out, a theatrical striptease, a voyeur celebrating his own body. He must have been aware that not everyone would be comfortable with his nakedness—that in stripping, he would, like any actor, be subjecting his body and behavior to audience scrutiny and opinion. He could not have been entirely surprised when the critics bashed him: *Blackwood's Magazine* reported that when he disrobed, "eyebrows nearly [went] through the roof."[190] An American reviewer, watching Knight perform his *Timon of Athens*, unkindly dubbed him "*Tarzan of Athens*." The same disparaging moniker also served as the title of John Van Domelen's 1987 biography.

On a personal note: I did not see Knight perform live, but I do own a copy of his *Symbol of Man: On Body-Soul for Stage and Studio* (1979). Having spent years familiarizing myself with Spiritualist materials, including Knight's oeuvre, I can appreciate Knight's Spiritualist vision and still recognize the easy comic fodder. Looking at these self-portraits of G. Wilson Knight, Shakespearean interpreter, Spiritualist, and all-too-apparently nudist thespian, I think to myself, how brave, how stupid, how naive, how knowing, how creative, how destructive, how brilliant, how nutty, how visionary, how blind. And then I think to myself, these were taken back in 1950, not at all the way he must have look 29 years later, at age 82, naked before his audience. An old man reciting the well-worn, pretending he was one of the virile; his desiccated muscles and shriveled phallus laid bare—exactly what he wanted, the sleepy turtle of death serenely looking on the immortality of life, the central mystery, the divine scheme. But Knight's occult interests had already put him beyond the ordinary cares of this plane of existence. Michael Dobson strikes the right note: Knight was "the founder of a spiritualist school of Shakespearian interpretation which no-one else—in the academy, at least—has felt able or willing to join."[191] He was both an unaccommodated and unaccommodating man.

In an interview conducted in 1982, Knight acquiesced that many theater reviewers did not like his work, but he was heartened by his awareness of "spirit reports from the higher dimension."[192] In his unpublished tribute to his mother, he was plainer still: "There has been also a sense *of the past itself watching and collaborating through spirit-communication.*"[193] Knight's stagings constitute a fascinating and perhaps unique example of a Shakespearean performing not for the living but for the dead.

POSTSCRIPT

On February 28, 2012, I received an e-mail from two student workers (Matt and Alex), who volunteer with the aged and indigent in Exeter. They related a message from Olivia Anderson (née Mordue), who served as G. Wilson Knight's secretary for more than thirty years. I had already exchanged some e-mails with Mrs. Anderson, many of which are cited in this chapter. This particular e-mail concerned a message from beyond. On February 17, 2012, Mrs. Anderson attended a séance conducted by Mrs. Moira Hawkins CSNU (Spiritualist National Union). Mrs. Anderson asked if G. Wilson Knight was present. He was not, but a Spirit Guide was in contact with him. Mrs. Anderson then asked if Knight was aware that Jeffrey Kahan was writing a book on Shakespeare and Spiritualism. A male voice speaking through medium replied, "The Californian professor thinks he has been inspired but he is not sure about the Spirits. But he is in touch and is indeed inspired by them. At times he thinks his inspiration comes from his own brain, also he ought to know that the gentleman he writes of is always there to help him along. If he opens his mind to him, to Wilson Knight, he will be surprised at the thoughts he gets, at first thinking that they are his own."

CHAPTER 6

BEYOND THE ACADEMIC
FIELDS WE KNOW . . .

THE YEAR IS 1920. COTTINGLEY DELL, JUST **outside of Bradford.** Sir
Arthur Conan Doyle opens a letter from Edward Gardner, a well-known
lecturer on occult subjects and president of the Blavatsky Lodge of Theosophy in London. Gardner reports an amazing discovery: fairies have been
photographed in the north of England. The same letter informed Doyle
that the images capture an angelic ten-year-old girl, Frances Griffiths,
playing with hand-sized and togaed pixies. The photographs were taken
about three years earlier by Frances's sister Elsie:

> Elsie said she wanted to photograph them, and begged her father to lend
> his camera. For long he refused, but at last she managed to get the loan of
> it and one plate. Off she and Frances went into the woods near a water-fall.
> Frances "ticed' them, as they call it, and Elsie stood ready with the camera.
> Soon the three fairies appeared, and one pixie dancing in Frances' aura.
> Elsie snapped and hoped for the best. It was a long time before the father
> would develop the photo, but at last he did, and to his utter amazement
> the four sweet little figures came out beautifully![1]

Gardner wrote excitedly to the girls' mother, Polly, asking for permission to see more photos and to interview the children. The mother, a
fellow Theosophist, was honored and agreed.[2] After just a single meeting with the girls, Gardner speculated that the fairies had appeared to
the children because they were both natural mediums, especially Frances,
whom Gardner describes as having "a beautifully clear, yet loosely knit,
etheric aura, yielding easily accessible ectoplasmic material."[3] (He did not
state how he came to this conclusion.) In the hopes that they might snap
some more pictures, Gardner gave the girls a new camera. In due course,
Gardner was rewarded with two more fairy photos, which he judged to
be genuine. Doyle, in a reply to Gardner, dated June 22, 1920, thought

that the images would prove to be "epoch-making if we can entirely clear up the circumstances." Not that he had any serious doubts: "It so happens that I am writing an article on fairies at present, and have accumulated quite a mass of evidence . . . We are all indebted to you as the channel by which this has come to the world. Yours sincerely. A. Conan Doyle."[4] Three days later, Gardner responded enthusiastically, stating that the girls had been playing with the fairies "since babyhood." Gardner, with a dash of Mesmerism, added that it was likely that the fairies appeared only to these girls because their joint "aura" strengthened "the very delicate etheric vehicle of the fairy and makes it more acitinic" [*sic*—he means "actinic"].[5] In short, the girl's magnetic fluid or "aura" allowed the fairies to be seen in UV light.

Doyle wrote about the case, first in *The Coming of the Fairies* (1922) and later in *Edge of the Unknown* (1930). In both narratives, he firmly believed that the pictures of the fairies were genuine. As part of his investigation, he also interviewed a number of other people who said that they too had seen fairies, though, unlike Elsie Griffiths, these witnesses lacked photographic evidence. A Miss Eva Longbottom of Bristol, who had been blind from birth, told Doyle that, in the mists of her mind, she often "saw" fairies, including "poem fairies" who "looked" like characters in Shakespeare: "If you could imagine Perdita [from *The Winter's Tale*] in the *Midsummer Night's Dream*, translated from the stage into a real fairy, you would have a good idea of the poem fairy. She has a very beautiful girlish character." Another witness discussed a "sentiment"—that is, sentimental—fairy, who answered to the name "Miranda," Prospero's daughter from *The Tempest*; still another swore that she had seen a "dancing little feminine elf so beloved by Shakespeare."[6] To Doyle and other Spiritualists, the fairy "spirites"—as Shakespeare referred to them—were yet further confirmation of the new faith.

DOYLE'S SPIRITUALISM

That the mustachioed and solemn Doyle, author of the *Sherlock Holmes* stories, was an ardent Spiritualist might surprise some. His conversion to the new faith was, in fact, a slow one. Between 1885 and 1888, Doyle attended a number of séances but remained a thorough skeptic. In a 1917 article for *Metropolitan* magazine, he recalled

> I tried some tableturning [séances], and got the usual banal messages. This deepened my distrust of the whole subject. If spirits do exist, I thought, they must be something superhuman, whereas these creatures who send such messages, if they really come from outside ourselves, must rather be

subhuman. I thought I had the scientific mind, and yet I was really doing, as many of my superiors in science were doing, the most unscientific thing possible, for I was arguing from a supposition instead of from a fact. My duty was not to imagine a spirit and then judge the messages by that imaginary standard, but it was to study the messages, presuming that they were genuine, and endeavor to learn the nature of those who sent them.

We may ask why he bothered to attend more than that first séance. After all, if he felt the entire event to be a waste of time, why continue year after year?

According to Doyle scholar Kelvin I. Jones, Doyle's initial interest in séances had nothing to do with the dead. Rather, it was to please his wife, Louise Hawkins, also known as "Touie." However, over the next 25 years, Doyle's life was marred by personal tragedy, enough to have him seek solace with the very mediums he had once considered to be charlatans. His wife was diagnosed with tuberculosis and died on July 4, 1906; his nephew Arthur was killed in the First World War (July 6, 1915); his son, Arthur Alleyne Kingsley, known as Kingsley, died from influenza aggravated by war wounds he suffered in the First World War (October 28, 1918); his brother Innes died four months later. While more deaths would soon follow—Doyle's sister, Aimée Monica Doyle, died in 1921; likewise, Aimée's husband, Ernest William Hornung, died of pneumonia on March 22 of the same year. It was Doyle's second wife, Jean Leckie, who seems to have been the prime mover in her husband's religious conversion. She, among others, acted as medium, receiving automatic writings from many of her husband's departed relations, specifically his brother Innes and his son Arthur Alleyne Kingsley Doyle.[7] The magician and popular entertainer Harry Houdini attended a session of Lady Doyle's automatic writing and recalled

> Sir Arthur, with his head bowed down, just like a simple child, uttered a prayer, calling upon the Almighty to let us have a sign from our friends from beyond. He placed his hands caressingly upon Lady Doyle's, to give her more power . . . I think that, in her heart of hearts, Lady Doyle is sincere, and I am positive that Sir Arthur is just as religious in his belief as it is possible for any human being to be. As from time to time Lady Doyle started to write, he would soothe her as if admonishing the spirit not to be too forcible with her.[8]

Still more oddly, when the aforementioned Houdini revealed to Doyle some of the simple tricks he used in his act to create the illusion of supernatural contact—aside from rescuing himself from police cuffs, ropes, and underwater safes, Houdini regularly pretended to read people's minds or to receive messages from the dead—Doyle refused to believe Houdini and insisted that the magician had actual supernatural powers.[9] When Houdini pressed the point, Doyle broke off their friendship.[10]

Doyle was not just refusing to see reason. He was also preferring to see nonreason. He described Spiritualism as a "force outside the rules of science" and "a call of hope." Houdini, on the other hand, was pursuing Spiritualism scientifically, but in so doing he was missing the point entirely.[11] Sometimes the cold clarity of empiricism is not just incongruous with the incredible; it is, moreover, inimical to the whimsical. The *Wales Argus* (1921), writing on the Cottingley Fairies, strikes the right note: "The day we kill Santa Claus with our statistics and our photographs we shall have plunged a glorious world into deepest darkness." States-side, *The Sun* (1921) agreed: "The soul of the fairy is its evanescence. Its charm is the eternal doubt, rose-tinted with the shadow of a hope. But the thrill is all in ourselves."[12] Indeed, Houdini's demystifications of magic constituted a form of creative discourtesy. If Doyle and other Spiritualists preferred to believe in other realms of existence, then who was Houdini to burst that joyous bubble?

In an odd role reversal, it was Houdini who favored reason and Doyle who preferred the occultations of the imagination. Further, Doyle sought and cited only those texts that confirmed his faith, among them those of C. W. Leadbeater, a Theosophist who commonly wrote on the subject of fairies.[13] In *The Astral Plane* (1895), Leadbeater explained that fairies are real because a "man will sometimes go through a long series of *imaginary* but most striking adventures" with them.[14] In *The Hidden Side of Things* (1913), he added that fairies were especially fond of forming long relationships with children, "especially for such as are dreamy and imaginative."[15] As to their size and shape, fairies, he wrote, are formed from "Ethertic [*sic*] matter" and, as such, have no actual shape but enjoy molding themselves to the local culture. Thus, while English fairies are often emerald green, reflective of England's green and pleasant land, the fairies of gold-rich California are white and gold; the fairies in the Dutch Indies are green and yellow, "like a football jersey."[16] He likewise argued for the existence of vampires and werewolves, ostensibly because such creatures would have been long forgotten, unless there was some evidence for their existence: "the general characteristics of such tales are too well known" to be deliberated.[17] If the imagination deems fairies, vampires, and werewolves to be real, then they are.

Long after Doyle died, Frances and her sister Elsie, who snapped the photographs, confessed that they had cut images of fairies from magazines of the period and set them on hatpins. The magazine images had, in part and turn, been based on Arthur Rackham's *Tales from Shakespeare* and still other illustrations of *A Midsummer Night's Dream*.[18] But Doyle, had he lived to hear the confession, would not have flinched. His faith was literal; it was also literary. As he wrote in *Edge of the Unknown*, the connection between fact and fantasy was not as important as the connection between poetry and a heightened reality: "anything which widens our conceptions of the possible, and shakes us out of our time-rutted lines of thought, helps us to regain our elasticity of mind and thus to be more open to new philosophies."[19] Doyle was here employing a standard catchall used by the new sect to dispel all doubts. It was invoked by Spiritualist Horace Greeley in *Recollections of a Busy Life* (1868); by Luther Calvin Tibbets in *Spirit of the South* (1869); by Eugene Crowell in *The Identity of Primitive Christianity and Modern Spiritualism* (1881); by James Martin Peebles in *Seers of the Ages: Embracing Spiritualism Past and Present* (1903); by Moses Hull and William F. Jamieson in *The Greatest Debate within a Half Century upon Modern Spiritualism* (1902); and by the spiritualist rags *The Medium and Daybreak* (1884) and *Theosophy* (1919).[20] The line was from *Hamlet*: "There are more things in heaven and earth, Horatio, / Than are dreamt of in your philosophy."[21]

One thing that was beyond Spiritualist philosophy, however, was even the *possibility* of fraud. Harry Houdini noted that, even when confronted with outright deception, Doyle's faith remained unshaken. For example, we may turn to the famous case of the medium Florence Cook, who once conducted a séance for a politician and member of the House of Commons, Sir George Sitwell, and a group of Spiritualists. In the murky light of candles, the Spirit of a female child, age 12 years, and answering to the name of "Marie," appeared. Sitwell noted that the medium was no longer present. Looking still closer at this messenger from another world, Sitwell and the others spied what seemed to be a corset beneath the robes of the ghost. At a subsequent séance, Sitwell heard what sounded like someone undressing. When the ghost Marie appeared, he and others around the séance table grabbed her by the wrist. The ghost turned out to be the medium dressed as a child.[22] Yet Doyle exonerated the medium, concluding that, even if Florence Cook had cheated this one time, there was no reason to believe that she had cheated every time: "The author is only aware of one occasion upon which the honesty of her mediumship was called in question, and that was when she was seized by Sir George Sitwell and accused of personating a spirit . . . It is a reflection of our own ignorance that a lifetime of proof should be clouded by a single episode of this nature."[23] Mediums, he insisted, were "passive agents in themselves and powerless. If left to themselves [i.e., severed from Spiritual contact] they guess and muddle," yet, "when the true connection is formed, all is clear. That connection depends on the forces beyond, which are repelled by frivolity or curiosity."[24] In short, Sitwell had encountered fraud because his doubt had somehow severed the "true connection" between the medium and her Spirit Guide. Had he just emitted the right amount of faith, fraud would not have been necessary. Likewise, when another Spiritualist, Sir Oliver Lodge, suspected that the Cottingley fairy photographs might be fraudulent, Doyle retorted, "Sir Oliver is too damn scientific."[25]

Ironically, it was this same Sir Olivier Lodge, a professor of mathematics and physics at University College, Liverpool, and a member of the Royal Society, who maintained that Spiritualism entailed religious faith, certainly, but required, above all, "poetic insight."[26] The best Spiritualists, he argued, were those who understood the power of poetry. He therefore suggested that future Spiritualist investigators be recruited from "trained students of literature."[27] And if these students of literature lacked the scientific acumen to do the job properly, that too was "comparatively unimportant."[28] What was important was that Spiritualism and literature stand together against the scientific conception of an indifferent, mechanical universe. Science can do many things, but it has no way of dealing with goodness, beauty, or desire, nor is science capable of appreciating a joke, and here he includes spiritual hoaxes: "The world is not limited to the serious. If a thing is big enough it can afford to have a humorous or a trivial side."[29] Typically, he then (slightly mis-)quotes Hamlet: "Providence is not above attending to the fall of a sparrow." He means not that our lives are fated but that there more to life than a slide rule. Call it poetic experience or religious intuition; it amounts to much the same thing.

THE LIMITS OF LOGICAL CRITICISM

Let's return to C. W. Leadbeater and his notion that fairies, vampires, and werewolves must be real because, in some sense, we need them to be. I would argue that Spiritualist appraisals of Shakespeare manifest for much the same reason—because what we academics are doing is somehow lacking. Science and logic appeal to the intellect; they favor the reproducible and the useful, but literature does not work like that at all. While we may find deeper experiences in some selections, repeated exposure to those same passages tends to leave us wanting new experiences; even our favorite passages in a given work may, on repeated readings, shift from novel and poignant to clichéd and hackneyed. The words on the page might remain the same, but their meanings shift mysteriously.

So much for the reproducible. The utilitarian value of literature is a still thornier issue. Such readings usually center on a moral precept or an educational message of some sort. Horace, Aristotle, and other ancient Greco-Roman writers set or followed strict literary rules concerning character, plot, and, above all, moral philosophy.[30] Likewise John Milton wrote *Paradise Lost* to explain or to "justify the ways of God to man."[31] George Crabbe (1781) may have called fiction a "strange art" and a "magic," but in the main he believed that the primary function of fiction was didactic: to "soothe the griev'd," to "chastise" the "stubborn," to "admonish" stupidity, and to "confirm" wisdom.[32] More recently, Lisa Zunshine (2006) argues that fiction often appeals to us because it "allows us to navigate our social world and also structures that world."[33] Likewise, Nicola S. Schutte and John M. Malouff (2006) link reading to a desire to learn vicariously.[34]

Yet when these sorts of practical uses are applied to Shakespeare, his works often fall flat. As Samuel Johnson (1765) admitted, "he [Shakespeare] sacrifices virtue to convenience, and is so much more careful to please than to instruct, that he seems to write without any moral purpose . . . he makes no just distribution of good or evil."[35] Johnson further argued that this same moral failing of Shakespeare's connects to other aspects of his art, including his use of "unnatural metaphors."[36] Johnson also endorsed fellow editors who took similar issue with Shakespeare: for example, William Warburton, who described Shakespeare's use of metaphor as "disjointed"—that is, unequal.[37] If metaphorical comparisons do not add up, then—argued Johnson—we can't be surprised if the scales of justice (i.e., poetic justice or "just distribution of good or evil") are also equally lopsided.

Intuiting that the plays offer more than they immediately divulge to rational thought, we might dismiss Johnson's approach as inadequate.[38] After all, just what are we to learn by treating *Othello* as if it were an instruction manual?—don't talk to strangers!—or by a utilitarian reading of *King Lear*?—finding a good retirement home can be so hard! Even Johnson, I think and hope, would acknowledge that to read Shakespeare for moral instruction or "just distribution" alone is to misapply the imagination for reasonable ends. Yet the repudiation of the nonutilitarian (or what we might here simply call the "poetic" or the "transcendent") is with us still. Ann and John O. Thompson (1987), in their collection of essays on Shakespearean metaphor, caution at the outset that "we do not claim to have found any theory of metaphor sufficiently comprehensive to account fully for Shakespearean usage. Indeed, we would be extremely sceptical about any such claim."[39] Shakespeare's art, it seems, cannot be contained in any logical system. Still, Thompson and Thompson urge us to imagine that it can be, because "thinking about this possibility [a solution to Shakespearean meaning] is good practice for liberating oneself from the circularity and mysticism of 'organic unity.'"[40]

A similar logic is apparent in James Wood's *The Broken Estate: Essays on Literature and Belief* (1999), in which he initially argues that imaginative and religious experiences are separable:

> Fiction . . . is the place of not-quite-belief. Precisely what is a danger in religion is the very fabric of fiction. In most orthodox religions, a belief that is only "as if" is either the prelude to a loss of faith, or an instance of bad faith . . . In fiction, by contrast, one is always free to choose not to believe, and this very freedom, this shadow of doubt, is what helps to constitute fiction's reality . . . It is for this reason that many readers dislike actual magic or fantasy in novels . . . [because magic forces] on us miracles which, because they are beyond reason, we cannot choose not to believe.[41]

Yet Wood then retreats from his thesis when dealing with Shakespeare, whose artistry is most discernible when his metaphors "burst beyond the reasonable"—that is, when the logical connection between the object and the description break down; when, in effect, we are pushed into a fantasy of language where "we cannot choose not to believe."[42]

Still others explain away Shakespeare's evocative language by relocating it in a prerational age—that is a neo–Dark Age of superstition, delusion, and irrationality. Gerald L. Bruns (1975) offers the following analysis of Shakespearean verse: "What distinguishes the language of Shakespeare from ordinary speech is that it is rather more symbolic than arbitrary—more symbol than sign—and accordingly it works to induce that original, primitive condition of the mind in which word and world appear to constitute a numinous and undifferentiated whole."[43] Brian Vickers (1984), while not mentioning Shakespeare *per se*, is in basic agreement: "In the scientific tradition . . . a clear distinction is made between words and things and between literal and metaphorical language. The occult tradition does not recognize this distinction."[44] While not referring directly to the occult in Shakespeare, Norman Rabkin (1981) argues that the function of Shakespeare's tragedies is to overwhelm our reason. The plays offer "disturbing mysteries," which reveal the "inadequacy of reasonable understanding."[45] Likewise, A. D. Nuttall (1983) points out that Shakespeare's power is located in "an almost surrealist transformation of nature."[46] That "transformation of nature" is poetical. It is also magical. By the process of language alone, one thing is turned into another.

Put these seemingly disparate dissatisfactions together and it appears fairly clear that unease over or outright dismissal of Shakespeare's occultism comes in two forms. The first is obvious: the poet-playwright's ability to use words to create images and comparisons that defy rational analysis. (This was, we might recall from Chapter 1, a key issue for nineteenth-century actors and critics alike.) The second is more awkward: our sense that our academic practices often undermine the delights of literary experience—the very point raised by Delia Bacon. True, the present generation has introduced a variety of technically sophisticated literary techniques that often dwell on the historical or subversive aspects of the text. These readings have sparked great excitement in Shakespeare Studies, but they have also damaged or delegitimized commonly held aesthetic values. The upshot is that a work's so-called timeless themes are habitually exposed as "cultural impositions," Belief in an author's "intention" is commonly dismissed as pure "fallacy," and a work's emotional or psychological impact is often put aside in pursuit of the political or the material.

Arthur Conan Doyle, we might here recall, argued that poetics were, even in his era, in danger of becoming "too damn scientific." One hundred or so years on, we seem to be at a profound turning point, so argue Keith Windschuttle (1997), John M. Ellis (1997), R. V. Young (1999), Tom McAlindon (2004), Edward Pechter (2011), and, above all, Harold Bloom, whose recent defenses of Shakespeare's spiritual or intrinsic elements have been dismissed as "amateur," or, worse, old-fashioned.[47] True, it's hard not to hear in such prose the grumblings of graybeards, yet even a comparatively youthful critic like Michael D. Bristol (1996) freely admits that contemporary practices, which dwell on the "repetitive chronicle of [Marxist] appropriation and return on investment" can only take us so far: "Shakespeare's plays are not just ephemeral products of the cultural industry . . . [I] would suggest that the supply side hypothesis is at best incomplete."[48] Likewise, Stephen Greenblatt (2001), perhaps our generation's most celebrated Shakespeare critic, expresses "dismay" over latter-day critical "insensitivity to the imaginative dimension"; many critics, he believes, have forgotten "the whole reason anyone bothers with the enterprise in the first place."[49]

It does not follow that any or all of these critics are ready to try automatic writing or to visit a medium, but it does suggest that literary "value"—no matter how quaint the term seems—is coming back into the conversation. Shakespiritualism marks an early attempt to bring together spiritual and critical engagements; and while the results may seem to some to be undisciplined, its intent prefigures our own growing sense that secular discourse can encircle but never fully grasp the culturally sacred.

"A Desire to Speak with the Dead"

It is not my intention to rouse my readers to endorse an unformulated or noncritical mode of reading or to belabor the apparent pitfalls of today's Shakespeare criticism, no matter how much of it tends to neglect, discount, or dismiss any literary experience that defies its own pragmatic, descriptive, or theoretical apparatus. The rules of the game of criticism have to be satisfactory to those who follow them; they do not need to be "right," only consistent to the game's own process. Change will come. It always does. It may take the form of Shakespiritualism, or, more likely, it may not. Even in the aftermath of postmodernism, which prides itself on the opening of the text to virtually *any* new reading, it is unlikely that a major research institution would embrace a candidate who claims that he or she had actually spoken with Shakespeare.

Still, if we were to engage in a bit of speculation, we might ask ourselves how an academic embracement of Shakespiritualism might have altered our critical enterprise. Certainly, we might see some differences, but in the main, I doubt the variances would astonish. We may note, for example, that the Spiritualist suspicion of multiple (living and dead) authors penning the supposedly single-author Shakespeare text was roughly contemporaneous with similar mainstream theories. Alexander Pope (1725) questioned Shakespeare's sole authorship of *Comedy of Errors*, *Love's Labour's Lost*, and *Winter's Tale*; Lewis Theobald (1734) probed the authorship of *Henry V*; Thomas Hamner (1743) had reservations concerning the authorship of *Two Gentlemen of Verona*; Johnson (1765), of *Richard II*; Richard Farmer (1767), of *The Taming of the Shrew*; Edmond Malone (1790), of the first *Henriad* and *Henry VII*. Samuel Taylor Coleridge (1808–19, pub. 1836) rejected Shakespeare's authorship of the Porter scene in *Macbeth* and some of the "low soliloquy" of *Richard III*; Charles Knight (1843) believed that Shakespeare only revised *Timon*; and William George Clark and William Aldis Wright (1874) contended that much of *Macbeth* was by Middleton. F. G. Fleay (1876 and 1886) maintained that many of Shakespeare's plays were coauthored: *1–3Henry VI*, *Richard III*, and *Titus*, he said, were by Shakespeare, Marlowe, Peele, Lodge, and Kyd; *Taming of the Shrew* was coauthored by Shakespeare, Peele, and Drayton; *Romeo and Juliet* was coauthored by Kyd; *Troilus and Cressida* had the debris of Dekker and Chettle; *Macbeth*, of Middleton; *Timon*, of Tourneur; *The Tempest*, of Francis Beaumont; and *Julius Caesar*, of Ben Jonson. J. M. Robertson's studies in the early twentieth century similarly argued that Marlowe helped write *1–3Henry VI*, *Titus Andronicus*, *Richard III*, *Richard II*, *Henry V*, *Julius Caesar*, and *Comedy of Errors*; Peele and Greene, he claimed, wrote parts of *Taming of the Shrew* and *All's Well That Ends Well*, while Chapman helped on *The Tempest*, *Hamlet*, *Merry Wives*, *All's Well*, *Measure for Measure*, *Troilus and Cressida*, *Timon*, and *Pericles*. Robertson also believed that these coauthors had been revised by still other writers—Chettle, Dekker, Drayton, Heywood, and Munday.[50]

Still other Spiritualist resonances appear in many of this generation's better-known literary studies. In *Meaning by Shakespeare* (1992), Terence Hawkes argues that Shakespeare is now integral to our expression and thought processes: "Shakespeare doesn't mean: we mean by Shakespeare"; likewise, in *Shakespeare: The Invention of the Human* (2008), Harold Bloom argues that Shakespeare was, through his dramatic characters, the inventor of our present conception of humanity, hence our conception of self. Both arguments were anticipated by Benjamin De Casseres, a Sephardic Jew from Philadelphia, who, in the 1920s, converted to Spiritualism. In his *Forty Immortals* (1926), De Casseres explains that Shakespeare's immortal characters are the blueprints for human thought and activity: "The persons in Shakespeare's drama are the archetypes of the race. If the universe were destroyed and only the works of Shakespeare left the Creator could make over the race from the Plays."[51] If claiming that fictional characters are somehow more real than flesh and blood seems a bit farfetched, De Casseres explains that the difficulty stems from a lack of religious faith. As he sees it, the physical plane is made up of three dimensions; the astral plane, of four dimensions. The issue is in the distinction of which plane is more worthy of our minds and aims: "Time [i.e., one of the aspects of the physical plane] confuses the 'real' [i.e., the astral plane] with the 'unreal.'"[52] Since Shakespeare is the god of the unreal, and our world is unreal, he is our god: "All the planets are named for a god except the one we live on. The Earth should be renamed Shakespeare."[53]

We might dismiss Spiritualist anticipations of our critical pronouncements as lucky guesses, or simply say that even a stopped clock is right twice a day, but—having read Spiritualist documents for nearly a decade in preparation for this book—I find that it is not enough to say that present-day scholars attempt to be logical and critical and that Shakespiritualists did not. To do so would suggest that Spiritualists recognized and accepted diacritical logic. Rather, Shakespiritualists, who were, for the most part, not academics, engaged literature nonacademically—not logically or illogically, but nonlogically; not critically or uncritically, but noncritically.

If that made Spiritualists encounters and arguments "wrong," well, these same worshippers often paid a price for their erring reason: Dodd and Allen were embarrassments to many in their own anti-Stratfordian circle; the new religion was a virtual career killer for Jackson Knight and his brother G. Wilson Knight. Then again, the vast majority of Spiritualists led ordinary lives and suffered no direct consequences for their faith. As with any group of religious adherents, they went about their day believing what they believed. Their approaches were not dictated by the conversations of the academy or the related peer-review processes of professional publication.

There is, however, a world elsewhere, and by that I don't necessarily mean the Spiritual Realm but rather the wider world of recreational reading. I would argue that outside the formal world of academia, most book lovers continue to read Shakespeare and other great writers for deep, ineffable experiences. Reading poetically and connecting texts intuitively is simply more pleasurable than, say, reading for mechanical facets or scanning for instances of oppression.

In the introduction to this study, I argued that Shakespeareans have some difficulty relating to Shakespeare's artistic faculty and, when their own academic discourse fails, often adopt Spiritualist concepts and terms. I subsequently argued that Shakespeare Studies is, collectively, a kind of game, perhaps not even an important one. Much of our literary gamesmanship is, nonetheless, undertaken with a formality that suggests something akin to religious ritual: invoking sacred names, renouncing scholastic shibboleths, and, more often than not, walking in rhetorical circles. That is by design. Our practice insists on no ending, only eternal beginning. That pseudoreligiosity is still more obvious when academics attempt to engage the general public. For example, the aforementioned Stephen Greenblatt, in his *New York Times* bestselling *Hamlet in Purgatory* (2001), reimagines Shakespeare as a Renaissance "conjurer." Likewise, Stanley Wells, coeditor of the *Oxford Shakespeare*, interviews the ghost of Shakespeare in the admittedly charming chapbook *Coffee with Shakespeare* (2008).[54]

The adoption of a Spiritualist lexis by so many academics may be a form of snobbery, akin to an astronomer talking to astrologers, a temporary adoption of a simplified, metaphorical language in order to communicate with the superstitious. I tend, however, to think it is more complex and bizarre than that. Perhaps these sorts of popularizations are less a debasement than they are a distilment; perhaps what we are getting is the pure essence of what academics are (at least sometimes) really seeking when they discuss literature, not so much a scientific analysis as an intuitive grasp of meaning, an incantation, a mystical manner entirely unsuited to the hard-nosed logic we tend to associate with formal academic discourse.

To those who have never experienced literary transcendence, this may simply seem nonsensical. But the same may be said for many descriptions of experience. There is no way to describe the taste of chocolate unless you've eaten chocolate, and if you have eaten chocolate, then there is no need to describe it, other than to say that chocolate tastes like chocolate. The same may be said of any mystical or transcendent experience. If you've had one, there is no need to describe it; if you haven't had one, there is no way to understand it. Then again, many of us have had such experiences or have at least experienced a desire to experience them. Moreover, since the desire for transcendent experiences is not limited to academics, we shouldn't be surprised that nonacademics have their own ways of seeking and expressing compatible sentiments. I note, for example, that some of the attractions of the séance circle are recreated in today's informal reading groups. Prior to tenure and the time-consuming teaching, research, committee, and administrative work associated with it, I hosted such informal reading groups for a number of years and still lecture on certain authors and texts from time to time. When it comes to Shakespeare, what the preponderance of participants want to know is what he was like, what his words and works mean, and, if he were alive today, what he would make of our world.

These questions are not so very different in their outward signs from those posed by Percy Allen, who, through the auspices of Hester Dowden, explored the authorship of the plays; by H. H. Furness, who asked "Shakespeare" the meaning of the seemingly inexplicable *Vllorxa*; or by G. Wilson Knight, who, in his dealings with "Tutu," wondered whether Shakespeare's Spirit was personally guiding him to a higher truth. Perhaps most important, it is today's readers, who, through sheer strength of number, aid traditional academia in keeping authors and their books alive. Whether today's readers are religiously minded or not, they, like the Shakespiritualists of yore, recognize the major authors who have shaped our culture and, in so doing, acknowledge the role so-called dead authors continue to play in the shaping of what is to come.

GLOSSARY OF SPIRITUALIST TERMS AND TECHNIQUES

AUTOMATIC WRITING. A Spirit uses the medium's hand to write replies to any number of questions posed; also practiced by amateurs as a way of strengthening their spiritual powers. As an added feature, a magic pencil sometimes floats. In such instances, the Spirits are asking the medium to begin writing. How it is done: The pencil hangs on thin metal or glass wires.

CLAIRGUSTANCE or CLAIRLIENCE. A taste or smell associated with the Spirit. For example, if you are trying to contact your mother, who was fond of gardening, a waft of rose water might be introduced. How it is done: aromatherapy.

DERMOGRAPHY, also known as SKIN WRITING. The Spirits literally write words or pictures on the medium's flesh. How it is done: Invisible ink, likely lemon juice, is used. When held up to a candle, the ink grows increasingly visible.

ECTOPLASM. A pale, filmy materialization of the soul, produced by the medium when in a trance state. Likely invented by Leah Fox (circa 1860). The last manifestation of ectoplasm seems to have taken place in 1939. Cambridge University has a sample; it looks and feels like cheesecloth or chiffon. Female mediums sometimes stuffed ectoplasm in their vaginas, necessitating strip-searches. See also SOUL and SPIRIT'S PROGRESS.

LAMPADOMANCY. Flame reading. The messages might be conveyed by changes in flame intensity, color, or direction. How it is done: Chemicals can be added to a segment of the candle to make the flame flicker or change color. On the direction of the flame: a small hole in the table may allow for a flue to affect air-current. A turkey baster, for example, might be used. See also PYROSCOPY, SCRYING, and TASSEOGRAPHY.

MAGIC BOX. Sometimes a curtained area from which the Spirit emerges or behind which clients could caress Spirits; sometimes a large trunk, like a magical cabinet used by magicians. Another version: a small, television-like box in which only a face or a miniature body might appear. The latter is likely a trick of projection. See also SOUL.

MEDIUM. The human conduit for spiritual communication. There are three forms of mediumship. The first is deep trance, in which the medium's body is possessed. In this state, the medium generally wakes somewhat groggily and without any knowledge of what transpired. Another form is light trance, in which the medium is aware of what is being said while it is said, but has, once the trance is broken, no knowledge of it. The rarest form of trance mediumship is called "trumpet mediumship," in which the medium relates messages and retains full knowledge of the communication. How it is done: simple acting.

MESMERISM. The use of magnets or "universal fluid" or "Odic force" to cure the living or to contact the dead. Founded by Anton Mesmer.

MIRROR WRITING, also known as MIRROR SCRIPTING. Writing backward from right to left or from bottom to top. When reflected in a mirror, the text is decipherable. The idea is that the Spirits exist in an opposite world, like a film negative. How it is done: practice. See also SCRYING and SPIRIT PHOTOGRAPHY.

OUIJA BOARD. Consists of a board with *yes* and *no* written on opposite corners. In the center of the board, letters of the alphabet are laid out in a fan-like display. Messages—"yes," "no," or the spelling of words—are provided via a small, heart-shaped piece of wood or movable indicator, called the *planchette* or *traveler*. The first Ouija board was patented in 1853, though David Fox, brother to the Fox sisters, invented a verbal form of this technique about a decade earlier. The word *Ouija* and the technique itself have been variously linked to ancient Egyptian and Chinese forms of divination. Game dynamics aside, *Ouija* is likely a simple combination of the French *oui* and the German *ja*—both meaning *yes*. Ouija Board manufacturers insisted that their device was a religious item and therefore not subject to taxation. The IRS disagreed, labeling the Ouija board a mere game. Court cases ensued in 1920, 1921, and 1922, in all of which the Courts either sided with the IRS or refused to overturn earlier decisions. In 1966, the toymaker Parker Brothers brought out a game version of this so-called religious tool that outsold even Monopoly. How it works: The person attempting to contact the Spirits holds the traveler, which "magically" moves across a board covered with letters. The faithful believe that the Spirit spells out replies; the less credulous might suspect fraud or autosuggestion at play. See also SPIRIT RAPPING and PLANCHETTE.

PELLET READING. A medium holds up a sealed envelope to his forehead and allows the Spirits to divine the question contained within and to respond appropriately. How it is done: The medium picks up the first envelope and says, for example, "Someone has an uncle named Fred who is ill; he will recover." He opens the envelope and reads, "Will Fred recover from surgery?" A stranger in the audience then comes forward to say that he wrote that message. This person is actually the medium's assistant, and the question has been preset. The envelope the medium has just opened is not the one supposedly written by the secret assistant, but the *next* question, which reads, "Will I make money?" The medium then holds up an envelope and says, "This person is worried about money." He thus stays one step ahead of the audience. Many North Americans of my age bracket might recall Johnny Carson doing a version of this vaudevillian trick in his recurring *Tonight Show* role as "Carnac the Magnificent."

PLANCHETTE or TRAVELER. A magical device that allows the Spirit Guide to spell out messages. Sometimes it is a mini table, with two legs on rollers. A third leg holds the point of a pencil or pen. The planchette is usually heart shaped but is sometimes round. Some can be utilized by a single medium; most planchettes require two mediums working in tandem. The planchette may be used to answer *yes* or *no*, or to spell out various messages. See also OUIJA BOARD.

PRAYER HEALING. This sometimes involves Mesmerism or simple group prayer. How it is done: autosuggestion or hypnosis provides temporary benefits.

PSYCHOMETRY. Emotional impressions of humans left on inanimate objects. How it's done: The questions begin generally. The medium holds an object and says, "First impression . . . intense excitement of the perceptive organ . . . of the intellect." The answer cannot be wrong. The object must have an emotional connection with the departed or it would not have been brought to the medium. The medium might continue by saying something about the considerable excitability and anxiety of the person who owned the object, or by stating that the person was somewhat harassed and overtasked with the details of business, or by stating that the person who owned the object was active in industry or of great resolution, and so on. Depending on the answer, the medium slowly zeroes in on the traits of the person in question.

PYROSCOPY. Candle reading. A candle is covered in blessed olive oil, lit, and allowed to burn for some time while the petitioner asks the Spirits a question. The candle is then blown out and placed on a white sheet of paper and rolled like sushi. The paper is then unrolled. The soot of the candle should leave some impressions on the paper, which can then be read like tea leaves. See also LAMPADOMANCY, SCRYING, and TASSEOGRAPHY.

SCRYING. Reading Spirit messages in crystal, glass balls, mirrors, polished copper, or what the Renaissance mystic John Dee termed the "shew stone." More recent versions include transparent plastic balls. The medium gazes into the ball and concentrates on a Spirit or a question. Many mediums report a mist or smoke, which then clears, revealing a picture. How it works: self-hypnosis or sheer fantasy. See also AUTOMATIC WRITING, MIRROR WRITING, and TASSEOGRAPHY.

SLATE WRITING. Consisting of a writing slate placed under the table, held in place with the hand of the medium, whose thumb remains visible on the upper surface of the table. After a time, writing is heard and, following three otherworldly knocks, the slate is produced and the Spirit message examined. How it is done: Either a trap door beneath the table opens and an assistant secretly switches the plate with one that has an appropriate message, or the medium uses sleight of hand to distract the observers while he or she scrawls a message.

SOUL. The essence of the person, still recognizable to the living. The age of the immortal image seems to vary. People usually see their parents as old, though generally in good health. On the other hand, G. Wilson Knight reported that his aborted brother existed as an adult in the Spirit Realm. Shakespeare seems to be eternally in his midtwenties. People missing limbs or otherwise wounded are healed and whole in the Spirit Realm. See also SPIRIT'S PROGRESS and SPIRIT WAVELENGTH.

SPIRIT GUIDE. The medium's contact in the Spirit Realm. Sometimes the Spirit Guide speaks or spells a message to the medium; sometimes the

Spirit Guide possesses the medium. The Spirit Guide is usually an ethnic minority of some sort. While this might have much to do with colonialism, it is more often associated with an affirmation of multiculturalism. On a more cynical note, the linguistic gaps in translation allow the medium an easy out for erroneous information.

SPIRIT PHOTOGRAPHY. Photographs that reveal the evidence of a Spirit's face floating near that of the medium; these floating heads have contemporary hairstyles or, in the case of men, Victorian beards. How it is done: A simple photography trick known as "double exposure." See also MIRROR WRITING.

SPIRIT RAPPING. Developed by the American Spiritualist Margaret Fox and her two sisters. The medium asks the Spirit a question, who replies with one rap for *no*, two raps for *doubtful*, and three raps for *yes*. The medium might also recite aloud the alphabet, the Spirit knocking when the right letter is called out. How it is done: A simple adaptation of the children's game Twenty Questions.

SPIRIT REALM, also known as SUMMERLAND. There are various theories concerning this happy land. Some say the Sprit Realm is divided into a series of hierarchies or cycles in which the earthly is slowly cast off and the soul is eventually reunited with a Group Soul or, possibly, with God. See SPIRIT'S PROGRESS. Most agree that the Spirits who return to earth do so on special dispensation to save or to guide mortals. Many other Spiritualists believe that souls are permanently on call and pass the time in what seem to be pleasant activities (reading, going for walks, attending the theater, drinking whiskey, and so forth).

SPIRIT VOICES. A voice seems to come from above or behind the medium. How it is done: likely, ventriloquism, commonly practiced by stage magicians and vaudevillian entertainers.

SPIRIT WAVELENGTH. Based on the theory that souls oscillate at different speeds. The radio-like medium tunes in to receive messages. See also SPIRIT'S PROGRESS.

SPIRIT'S PROGRESS. Almost all Spiritualists agree that the soul literally and metaphysically jumps through reincarnative hoops, each helpfully color-coded. According to Spiritualist thought, Spirits closest to God are white. Color is also linked to the soul's vibration. See SPIRIT WAVELENGTH.

SWEDENBORGISM. A foundational sect for Spiritualism, created by Emmanuel Swedenborg and typified by the belief that the Spirit World, filled with universities, libraries, and academic debate, can be reached in dreams.

TABLE TAPPING, or TABLE TILTING or TABLE TURNING. The table is used by a group, all of whom rest their fingers on the table's edge. The medium makes contact with a Spirit Guide, who then answers questions by rocking the table up or down or knocking it over. As with a PLANCHETTE, the number of people involved supposedly mitigates the possibility of fraud. The medium calls out a question, then either demands that the Spirit tilt the table once for *yes*, twice for *maybe*, or three times for *no* or asks for a name or short answer by running through the alphabet. For example, "What is your name?" The medium then runs through the alphabet. At *M* the table tilts. The medium moves on to the second letter; a tilt is felt at *I*. The medium might then shout out, "Is your name Michael?" If a single tilt is then felt, he or she may move on to the next question. How it is done: a cord is lanced to one of the table legs. That same leg is slightly shorter than the rest. The medium tugs the cord, thus wobbling the table. Sometimes a three-legged table is used, as a shortened leg on such a table is still more unstable.

TASSEOGRAPHY. The reading of messages in tea leaves found in the bottom of a shallow cup. The medium sips from the cup three times, then swirls the leaves while asking a question. The cup is then turned over, the liquid draining into the accompanying saucer. The cup is then examined for images. The depth of the images (i.e., how closely they rest to the lip or bottom of the cup) is deemed to be important: a message left near the top of the cup suggests a Spirit who has made great progress; a message at the bottom of the cup suggests a younger or inferior Spirit. The images are formed by the remnants of tea leaves or coffee grounds. How it is done: No trick is involved, since the images are entirely interpretive. See also LAMPADOMANCY, SCRYING, SPIRIT'S PROGRESS, and PYROSCOPY.

THEOSOPHY. Spiritualism, with elements of Buddhist and Egyptian mythology.

A NOTE ON THE SPELLING OF *SPIRIT*

To CAP OR NOT TO CAP THE word *Spirit*, that is the question. Devotional texts offer no standardized approach. While I have retained all original spellings in citations, I have wrestled with the issue in my own narrative. On the one hand, we might read the word as a generic, in which case, it would not be capitalized. In this sense *spirit* would be used in much the same way we would refer to a "king" or a "prince." But this doesn't sit right. On the other hand, to capitalize *Spirit* might imply that I am a practitioner of "Spiritualism." I am not. In the context of this work, however, capitalization is, I think, appropriate, insofar as the majuscule encourages the reader to distinguish within its nominative uses a certain force, presence, or individuality. For the same reason, *Spirit Guide* and some other Spiritualist terms are also capitalized. However, *fairies*, *vampires*, and *werewolves* remain in lower case.

NOTES

INTRODUCTION

1. "Shakespeare Ghost Revises 'Hamlet,'" *New York Times*, April 4, 1921.
2. An account of this incident appeared in the March 17, 1909 Meridian, CT, *Journal*; see the facsimile of this article appended to John Armstrong Chaloner, *Robbery Under Law or, The Battle of the Millionaires: A Play in Three Acts and Three Scenes*, 2nd ed. (Roanoke Rapids, NC: Palmetto Press, 1915), 248.
3. See "Declared Sane," *Wanganui Chronicle*, December 12, 1919.
4. "Shakespeare Ghost Revises 'Hamlet'" emphasis my own.
5. Lizzie Doten, *Poems From the Inner Life*, 17th ed. (Boston: Colby and Rich, 1863), 86.
6. Henry Kiddle, ed., *Spiritual Communications* (New York: Authors' Publishing, 1879), 66. That Shakespeare was not religious or moral enough is an old bugbear. Samuel Johnson (1765) expressed similar qualms: "He [Shakespeare] seems to write without any moral purpose . . . he makes no just distribution of good or evil" (Samuel Johnson, *Johnson on Shakespeare: Essays and Notes Selected and Set Forth with an Introduction*, ed. Walter Raleigh (London: Henry Frowde, 1908), 20–21.
7. Sarah Taylor Shatford, *Shakespeare's Revelations by Shakespeare's Spirit* (New York: Torch Press, 1919), 45.
8. Hudson Tuttle and J. M. Peebles, *The Year-Book of Spiritualism for 1871* (Boston: William White, 1871), 156. Balfour was also president of the Society of Psychical Research. See John Gray, *The Immortalization Commission: Science and the Strange Quest to Cheat Death* (New York: Farrar, Straus and Giroux, 2011), 2.
9. Emma Hardinge Britten, *Modern American Spiritualism: A Twenty Years' Record* (New York: self-published, 1870), 13, 273; R. Laurence Moore also counts the number of American Spiritualists at 11 million—in an America with a total population of 35 million, that seems absurdly high (R. Laurence Moore, "Spiritualism and Science: Reflections on the First Decade of Spirit Rappings," *American Quarterly* 24, no. 4 [1972]: 474–500; 481). Johann Joseph Ignaz von Döllinger believed that American Spiritualists numbered "over two millions [*sic*]" (Johann Joseph Ignaz von Döllinger, *Addresses on Historical and Literary Subjects*, trans. Margaret Warre [London: John Murray, 1894], 293). Frederic Marvin, a Spiritualist debunker, puts the number of American practitioners at around 4 million. For an overview of the numerical debate, see Molly McGarry, *Ghosts of Futures Past: Spiritualism and the Cultural Politics of Nineteenth-Century*

America (Berkeley: University of California Press, 2008), 3. As late as 1941, there were over 300 Spiritualist Churches in England alone. See Rene Kollar, *Searching for Raymond: Anglicanism, Spiritualism, and Bereavement between the Two World Wars* (Lanham, MD: Lexington Books, 2000), 140. Kollar puts the number of British worshipers at just over 10,000. However, the registered numbers do not tell the entire story. As Alex Owen points out, British Spiritualists often paid dues. Subscriptions to Spiritualist societies and newsletters might cost as much as a full guinea a year, the equivalent of about 110 pounds in 2009 funds. (Conversion based on Bank of England Inflation Calculator; updates for 2010–13 not yet, as of this writing, available). Counting paid subscribers, members, and one-time fee-payers (i.e., those who hired a medium on a pay-as-you-go basis), the number of adherents in England was probably around 100,000. The number of casual adherents, or believers who did not practice, was likely significantly higher. See Alex Owen's *The Darkened Room: Women, Power and Spiritualism in Late Victorian England* (Philadelphia: University of Pennsylvania Press, 1989), 25. On the worldwide figure, see Molly McGarry, "'The Quick, the Dead, and the Yet Unborn': Untimely Sexualities and Secular Hauntings," in *Secularisms*, ed. Janet R. Jakobsen and Ann Pellegrini (Durham, NC: Duke University Press, 2008), 247–79; 253.

10. Quoted in Ilya Vinitsky, *Ghostly Paradoxes: Modern Spiritualism and Russian Culture in the Age of Reason* (Toronto: University of Toronto Press, 2009), 61.

11. On historical studies, see, for example, Janet Oppenhiem, *The Other World: Spiritualism and Psychical Research in England, 1850–1914* (Cambridge: Cambridge University Press, 1985); Antoine Faivre, *Access to Western Esotericism* (Albany: State University of New York Press, 1994); and Jack Monroe, "Making the Séance 'Serious': *Tables Tournantes* and the Second Empire Bourgeois Culture, 1853–1861," *History of Religions* 38, no. 3 (February 1999): 219–46. Martin Rudoy Scherzinger links Spiritualism to Romanticism, especially the latter's common trope of a Muse-like agency (Martin Rudoy Scherzinger, "Music, Spirit Possession and the Copyright Law: Cross-Cultural Comparisons and Strategic Speculations," *Yearbook for Traditional Music* 31 [1999]: 102–25, esp. 106–7). On the continued growth of Spiritualism between the First and Second World Wars, see Jenny Hazelgrove, *Spiritualism and British Society Between the Wars* (Manchester: Manchester University Press, 2000), passim; Kollar, *Searching for Raymond*, passim; Jerusha Hull McCormack, "Domesticating Delphi: Emily Dickinson and the Electro-Magnetic Telegraph," *American Quarterly* 55, no. 4 (December 2003): 569–601; Daniel Herman, "Whose Knocking? Spiritualism as Entertainment and Therapy in Nineteenth-Century San Francisco," *American Nineteenth Century History* 7, no. 3 (September 2006): 417–42; John Harvey, "The Photographic Medium: Representation, Reconstruction, Consciousness, and Collaboration in Early-Twentieth-Century Spiritualism," *Technoetic Arts: A Journal of Speculative Research* 2, no. 2 (2004): 109–23; John Warne Monroe, *Laboratories of Faith: Mesmerism, Spiritism, and Occultism in Modern France* (Ithaca, NY: Cornell University Press, 2008); Tatiana Kontou, *Spiritualism and Women's Writing: From the Fin de Siècle to*

the Neo-Victorian (New York: Palgrave Macmillan, 2009); Amy Lehman, *Victorian Women and the Theatre of Trance: Mediums, Spiritualists and Mesmerists in Performance* (Jefferson, NC: McFarland, 2009); Shane McCorristine, *Spectres of the Self: Thinking About Ghosts and Ghost-Seeing in England, 1750–1920* (New York: Cambridge University Press, 2010); and Gray, *The Immortalization Commission.*

12. Ewan Fernie, ed., introduction to *Spiritual Shakespeares* (New York: Routledge, 2005), 1–27; 8. On the uses of theological language, Jacques Derrida observes, "there has never been a scholar who really, and as scholar, deals with ghosts. A traditional scholar does not believe in ghosts—nor in all that could be called the virtual space of spectrality. There has never been a scholar who, as such, does not believe in the sharp distinction between the real and the unreal, the actual and the inactual, the living and the non-living, being and non-being ('to be or not to be,' in the conventional reading), in the opposition between what is present and what is not, for example in the form of objectivity" (Jacques Derrida, *Specters of Marx: The State of the Debt, the Work of Mourning, and New International*, trans. Peggy Kamuf [New York: Routledge, 1994], 11).

13. Even Courtney Lehmann is reluctant to use religiously-tinged language. Instead of writing the word "ghost," she prefers "signifying void" (Courtney Lehmann, *Shakespeare's Remains: Theater to Film, Early Modern to Postmodern* [Ithaca, NY: Cornell University Press, 2002], xiv, 2).

14. Roland Barthes, "The Death of the Author," in *Image—Music—Text*, trans. Stephen Heath (New York: Noonday Press/Farrar, Straus and Giroux, 1977), 142–48; 146; and Michel Foucault, "What is an Author?," in *The Foucault Reader*, ed. Paul Rabinow (New York: Vintage Books, 2010), 101–20; 118–19. A fuller treatment of Foucault and Barthes is found in Chapter 4 of the present study.

15. Paul Adrien Maurice Dirac, *The Principles of Quantum Mechanics*, in *The Collected Works of P.A.M. Dirac, 1924–1948*, ed. R. H. Dalitz (Cambridge: Cambridge University Press, 1995), 456.

16. Margreta de Grazia and Peter Stallybrass, "The Materiality of the Shakespearean Text," *Shakespeare Quarterly* 44, no. 3 (1993): 255–83; 256, 283.

17. Michael D. Bristol, *Big-Time Shakespeare* (New York: Routledge, 1996), 11.

18. Charles H. Frey, *Making Sense of Shakespeare* (Teaneck, NJ: Fairleigh Dickinson University Press, 1999), 21.

19. Terence Hawkes, *Shakespeare in the Present*, Accents on Shakespeare (New York: Routledge, 2002), 141.

20. Stephen Greenblatt, *Will in the World: How Shakespeare Became Shakespeare* (New York: W. W. Norton, 2004), 53.

21. Eric S. Mallin, *Godless Shakespeare*, Shakespeare Now (London: Continuum, 2007), 22, 23.

22. Slavoj Žižek, reviewing Derrida's use of occult language, concludes that the specter represents "the ultimate horizon of ethics" (Slavoj Žižek, "The Spectre of Ideology," in *The Žižek Reader*, ed. Elizabeth Wright and Edmond Wright [Malden, MA: Blackwell Publishers, 1999], 53–86; 74, 79, 77). Freud defines

the "uncanny" as something that is identical with its opposite, something which is "secretly familiar" but has undergone a "repression and then returned from it" (quoted in Antony Easthope, "Freud's Spectres," in *Evil Spirits: Nihilism and the Fate of Modernity*, ed. Gary Banham and Charlie Blake [New York: Manchester University Press, 2000], 146–64; 155). Historians have explored the polysemies of Spiritualism and literary criticism. Logie Barrow writes, "Elitist epistemologies . . . derive further power from their confusion about their own naturalness and inevitability"—i.e., by creating liturgy or jargon (Logie Barrow, *Independent Spirits: Spiritualism and English Plebeians, 1850–1910* [London: Routledge and Kegan Paul, 1986], 148). On the debunking of literary terms by a literary critic, see Stanley Stewart, *"Renaissance" Talk: Ordinary Language and the Mystique of Critical Problems* (Pittsburgh, PA: Duquesne University Press, 1997), esp. 103.

23. Harold Boom, *Genius: A Mosaic of One Hundred Exemplary Creative Minds* (New York: Warner Books, 2002), xviii, 12. He also refers to Shakespeare's "miraculous rendering of reality" (4). Bloom professes that his own interest in all canonical literature is fueled by a "desire for the transcendental" (7).

24. Ibid., 7. Bloom also traces the word "influence" to an "occult and astral sense" (Harold Bloom, *Kabbalah and Criticism* [New York: Continuum, 1993], 52).

25. Gary Taylor, *Reinventing Shakespeare: A Cultural History from the Restoration to the Present* (New York: Oxford University Press, 1989), 6; Terence Hawkes, *Meaning by Shakespeare* (New York: Routledge, 1992), 141–53; and Bristol, *Big-Time Shakespeare*, 4.

26. On bardolatry, see F. E. Halliday, *The Cult of Shakespeare* (London: Gerald Duckworth, 1957); Martha Winburn England, *Garrick's Jubilee* (Columbus: Ohio University Press, 1964); Howard Felperin, "Bardolatry Then and Now," in *The Appropriation of Shakespeare: Post-Renaissance Reconstructions of the Works of the Myth*, ed. Jean I. Marsden (New York: St. Martin's Press, 1991), 129–44; Barbara Hodgdon, *The Shakespeare Trade: Performances and Appropriations* (Philadelphia: University of Pennsylvania Press, 1998), passim; Samuel Schoenbaum, *Shakespeare's Lives*, new ed. (1991; repr., New York: Oxford University Press, 1993); Jeffrey Kahan, "Shakespeare and the Forging of Belief," *Critical Quarterly* 43, no. 2 (2001): 19–33; and Jack Lynch, *Becoming Shakespeare: The Unlikely Afterlife That Turned a Provincial Playwright into the Bard* (New York: Walker, 2007). For the purposes of this study, the most pertinent critic is probably Charles Laporte (2007), who argues that bardolatry often centered on Shakespeare as an inspired author. His basic argument is that bardolatry—the worship of Shakespeare—stemmed from an inability to believe that an ordinary mortal, particularly one from such humble origins, could have composed the works ascribed to him. He notes, for example, a number of eighteenth- and nineteenth-century critics and poets who compared Shakespeare's "divine" authoring to the inspired writings of Homer or to the biblical prophets. See Charles Laporte, "The Bard, the Bible, and the Victorian Shakespeare Question," *ELH* 74 no.3 (2007): 609–28. Laporte's study enhances our understanding of bardolatry, and certainly his thoughts on the difficulties of connecting

Shakespeare's bucolic upbringing to his dramatic and poetic sophistication help explain some of the reasons Bacon and others have been proposed as the "true" author(s) of Shakespeare's work. We will turn to the so-called authorship question in Chapters 2 and 3 of this study.

27. William F. Friedman and Elizabeth S. Friedman, *The Shakespearean Ciphers Examined: An Analysis of Cryptographic Systems Used as Evidence that Some Author Other Than William Shakespeare Wrote the Plays Commonly Attributed to Him* (Cambridge: Cambridge University Press, 1957), 282.

28. The anonymous critic is cited in Friedman and ibid., 50.

29. G. Wilson Knight, *Starlit Dome: Studies in the Poetry of Vision* (London: Oxford University Press, 1943), 323.

30. G. Wilson Knight, *The Christian Renaissance* (London: Methuen, 1962), 329; and G. Wilson Knight, *Starlit Dome*, 319.

31. Margaret J. Somerville, "Editorial: 'Waiting in the Chaotic Place of Unknowing': Articulating Postmodern Emergence," *International Journal of Qualitative Studies in Education* 21, no. 3 (May–June 2008), 209–20; 209.

32. John M. Ellis, *Literature Lost: Social Agendas and the Corruption of the Humanities* (New Haven, CT: Yale University Press, 1997), 37.

33. Percy Allen, *Talks with Elizabethans* (New York: Rider, 1947), 45.

34. R. S. White, "Where is Shakespeare's Autobiography?," in *Early Modern Autobiography: Theories, Genres, Practices*, ed. Ronald Bedford, Lloyd Davis, and Philippa Kelly (Ann Arbor: University of Michigan, 2006), 174–88; 178.

35. Ibid., 178.

36. On Spiritualism during the First World War, see Michael Snape, "Civilians, Soldiers and Perceptions of the Afterlife in Britain during the First World War," in *The Church, the Afterlife, and the Fate of the Soul*, ed. Peter Clarke and Tony Claydon (Rochester, NY: Boydell Press, 2009), 371–403. Shakespeare, however, is not mentioned.

37. On Louis Benjamin, see Albert Durrant Watson, *The Twentieth Plane: A Psychic Revelation* (Philadelphia: George W. Jacobs, 1919), 98.

38. Daisy O. Roberts and Collin E. Woolcock, *Elizabethan Episode Incorporating Shakespeare and Co., Unlimited* (London: Regency Press, [1961]), 33. The first time Olivier came into view, Shakespeare lamented "not like that—he was sleeker, much sleeker"; when Jean Simmons's Ophelia occupied the screen, the voice said, "not just a child like this. But she acts well, it serve. for the play" (33). Over time, Roberts learned to speak to the voice and to allow her body to become a seismic needle, recording Shakespeare's "wavelength" through automatic writing (9). On "wavelength," see "Spirit Wavelength" in the Glossary of Spiritualist Terms and Techniques appended to this study.

39. James Merrill, *Changing Light at Sandover* (New York: Atheneum, 1982), 164.

40. See J. M. E. McTaggart, "The Unreality of Time," *Mind: A Quarterly Review of Psychology and Philosophy* 17 (1908): 456–73; Dunne's other books offer a variety of mathematical formulae and vector diagrams validating this idea. The novelist Andrew Crumey, who also holds a PhD in theoretical physics from Imperial College, London, recently looked at Dunne's math and labeled

it multiply as "speculation, pseudo-science or crank theory, depending on your point of view" ("An Experiment with Time," *Picador* [blog], March 2008, http://www.crumey.toucansurf.com/an_experiment_with_time.html). In his study of McTaggart, Gerald Rochelle argues for a higher reality that is "substantial but non-material"; J. R. Lucas states that the differences between past and present are an "illusion." See Gerald Rochelle, *Behind Time: The Incoherence of Time and McTaggart's Atemporal Replacement* (Brookfield, VT: Ashgate, 1998), 15; and J. R. Lucas, *The Future: An Essay on God, Temporality, and Truth* (New York: Blackwell, 1989), 4, and his *Space, Time and Causality: An Essay in Natural Philosophy* (Oxford: Clarendon Press, 1984), in which he suggests that science needs to adopt an "opaque contingency in our encounters with the external world" (12).

41. G. Wilson Knight, "Spirit-Writing," 1950–71, Manuscript Collection of the University of Exeter, 57; see also G. Wilson Knight, "Caroline: Life after Death," circa 1952; last revised 1985 Manuscript Collection of the University of Exeter, 385–86. In *Shakespearian Dimensions* (Brighton, Sussex: Harvester Press, 1984), Knight argues that Shakespeare received his plays via his spiritual "inspirers" (109).

42. John Sullivan Dwight, *Dwight's Journal of Music: A Paper of Art and Literature* 23–24 (1863–64): 354.

43. Hugh Junor Browne, *The Holy Truth, or, the Coming Reformation* (London: A. Hall, 1876), 106.

44. Kiddle, *Spiritual Communications*, 68.

45. Gerald Massey, *Shakspeare's Sonnets Never Before Interpreted: His Private Friends Identified: Together with a Recorded Likeness of Himself* (London: Longmans, Green, 1866), 145. In 1872, Massey explained that his own occult investigations had revealed that Christopher Marlowe had not translated *Pharsalia*; he had merely recorded the dictation of a spirit (Gerald Massey, *Concerning Spiritualism* [London: J. Burns, 1872], 95). Sixteen years later, Massey argued that Marlowe was a Faustus-like figure, who, were he alive today, would have been regarded as a "phenomenal spiritualist" (Gerald Massey, *The Secret Drama of Shakespeare's Sonnets* [N.p.: Richard Clay, 1888], 170).

46. James Hervey Hyslop, *Contact with the Other World: The Latest Evidence as to Communication with the Dead* (New York: Century, 1919), 266.

47. Watson, *The Twentieth Plane*, 143.

48. Benjamin De Casseres, *Forty Immortals* (New York: Seven Arts, 1926), 363.

49. Roberts and Woolcock, *Elizabethan Episode*, 35.

50. Watson, *The Twentieth Plane*, 98.

51. Alfred Dodd, *The Immortal Master* (London: Rider, [1943]), 74.

52. Ibid., 66.

53. Allen, *Talks with Elizabethans*, 20, 41. I am here supposing that both *Taming* and *Titus* were written around 1591. Fetcher was born in 1579; Beaumont in 1584.

54. William Bliss, *The Real Shakespeare: A Counterblast to Commentators* (London: Sidwick and Jackson, 1947), 301–2.

55. Browne, *The Holy Truth, or, the Coming Reformation*, 206; James Hervey Hyslop, *Proceedings of the American Society for Psychical Research: A Further Record of Mediumistic Experiments* 19 (1925): 80–81.

56. Shatford, *Shakespeare's Revelations by Shakespeare's Spirit*, 298.

57. G. Wilson Knight, *This Sceptered Isle: Shakespeare's Message for England at War* (1950; repr., Folcroft, PA: Folcroft Library Editions, 1969), 18, 16. To his credit, Knight openly questions his own logic; perhaps he has gone too far in merging the poetry of Shakespeare to reality: "Is this really the England of Shakespeare's day? Does such a Great Britain exist? Can it exist?" (31–32). Still, Knight's belief in spiritual communication cannot be questioned. See Chapter 5 of this study.

58. Dodd, *The Immortal Master*, 101.

59. Harriet M. Shelton, *Abraham Lincoln Returns* (New York: Evans, 1957), passim, 30, 36–37, 97; E. Lee Howard, *My Adventure into Spiritualism* (New York: Macmillan, 1935), 111; Gerald Massey was the author of *Ancient Egypt: The Light of the World* (London: T. F. Unwin, 1907); Ignatius Donnelly was author of *Atlantis: The Antediluvian World* (New York: Harper, 1882). A last bit of evidence: while not mentioning Shakespeare, W. G. Langworthy Taylor compared the messages Kate Fox received from the Spirit Realm to the "hieroglyphics, on excavated pottery, on reopened tombs, [and] on papyri unrolled from mummies" (W. G. Langworthy Taylor, preface to *Fox-Taylor Automatic Writing 1869–1892 Unabridged Record*, by Kate Fox, ed. Sarah E. L. Taylor [Minneapolis, MN: Tribune-Great West self-published, 1932], ii).

60. On Emerson, see the review of Musle-Huddeen Sheik Saadi's *The Gulistan, or Rose Garden*, in *The North American Review* 102 (1866): 260–64; 261.

61. See "An Easter Address by Rev. M. J. Savage," *Light: A Journal of Psychical, Occult, and Mystical Research* 9 (May 25, 1889): 251–54, esp. 253. On Buddhism and Spiritualist parallels and links, see Lynn L. Sharp, who connects the rise of Spiritualism to the "newly discovered" religions of the east, including Hinduism and Buddhism (*Secular Spirituality: Reincarnation and Spiritism in Nineteenth-Century France* [Lanham, MD: Lexington Books, 2006], xi); see also J. Jeffrey Franklin, *The Lotus and the Lion: Buddhism and the British Empire* (Ithaca, NY: Cornell University Press, 2008), 55, 59; and David R. Loy, *Awareness Bound and Unbound: Buddhist Essays* (Albany: State University of New York, 2009), 109. On British Spiritualism and/or its links to Indian-influenced Theosophy, see Oppenhiem, *The Other World*, 20, 163–70, 173, 180–82; Alvin Boyd Kuhn, *Theosophy: A Modern Revival of Ancient Wisdom* (New York: Henry Holt, 1930), 33–35; and Rudolf Steiner, *Spiritualism, Madame Blavatsky, and Theosophy: An Eye Witness View of Occult History*, ed. Christopher Bamford (Great Barrington, MA: Anthroposophic Press, 2001), 67–82. G. Wilson Knight linked Spiritualism to Buddhism in G. Wilson Knight, *The Imperial Theme: Further Interpretations of Shakespeare's Tragedies Including the Roman Plays* (1931; London: Methuen, 1965), 358; in G. Wilson Knight and W. F. Jackson Knight, *Elysion: On Ancient Greek and Roman Beliefs Concerning a Life after Death* (New York: Barnes and Noble, 1970), 10; in G. Wilson Knight, *Christian Renaissance*

(London: Methuen, 1962), 327; and in G. Wilson Knight, *Shakespeare's Dramatic Challenge: On the Rise of Shakespeare's Tragic Heroes* (New York: Barnes and Noble Books, 1977), 146.

62. Richard Maurice Bucke, *Cosmic Consciousness* (Philadelphia: Conservator, 1894), 311.

63. William Stanley, *The Case of The Fox: Being His Prophecies, Under Hypnotism, of the Period Ending A.D. 1950: A Political Utopia* (London: Truslove and Hanson, 1903), 107.

64. Stan McMullin argues that the accommodating nature of Spiritualism allowed for a "core institution common to the various marginalized groups committed to spiritualist communication regardless of their individual beliefs" (Stan McMullin, *Anatomy of a Seance: A History of Spirit Communication in Central Canada* [Montreal: McGill-Queen's University Press, 2004], 224).

65. Tyatafia soon put him in touch with Shakespeare, who spoke to Hugo in perfect French. See John Chambers, *Victor Hugo's Conversations with the Spirit World: A Literary Genius's Hidden Life* (Rochester, VT: Destiny Books, 1998), 217.

66. The same device automatically updated Shakespeare's thoughts into "ordinary language for ordinary people" (Daisy O. Roberts, *Why in the World?* [London: Linden Press, 1961], 169). On Shakespeare's surprisingly modern language, see also Browne, *The Holy Truth, or, the Coming Reformation*, 209, and Bliss, *The Real Shakespeare*, 296–97. On a related note, Donald W. Foster, reading the "Shakespeare" poems and writings transcribed by Sarah Taylor Shatford, comments, "it is hard to reconcile the Shakespeare whose voice I think I know with the Shakespeare responsible for Miss Shatford's book of *Revelations*" (Donald W. Foster, "Commentary: In the Name of the Author," *New Literary History* 33, no. 2 [Spring 2002]: 375–96; 391).

67. James M. Frederick and Olga A. Tildes, *The Silver Cord: Life Here and Hereafter* (N.p.: self-published, 1946), 261; Johann Carl Friedrich Zöllner, *Transcendental Physics*, trans. Charles Carleton Massey (New York: W. H. Harrison, 1880), 7, 29; and Bliss, *The Real Shakespeare*, 295. Spiritualists of the Gilded Age began to refer to an "X-Faculty" or an "'X' consciousness"; others wrote of "some general inter-atomic repulsive force"; the Spiritualist L. Kelway Bamber (1919) explained that souls "vibrate at a higher rate than our reality," but that mediums could apprehend their existence in the "Etheric" sphere by making the right harmonic sounds. See Donna M. Lucey, *Archie and Amélie: Love and Madness in the Gilded Age* (New York: Three Rivers Press, 2006), 202, 248; L. Kelway Bamber, *Claude's Book* (London: Methuen, 1918), 68; see also her followup, *Claude's Second Book* (New York: H. Holt, 1919), ix, 72.

68. R. G. Pressing, *Rappings That Startled the World: Facts About the Fox Sisters* (Lily Dale, NY: Dale News, [1940?]), 47. See the terms "clairgustance," "lampadomancy," and "pyroscopy" in the Appendix of this study.

69. On the variety of mediums, see Oppenhiem, *The Other World*, 28–44; and Jenny Hazelgrove, *Spiritualism and British Society Between the Wars*, 6–7.

70. Oppenhiem, *The Other World*, 22. On professional medium fees: In 1852, for example, the medium Mrs. Hayden was charging half a guinea for her spiritual services, about 65 pounds in 2009 money (Owen, *The Darkened Room*, 19).

71. On feminist Spiritualism, see Nina Auerbach, *Daphne du Maurier, Haunted Heiress* (Philadelphia: University of Pennsylvania Press, 2000), 154; Ann Braude, *Radical Spirits: Spiritualism and Women's Rights in Nineteenth-Century America* (Boston: Beacon Press, 1989), 82; and Marlene Tromp, *Altered States: Sex, Nation, Drugs, and Self-Transformation in Victorian Spiritualism* (Albany: State University of New York Press, 2006), 22. On the physical charms of many young female mediums, see Oppenhiem, *The Other World*, 19–21. On the "sexy" séance: Jack Monroe argues that the séance "fostered the lifting of social restraint," both on a personal and political level (Monroe, "Making the Séance 'Serious,'" esp. 226, 228).

72. In 1856, one New Yorker suggested that he and friends should see Kate Fox perform a séance because it was a "good show" and "cheap" (Ronald Pearsall, *The Table-Rappers: The Victorians and the Occult* [1972; repr., Stroud, Gloucestershire: Sutton, 2004], 65). On theatrical fun: Janet Oppenhiem suggests that séances were "jolly good shows" (Oppenhiem, *The Other World*, 25); John Monroe argues that many in France saw séances as pure amusement (Monroe, "Making the Séance 'Serious,'" 221).

73. John Worth Edmonds, George T. Dexter, and Nathaniel Pitcher Tallmadge, *Spiritualism* (New York: Partridge and Brittan, 1853–55), 1:158. Writes John Gray, "The dead were given the task of saving the living; the posthumously designed messiah would save humanity from itself" (Gray, *The Immortalization Commission*, 4).

74. On chariots and sailing, see "Owen Says Heaven Needs Active Men: Sailing One of the Pastimes," *New York Times*, February 5, 1923; on novels and theatre, see Hester Dowden's interviews with Oscar Wilde (Chapter 3, this study); on universities and time travel, see Dodd, *The Immortal Master*, 97; on cities, see Lehman, *Victorian Women and the Theatre of Trance*, 102–14, esp. 111–14 and Jean-Baptiste Delacour, *Glimpses of the Beyond: The Extraordinary Experiences of People Who Have Crossed the Brink of Death and Returned*, trans. E. B. Garside (New York: Delacorte Press, 1974), 168; on fruits and vegetables, see John Worth Edmonds, George T. Dexter, and Nathaniel Pitcher Tallmadge, *Spiritualism*, 1:157; on cigars and whiskey sodas, see Edward Clodd, *The Question: "If a Man Die, Shall He Live Again?": Job XIV 14. A Brief History and Examination of Modern Spiritualism* (New York: E. J. Clode, 1918), 227–28; on flowers, trees, and so on, see G. Wilson Knight's mother's report in Chapter 5 of this study.

75. Henry J. Triezenberg, *Spiritualism: Asking the Dead* (Grand Rapids, MI: Zondervan, 1939), 45.

76. Richard S. Westfall, *The Life of Isaac Newton* (Cambridge: Cambridge University Press, 1994), 117. These and other like theories prompted the modern economist John Maynard Keynes, a keen collector of Newtonia, to opine that "Newton was not the first of the age of reason. He was the last of the magicians"

(quoted in Michael White, *Isaac Newton: The Last Sorcerer* [New York: Basic Books, 1999], 3).

77. Elliott O'Donnell, *The Menace of Spiritualism* (New York: Frederick A. Stokes, 1920), 52. As the title suggests, O'Donnell was not a Spiritualist, though he was far from a rationalist. Wrote O'Donnell: "I believe in ghosts but am not a spiritualist" (quoted in Leslie Shepard, Lewis Spence, and Nandor Fodor, eds., *Encyclopedia of Occultism and Parapsychology*, 3rd ed., s.v. "O'Donnell, Elliott [1872–1965]" [Detroit, MI: Gale Research, 1991], 2:1211).

CHAPTER 1

1. For his part, Foster, an alcoholic, must have enjoyed his evenings with Browne, a whiskey distiller. Within five years of meeting Browne, Foster was taken to Danvers Insane Asylum, Boston, suffering, according to reports, from advanced alcoholism and softening of the brain (Leslie Shepard, Lewis Spence, and Nandor Fodor, eds., *Encyclopedia of Occultism and Parapsychology*, 3rd ed., s.v. "Foster, Charles H. [1838–1888]" [Detroit, MI: Gale, 1991], 1:606–7).

2. Hugh Junor Browne, *The Holy Truth, or, the Coming Reformation* (London: A. Hall, 1876), 59. On how these tricks are performed, see "Skin Writing" and "Pellet Reading" in the Glossary of Spiritual Terms and Techniques in this study. Foster's incantations were not recorded; the version I have inserted is from H. P. Lovecraft's classic story of spiritual possession, "The Rats in the Walls" (1923), from *Tales of H. P. Lovecraft*, ed. Joyce Carol Oates (New York: HarperCollins, 2000), 14–29; 29. Parker himself said that the language was Zulu or Kafar.

3. The prayer is found in National Spiritualist Association of the United States of America, *Spiritualist Manual*, rev. ed. (Washington, DC: National Spiritualist Association of the United States of America, revised, 1925), 27.

4. The hymn, "Abide With Me," was written by Henry F. Lyte in 1847, with music added by William H. Monk in 1861. The penultimate line likely derives from 1 Corinthians 15:55—"O death, where is thy sting?" There is, too, an echo of Shakespeare's *The Passionate Pilgrim*: "death's sharp sting!" (stanza 10, line 4), but I remain doubtful of the synecdoche.

5. Browne, *The Holy Truth*, 207. See also 79, 81, 83, 206.

6. Ibid., 308, 426, 230. The hymn and other preliminary activities of the séance are culled from Arthur Findlay, *On the Edge of the Etheric, or Survival after Death Scientifically Explained* (London: Psychic Books, [1949?]), 75–76; and Gladys Osborne Leonard, *My Life in Two Worlds* (London: Cassell, 1931), 43.

7. Emmanuel Swedenborg, *Dream Diary*, 10ff. quoted in Signe Toksvig, *Emanuel Swedenborg: Scientist and Mystic* (London: Faber, 1949), 142–43. Swedenborg's first name is often spelled as "Emanuel." Where possible, I have regularized to "Emmanuel."

8. The son of god advised him, "Don't eat so much!" (Olof Lagercrantz and Anders Hallengren, *Epic of the Afterlife: A Literary Approach to Swedenborg* [West Chester, PA: Swedenborg Foundation, 2002], 10). Swedenborg seems to

have been a classic binge eater. He began his day with a high-calorie breakfast of cookies, gingerbread, and syrupy-sweet coffee but skipped dinners.

9. Johann Friedrich Immanuel Tafel, *Documents Concerning the Life and Character of Emanuel Swedenborg* (Manchester: Joseph Hayward, 1841), 127.

10. Quoted in Sir Oliver Lodge, *The Survival of Man: A Study in Unrecognized Human Faculty* (New York: George H. Doran, 1909), 121.

11. Emmanuel Swedenborg, *Spiritual Diary*, para. 2542 quoted in David Lorimer, *Survival? Body, Mind and Death in the Light of Psychic Experience* (London: Routledge, 1989), 198.

12. Ian Wilson, *The After Death Experience: The Physics of the Non-Physical* (London: Sidgwick and Jackson, 1987), 58.

13. Tafel, *Documents Concerning the Life and Character of Emanuel Swedenborg*, 119–20.

14. Lagercrantz and Hallengren, *Epic of the Afterlife*, 72–73.

15. Swedenborg discovered this by way of an experiment. He had a spirit "go outside and write a sentence in heavenly characters." He was then asked to read it, only to discover that certain heavenly symbols had no human translation. See Ernst Benz, *Emanuel Swedenborg: Visionary Savant in the Age of Reason*, trans. Nicholas Goodrick-Clarke (West Chester, PA: Swedenborg Foundation, 2002), 328.

16. Samuel M. Warren, *A Compendium of the Theological Writings of Emanuel Swedenborg* (New York: Board of Publication of the General Convention of the New Jerusalem in the U.S., 1875), 721, 723, 724, 727.

17. Ibid., 726.

18. Emanuel Swedenborg, *True Christian Religion: Containing the Universal Theology of the New Church*, 3rd ed. (London: J.Phillips, 1781), 2:60ff.

19. Benz, *Emmanuel Swedenborg*, 334–35. Regarding this debate: Considering Spinoza believed that God exists only as a philosophical concept, this argument should not have been very difficult for Swedenborg to win, as it took place in the Spirit world.

20. Swedenborg, *True Christian Religion*, 605. Swedenborg's Spiritual Library would prove to be important to Baconians, discussed in the next chapter.

21. On Pythagorean thought, see D. P. Walker, *Spiritual and Demonic Magic from Ficino to Campanella* (London: Warburg Institute, University of London, 1958), 12–14; Pythagoras is also discussed in Chapter 2 of this study. On Kabbalah, writes Karen Silvia de León-Jones: "Kabbalah, theology, and philosophy are aspects of an integrated unity. The three cannot be analyzed separately, but must be considered as a whole. The linguistic game of recombining the three terms is itself Kabbalistic" (Karen Silvia de León-Jones, *Giordano Bruno and the Kabbalah: Prophets, Magicians, and Rabbis* [Lincoln: University of Nebraska Press, 2004], 24).

22. George Beaumont, *The Anti-Swedenborg: Or, a Declaration of the Principal Errors Contained in the Theological Writings of E. Swedenborg* (London: Richard Baynes, 1824), 2–3.

23. David George Goyder, *Swedenborg and His Mission* (London: Fred Pitman, 1853), 78.

24. Likely due to rain, commerce was curtailed and the event lost 2,000 pounds, but Garrick paid the difference out of his own pocket. See Christian Deelman, *The Great Shakespeare Jubilee* (New York: Viking Press, 1964), 259; and Jean Benedetti, *David Garrick and the Birth of Modern Theatre* (London: Methuen, 2001), 211.

25. F. E. Halliday, *The Cult of Shakespeare* (London: Gerald Duckworth, 1957), 69.

26. Deelman, *The Great Shakespeare Jubilee*, 7.

27. See Eneas Sweetland Dallas, ed., "The Shakespeare Jubilee," in *Once a Week* 10 (January 16, 1864): 104–12; 105. On "attitude of inspiration," Deelman records that the image "showed Shakespeare caught in a spirited attitude" (Deelman, *The Great Shakespeare Jubilee*, 203).

28. Karl Elze, *William Shakespeare: A Literary Biography*, trans. L. Dora Schmitz (London: G. Bell and Sons, 1888), 532; the poem appears in n. 2. The chalice image was so important that the printed version of the poem takes its form.

29. Thomas Davies, *Memoirs of the Life of David Garrick* (London: self-published, 1780): 2:226. On presentation of the wand, see Deelman, *The Great Shakespeare Jubilee*, 182.

30. Davies, *Memoirs of the Life of David Garrick*, 2:226–27.

31. Deelman, *The Great Shakespeare Jubilee*, 204.

32. Arthur Murphy, *The Life of David Garrick* (Dublin: Brett Smith, 1801), 1:459.

33. George Saville Carey, *Shakespeare's Jubilee, a Masque* (London: T. Becket and P. A. De Hondt, 1769), 14, 23. Carey's poem is given brief treatment in David A. Brewer, *The Afterlife of Character, 1726–1825* (Philadelphia: University of Pennsylvania Press, 2005), 2.

34. Davies, *Memoirs of the Life of David Garrick*, 2:227.

35. John Aubrey, *Brief Lives* (Oxford: Clarendon, 1898), 2:225–27; 226. Dogberry is referred to as the "Constable" but is inexplicably cited as coming from *A Midsummer Night's Dream* (226).

36. Quoted in Edmond Malone and James Boswell Jr., eds., *The Plays and Poems of William Shakespeare* (London: J. R. Rivington, etc., 1821), 20:306n. 4.

37. Charles Dickens, *The Letters of Charles Dickens*, ed. Georgina Hogarth and Mary Dickens, 2nd ed. (London: Chapman and Hall, 1880), 1:178. On P. T. Barnum, see Kim C. Sturgess, *Shakespeare and the American Nation* (New York: Cambridge University Press, 2004), 183.

38. Joseph Ritson, *Remarks, Critical and Illustrative, on the Text and Notes of the Last Edition of Shakspeare* (London: J. Johnson, 1783), vi.

39. Walter Scott, *The Journal of Sir Walter Scott, From the Original Manuscript at Abbotsford* (Edinburgh: David Douglas, 1890), 2:154.

40. Matthew Arnold ["A." on title page], "Shakespeare," in *The Strayed Reveller, and Other Poems* (London: B. Fellowes, 1849), 50.

41. Francis Jeffrey, review of *The Family Shakespeare*, by Thomas Bowdler, *Edinburgh Review* 71 (1821): 52–54; 53. Those who read Shakespeare in secular modes were often more critical. Lewis Theobald (1726) mocked the premise

that Shakespeare's texts should be treated as "sacred Writings"; likewise, William Goodman (1816) considered the apotheosis of Shakespeare to be without merit: "there be persons, who are charmed with the puns and smut and rant and hobgoblins of our . . . '*Divine* Bard,' surely I may be allowed to express my dislike of these without being *abused*." See Lewis Theobald, *Shakespeare Restored: Or, a Specimen of Many Errors, As Well Commited, and Unamended, by Mr. Pope in His Late Edition of This Poet* (London: Francklin, J. Woodman and D. Lyon, and C. Davis, 1726), iv; and William Goodman, "Milton, Shakespear, and Potatoes," letter to *Cobbett's Political Register* 30 (January 20, 1816): 82–84; 82. Scholarly editions of Shakespeare, unaffected by Bowdler, were also produced, but, as the nineteenth century wore on, general readers, particularly religiously minded readers, preferred Bowdlerization. In the *Morning Light: The New-Church Weekly* (1880), we read of a group of boys who wanted to buy an edition of Shakespeare as a wedding gift for their teacher, Mr. Page: "In the two previous instances the class had taken the opportunity of presenting superb editions of the Holy Scriptures, as being the worthiest gift they could offer to those entering upon the blessings and duties of married life. In the present case they had learned that their friend was possessed of a beautiful copy of the Bible . . . They were therefore gratified in offering to him the noblest monument of English literature in a copy of the works of William Shakespeare." This was not, however, a culled edition, but one "in which virtue and vice were inextricably intermingled." The distressed boys therefore trusted that Mr. and Mrs. Page would self-edit the text, dwelling only on those passages in which "the human heart expressed" itself "in fittest and finest language." See "News of the New Church," *Morning Light: The New-Church Weekly* 3 (December 11, 1880): 498–500; 499.

42. William Dodd, *The Beauties of Shakespeare* (London: Chiswick Press, 1821), viii.

43. Thomas Carlyle, "The Hero as Poet: Dante; Shakspeare," in *On Heroes, Hero-worship, and the Heroic in History: Six Lectures* (New York: John Wiley, 1849), 70–102; 99, 100, 101, 100.

44. J. M., *Shakespeare Self-Revealed in His "Sonnets" and "Phoenix and Turtle"* (London: Sherratt and Hughes, 1904), 137.

45. Joseph Howard Jr., *Life of Henry Ward Beecher, the Eminent Pulpit and Platform Orator* (Philadelphia: Hubbard, 1887), 254, 256–57.

46. William Burgess, *The Bible in Shakspeare: A Study of the Relation of the Works of William Shakspeare to the Bible* (New York: Thomas Y. Crowell, 1903), xiii. The critic and artist John Ruskin, for example, wrote that when the troubles of the world overwhelmed him, he put himself into a "strange lethargy and trance" in which he could commune with the spirit of Shakespeare. Ruskin then rhapsodized passages from *Hamlet* and *Lear* as if they were biblical divination and instruction of moral laws: "The gods are just, and of our pleasant vices make instruments to scourge us"; "There's a divinity that shapes our ends, rough hew them how we will" (John Ruskin, *Sesame and Lilies*, rev. ed. [New York: John Wiley and Son, 1873], 137, 141). More recently, Jack Lynch described

eighteenth- and nineteenth-century visits to Stratford thus: "They [visitors] wanted to stand over his remains and contemplate their own mortality" (Jack Lynch, *Becoming Shakespeare: The Unlikely Afterlife That Turned a Provincial Playwright into the Bard* [New York: Walker, 2007], 245).

47. See, for example, Henry James, "The Birthplace," in *The Altar of the Dead: The Beast in the Jungle; The Birthplace, and Other Tales* (New York: Charles Scribner's Sons, 1909), 128–213; 153. See also Jean I. Marsden, *The Re-Imagined Text: Shakespeare, Adaptation, and Eighteenth-Century Literary Theory* (Lexington: University Press of Kentucky, 1995), 127. The present worship of Shakespeare, and the monies still generated from tourists who descend upon Stratford-upon-Avon, is ably covered in Barbara Hodgdon's *The Shakespeare Trade: Performance and Appropriations* (Philadelphia: University of Pennsylvania Press, 1998).

48. James Walter, *Shakespeare's True Life* (London: Longmans, Green, 1890), 285.

49. William Shakespeare, *The Winter's Tale*, in *The Riverside Shakespeare*, ed. G. Blakemore Evans and J. J. M. Tobin, 2nd ed. (New York: Houghton Mifflin, 1997), 5.3.110–11. All subsequent citations of Shakespeare's texts, unless otherwise indicated, are from this source.

50. William Shakespeare, *1 Henry IV*, 3.1.14–17, 17–19, 20–22, 52–54.

51. *The Lancet* 2 [now 76] (November 10, 1860): 466.

52. Shakespeare, *1Henry IV*, 3.1.148–52.

53. Charles Lamb, "On the Tragedies of Shakespeare," *Reflector 1810–1811* in *The Complete Works in Prose and Verse of Charles Lamb*, ed. R. H. Shepherd (London: Chatto and Windus, 1875), 253–65; 254, 263, 261, 262, 264.

54. The remark was made by actress Fanny Kemble (1833). See Marvin Rosenberg, *The Masks of Macbeth* (Newark: University of Delaware Press, 1992), 9. The Regency actor John Philip Kemble dismissed Macbeth's fear of ghosts as a "superstition" that proceeds not from a fear of real supernatural activity but from simple "credulity"; Richard III was not haunted by ghosts but by his own conscience (John Philip Kemble, *Macbeth, and King Richard the Third: An Essay, in Answer to Remarks on Some of the Characters of Shakspeare* [London, John Murray, 1817], 122, 127).

55. Diane Long Hoeveler, *Gothic Riffs: Secularizing the Uncanny in the European Imagery, 1780–1820* (Columbus: Ohio State University Press, 2010), 57.

56. In terms of full stagings, *Winter's Tale* had a score of London performances throughout the eighteenth century; *Pericles*—often dismissed as a non-Shakespearean play—had none. See the entries for each play in Ben Ross Schneider Jr., ed., *Index to the London Stage, 1660–1800* (Carbondale: Southern Illinois University Press, 1979).

57. R. A. Foakes, "'Armed at Point Exactly': The Ghost in *Hamlet*," *Shakespeare Survey* 58 (2005): 34–47; 40. On embarrassment, albeit of nonsupernatural Shakespeare, see also Michael Dobson, *The Making of the National Poet: Shakespeare, Adaptation and Authorship, 1660–1769* (New York: Oxford University Press, 1992), 187; in the same study, he suggests that bardolatry was linked to nature (217). This may account for the reluctance to discuss or to stage the Supernatural (which throws the natural order into disorder). The

well-respected eighteenth-century theater critic James Boaden suggested that actors should abandon the ghost scenes in *Hamlet*. He presented this suggestion in a play, *Fountainville Forest* (Diane Long Hoeveler, *Gothic Riffs: Secularizing the Uncanny in the European Imagery, 1780–1820*, 130–31). On ghosts and witches as an offense to modern sensibilities, see also Robert Hunter West, *Shakespeare and the Outer Mystery* (Lexington: University of Kentucky Press, 1968), 42. Marvin Rosenberg notes that post-Jacobean theater was "increasingly sceptical of the supernatural" elements in Hamlet, but cites no specific dates or examples (Marvin Rosenberg, *The Masks of Hamlet* [Newark: University of Delaware Press: Associated University Presses, 1992], 21).

58. "*The Tempest*: An Old Playgoer's Appreciation of the Important Shakespearean Revival at the Royal," *The Irish Playgoer and Amusement Record* 1, no. 15 (February 15, 1900): 4.

59. In Richard Wilson's *Shakespeare in French Theory: King of Shadows* (New York: Routledge/Francis and Taylor, 2007), Shakespeare is depicted as a shadow "menacing" the clarity of neoclassical logic and decorum. Likewise, we can glimpse in that argument the very reason why Shakespirtualism had been hitherto shunned by Shakespeareans; it links their revered subject of study and their legitimate practice to an anarchic, anti-intellectualism (35–39).

60. Antonio Melechi, *Servants of the Supernatural: The Night Side of the Victorian Mind* (London: William Heinemann, 2008), 11. Mesmer's fame later influenced Mary Shelley, who had her Victor Frankenstein attend Ingolstadt for medical, rather than theological, training (Jane R. Goodall, *Stage Presence* [New York: Routledge, 2008], 89).

61. Charles Knight, *The English Cyclopaedia: A New Dictionary of Universal Knowledge*, vol. 5 (London: Bradbury and Evans, 1860), 679. On Mesmer's clothing, see Ronald Pearsall, *The Table-Rappers: The Victorians and the Occult* (1972; repr., Stroud, Gloucestershire: Sutton, 2004), 17.

62. Pearsall, *The Table-Rappers*, 16; and Goodall, *Stage Presence*, 85. The supernaturalism of Mesmer's cures was doubtless aided by the creator of his magnets, Maximillian Hell—his real name. Hell was a Jesuit professor of astronomy. See Melechi, *Servants of the Supernatural*, 11.

63. Robert Darnton, *Mesmerism and the End of the Enlightenment in France* (New York: Schocken Books, 1970), 8.

64. Pearsall, *The Table-Rappers*, 17.

65. Margaret Goldsmith, *Franz Anton Mesmer: A History of Mesmerism* (Garden City, NY: Doubleday, Doran, 1934), 164.

66. Vincent Buranelli, *The Wizard From Vienna* (London: Peter Owen, 1975), 128–29; see also 14, 83. It wasn't all hypnotic fun and games. Mesmer also founded the "Society of Harmony," a secretive group that was said to promote science, humanitarianism, and, of course, Mesmerism—Hogwarts avant la lettre (149). See also Wouter J. Hanegraaff, *New Age Religion and Western Culture: Esotericism in the Mirror of Secular Thought* (Albany: State University of New York Press, 1998), 436, 431–33.

67. Melechi, *Servants of the Supernatura*, 12–16; and Franz Anton Mesmer, *Mesmerism: A Translation of the Original Scientific and Medical Writings of F. A. Mesmer* (Los Altos, CA: Kaufmann, 1980), 27.

68. See Jean-Sylvain Bailly, *Exposé* (1784), translation found in Jessica Riskin, *Science in the Age of Sensibility: The Sentimental Empiricists of the French Enlightenment* (Chicago: University of Chicago Press, 2002), 223; and Pearsall, *The Table-Rappers*, 16. See also D. Scott Rogo, *Parapsychology: A Century of Inquiry* (Los Angeles: Taplinger, 1975), 37. For more on Mesmerism and revolutionary politics, see Darnton, *Mesmerism and the End of the Enlightenment in France*, 70–73.

69. For an overview, see G. S. [Hugh Macneile, Dean of Ripon], *Mesmerism the Gift of God: In Reply to "Satanic Agency and Mesmerism"* (London: William Edward Painter, 1843), esp. 12.

70. On interchangeable aspects of Swedenborgism, Mesmerism, and Spiritualism, see J. W. Jackson, "To the Editor of the Intellectual Repository," *The Zoist: A Journal of Cerebral Physiology and Mesmerism, and Their Applications to Human Welfare* 12 (1855): 367; George Bush, *Mesmer and Swedenborg: Or, the Relation of the Developments of Mesmerism to the Doctrines and Disclosures of Swedenborg* (New York: John Allen, 1847), 199; James R. Lewis, ed., *Odd Gods: New Religions and the Cult Controversy* (Amherst, NY: Prometheus Books, 2001), 339; Peter Washington, *Madame Blavatsky's Baboon: A History of the Mystics, Mediums, and Misfits Who Brought Spiritualism to America* (1993; repr., New York: Schocken Books, 1995), 16–18; and Fredrik Johan Björnström, *Hypnotism: Its History and Present Development*, trans. Baron Nils Posse (New York: Humboldt, 1889), 9. In America, the teachings of Swedenborg and Mesmer took root in part because of the French Mesmerist Charles Poyen, who visited New England in 1837 to promote "magnetic healing" (Nancy Rubin Stuart, *The Reluctant Spiritualist: The Life of Maggie Fox* [New York: Harcourt, 2005], 45). An 1852 pamphlet by Rev. John Bywater of Rochester, New York, entitled *The Mystery Solved*, informed the public that one apparition, Samuel C. Wood, had explained to him that ghosts were created by electrical power. Mediums were necessary only insofar as they had an unique overcapacity of "nerve-vital fluid," and were thus "better conductors of electricity" (cited in R. G. Pressing, *Rappings That Startled the World: Facts About the Fox Sisters* [Lily Dale, NY: Dale News, (1940?)], 37); WorldCat gives the date as 1852, but Pressing dates Bywater's work to 1842. In the 1850s, the American mystic Andrew Jackson Davis claimed that while in a trance he could communicate with the dead and included Swedenborg among his many contacts (Andrew Jackson Davis, *The Principles of Nature, Her Divine Revelations* [New York: S. S. Lyon and W. Fishbough, 1851], 587, and Andrew Jackson Davis, *The Magic Staff: An Autobiography* [New York: J. S. Brown, 1857], 333). See also Bush, *Mesmer and Swedenborg*, 189; Harvey L. Eads, *Shaker Sermons: Scripto-Rational. Containing the Substance of Shaker Theology. Together With Replies and Criticisms Logically and Clearly Set Forth*, 3rd ed. (South Union, KY: no publisher, 1884), 232; and Rogo, *Parapsychology: A Century of Inquiry*, 42–43. Mesmer's theories

have also been connected to the Theosophy movement (Goodall, *Stage Presence*, 105). Swedenborgian thought also informs Theosophy. See Alvin Boyd Kuhn, who notes that Theosophists believed that a metaphysical double existed for all objects, including other planets (*Theosophy: A Modern Revival of Ancient Wisdom* [New York: Henry Holt, 1930], 230, 310).

71. James Wyckoff, *Franz Anton Mesmer: Between God and Devil* (Englewood Cliffs, NJ: Prentice-Hall, 1975), 136–37. In 1884, Edmund Gurney argued that the unconscious might be responsible for some seemingly Spiritual phenomena, like automatic writing, but his views were generally ignored by Spiritualist believers (*Proceedings of the Society for Psychical Research* 2 [November 28, 1884]: 223–24). On the spreading of Mesmerism, see also Rudolf Steiner, *Spiritualism, Madame Blavatsky, and Theosophy: An Eye Witness View of Occult History*, ed. Christopher Bamford (Great Barrington, MA: Anthroposophic Press, 2001), 73.

72. To Bush, it was self-evident that Mesmerism, with its séance trappings, served as a "providential attestation" to Swedenborg's conversations with Spirits. See his *Mesmer and Swedenborg*, vii.

73. On Kate Fox, see entry for December 6, 1870 in Kate Fox, *Fox-Taylor Automatic Writing 1869–1892 Unabridged Record*, ed. Sarah E. L. Taylor (Minneapolis, MN: Tribune-Great West, privately published, 1932), 162. On skepticism as a force capable of dispersing psychical energy, see also Stephen E. Braude, *The Limits of Influence: Psychokinesis and the Philosophy of Science* (New York: Routledge and Kegan Paul, 1986), 285.

74. Fox, *Fox-Taylor Automatic Writing 1869–1892*, 162). However, Franklin urged perseverance, since the main conductor of Spiritualism was not electricity or magnets but belief itself: "Faith guides the honest heart in all things, and is one of the strongest magnets between earth and heaven" (363). On electromagnetism and Spiritual communication: On January 10, 1870, Kate failed to reach the Spirits because the "earth is full of dampness, very little electricity in the air, therefore we failed"; on June 29, 1870, a spirit, Olin, complained that "If we only had a cool, clear atmosphere there would be no difficulty"; on June 30, 1870, Kate was pleased because "the atmosphere is not heated . . . and we have worked with power"; and so forth (8, 96, 96–97).

75. Horace Howard Furness, *Letters of Horace Howard Furness* (Boston: Houghton Mifflin, 1922), 2:261.

76. Darnton, *Mesmerism and the End of the Enlightenment in France*, 47. Likewise, Jane Goodall notes that many nineteenth-century theatergoers often described being "galvanized" or "mesmerized" by star actors. She then links this language to Mesmer. (Goodall, *Stage Presence*, 58, 127, 84–121).

77. Goodall, *Stage Presence*, 11; and Augustine of Hippo, *The City of God*, trans. Marcus Dods (Edinburgh: T. and T. Clark, 1888), 1:241, 240.

78. For a useful overview, see Ronald W. Vince, *Ancient and Medieval Theatre: A Historiographical Handbook* (Westport, CT: Greenwood Press, 1984), 89–129.

79. Stephen Greenblatt, *Shakespearean Negotiations: The Circulation of Social Energy in Renaissance England* (Berkeley: University of California Press, 1988),

125–27; 127. A similar argument is presented in Greenblatt's *Hamlet in Purgatory* (Princeton, NJ: Princeton University Press, 2001), 258–61. This time, however, the process is unconscious and uncalculated.

80. On the question of fakery: Marion Gibson points out that defining witchcraft is a complicated business; the term must be "defined here as agreed patterns used by communities and members of those communities to identify individual events or people as connected with the impossible crime of witchcraft" (Marion Gibson, *Reading Witchcraft: Stories of Early English Witches* [New York: Routledge, 1999], 5).

81. Bridget Bennett, *Transatlantic Spiritualism and Nineteenth-Century American Literature* (New York: Palgrave Macmillan, 2007), 85. We should note one major exception: French Spiritualism, in which Shakespeare played almost no religious role at all. This was almost entirely due to Allan Kardec (actual name: Hippolyte Léon Denizard Rivail). In 1858 Kardec, a born bureaucrat, set up a national network—the Société d'Etudes Spirites—to record psychic phenomena. (Kardec served as both its leader—his followers called him "master"—and adjudicator.) Spiritual revelations had to be first submitted to a local Société Spirite, then passed along to a central Parisian office, where Kardec would judge whether the new experience fit within his system. If acceptable, it might thereafter be published in one of his forthcoming books; if not, the revelation would be rejected. The chief elements that Kardec wanted wheedled from the séance were its gimmickry, its "charlatanism and jugglery," and its "parlour trick" aspects—in sum, its theatricality. See Lynn L. Sharp, *Secular Spirituality: Reincarnation and Spiritism in Nineteenth-Century France* (Lanham, MD: Lexington Books, 2006), 77; and Jack Monroe, "Making the Séance 'Serious': *Tables Tournantes* and the Second Empire Bourgeois Culture, 1852–1861," *History of Religions* 38, no. 3 (February 1999): 219–46; 239, 241.

82. *The Medium and Daybreak* (1878): 393; Reuben Briggs Davenport, *The Death-Blow to Spiritualism* (New York: G. W. Dillingham, 1888), 197; and Maurice Leonard, *People from the Other Side: The Enigmatic Fox Sisters and the History of Victorian Spiritualism* (Stroud, Gloucestershire: History Press, 2008), 112. See also Leonard Zusne and Warren H Jones, *Anomalistic Psychology: A Study of Magical Thinking* (Hillsdale, NJ: L. Erlbaum, 1989), 99.

83. Raymond Buckland, *Solitary Séance: How You Can Talk With Spirits on Your Own* (Woodbury, MN: Llewellyn Publications, 2011), 73.

84. Earnest Isaacs, "The Fox Sisters and American Spiritualism," in *The Occult in America: New Historical Perspectives*, ed. Howard Ker and Charles L. Crow (Chicago: University of Illinois Press, 1986), 79–110; 102.

85. On Margaret, see Barbara Weisberg, *Talking to the Dead: Kate and Maggie Fox and the Rise of Spiritualism* (New York: HarperCollins, 2004), 244; on Kate, see Fox, *Fox-Taylor Automatic Writing 1869–1892*, 97; on Leah and the sisters' theatricality in general, see Charles Robert Richet, *Thirty Years of Psychical Research: Being a Treatise on Metaphysics*, trans. Stanley De Brath (London: Collins and Sons, 1923), 479; and Ann Braude, *Radical Spirits: Spiritualism and*

Women's Rights in Nineteenth-Century America (Boston: Beacon Press, 1989), 17.

86. Robert Dale Owen, *The Debatable Land Between This World and the Next: With Illustrative Narrations* (London: Trübner, 1871), 270.

87. Mary Roach, *Spook: Science Tackles the Afterlife* (New York: W. W. Norton, 2005), 196.

88. E. Lee Howard, *My Adventure into Spiritualism* (New York: Macmillan, 1935), 109, 39. Writes Clarke Garrett, "spirit possession is a kind of theater, communicating the experience of the sacred through culturally comprehensible words and gestures to the believing community" (Clarke Garrett, *Origins of the Shakers: From the Old World to the New World* [Baltimore, MD: Johns Hopkins University Press, 1998], 10).

89. Harry Houdini, *A Magician Among the Spirits* (1924; repr., Amsterdam: Fredonia Books, 2002), 145.

90. J. Saunders, "Civic Government," *London* 5–6 (1843): 81–96; 95. See also "On a Visit to the Egyptian Hall," *Punch* 68–69 (February 20, 1875): 81–96; 85–86. Smaller séances were sometimes held under the main stage of a theater, the portion Shakespeare's contemporaries would call the "Hell." So recalls the medium Gladys Osborne Leonard (1931), "We [she and her husband] used to wander about the theatre, looking for a quiet spot. It seemed hopeless, till one night we discovered a very steep, narrow staircase leading down from the stage. We climbed down it, though actually we had no right to do so, and found ourselves in a large deserted place, among all the different engines and machinery that were used for the heating, lighting and other purposes of the theatre . . . We took them down the stairs with all secrecy, desperately hoping we should not be discovered. Between nine and ten o'clock we had a 'wait,' so we determined to sit every evening at this time" (Leonard, *My Life in Two Worlds*, 43–44).

91. May Wright Sewall, *Neither Dead Nor Sleeping* (Indianapolis, IN: Bobbs-Merrill, 1920), 97–99. *The Phreno-Magnet, and Mirror of Nature* 1 (1843) details similar manifestations of ordinary people suddenly able to play the parts of Coriolanus, Juliet, and Macbeth (11, 93, 189). However, in these instances, the behavior is explained away as a trick of hypnosis or, as the *Phreno-Magnet* terms it, "Magnetism" (1). See also Ilana Kurshan, "Mind Reading: Literature in the Discourse of Early Victorian Phrenology and Mesmerism," in *Victorian Literary Mesmerism*, ed. Martin Willis and Catherine Wynne (New York: Rodopi, 2006), 17–38; 28. Jane Goodall connects acting to self-hypnosis (Goodall, *Stage Presence*, 102).

92. On the link between method acting and the séance, see Tatiana Kontou, *Spiritualism and Women's Writing: From the Fin de Siècle to the Neo-Victorian* (New York: Palgrave Macmillan, 2009), 10, 16, 26, 27.

93. Frances H. Green, *Biography of Mrs. Semantha Mettler, The Clairvoyant* (New York: Harmonial Association, 1853), 103; see also 90.

94. Zenor was memorialized in James Crenshaw, *Telephone Between Worlds*, 6th printing (Los Angeles: De Vorss, 1957. Zenor's demonstrations of psychic ability included alleged conversations with Spirits on (I) the state of the soul after

death and (II) prognostications on earthly events. On the latter, the Spirits were rather vague in virtually all cases. For example, on January 12, 1945, Zenor received the following message: "Some very startling news comes out, very important news, about Hitler that the American people have been waiting for"; on February, 23 1945, "There will be some startling news soon about Goering"; on March 16, 1945, "You are going to read some very startling news about Hitler. I can see that in big black letters on the front page, of course, and it seems as though it's startling news and good news, of course, so far as the American people are concerned"; on March 23, 1945: "Some startling news will be brought to bear about Hitler, some awful things," and so on (179).

95. Crenshaw, *Telephone Between Worlds*, 225.

CHAPTER 2

1. These were standard nineteenth-century treatments for madness. See Indiana Commission on Public Records, "Medical Treatment for Insanity," Accessed September 1, 2012. http://www.in.gov/icpr/2704.htm.

2. Ignatius Donnelly quotes this story, as reported in the December 26, 1886 Philadelphia *Times*, in his *The Great Cryptogram: Francis Bacon's Cipher in the So-Called Shakespeare Plays* (New York: R. S. Peale, 1887), 902.

3. Delia Bacon, *The Philosophy of the Plays of Shakspere Unfolded* (Boston: Ticknor and Fields, 1857), xxii.

4. Ibid., xix

5. Ibid., xciii, xcvii

6. Nathaniel Hawthorne, "Recollections of a Gifted Woman," in *Our Old Home* (London: Smith, Elder, 1864), 78–105; 91–92. Delia Bacon believed that Providence was guiding her work, even setting up tests of her faith (Vivian C. Hopkins, *Prodigal Puritan: A Life of Delia Bacon* [Cambridge, MA: Belknap Press of Harvard University Press, 1959], 265).

7. Mrs. John Farrar, *Recollections of Seventy Years* (Boston: Ticknor and Field, 1865), 320–21. This might be an appropriate moment to point out that Henry James argued that doubters of Shakespeare's authorship underwent a crisis of faith. On James, see Charles Laporte, "The Bard, the Bible, and the Victorian Shakespeare Question," *ELH* 74 (2007): 609–28; esp. 623. As this chapter attests, quite the opposite was true: Doubters of Shakespeare's authorship relied upon Spiritual faith as a form of evidence.

8. Hawthorne, "Recollections of a Gifted Woman," 94.

9. Ibid., 97–98.

10. Delia Bacon was an inmate at Bloomingdale Asylum, New York, from mid-April to late-July 1859 (Hopkins, *Prodigal Puritan*, 259). See also Theodore Bacon, *Delia Bacon: A Biographical Sketch* (Boston: Houghton, Mifflin, 1888), 12; and John Michell, *Eccentric Lives and Peculiar Notions*, 2nd ed. (New York: Black Dog and Leventhal, 1999), 184–91.

11. Edmund Routledge, ed. *Every Boy's Book: A Complete Encyclopædia of Sports and Amusements* (London: George Routledge and Sons, 1881), 769.

12. Donnelly, *The Great Cryptogram*, 545.

13. Ibid., 515.

14. Walter Begley, *Is it Shakespeare? The Great Question of Elizabethan Literature* (New York: E. P. Dutton, 1903), 305.

15. Larry Richard Peterson, *Ignatius Donnelly: A Psychohistorical Study in Moral Development Psychology, Dissertations in American Biography* (PhD Thesis, University of Minnesota, 1977; repr., New York: Arno Press, 1982), 90–91.

16. *Case and Comment: The Lawyer's Magazine* 22 (June 1916–May 1917): 57.

17. Gerald W. Johnson, *The Lunatic Fringe* (Westport, CT: Greenwood Press, 1957), 137; and Peterson, *Ignatius Donnelly*, 151–52. On insults of Donnelly: Algernon Charles Swinburne renamed Ignatius Donnelly as "Athanasius Dogberry"—St. Athanasius (ca. 296–373) is known among Protestants as "Father of The Canon"; Dogberry is a comical character in Shakespeare who misuses words (Algernon Charles Swinburne, *A Study of Ben Jonson* [London: Chatto and Windus, 1889], 181).

18. William Shakespeare, *Macbeth*, in *The Riverside Shakespeare*, ed. G. Blakemore Evans and J. J. M. Tobin, 2nd ed. (New York: Houghton Mifflin, 1997), 5.5.48. All subsequent citations of Shakespeare's texts, unless otherwise indicated, are from this source.

19. Ignatius Donnelly, *The Cipher in the Plays and on the Tombstone* (Minneapolis, MN: Verulam, 1899), 335. In 1899 Horace Howard Furness argued, perhaps seriocomically, that Shakespeare wrote Bacon—at least his magisterial *Advancement of Learning*. According to Furness, Bacon then came to believe that he actually wrote the book, a wish-fulfillment that then led to his later claim that he was actually the author of Shakespeare's plays: "he [Bacon] thought, he would make sure of a posthumous revenge should the [supposed] anagram [placed on the prefatory material of the First Folio] be deciphered: 'If Shakespeare succeeds in claiming my philosophy, I will take his plays in exchange'" (Horace Howard Furness, "The Argument for Shakespeare as Shakespeare," in *Shakespeare and His Rivals: A Casebook on the Authorship Controversy*, ed. George McMichael and Edgar M. Glenn [New York: Odyssey Press, 1962], 225–30; 228).

20. Peterson, *Ignatius Donnelly*, 168.

21. Donnelly, *The Cipher in the Plays and on the Tombstone*, 364–65.

22. Ibid., 364.

23. Ibid., 94.

24. Ibid., 365.

25. Peterson, *Ignatius Donnelly*, 151.

26. Donnelly, *The Cipher in the Plays and on the Tombstone*, 348, 336. Likewise, Percy Allen writes of the bliss of the "Greater Initiation," presumably, being one of the select few who understands the "three-fold drama"—three-fold in that we have (1) the play, (2) the drama of finding the clues to unlock the cipher, and (3) the deciphered text, which reveals the true "author" of the plays and their mystical meanings (*The Oxford-Shakespeare Case Corroborated* [London: Cecil Palmer, 1931], 69).

27. J. Henderson, "A Remarkable Seance," *Light: A Journal of Psychical, Occult, and Mystical Research* 10 (June 7, 1890): 278–79.

28. See the advertisement at the end of volume 2 of Orville Ward Owen, *Sir Francis Bacon's Cipher Story* (Detroit, MI: Howard, 1893). Fact check: In 1576, Queen Elizabeth appointed Sir Amias Paulet ambassador to Paris and put the young Francis Bacon under his charge. That hardly sounds like banishment. Besides, Bacon was only 15 years old at the time, so it's difficult to imagine him having committed a crime worthy of exile. On the creation of the Bacon cipher while the author was in Paris, see Baxter, *The Greatest of Literary Problems*, 530.

29. Owen, *Sir Francis Bacon's Cipher Story*, 1:175.

30. G. Ward Price, *Extra-Special Correspondent* (London: G. Harrap, 1957), 21, 22. A similar latent violence informs Penn Leary's *The Second Cryptographic Shakespeare* (Omaha, NE: Westchester House, 1990), in which Shakespeare is an eternal vampire that must be destroyed so that the text may be freed: "Through the leaded, dusty glasswork of our illusory casement window we may glance into Stratford Church itself. There, where it has anonymously rested upon the floor of the Chancel since 1616, is Mr. Shake-speare's purported gravestone. We intend to pursue this plebeian to the edge of the hereafter; we shall hound him into his very tomb; we shall drive our cryptographic quill into his rustic heart" (4–5).

31. Price, *Extra-Special Correspondent*, 20. See also "Seeking Bacon Manuscripts in the River Wye: Dr. Orville W. Owen's Curious Search to Prove That Bacon Wrote the Shakespeare Plays Interests and Amuses England," *The New York Times*, May 14, 1911, SM6; and "Bacon-Shakespeare Riddle in River Bed: Detroit Doctor Excavates the Wye for Proof That Bacon Wrote Bard's Works," *The New York Times* February 26, 1911, C1. Marjorie Garber states that Colonel Fabyan, a financial backer of Elizabeth Wells Gallup, also contributed funds (Marjorie Garber, *Shakespeare's Ghost Writers* [New York: Methuen, 1987], 5).

32. Price, *Extra-Special Correspondent*, 23.

33. Ibid., 24. Owen's behavior was by no means unique. John Mackinnon Robertson complained that Baconians were nothing more than a group of "enthusiasts, impostors, and dupes" intent upon exposing one "of the grossest frauds" of all time—i.e., the "true" identity/identities of Shakespeare (*Pioneer Humanists* [London: Watts, 1907], 42).

34. On Owen as fraudster, see William F. Friedman and Elizabeth S. Friedman, *The Shakespearean Ciphers Examined: An Analysis of Cryptographic Systems Used as Evidence that Some Author Other Than William Shakespeare Wrote the Plays Commonly Attributed to Him* (Cambridge: Cambridge University Press, 1957), 69–71.

35. Elizabeth Wells Gallup, *The Bi-literal Cypher of Sir Francis Bacon, Discovered in His Works* rev. ed. (Detroit, MI: Howard, 1910), 1:22. On authorial attributions for Jonson, see 2:62–71; for Greene, 2:80, 175; for Marlowe, 2:173; for Spenser, 2:180; for *Sir John Oldcastle*, 2:15–16; and for *Yorkshire Tragedy*, 2:78–79. The aforementioned plays are often grouped as part of the *Shakespeare Apocrypha*. More recently, the *Yorkshire Tragedy* has been regularly attributed to Thomas Middleton.

36. Gallup, *Bi-literal Cypher of Sir Francis Bacon*, 2:28.

37. Elizabeth Wells Gallup, *The Tragedy of Anne Boleyn: A Drama in Cipher Found in the Works of Sir Francis Bacon* (Detroit, MI: Howard, 1901), 135. See Elizabeth Wells Gallup, "Announcement," in *The Bi-literal Cypher of Sir Francis Bacon, Discovered in His Works*, 3:136–37.

38. Gallup, *Bi-literal Cypher of Sir Francis Bacon*, 2:55.

39. Gallup, *Tragedy of Anne Boleyn*, xxii.

40. Gallup, *The Bi-literal Cypher of Sir Francis Bacon*, 1:2, 22.

41. Ibid., 3:4.

42. Ibid., 3:5.

43. Ibid., 3:3.

44. Ibid., 3:8.

45. Ibid., 3:13.

46. Ibid., 3:8.

47. See review of her work in *Baconiana*, 3, no. 1 (1903): 58.

48. See his letter to Sanborn Pitts (June 27, 1927), Huntington Library Manuscript Collection.

49. See Walter Conrad Arensberg, Letters, Huntington Library Manuscript Collection. William Carlos Williams, while not mentioning Arensberg, dismissed the possibility that Bacon was Shakespeare (William Carlos Williams, *The Embodiment of Knowledge*, introduction by Ron Loewinsohn [New York: New Directions, 1977], 136). William Carlos Williams won the Pulitzer in 1964, well after his correspondence with Arensberg, but his fame had been cemented as early as the 1930s.

50. Christopher Isherwood, *Lost Years: A Memoir 1945–1951*, ed. Katherine Bucknell (New York: HarperCollins, 2000), 29–30.

51. Herbert Silberer, *Problems of Mysticism and Its Symbolism* (New York: Moffat, Yard, 1917), 228.

52. S. L. MacGregor, *Kabbala Denudata: The Kabbalah Unveiled, Containing the Following Books of the Zohar* (London: Kegan Paul, Trench, Trubner, 1926), 117.

53. Walter Conrad Arensberg, *The Shakespearean Mystery* (Pittsburgh: self-published, 1927), 24.

54. Walter Conrad Arensberg, *The Secret Grave of Francis Bacon at Lichfield* (San Francisco: John Howell, 1923), 38–39, 40.

55. Arensberg, *The Shakespearean Mystery*, 163.

56. Walter Conrad Arensberg, *Burial of Francis Bacon and His Mother in the Lichfield Chapter House* (Pittsburgh, PA: self-published, 1924), 20.

57. Arensberg, *The Secret Grave of Francis Bacon at Lichfield*, 16.

58. The same counterargument can be applied to Bacon's use of a secret code: Arensberg argued that Bacon "intended to express a meaning which is intentionally concealed" or, still more convolutedly, that "the Shakespearean mystery was created by Bacon for the purpose of being discovered as the result of the discovery of the method in accordance with which it is expressed." See Arensberg, *The Shakespearean Mystery*, 13, 24.

59. In fact, Arensberg argued, Freemasonry was created as a functional subsidiary for Bacon's secret. See Arensberg, *Burial of Francis Bacon and His Mother*, 8.

60. Arensberg, *The Secret Grave of Francis Bacon at Lichfield*, 16, 45. In *The Shake-spearean Mystery*, Arensberg adds that he has "conclusive [though unstated] evidence that the Shakespearean mystery has been guarded continuously, and is guarded today, by members of the Fraternitas R.C (R.C. = Rosicrcusians)," 323.

61. Arensberg, *Burial of Francis Bacon and His Mother*, 45. See also Arensberg, *The Secret Grave of Francis Bacon at Lichfield*, 20.

62. Arensberg, *The Secret Grave of Francis Bacon at Lichfield*, 17–18. Arensberg was not alone in the belief that the official tomb did not house Bacon's bones. See C. Le Poer Kennedy, *Notes and Queries*, 2nd ser., 9 (February 1918): 132, cited in David Ovason, *Shakespeare's Secret Booke: Deciphering Magical and Rosicrucian Codes* (Forest Row, East Sussex: Clairview, 2010), 43. On other theories as to Bacon's final resting place, see Maria Bauer, who supported Owen's contention that Bacon was the true heir of Queen Elizabeth but believes that Bacon's remains were placed in a Virginian vault—the territory named after his supposed mother—along with his manuscripts; however, she explained that "vested money interests have thus far prevented the actual opening of the vault" (Margaret Storm, *Return of the Dove* [Baltimore, MD: Margaret Storm, 1957], 267). See also Maria Bauer, *Francis Bacon's Great Virginia Vault* (self-published, 1939) and her *Foundations Unearthed* (Glendale, CA: Veritas Press, 1944).

63. Arensberg, *The Secret Grave of Francis Bacon at Lichfield*, 18.

64. Ibid., 15.

65. Ibid., 13.

66. The application was submitted to the Dean of Litchfield Cathedral on April 19, 1923. See Ibid., 46.

67. Isherwood, *Lost Years*, 30.

68. Alfred Dodd, *The Immortal Master* (London: Rider, [1943]), 45–49; 48.

69. Ibid., 50. The Marlowe Society links this same sonnet to the allegedly faked death of Christopher Marlowe. See "Marlowe in Exile? 3. Sonnet 74," The Marlowe Society, accessed September 1, 2012. http://www.marlowe-society .org/marlowe/life/exile3.html.

70. The foundation stone was laid in 1929. Alfred Dodd, *Shakespeare: Creator of Freemasonry* (London: Rider, [1937], 267.

71. Alfred Dodd, *The Marriage of Elizabeth Tudor* (London: Rider, 1940), 169–70.

72. Alfred Dodd, *Sir Francis Bacon's Diary* (London: George Lapworth, 1947), 21.

73. The colophon to his book *The Secret History of Francis Bacon (Our Shake-speare) The Son of Queen Elizabeth* (1931) bears the Freemason symbol of square and compass.

74. Dodd, *Shakespeare: Creator of Freemasonry*, 230, 183.

75. Dodd, *Sir Francis Bacon's Diary*, 16–17.

76. Dodd, *The Secret History of Francis Bacon (Our Shake-speare) The Son of Queen Elizabeth*, 7th ed. (1931; repr., London: C. W. Daniel, 1941), 12.

77. Alfred Dodd, *The Martyrdom of Francis Bacon* (London: Rider, [1945?]), 139.

78. Rudyard Kipling, "The Judgment of Dungara," in *The Works of Rudyard Kipling* (New York: Doubleday and McClure, 1899), 2:226–37; 236.

79. For this and other code systems, I consulted three handbooks: Stephen Pincock, *Codebreaker: The History of Codes and Ciphers, from the Ancient Pharaohs to Quantum Cryptography* (New York: Walker, 2006) Sybil Leek, *Numerology: The Magic of Numbers*, 2nd ed. (New York: Macmillan, 1969) and Geoffrey Hodson, *The Hidden Wisdom in the Holy Bible*, 3 vols. (Wheaton, IL.: Theosophical Publishing, 1967), esp. vol. 2.

80. Charles Singer, *From Magic to Science: Essay on the Scientific Twilight* (New York: Dover Publications, 1968), 144–45. See also Thomas Taylor, *The Theoretic Arithmetic of Pythagoreans* (Los Angeles: Phoenix Press, 1934), vii-viii.

81. On Pythagorean harmonies, see O. B. Hardison Jr., "A Tree, a Streamlined Fish, and a Self-Squared Dragon: Science as a Form of Culture," in *Poetics and Praxis, Understanding and Imagination: The Collected Essays of O. B. Hardison, Jr.*, ed. Arthur F. Kinney (Athens: University of Georgia Press, 1997), 328–60; 332–33.

82. Quoted in Hodson, *The Hidden Wisdom in the Holy Bible*, 2:x.

83. Quoted in Marilynn Hughes, *The Mysteries of the Redemption: A Treatise on Out-of-Body Travel and Mysticism* (Morrisville, NC: Lulu.com, 2003), 149.

84. Quoted in Alan Silver, *Jews, Myth and History: A Critical Exploration of Contemporary Jewish Belief* (Leicester: Matador/Troubadour, 2008), 41.

85. The Tree of Life is an ancient symbol that predates Judaism. Egyptians, Buddhists, and Greeks had similar concepts. See Hardison Jr., "A Tree, a Streamlined Fish, and a Self-Squared Dragon," 332–33.

86. See Geoffrey Chaucer, *The Equatorie of the Planets*, ed. Derek J. Price (Cambridge: Cambridge University Press, 1955), 156–63, 182–87; and Kari Anne Rand Schmitt, *The Authorship of The Equatorie of the Planetis* (Woodbridge: D. S. Brewer/Boydell and Brewer, 1993), 3–54.

87. The messages were intercepted and decoded by England's master code-breaker, Thomas Phelippes. See John Bossy, *Under the Molehill: An Elizabethan Spy Story* (New Haven, CT: Yale University Press, 2001), 20, 37; Stephen Budiansky, *Her Majesty's Spymaster: Elizabeth I, Sir Francis Walsingham, and the Birth of Modern Espionage* (New York: Viking, 2005), 145–46; Derek Wilson, *Sir Francis Walsingham: A Courtier in an Age of Terror* (New York: Carroll and Graf, 2007), 210; and Robert Hutchinson, *Elizabeth's Spymaster: Francis Walsingham and the Secret War that Saved England* (New York: Thomas Dunne Books, 2007), 267–68.

88. Anthony B. Dawson and Paul Yachnin, eds., introduction to *Richard II* (New York: Oxford University Press, 2011), 1–117; 4. A variety of "Caesar Shifts" and substitutions were also used in private correspondences during the English Civil War. See Lois Potter, *Secret Rites and Secret Writing: Royalist Literature, 1641–1660* (Cambridge: Cambridge University Press, 1989), esp. 40–41.

89. Francis Bacon, *The Advancement of Learning*, ed. Michael Kiernan, The Oxford Francis Bacon (Oxford: Clarendon Press, 2000), 4: 126.

90. Francis Bacon, *De Augmentis Scientiarum*, BK VI, Chapter 1, in *The Works of Francis Bacon, Baron of Verulam, Viscount St. Alban, and Lord High Chancellor of England.* (London: C. and J. Rivington, etc., 1826), 7:263–4

91. Walter Conrad Arensberg, *The Magic Ring of Francis Bacon* (Pittsburgh, PA: self-published, 1930), 7.

92. Walter Conrad Arensberg, *The Cryptography of Shakespeare* (Los Angeles: Howard Brown, 1922), 1:3.

93. Ironically, Arensberg was aware of the limitations of this sort of thinking, though he was only able to see the flaw in the writings of others. While sure that his system was correct, he was critical of Ignatius Donnelly's attempt to decipher Shakespeare: "Many of the so-called discoveries in the Shakespeare plays, as, for instance, Donnelly's *Great Cryptogram*, are cases in point. They are not cryptograms at all, but merely arbitrary readings foisted into the text by mistaken ingenuity." See Walter Conrad Arensberg, *The Cryptography of Dante* (New York: Alfred A. Knopf, 1921), 5.

94. Walter Conrad Arensberg, *The Cryptography of Shakespeare*, 1:227.

95. Walter Conrad Arensberg, *The Baconian Keys*, rev. ed. (Pittsburgh, PA: self-published, 1928), 11.

96. Arensberg, *The Magic Ring of Francis Bacon*, 8–9.

97. Ibid., 51.

98. Margaret Barsi-Greene, *I, Prince Tudor, Wrote Shakespeare: An Autobiography From His Two Ciphers in Poetry and Prose* (Boston: Branden Press, 1973), 24.

99. Wallace McCook Cunningham, ed., *The Tragedy of Sir Francis Bacon Prince of England* (Los Angeles: Philosopher's Press, 1940), 88. On this point, see also Margaret Barsi-Greene, who argues that "secret chronicle, repeated over and over again, is like a broken record" scattered throughout the First Folio (Barsi-Greene, *I, Prince Tudor, Wrote Shakespeare*, 12). Lastly, we might here note that Bacon's *Advancement of Learning* has "frequent and extensive press corrections." See Michael Kiernan's introduction to Bacon, *The Advancement of Learning*, 4: LXXVIII.

100. Dodd, *The Secret History of Francis Bacon*, 39, 211.

101. Ibid., 46–47.

102. Ibid., 213.

103. Alfred Dodd, *Who Was Shake-speare? Was He Francis Bacon, The Earl of Oxford or William Shaksper?* (London: George Lapworth, 1947), 20.

104. Dodd, *The Secret History of Francis Bacon*, 211.

105. Edward D. Johnson, *The First Folio of Shake-speare* ([London]: C. Palmer, [1932]), 10–11. Johnson uses the same logic, by the way, to "prove" that Bacon is also the "true" author of Cervantes's *Don Quixote*, though that book was published, of course, in Spain—their common errors do not reveal common print house accidentals but are signs that Bacon and his friends left for careful readers (71).

106. Johnson, *The First Folio of Shake-speare*, 15–16.

107. W. B. Venton, *Analyses of Shake-speares Sonnets Using the Cipher Code* (London: Mitre Press, 1968), 36–37.

108. Jane W. Beckett, *The Secret of Shakespeare's Doublet* (Hampton, NH: P. E. Randall, 1977), passim; and Ovason, *Shakespeare's Secret Booke*, 53.

109. William Shakespeare, *Much Ado about Nothing*, 2.3.258–59.

110. Jeffrey Kaplan and Heléne Lööw go on to note that "the ideas generated within the cultic milieu may eventually become mainstream, but before they come to the attention of the dominant culture, they will have to be thoroughly vetted, debated, reformulated" (Jeffrey Kaplan and Heléne Lööw, introduction to *The Cultic Milieu: Oppositional Subcultures in an Age of Globalization* [Walnut Creek, CA: Altamira Press/Roman and Littlefield, 2002], 1–11; 3–4).

111. Stritmatter is quoted in Jennifer Howard, "A Shakespeare Scholar Takes on a 'Taboo' Subject," *The Chronicle of Higher Education*, March 28, 2010, http://chronicle.com/article/A-Shakespeare-Scholar-Takes-on/64811. Relatedly, Shane McCorristine argues that Spiritualistic thought operates as an "institute of cultural disembarrassment" (Shane McCorristine, *Spectres of the Self: Thinking About Ghosts and Ghost-seeing in England, 1750–1920* [New York: Cambridge University Press, 2010], 134).

112. Dobson is quoted in Howard, "A Shakespeare Scholar Takes on a 'Taboo' Subject."

113. On this point, I am indebted to Shawn James Rosenheim, *The Cryptographic Imagination: Secret Writing from Edgar Poe to the Internet* (Baltimore, MD: Johns Hopkins University Press, 1997), 153.

114. William Shakespeare, *Pericles*, 1.1.64–71.

115. William Shakespeare, *The Merchant of Venice*, 2.7.4–9.

116. Terence Hawkes, *Meaning by Shakespeare* (New York: Routledge, 1992), 1–2, emphasis my own.

117. James Shapiro, *Contested Will: Who Wrote Shakespeare?* (New York: Simon and Schuster, 2010), 40. Shapiro dates this practice to Malone's 1790 edition of Shakespeare. Malone's practice is, arguably, still older. As discussed in Chapter 1, the first systematic attempt to understand Shakespeare by visiting Stratford-upon-Avon was undertaken by John Aubrey.

118. See Caroline Spurgeon, *Shakespeare's Imagery and What It Tells Us* (Cambridge: Cambridge University Press, 1958), 195.

119. Ludwig Wittgenstein, *On Certainty*, ed. G. E. M. Anscombe and G. H. von Wright; trans. Denis Paul and G. E. M. Anscombe (New York: Harper and Row, 1969), 8e.

120. Norman Rabkin, *Shakespeare and the Problem of Meaning* (Chicago: University of Chicago Press, 1981), 4.

121. Sinfield adds: "it is the mismatch with present-day assumptions that allows us to make what we will of them [the plays]." Alan Sinfield, *Cultural Politics— Queer Reading* (Philadelphia: University of Pennsylvania Press, 1994), 4. One must admire such honesty.

122. Terence Hawkes, general editor's preface to *Alternative Shakespeares*, vol. 2 (New York: Routledge, 1996), xi-xii; emphasis my own.

123. Catherine Belsey, *Critical Practice* (New York: Methuen, 1980), 116, 117; emphasis my own.

124. Both Hawkes and Belsey are practitioners of a game set by Paul De Man (1986), who offers the following definition of *ideology*: "What we call ideology is precisely the confusion of linguistic with natural reality, of reference with phenomenalism." See Paul De Man, *The Resistance to Theory*, ed. Wlad Godzich (Minneapolis: University of Minnesota Press, 1986), 11. On second reading, we can see the imprecision of this seemingly precise statement. Remove the extraneous phrases and we read, "Ideology is precisely the confusion"; remove the adverb and we strike at the heart of the sentence: "Ideology is the confusion."

125. Annabel Patterson, *Censorship and Interpretation: The Conditions of Writing and Reading in Early Modern England* (Madison: University of Wisconsin Press, 1984), 3–23; and Louis Montrose, *The Purpose of Playing: Shakespeare and the Cultural Politics of the Elizabethan Theatre* (Chicago: University of Chicago Press, 1996), 211. Montrose cleverly argues that the players and even the playwrights themselves might have been innocent of seditious intent, although the audience might have read the situation differently (70).

126. Richard Wilson, *Secret Shakespeare: Studies in Theatre, Religion and Resistance* (New York: Manchester University Press, 2004), 10.

127. Wilson, *Secret Shakespeare*, 298.

128. Clare Asquith, *Shadowplay: The Hidden Beliefs and Coded Politics of William Shakespeare* (New York: PublicAffairs, 2005), title page and 289.

129. Leah S. Marcus, *Puzzling Shakespeare: Local Reading and Its Discontents* (Berkeley: University of California Press, 1988), 144.

130. Marcus, *Puzzling Shakespeare*, 145.

131. Ibid., 213.

132. Ibid. emphases my own.

133. Ibid., 1.

134. Ibid., 213.

135. Immanuel Kant, in his *Critique of Pure Reason*, trans. Max Müller (1781; repr., Garden City, NY: Anchor Books/Double Day, 1966), 362. The quotation is Kant's, though the example of the piecemeal body is my own.

136. Leah S. Marcus, *Unediting the Renaissance: Shakespeare, Marlowe, Milton* (London: New York: Routledge, 1996), 227.

137. Graham Bradshaw, *Misrepresentations: Shakespeare and the Materialists* (Ithaca, NY: Cornell University Press, 1993), 204.

138. H. R. Coursen, *Shakespeare: The Two Traditions* (Teaneck, NJ: Fairleigh Dickinson University Press, 1999), 239.

139. Cunningham, *The Tragedy of Sir Francis Bacon Prince of England*, 67.

140. Granville C. Cuningham, *Bacon's Secret Disclosed in Contemporary Books* (London: Gay and Hancock, 1911), 33. On the plays as pointless, Wallace McCook Cunningham, writes that they are "botched by the coded burden, by the sacrifice of the cover play in the true play" (Cunningham, *The Tragedy of Sir Francis Bacon Prince of England*, 65).

141. Dodd, *The Martyrdom of Francis Bacon*, 5. Likewise, Bacon, according to Margaret Barsi-Greene, was "Chafing under the cloud of his birth, the victim of a

destiny beyond his control which ever placed him in a false position, defrauded
of his birthright, [consequently] Francis Bacon committed to the Cipher the
plaints of an outraged soul" (Barsi-Greene, *I, Prince Tudor, Wrote Shakespeare*, 13).

142. See also Shapiro, *Contested Will*, 4.

143. Charles Alexander Montgomery, cited in Friedman and Friedman, *The Shake-spearean Ciphers Examined*, 57–58; Arensberg, *The Magic Ring of Francis Bacon*, 51–52; and Cunningham, *The Tragedy of Sir Francis Bacon Prince of England*, 91, emphasis my own.

CHAPTER 3

1. Gordon McMullan, *Shakespeare and the Idea of Late Writing: Authorship in the Proximity of Death* (New York: Cambridge University Press, 2007), 157. Dowden's narrative had, perhaps even has, remarkable staying power. A. C. Bradley (1904) thinks it likely that Shakespeare's plays reflected his emotional life, though he doubts if Shakespeare was ever "overwhelmed by such feelings." Nonetheless, he espies in Prospero "the whole mind of Shakespeare in his last years" (A. C. Bradley, *Shakespearean Tragedy* [New York: St. Martin's Press, 1992], 238ff, 288). In *Shakespeare's Last Plays* (London: Chatto and Windus, 1938), E. M. W. Tillyard argues that Shakespeare wanted to complete the final phase of a tragic pattern—but here, too, we have Dowden in another key, for how would Shakespeare know he had to complete the final phase of his work unless he anticipated his quick exit from this world into the next? Thus, Shakespeare's last plays demonstrate the playwright's new turn for contemplation and his immediate and acute awareness of the "different planes of reality"—a phrase Tillyard used on three separate occasions (68, 76, 81). Even Lytton Strachey's (1922) famous contention that Shakespeare's late plays represent a writer "bored with people, bored with real life, bored, in fact, with everything except poetry and poetical dreams" suggests someone who is looking beyond the material veil of this world (Lytton Strachey, "Shakespeare's Final Period," in *Books and Characters* [New York Harcourt, Brace, 1922], 49–69; 64). Northrope Frye (1986) sees some "self-identification" between Shakespeare and his character Prospero (Northrope Frye, *Northrop Frye on Shakespeare* [Markham, Ontario: Fitzhenry and Whiteside, 1986], 171). David Bevington (1988) insists that the "themes that dominate Shakespeare's later romances suggest retirement—from the responsibilities of parenthood, from art, from the theater, from life itself" (David Bevington, "The Late Romances," in *Shakespeare: The Late Romances* [Toronto: New York: Bantam Books, 1988], xxv—xxxiii; xxvii). More recent studies continue to situate Shakespeare's late plays in relation to the playwright's life. Simon Palfrey (1997), for example, insists that Shakespeare was increasingly consumed by "self-reflection," which paradoxically transcended any sense of the self in favor of "things diffuse, accelerating, polysemous" (Simon Palfrey, *Late Shakespeare: A New World of Words* [Oxford: Clarendon Press, 1997], 265).

2. Edward Dowden, *Shakspere: A Critical Study of His Mind and Art* (London: Henry S. King, 1875), 417, 425–26.

3. Edward Dowden, *Shakespeare Primer* (London: Macmillan, 1877), 60. In the same text, he suggests that *The Winter's Tale* is Shakespeare's last play (57).

4. Edward Dowden, *Introduction to Shakespeare* (1907; repr., Freeport, NY: Books for Libraries Press, 1970), 85.

5. Dowden, *Shakespeare Primer*, 59.

6. Ibid.

7. Edward Dowden, *The Sonnets* (London: Kegan, Paul, Trench, 1881), 11; and Dowden, *Shakespeare Primer*, 60.

8. Edward Dowden, "The Interpretation of Literature," in *Transcripts and Studies* (London: Kegan Paul, Trench, Trübner, 1896), 237–68; 264–65.

9. Edward Dowden, "Shakespeare as Man of Science (Bacon-Shakespeare Controversy)," in *Essays Modern and Elizabethan* (New York: E. P. Dutton, 1910), 282–307; 282.

10. Ibid., 288.

11. See Geraldine Cummins's memoir, *Unseen Adventures* (London: Rider, 1951), 21. Years later, Hester would tell her clients and guests that her first psychic intuition was the death of her father, a telling detail, though not too great a prediction, since Dowden's health had been deteriorating for a number of years; he finally succumbed to heart failure in 1913. See Kathryn R. Ludwigson, *Edward Dowden* (New York: Twayne, 1973), 47, 52.

12. Alfred Dodd, *The Immortal Master* (London: Rider, [1943]), 76.

13. E. C. Bentley, *Far Horizon* (London: Rider, 1951), 21.

14. William Watson's opposition to the war probably cost him the laureateship too, which was bestowed on Alfred Austin in 1896.

15. Edward Dowden, "The Interpretation of Literature," 241.

16. Edward Dowden, *Letters of Edward Dowden and His Correspondents*, ed. Elizabeth D. Dowden and Hilda M. Dowden (London: J. M. Dent, 1914), 92–94.

17. *British Medical Journal* 1 (1899): 1162; *The British Journal of Dermatology* 8 (1896): 488; and *Modern Medicine* 11, no. 9 (1902): 208.

18. Ludwigson, *Edward Dowden*, 19; and Terence Brown, *Ireland's Literature: Selected Essays* (Totowa, NJ: Rowman and Littlefield, 1988), 34.

19. The official separation came legally in 1916, but the war began in 1914 and lasted to 1918, so, likely, he granted the separation in absentia. He was serving as a surgeon in the First World War. Further, Hester traded on her father's fame. A young Geraldine Dorothy Cummins was thrilled to meet Hester because she was the "daughter of an internationally famous scholar" (Geraldine Cummins, *Swan on a Black Sea: A Study in Automatic Writing: The Cummins-Willett Scripts*, ed. Signe Toksvig, foreword by C. D. Broad, rev. ed. [New York: S. Weiser, 1970], 151).

20. Bentley, *Far Horizon*, 87. In *The Gospel of Philip the Deacon* (1932), we learn that Johnannes is the spirit of a "Jewish rabbinical doctor, who habitually controls the hand and mind of the automatist" (Frederick Bligh Bond and Hester Dowden, *The Gospel of Philip the Deacon 1932* [New York: Macoy, 1932], 209). This same Johannes reveals that Shakespeare was an anti-Semite: Shylock would have been "a hateful figure," but Shakespeare was overruled

by Oxford, who "would fain have excited the pity of the public for the Jew" (Percy Allen, *Talks with Elizabethans* (New York: Rider, 1947), 44). Hester Dowden was Irish, and anti-Semitism was common among the Irish of this era. In 1904, the year in which *Ulysses* takes place, a priest-led pogrom against the Jews occurred in Limerick—but Hester Dowden's spiritual communiqué took place in 1946, just after the Nuremberg Trials. It is plausible that Allen and Dowden were merely branding Shakespeare as anti-Semitic as a way of weakening our positive associations with him.

21. Roger Nyle Parisious, "Occultist Influence on the Authorship Controversy," *The Elizabethan Review* 6, no. 1 (Spring 1998): 9–43; 22. Bond worked as Hester Dowden's assistant, a point to which we will return. On William Lyon MacKenzie King, see Stan McMullin, *Anatomy of a Seance: A History of Spirit Communication in Central Canada* (Montreal: McGill-Queen's University Press, 2004), 215, 217.

22. Alfred Dodd, *The Immortal Master*, 75.

23. Ibid., 76. Emphasis is in Dodd's text.

24. Alfred Dodd, *Francis Bacon's Personal Life-Story* (London: Rider, 1949), 96.

25. Alfred Dodd, *The Martyrdom of Francis Bacon* (London: Rider and Company, [1945?]), 11; and Dodd, *The Immortal Master*, 9, 39, 9.

26. Alfred Dodd, *Who Was Shake-Speare? Was He Francis Bacon, The Earl of Oxford or William Shaksper?* (London: George Lapworth, 1947), 3–4. The particular value of the number 33 is discussed in Chapter 2 of the present study.

27. Dodd, *The Immortal Master*, 87.

28. For "Higher Truth," see Dodd, *The Martyrdom of Francis Bacon*, 9; for the rest, Dodd, *Francis Bacon's Personal Life-Story*, 96.

29. Dodd, *The Immortal Master*, 79, 92, 101.

30. Ibid., 78.

31. Ibid., 71. For the significance of white light, see "Spirit Realm" in the Glossary of Spiritualist Terms and Techniques appended to this study.

32. Ibid., 56.

33. Ibid., 73.

34. Ibid., 71.

35. Ibid., 76.

36. Ibid., 67.

37. Ibid., 88, 90.

38. Dodd, *Who Was Shake-Speare?*, 12.

39. Parisious, "Occultist Influence on the Authorship Controversy," 21, 22.

40. Percy Allen, *Shakespeare, Jonson, and Wilkins as Borrowers* (London: Cecil Palmer, 1928), xvii.

41. David Scott Kastan, *Shakespeare after Theory* (New York: Routledge, 1999), 39, 33, 38.

42. Allen, *Shakespeare, Jonson, and Wilkins as Borrowers*, 185.

43. Percy Allen, *The Oxford-Shakespeare Case Corroborated* (London: Cecil Palmer, 1931), 235–37, 305.

44. Percy Allen, *The Life Story of Edward de Vere as William Shakespeare* (London: Cecil Palmer, 1932), 234. Allen was also elected president of the Shakespeare Fellowship in 1945. The Fellowship (founded in 1922) had hitherto searched in vain to identify "the personality of the one creative genius that our race produced, whose works appear to have been published under the pen-name of 'William Shakespeare.'" See the Mission Statement cited in Flodden W. Heron, *Who Wrote Shakespeare? Recent Discoveries by Members of the Shakespeare Fellowship* (San Francisco: Literary Anniversary Club, 1943), 3. Note "one creative genius." The effect of the one-artist approach was to pit one camp against another: followers of Francis Bacon versus the followers of Edward de Vere, the Earl of Oxford, versus the admirers of Christopher Marlowe, and so forth. Allen's collaborative theory was, therefore, a compromise likely to attract a wide following.

45. Allen, *Talks with Elizabethans*, 30.

46. Ernest Allen was also an Oxfordian. With his brother Percy, he wrote *Lord Oxford and Shakespeare: A Reply to John Drinkwater* (London: Dennis Archer, 1933).

47. Allen, *Talks with Elizabethans*, 34–35.

48. Emmanuel Swedenborg writes of "a large library," in which all books exist in their "perfection." See Chapter 1.

49. Allen, *Talks with Elizabethans*, 41–42, 49.

50. Ibid., 92.

51. Ibid. The manuscripts were wrapped in three bundles, one serving as a pillow for Shakespeare's head, another for his feet, while a third had been placed into his hands, which were crossed over his heart.

52. Bentley, *Far Horizon*, 152.

53. Samuel Schoenbaum, *Shakespeare's Lives*, new ed. (1991; repr., New York: Oxford University Press, 1993), 439.

54. On May 20–21, 1947, Dodd and Percy debated the authorship of Shakespeare's plays at Mason Croft, Stratford-upon-Avon. Dodd published his argument; Allen did not. No one seems to have supported Shakespeare's candidacy for author of his own plays. See Dodd, *Who Was Shake-Speare?*, 3. Mason Croft is now the home of the University of Birmingham's Shakespeare Institute.

55. David Macey, *The Lives of Michel Foucault* (New York: Vintage/Random House, 1993), 472; and Louis-Jean Calvet, *Roland Barthes: A Biography*, trans. Sarah Wykes (Indianapolis: Indiana University Press, 1995), 39, 253–54. While family may have had a role to play in these arrangements, neither critic specified in their wills that they did not wish to have traditional religious burials.

56. Roland Barthes, "The Death of the Author," in *Image—Music—Text*, trans. Stephen Heath (New York: Noonday Press/Farrar, Straus and Giroux, 1977), 142–48; 142.

57. Ibid., 144.

58. Michel Foucault, *The Order of Things: An Archaeology of the Human Sciences* (New York: Routledge, 2002), 221. On this point, see also Clare O'Farrell, *Michel Foucault* (London: Sage Publications, 2005), 72.

59. Michel Foucault, *The Politics of Truth*, ed. Sylvre Lotringer, trans. Lysa Hochroth and Catherine Porter (Los Angeles: Semiotext[e], 1997), 45.

60. Ibid., 141, 143; emphases my own.

61. J. Joyce Schuld, *Foucault and Augustine: Reconsidering Power and Love* (Notre Dame, IN: University of Notre Dame Press, 2003), 8.

62. Ibid., 14–15. On Foucault and Augustine, see also David Galston, *Archives and the Event of God: The Impact of Michel Foucault on Philosophical Theology* (Montreal: McGill-Queen's University Press, 2011), 107–10. In *Foucault and Theology* (New York: Continuum, 2011), Jonathan Tran refers to Foucault's "quasi-metaphysical philosophy" (42).

63. On this point, see Jonathan Tran, *Foucault and Theology*, 18.

64. Michel Foucault, *History of Sexuality*, trans. Robert Hurley, vol. 1, *An Introduction* (New York: Vintage, 1978), 96; emphases my own.

65. Rux Martin, "Truth, Power, Self: An Interview with Michel Foucault October 25, 1982," in *Technologies of the Self: A Seminar With Michel Foucault*, ed. Luther H. Martin, Huck Gutman, and Patrick H. Hutton (Amherst: University of Massachusetts Press, 1988), 9–15; 9; emphasis my own.

66. Michel Foucault, "What is an Author?," in *The Foucault Reader*, ed. Paul Rabinow (New York: Vintage Books, 2010), 101–20; 119. On this point, Barthes agrees. Authorship, he contends, is the "culmination of capitalist ideology, which has attached the greatest importance to the 'person' of the author" (Barthes, "The Death of the Author," 143).

67. Foucault, "What is an Author?," 111.

68. Ibid., 106.

69. Michel Foucault, *L'Order du discourse* [*The Order of Discourse*] (Paris: Gallimard, 1971), translation as found in Simon During, *Foucault and Literature: Towards a Genealogy of Writing* (New York: Routledge, 1992), 120; emphases my own.

70. On neutralization, see Foucault, "What is an Author?," 105. On the subject of fixed versus unfixed power relations, Foucault himself admits that paradigms that are too rigid (one assumes he includes those of his own creation) are subject to rapid reappraisal and overthrow: "There is always a possibility, in a given game of truth, to discover something else and to more or less change such and such a rule and sometimes even the totality of the game of truth." See Foucault's interview in James William Bernauer and David M. Rasmussen, eds., *The Final Foucault* (Cambridge, MA: MIT Press, 1987), 17.

71. Jack Stillinger, *Multiple Authorship and the Myth of Solitary Genius* (New York: Oxford University Press, 1991), 9. All these forms, he writes, are "channeled through the author into a work" (9). We may note that channeling is an occult term relating to mediumistic reception of Spirits, though, in this case Stillinger may have in mind something synonymous with the free-flow or circulation that so rivets Foucault's imagination.

72. Allen, *Talks with Elizabethans*, 40.

73. Ibid., 118.

74. Ibid., 26. Likewise, in his *Sir Francis Bacon's Diary*, Alfred Dodd suggests that Hester Dowden was unimportant to the process of revelation: "I found the True Order—or, rather, the True Order Found me" (Alfred Dodd, *Sir Francis Bacon's Diary* [London: George Lapworth and Co., 1947], 21).

75. Allen, *Talks with Elizabethans*, 118.

76. Ibid., 5–6.

77. Michael Schrage, "Writing to Collaborate: Collaborating to Write," in *Authority and Textuality: Current Views of Collaborative Writing*, ed. James S. Leonard, Christine E. Wharton, Robert Murray Davis, and Jeanette Harris (West Cornwall, CT: Locust Hull Press, 1994), 17–22; 21.

78. Jill R. Ehnenn, *Women's Literary Collaboration, Queerness, and Late-Victorian Culture* (Burlington, VT: Ashgate, 2008), 3.

79. Cummins, *Swan on a Black Sea*, 149.

80. Cummins, *Unseen Adventures*, 18, 17.

81. Ibid., *Unseen Adventures*, 18.

82. Hester Travers Smith, *Oscar Wilde from Purgatory*, new ed. (Whitefish, MT: Kessinger, 2004), 11, 18.

83. Smith, *Oscar Wilde from Purgatory*, 76.

84. Ibid., 12.

85. Ibid., 76, 75, 76.

86. The play was never produced and does not seem to have been published anywhere, though it did receive some attention at the 2008 Irish Society for Theatre Research, where Velma O'Donoghue Greene presented a paper entitled "Wild(e) Imaginings in *The Extraordinary Play* (1924) by Geraldine Cummins and Hester Travers Smith (nee Dowden)." As a variety of scholars have noted, Dowden's reluctance to call herself "author" fits within a complex web of writing that allowed a woman to retain a sense of decorum in a male-dominated industry. In any case, Cummins received no authorial or collaborative credit for "Wilde's" new play.

87. Hester Dowden, "How I Received Oscar Wilde's 'Spirit Play,'" *The Graphic*, 10 March 1928, 401. Wilde was particularly loquacious in death. In 1928, someone else, the pseudonymous "Lazar," published *The Ghost Epigrams of Oscar Wilde as Taken Down through Automatic Writing* (New York: Covici Friede, 1928). A sample: "Genius has limitations; stupidity is boundless" (xxxv).

88. See Leah Price, "From Ghostwriter to Typewriter: Delegating Authority at *Fin de Siècle*," in *The Faces of Anonymity: Anonymous and Pseudonymous Publication from the Sixteenth to the Twentieth Century*, ed. Robert J. Griffin (London: Palgrave Macmillan, 2003), 211–31. Christine Ferguson argues that mediums occupied a similar position to that of secretary (Christine Ferguson, "Zola in Ghostland: Spiritualist Literary Criticism and Naturalist Supernaturalism," *SEL: Studies in English Literature 1500–1900* 50, no. 4 [2010]: 877–94; 888). Sarah Edwards asserts that automatic writing is essentially female (Sarah Edwards, "Co-Operation and Co-Authorship: Automatic Writing, Socialism and Gender in Late Victorian and Edwardian Birmingham," *Women's Writing: The Elizabethan to Victorian Period* 15, no. 3 [2008]: 371–89; 372).

89. Eleanor Touhey Smith, *Psychic People* (New York: William Morrow, 1968), 66.
90. Hester Dowden, *Oscar Wilde from Purgatory: Psychic Messages*, new ed. (Whitefish, MT: Kessinger, 2004), 37. For more on Wilde's ghost, see Smith, *Psychic People*, 66.
91. Allen, *Talks with Elizabethans*, 116–17. On the function of Mr. V., for example, Eleanor Sidgwick pointed out that Hester Dowden guided the planchette of at least three different automatic writers. Since she was literally the guiding hand, we can assume that Hester was the author. On the other hand, Sidgwick noted that in some instances Mr. V. communicated with Wilde independent of Hester, just as Hester communicated with Wilde independent of Mr. V. See Bette London, *Writing Double: Women's Literary Partnerships* (Ithaca, NY: Cornell University Press, 1999), 175.
92. Lewis C. Roberts suggests that collaborative writing undermines any sense of originality; each writer becomes merely a "cog in the publishing machine" (Lewis C. Roberts, "'The Production of a Female Hand': Professional Writing and the Career of Geraldine Jewsbury," *Women's Writing* 12, no. 3 [2005]: 399–418; 400). See also Jane Donawerth, who argues for two models: (1) hierarchical—wherein each writer has a designated role—and (2) dialogical—wherein the writing duties and activities are more fluid (Jane Donawerth, "Authorial Ethos, Collaborative Voice, and Rhetorical Theory by Women," in *Rhetorical Women: Roles and Representations*, ed. Hildy Miller and Lillian Bridwell-Bowles [Tuscaloosa: The University of Alabama Press, 2005], 107–24; 119). Mediums and their copyists seem to merge both models.
93. Complicating the authorial process still more, Cummins's assistant, Frederick Bligh Bond, had also assisted Hester Dowden. Dowden and Bond had, together, "authored" *The Gospel of Philip the Deacon*.
94. Frederick Bligh Bond, *The Return of Johannes* (London: J. O. Hartes, 1925).
95. To complicate matters still more, Dowden herself (later) admitted that her Spirit Guide Johannes was Bond's creation: "At this time I was reading [Frederick] Bligh Bond's book, *The Gate of Remembrance*, in which the monk, Johannes, was the spokesman" (quoted in Bentley, *Far Horizon*, 80). The full title is *The Gate of Remembrance: The Story of the Psychological Experiment which Resulted in the Discovery of the Edgar Chapel at Glastonbury* (Oxford: Blackwell, 1918). Johannes also pops up in Bond's book, *The Hill of Vision: A Forecast of the Great War and of Social Revolution With the Coming of the New Race* (London: Constable, 1919), xi, xii, xiv, xx, 9.
96. All references to the court case are derived from Cummins v. Bond [1926. C. 1059.] [Chancery Division] [1927] 1 Ch 167; hearing dates: 21, 22 July 1926, accessed through LexisNexis database.
97. For more on this case, see Helen Sword, *Ghostwriting Modernism* (Ithaca, NY: Cornell University Press, 2002), 25; and London, *Writing Double: Women's Literary Partnerships*, 165–68. Despite having penned and published a variety of (traditionally-deemed) literary works, including *The Land they Loved* (1919) and *Fires of Beltane* (1936), as well as collaborating on three plays with Suzanne R. Day—*Out of a Deep Shadow* (1912), *Toilers* (1912), and *Broken Faith*

(1913), all professionally produced at Abbey Theatre, Dublin—literary distinction often eluded Cummins. The afterword to another of her Spiritualist dictations refers to her as an "amateur trance-writer" (Geraldine Cummins, *The Fate of Colonel Fawcett: A Narrative of His Last Expedition* [London: Aquarian Press, 1955], 144). Still, Cummins described herself as an author and playwright; her presumed psychic gifts merely aided in her literary production or "transmission" (Cummins, *Swan on a Black Sea*, 147). On Cummins's traditional literary efforts, see Lorna Sage, Germaine Greer, and Elaine Showalter, eds., *The Cambridge Guide to Women's Writing in English* (New York: Cambridge University Press, 1999), 175. See also Edwards, who points out that literary collaboration, especially among women, was often dismissed as amateur (Edwards, "Co-Operation and Co-Authorship," 382).

98. There does not seem to have been any animosity over Fripp's theft. Hester Dowden's biographer, E. C. Bentley, refers to *The Book of Johannes* as "his"/ Fripp's. See the acknowledgments page in Bentley's *Far Horizon*.

99. Peter Fripp and the spirit Carneades ("Johannes") through the mediumship of Hester Dowden, *The Book of Johannes* (New York: Rider, [1945?]), 11. Fripp later put aside Spiritualism and wrote a book on the Sant Mat movement, an esoteric philosophy combining aspects of Sikhism and Hinduism. See his *The Mystic Philosophy of Sant Mat* (London: Neville Spearman, 1964).

100. Fripp and Dowden, *Book of Johannes*, 86, 22.

101. Ibid., 22, 13, emphasis my own.

102. Ibid., 9; and Foucault, "What Is an Author?"

103. Fripp and Dowden, *Book of Johannes*, 98.

104. Bentley, *Far Horizon*, 146.

105. The title *Hero: A Story for Dog Lovers of All Ages* may be a pun. Among her early, unpublished work is a complete translation from the German of the Romantic poet Franz Seraphicus Grillparzer's *Hero and Leander* (see Parisious, "Occultist Influence on the Authorship Controversy," 22).

106. Allen, *Talks with Elizabethans*, 194–96. See also Bentley, *Far Horizon*, 160–61.

107. Allen, *Talks with Elizabethans*, 191.

108. Hester Dowden, *Oscar Wilde from Purgatory: Psychic Messages*, 40. See also Allen, *Talks with Elizabethans*, 116–17.

109. Allen, *Talks with Elizabethans*, 196; reprinted, with slight emendations, in Bentley, *Far Horizon*, 161.

110. Allen, *Talks with Elizabethans*, 195, 191.

111. Bentley, *Far Horizon*, 181–82.

112. See Parisious, "Occultist Influence on the Authorship Controversy," 24.

CHAPTER 4

1. Arthur Conan Doyle, *The History of Spiritualism* (1926; repr., New York: Arno Press, 1975), 1:62–69.

2. Ibid., 1:62.

3. Ibid., 1:62–63.

4. Ibid., 1:63.

5. Ibid.

6. Ibid., 1:64.

7. Ibid.

8. Maurice Leonard, *People from the Other Side: The Enigmatic Fox Sisters and the History of Victorian Spiritualism* (Stroud, Gloucestershire: History, 2008), 19–20, 33.

9. Ibid., 33. See also Earnest Isaacs, "The Fox Sisters and American Spiritualism," in *The Occult in America: New Historical Perspectives*, ed. Howard Ker and Charles L. Crow (Chicago: University of Illinois Press, 1986), 79–110; 83. Ann Braude states that Leah learned that she was a medium by being magnetized/hypnotized by a friend of the family (Ann Braude, *Radical Spirits: Spiritualism and Women's Rights in Nineteenth-Century America* [Boston: Beacon Press, 1989], 15), but the timing of her self-discovery seems suspicious.

10. Isaacs, "The Fox Sisters and American Spiritualism," 85, 90.

11. Reuben Briggs Davenport, *The Death-Blow to Spiritualism* (New York: G. W. Dillingham, 1888), 127, 36, 127; Barbara Weisberg, *Talking to the Dead: Kate and Maggie Fox and the Rise of Spiritualism* (New York: HarperCollins, 2004), 239. On the management of the sisters, Earnest Isaacs states that in the early days they were managed by the newspaper editor Eliab Wilkinson Capron (Isaacs, "The Fox Sisters and American Spiritualism," 84, 86, 92). The view is disputed by A. Leah Underhill (née Fox), who writes that Capron heaped "ridicule" on the idea of live performances but did consent to give lectures for each of the four Rochester dates at the Corinthian Hall in Rochester (A. Leah Underhill, *The Missing Link in Modern Spiritualism* [New York: Thomas R. Knox, 1885], 62–63).

12. Davenport, *The Death-Blow to Spiritualism*, 127.

13. Ibid., 115–16. Their mother, however, was superstitious. Margaret described her mother as "a fanatic, I call her that because she . . . believed in these things" (quoted in Weisberg, *Talking to the Dead*, 239).

14. Earnest Isaacs attributes the rolling alphabet method to Isaac Post (Isaacs, "The Fox Sisters and American Spiritualism," 83).

15. Leonard, *People from the Other Side*, 25.

16. David Chaplin, *Exploring Other Worlds: Margaret Fox, Elisha Kent Kane and the Antebellum Culture of Curiosity* (Amherst: University of Massachusetts Press, 2004), 47. See also Isaacs, "The Fox Sisters and American Spiritualism," 84.

17. Todd Jay Leonard, *Talking to the Other Side: A History of Modern Spiritualism and Mediumship* (New York: iUniverse, 2005), 28. Barnum himself thought that Spiritualism was one of the "Humbugs of the World" (P. T. Barnum, *The Humbugs of the World* [New York: Carleton, 1866], 119–51).

18. A. Leah Underhill, *The Missing Link in Modern Spiritualism*, 129–30.

19. *The Medium and Daybreak* (1878), 393.

20. Robert Dale Owen, *The Debatable Land Between This World and the Next: With Illustrative Narrations* (London: Trübner, 1871), 367–68. See also Isaacs, "The Fox Sisters and American Spiritualism," 98.

21. Underhill, *The Missing Link in Modern Spiritualism*, 349–50. On Leah Fox's invention of ectoplasm, see also Ruth Brandon, *The Spiritualists: The Passion for the Occult in the Nineteenth and Twentieth Centuries* (New York: Alfred A. Knopf, 1983), 98 and Marlene Tromp, *Altered States: Sex, Nation, Drugs, and Self-Transformation in Victorian Spiritualism* (Albany: State University of New York Press, 2006), 103. On theories as to how ectoplasm is created in the Spirit Realm and then issued gaseously in our realm, see Arthur Findlay, *Looking Back*, 4th ed. (London: Psychic News, 1961), 209–10.

22. Isaacs, "The Fox Sisters and American Spiritualism," 100–101. In 1854, Kate made another easy score: the inventor Horace H. Day paid her $1,200 for a year's worth of sittings. On Kate's likely appropriation of Leah's trick, see Brandon, *The Spiritualists*, 103.

23. *Report on Spiritualism of the Committee of the London Dialectical Society* (London: Longmans, Green, Reader and Dyer, 1871), 165–66.

24. *The Spiritual Magazine* 6 (1871): 525–26.

25. Weisberg, *Talking to the Dead*, 214. The writings themselves were published as Kate Fox, *Fox-Taylor Automatic Writing 1869–1892 Unabridged Record*, ed. Sarah E. L. Taylor (Minneapolis, MN: Tribune-Great West, privately published, 1932). The book contains portraits of the children, composed by the Spirits on magnetized paper.

26. Her "Ben Franklin" Spirit Guide was among Kate's earliest creations. She first "communicated" with him in 1848. See Emma Hardinge, *Modern American Spiritualism*, 3rd ed. (New York: self-published, 1870), 53.

27. Nancy Rubin Stuart, *The Reluctant Spiritualist: The Life of Maggie Fox* (New York: Harcourt, 2005), 279–80.

28. Elisha Kent Kane and Margaret Fox, *The Love-Life of Dr. Kane: Containing the Correspondence, and a History of the Acquaintance, Engagement, and Secret Marriage Between Elisha K. Kane and Margaret Fox* (New York: Carleton, 1866), 269.

29. Chapin, *Exploring Other Worlds*, 4.

30. Dennis Drabelle, "Explorer in a Hurry," *The Pennsylvania Gazette*, March/April 2008, 30–35; 34.

31. Kane and Fox, *The Love-Life of Dr. Kane*, 186.

32. Dennis Drabelle, "Explorer in a Hurry," 33.

33. Ibid., 34.

34. Davenport, *The Death-Blow to Spiritualism*, 166.

35. Ibid., 165.

36. On June 2, 1870, Kate Fox reported that Margaret was "found away from home in a fearful state of intoxication" (Fox, *Fox-Taylor Automatic Writing 1869–1892*, 84). See also Chaplin, *Exploring Other Worlds*, 213. She may have also been addicted to drugs; see Nancy Rubin Stuart, who writes that Margaret was addicted to laudanum, a mild opiate cheaper than gin (Stuart, *Reluctant Spiritualist*, 280).

37. Isaac K. Funk, *The Widow's Mite and Other Psychic Phenomena* (New York: Funk, 1911), 241.

38. The Shakespeare actress Fanny Kemble had dined with the elder Furness. See *Shakespeariana, Shakespeare Society of New York* 5 (October 1888): 439.

39. James M. Gibson, "Horace Howard Furness: Book Collector and Library Builder," in *Shakespeare Study Today: The Horace Howard Furness Memorial Lectures*, ed. Georgianna Zeigler (New York: AMS Press, 1986), 169–89; 170.

40. Gibson, "Horace Howard Furness," 172.

41. Ibid., 170.

42. *Shakespeariana*, 440; and Gibson, "Horace Howard Furness," 172.

43. M. A. Shaaber, "The Furness Variorum Shakespeare," in *Proceedings of the American Philosophical Society* 75 (1935): 281–85; 282.

44. Furness would go on to complete still more editions: *Othello* (1886), *Merchant of Venice* (1888), *As You Like It* (1890), *The Tempest* (1892), *A Midsummer Night's Dream* (1895), *The Winter's Tale* (1898), *Twelfth Night* (1901), *Much Ado About Nothing* (1904), *Love's Labors Lost* (1904), *Anthony and Cleopatra* (1907), and *Richard III* (1908); a last edition, *Cymbeline* (1913), was published posthumously.

45. The bequest was sizeable—$60,000—but this money also included the establishment of an endowed chair in philosophy at the University of Pennsylvania (see Herbert G. Jackson, *The Spirit Rappers* [Garden City, NY: Doubleday, 1972], 189).

46. Quoted in Michael D. Bristol, *Shakespeare's America, America's Shakespeare* (New York: Routledge, 1990), 68.

47. Bristol, *Shakespeare's America, America's Shakespeare*, 69.

48. Gary Taylor, *Reinventing Shakespeare: A Cultural History, from the Restoration to the Present* (New York: Weidenfeld and Nicolson, 1989), 198.

49. Colin Franklin, *Shakespeare Domesticated: The Eighteenth-Century Editions* (Brookfield, VT: Scolar Press, 1991), 133.

50. Thomas Warton, *An Enquiry into the Authenticity of the Poems Attributed to Thomas Rowley* (London: J. Dodsley, 1782), 124. It should be noted that both Malone and Warton, using their respective systems, correctly judged the Rowley poems to be forgeries.

51. Horace Howard Furness, quoted in Joseph Jastrow, "The Psychology of Spiritualism," *The Popular Science Monthly* 34 (1889): 721–32; 727 n.

52. A "Magic Box" was also known as a "Magic Cabinet" or a "Magic Escape" apparatus and was used by stage magicians to saw women in half or to make them disappear entirely. While these sorts of tricks are common today, in the 1880s they were still associated with séances, not public stage shows. Illusionist Jean-Eugène Robert-Houdin remembers seeing the trick in 1858. However, many believe Houdin's reminiscence to be a fiction and generally date the public demonstration of the illusion to 1921. See Jean-Eugène Robert-Houdin, *Memoirs of Robert-Houdin: Ambassador, Author, and Conjurer*, trans. R. Shelton Mackenzie (Philadelphia: G. G. Evan, 1859), 234–35; and *Goldin v. Clarion Photoplays*, mentioned in the *Yale Law Journal* 32, no. 2 (December 1922): 201.

53. Horace Howard Furness, *Preliminary Report of the Commission Appointed by the University of Pennsylvania to Investigate Modern Spiritualism* (Philadelphia: J. B. Lippincott, 1887), 158.

54. Ibid.

55. I am indebted to Samuel A. Tannenbaum's useful overview of the crux; see his "Farewell to 'Vllorxa,'" *Shakespeare Association Bulletin* 11, no. 1 (January 1936): 41–45. Tannenbaum's own solution was a combination of words and utterance: "all—or—ha, all!" Other solutions have been offered by G. Joicey (1893), who favored "villains" (G. Joicey, "Shakspeariana," in *Notes and Queries* 87 [February 1893]: 102); Harold Littledale (1901), who gambled with "seven or ten in all" (cited in Henry Cunningham, "On 'Vllorxa' in 'Timon of Athens,'" *The Athenæum*, July 13, 1901, 71); Henry Cunningham (1901), who called "Vllorxa" a "mysterious word" but attempted to demystify it by offering "All lords, ay" ("On 'Vllorxa' in 'Timon of Athens,'" 71); and a desperate Leon Kellner (1925), who came up with "etcetera" (Leon Kellner, *Restoring Shakespeare: A Critical Analysis of the Misreadings in Shakespeare's Works* [1925; repr., New York: Biblo and Tannen, 1969], 12).

56. Horace Howard Furness, *On the Text of Shakespeare* (Philadelphia: Poet-Lore, 1891), 339–40.

57. Letter dated October 22, 1884, cited in Davenport, *The Death-Blow to Spiritualism*, 169–70.

58. Horace Howard Furness, *Letters of Horace Howard Furness* (Boston: Houghton Mifflin, 1922), 1:202.

59. Ibid., 1:203–4.

60. Horace Howard Furness, *Preliminary Report of the Commission Appointed by the University of Pennsylvania to Investigate Modern Spiritualism*, 47.

61. On the erotica of automatic writing, see Jack Monroe, "Making the Séance 'Serious': *Tables Tournantes* and the Second Empire Bourgeois Culture, 1852–1861," *History of Religions* 38, no. 3 (February 1999): 219–46; 226–28.

62. Davenport, *The Death-Blow to Spiritualism*, 197. See also Furness, *Letters of Horace Howard Furness*, 1:204–5; James M. Gibson, *The Philadelphia Shakespeare Story: Horace Howard Furness and the New Variorum Shakespeare* (New York: AMS Press, 1990), 141.

63. Furness, *Letters of Horace Howard Furness*, 1:205–6.

64. Ann Braude (1989) states that female mediums had the same social standing as prostitutes (Braude, *Radical Spirits*, 124).

65. Perhaps this was a team act? Sir William Crookes noted that Florence reappeared "not more than three seconds" after Katie's disappearance (William Crookes, *Researches in the Phenomena of Spiritualism* [London, J. Burns, 1874] 105). The *Philadelphia Inquirer* (December 15, 1874) tracked a woman who looked suspiciously like the ghostly Katie. She turned out to be a youthful-looking widow and single mother living in a boarding house. See also Earl Wesley Fornell, *The Unhappy Medium: Spiritualism and the Life of Margaret Fox* (Austin: University of Texas, 1964), 139.

66. Jenny Hazelgrove argues that female mediums sparked a "readjustment" in perceptions of a woman's enjoyment of sexual acts (Jenny Hazelgrove, *Spiritualism and British Society Between the Wars* [Manchester: Manchester University Press, 2000], 155).

67. On magic groping, see Tromp, *Altered States*, 43; see also Stephen E. Braude, *The Limits of Influence: Psychokinesis and the Philosophy of Science* (New York: Routledge and Kegan Paul. 1986), 145–48; C. D. Broad, "Cromwell Varley's Electrical Tests with Florence Cook," *Proceedings of the Society for Psychical Research* 54 (March 1964): 158–72; Peter Brookesmith, "What Katie Did," *Fortean Times* 179 (January 2004): http://www.forteantimes.com/features/articles/174/what_katie_did.html; Crookes, *Researches in the Phenomena of Spiritualism*, 108–12; Molly McGarry, *Ghosts of Futures Past: Spiritualism and the Cultural Politics of Nineteenth-Century America* (Berkeley: University of California Press, 2008), 104.

68. Ruben Briggs Davenport, *The Death Blow to Spiritualism*, 51. On the physical charms of many young female mediums, see Janet Oppenhiem, *The Other World: Spiritualism and Psychical Research in England, 1850–1914* (Cambridge: Cambridge University Press, 1985), 19–21. On the "sexy" séance: Jack Monroe argues that the séance "fostered the lifting of social restraint," both on a personal and political level (Monroe, "Making the Séance 'Serious,'" 219–46, esp. 226, 228). See also Tromp, *Altered States*, 29; and Braude, *Radical Spirits*, 121–23. Cathy Gutierrez offers an overview of this issue in *Plato's Ghost: Spiritualism in the American Renaissance* (New York: Oxford University Press, 2009), 92–93. The topic of sexual license was a common theme in both pro- and anti-Spiritualist pamphlets: Emil F. Ruedebusch (1896), for example, argued that sexual attraction within the bounds of Spiritualism was permissible because it wasn't really physical love, but Spirits seeking soul mates. That being said, Spiritualists were not naive. They understood that the séance, with all its groping and kissing, was (potentially) yet another arena in which men victimized women (Emil F. Ruedebusch, *The Old and the New Ideal* [Mayville, WI: privately published, 1896]).

69. June 9, 1870, Fox, *Fox-Taylor Automatic Writing 1869–1892*, 88. Marlene Tromp argues that Margaret and her sister became drunks not because they were addicted to drink or because they were trying to forget their present, reduced, and immoral circumstances, but because they were seeking to prolong throughout the days between shows the drug-like high they experienced around the séance table (Tromp, *Altered States*, 17, 175–76).

70. Furness, *Preliminary Report of the Commission*, 5, 82.

71. The commission was made up entirely of university personnel: William Pepper, Dr. Joseph Leidy, Dr. George A. Koenig, Professor Robert Ellis Thompson, Professor George S. Fullerton, and Dr. Horace Howard Furness, to whom were afterwards added Mr. Coleman Sellers, Dr. James W. White, Dr. Calvin B. Knerr, and Dr. S. Weir Mitchell. Of this commission, Dr. Pepper, as provost of the university, was, ex officio, chairman; Dr. Furness, acting chairman; and Professor Fullerton, secretary. See Furness, *Preliminary Report of the Commission*,

5; on respective personnel for Mrs. Lord's and Margaret Fox's interviews, see 33–35.

72. Furness, *Letters of Horace Howard Furness*, 1:203.

73. Ibid., 1:206.

74. Ibid., 1:202.

75. Ibid., 1:203.

76. Ibid., 1:207–8.

77. Houdini, *A Magician Among the Spirits*, 80.

78. John Nevil Maskelyne, quoted in Houdini, *A Magician Among the Spirits*, 80.

79. The Witchcraft Act was only overturned in 1950. See Findlay, *Looking Back*, 429.

80. Michael Sherme, *In Darwin's Shadow: The Life and Science of Alfred Russel Wallace: A Biographical Study on the Psychology of History* (New York: Oxford University Press, 2002), 194, 197. For more on this trial, see Ronald Pearsall, *The Table-Rappers: The Victorians and the Occult* (1972; repr., Stroud, Gloucestershire: Sutton, 2004), 233.

81. Houdini, *A Magician Among the Spirits*, 81.

82. Deborah Blum, *Ghost Hunters: William James and the Search for Scientific Proof of Life after Death* (New York: Penguin Press, 2006), 336.

83. Houdini, *A Magician Among the Spirits*, 80.

84. Furness, *Preliminary Report of the Commission*, 77; emphasis my own. Harry Houdini reprinted the letter but emended Zoellner to Zollner (Houdinin, *A Magician Among the Spirits*, 195–96).

85. Pearsall, *The Table-Rappers*, 232.

86. Were all of Furness's trips on behalf of the Seybert Commission a lie? No, some must have been real. For example, on November 14, 1885, Furness attempted to arrange a visit with a Spirit photographer, but the interview was refused. See Furness, *Letters of Horace Howard Furness*, 1:210.

87. Neuralgia was and is a very serious and painful complaint, but in this era it was often used as code for someone who was fall-down drunk, or so we gather from Anna Alice Chapin, *Greenwich Village* (New York: Dodd, Mead, 1917): "It is fairly late in the evening. In one of the little tea shops is a group of girls and men smoking. To them enters a youth, who is hailed with 'How is Dickey's neuralgia?' The newcomer grins and answers: 'Better, I guess. He's had six drinks, and is now asleep upstairs on Eleanore's couch. He'll be all right when he wakes up.' They laugh, but quite sympathetically, and the subject is dismissed" (276).

88. Letter dated November 22, 1884. This and all other Margaret Fox letters cited are housed in the Seybert Commission Correspondence (Ms. Coll. 412 Folder 73), Rare Book and Manuscript Library, University of Pennsylvania.

89. Furness, *Letters of Horace Howard Furness*, 1:214.

90. Ibid., 1:217.

91. Furness, *Preliminary Report of the Commission*, 133–34, 139–41. See also Gibson, *The Philadelphia Shakespeare Story*, 140–42; on the identity of Cooke's skull, see Jeffrey Kahan, *The Cult of Kean* (Aldershot: Ashgate, 2006), 165. On

Hemans's poem, see "To a Departed Spirit," in *Songs of the Affections with Other Poems* (London: William Blackwood, 1830), 41.

92. Hugh Macmillan, *Two Worlds Are Ours* (London: Macmillan, 1880), 46; see also Preston Kavanagh, *Secrets of the Jewish Exile: The Bible's Codes, Messiah, and Suffering Servant* (Tarentum, PA: Word Association, 2005), 201.

93. Baron Ludwig de Güldenstubbé, *Pneumatologie Positive et Experimentale: La Realité des Esprits et le Phénomène Merveilleux de leur Ecriture Directe Démontrées* (Paris: Librairie A. Franck, 1857). See also *The Spiritual Magazine* 8 (1873): 329–32; and John Michell, *Eccentric Lives and Peculiar Notions*, 2nd ed. (New York: Black Dog and Leventhal, 1999), 75–76.

94. Furness, *Letters of Horace Howard Furness*, 1:214, 217; see also Gibson, *The Philadelphia Shakespeare Story*, 142, and *Proceedings of the Society for Psychical Research* 5 (1889): 261. Furness likely bought the paper locally. The largest producer of the stuff was James A. Bliss of Philadelphia (Robert S. Cox, *Body and Soul: A Sympathetic History of Spiritualism* [Charlottesville: University of Virginia Press, 2003], 189). Bliss states that he got the idea from the Spirit of an Indian named Blackfoot. Margaret Fox, we recall, spoke to a Spirit calling itself Splitfoot.

95. Furness, *Letters of Horace Howard Furness*, 1:219.

96. Mary E. Cadwallader, *Hydesville in History* (Chicago: Progressive Thinker, 1917), 57.

97. Furness, *Preliminary Report of the Commission*, 4.

98. See Horace Howard Furness, *The Tempest: A New Variorum Edition of Shakespeare* (Philadelphia: J. B. Lippincott, 1892), 153.

99. Davenport, *The Death-Blow to Spiritualism*, 31

100. Ibid., 38.

101. See Tom Ogden, *The Complete Idiot's Guide to Ghosts and Hauntings*, 2nd ed. (New York: Penguin, 2004), 81–82; and Joel Martin, Patricia Romanowski, and George P. Anderson, *We Don't Die: George Anderson's Conversations with the Other Side* (New York: G. P. Putnam's Sons, 1988), 286–90.

102. Davenport, *The Death-Blow to Spiritualism*, 236.

103. D. Scott Rogo, *Parapsychology: A Century of Inquiry* (New York: Taplinger, 1975), 45.

104. Houdini, *A Magician Among the Spirits*, 16.

CHAPTER 5

1. G. Wilson Knight, *Jackson Knight: A Biography* (Oxford: Alden Press, 1975), 44.

2. Ibid., 45.

3. Ibid., 92.

4. Ibid.

5. Ibid., 312.

6. G. Wilson Knight, "Caroline: Life after Death," last revised March 20, 1985, Manuscript Collection of the University of Exeter, 21.

7. G. Wilson Knight, "Caroline," 52.

8. G. Wilson Knight, *Jackson Knight*, 338.

9. Ibid., 100.

10. G. Wilson Knight, "The Poet and Immortality," in *Shakespeare and Religion: Essays of Forty Years* (London, Routledge and K. Paul, 1967), 43–51; 48.

11. John Jones presents a less rosy picture: "From 1929 when his [Knight's] first book came out, until 1946 when he went to Leeds, he had been unable to get a university job at any level in Britain. At Birmingham, his eleventh shot, they said they would like to make him a lecturer, but he was too old" (John Jones, "Shakespeare and Wilson Knight [Revisited]," *Scripsi* 4, no. 1 [July 1986]: 51–57; 51).

12. Robert Blackmore, introduction to *The Letters of John Cowper Powys to G. R. Wilson Knight* by G. Wilson Knight and John Cowper Powys, ed. Robert Blackmore (London: Cecil Woolf, 1983), 7–21; 12.

13. Hugh Grady, *The Modernist Shakespeare: Critical Texts in a Material World* (Oxford: Clarendon Press, 1991), 95.

14. Janet Clare, "*Hamlet* and Modernism: T. S. Eliot and G. Wilson Knight," in *Shakespeare and European Politics*, ed. Dirk Delabastita, Jozef de Vos, and Paul Franssen (Newark: University of Delaware Press, 2008), 234–45; 243.

15. John E. Van Domelen, *Tarzan of Athens: A Biographical Study of G. Wilson Knight* (Bristol: Redcliffe, 1987), 52.

16. Robert Sale, "G. Wilson Knight," *Modern Language Quarterly* 29 (March 1968): 77–83; 77.

17. Graham Bradshaw, *Shakespeare's Skepticism* (Ithaca, NY: Cornell University Press, 1987), 97.

18. J. H. Crouch, review of *Shakespeare's Dramatic Challenge: On the Rise of Shakespeare's Tragic Heroes*, by G. Wilson Knight, *Library Journal* 102 (May 15, 1977): 1188.

19. Gordon McMullan, *Shakespeare and the Idea of Late Writing: Authorship in the Proximity of Death* (New York: Cambridge University Press, 2007), 56.

20. René Welleck, *A History of Modern Criticism: 1750–1950* (New Haven, CT: Yale University Press, 1986), 5:138.

21. John C. Briggs, "Within Athens' Shadow: The Ghost of Plutarch in Shakespeare's *Timon of Athens*," *Poetica* 48 (1997): 119–40; 120.

22. Martin Blocksidge, "'Professionally Defunct but Invigorating': G. Wilson Knight and *Timon of Athens*," *Use of English* 59 (1998–99): 132–45; 134.

23. Victor Kiernan, *Eight Tragedies of Shakespeare: A Marxist Study* (New York: Verso, 1996), 106.

24. John W. Velz, review of *Shakespearian Dimensions*, by G. Wilson Knight, *Shakespeare Studies* 18 (1986): 292–94; 292.

25. Michael Dobson, "Wilson Knight's *Wheel of Fire*," *Essays in Criticism* 52, no. 3 (July 2002): 235–44; 240.

26. John Jones, summing up critical opinion in his article "Shakespeare and Wilson Knight (Revisited)," 57.

27. Northrop Frye, *Spiritus Mundi: Essays on Literature, Myth, and Society* (Bloomington: Indiana University Press, 1976), 12–13. Terence Hawkes notes that the Globe edition first appeared in 1864 (Terence Hawkes, *Meaning By Shakespeare* [New York: Routledge, 1992], 148). Regarding Knight's reputation, it's not all bad. Kenneth Muir described Knight as "the most influential of Shakespeare critics," but noted that Knight felt himself unfairly "ostracized by the critical establishment" (Kenneth Muir, review of *Shakespearian Dimensions*, by G. Wilson Knight, *Modern Language Review* 83 [1988]: 406–7; 406). As an example of continued ostracism, Knight's live performances of Shakespeare, stretching over 50 years, were often ignored. Writes Emma Smith, "Wilson Knight's Shakespeare is linguistic and rhetorical" (Emma Smith, "The Critical Reception of Shakespeare," in *The New Cambridge Companion to Shakespeare*, ed. Margreta de Grazia and Stanley Wells [Cambridge: Cambridge University Press, 2010], 253–67; 259). We may further note that Knight, whose books repeatedly discuss aspects of Shakespeare and Spiritualism, is not mentioned even once in the recent and otherwise excellent *Spiritual Shakespeares*, ed. Ewan Fernie (New York: Routledge, 2005).

28. Spiritualists were often persecuted for their beliefs. See Daniel Cottom, *Abyss of Reason: Cultural Movements, Revelations, and Betrayals* (New York: Oxford University Press, 1991), 124.

29. William Kurtz Wimsatt, *The Verbal Icon: Studies in the Meaning of Poetry* (1954; repr. Lexington: University of Kentucky, 1982), 18.

30. Terence Hawkes, ed., introduction to *Alternative Shakespeares 2* (New York: Routledge, 1996),1–16; 13.

31. Helen Sword, *Ghostwriting Modernism* (Ithaca, NY: Cornell University Press, 2002), 57.

32. G. Wilson Knight, *The Christian Renaissance* (London: Methuen, 1962), 326.

33. G. Wilson Knight, *Myth and Miracle: An Essay on the Mystic Symbolism of Shakespeare* (London: Ed. J. Burrow, 1929), 28, 14.

34. G. Wilson Knight, "Mystic Symbolism," in *Shakespeare and Religion*, 65–68; 66.

35. G. Wilson Knight, *The Shakespearian Tempest* (London: Methuen, 1953), 11.

36. G. Wilson Knight, *The Burning Oracle: Studies in the Poetry of Action* (Toronto: Oxford University Press, 1939), 22.

37. G. Wilson Knight, *Starlit Dome: Studies in the Poetry of Vision* (London: Oxford University Press, 1943), 316.

38. G. Wilson Knight, introduction to *Shakespeare and Religion*, 1–38; 31.

39. G. Wilson Knight, "Caroline: Life after Death," 1. Likewise, in G. Wilson Knight, *Shakespearian Dimensions* (Brighton, Sussex: Harvester Press, 1984), xi.

40. Olivia Anderson, e-mail to this author, dated February 7, 2012.

41. G. Wilson Knight, "Caroline: Life after Death," 386. On January 4, 1955, Knight writes that the Spirits congregate in a "grand amphitheatre" (G. Wilson Knight, "Spirit-Writing," 1950–71, Manuscript Collection of the University of Exeter, 57).

42. G. Wilson Knight, "Caroline: Life after Death," 404; see also 405.

43. G. Wilson Knight, *Shakespearian Dimensions*, 123. On poetic x-rays, Spirits, and flying saucers, see G. Wilson Knight, *Neglected Powers: Essays in Nineteenth and Twentieth Century Literature* (New York: Barnes and Noble, 1971), 65.

44. G. Wilson Knight, *The Wheel of Fire* (1930; repr., London: Methuen, 1949), 225.

45. G. Wilson Knight, *Starlit Dome*, 101, 99, 189.

46. Ibid., 85; emphasis my own. On the general distrust of Knight's correspondences and word-linkages, we may here note Heather Dubrow's observation that contemporary readers have a "distrust of elaborate rhetorical devices . . . many modern readers . . . devalue works that delight in word play" (Heather Dubrow, *Captive Victors: Shakespeare's Narrative Poems and Sonnets* [Ithaca, NY: Cornell University Press, 1987], 16).

47. G. Wilson Knight, *Wheel of Fire*, 3.

48. G. Wilson Knight, *Lord Byron: Christian Virtues* (New York: Oxford University Press, [1952]), 47.

49. G. Wilson Knight, *Sovereign Flower* (1958; repr., London: Methuen, 1966), 258.

50. G. Wilson Knight, "Caroline: Life after Death," insert 326–41 F. Elsewhere, he calls his approach an "interpretative study" (G. Wilson Knight, *The Poetry of Pope: Laureate of Peace* [1955; repr., New York: Barnes and Noble, 1965], 15). John Veltz refers to Knight's methodology as "intuitive" ("G. Wilson Knight Revisited: *The Shakespearian Tempest* and the Symbolic Interpretation of Shakespeare," *Symbolism: An International Journal of Critical Aesthetics* 1 [January 2000]: 21–40; 21).

51. G. Wilson Knight, *Byron and Shakespeare* (New York: Barnes and Noble, 1966), 39; and appendix A and additional note "1966," in *Shakespeare and Religion*, 327.

52. G. Wilson Knight, "Caroline: Life after Death," ii. Knight wrote that "The *Psychic News* is a constant companion" (ii).

53. G. Wilson Knight, *Shakespearian Dimensions*, xx; G. Wilson Knight, *Neglected Powers*, 39ff; G. Wilson Knight, *The Christian Renaissance*, 333, 335; G. Wilson Knight, *The Dynasty of Stowe* (1945, repr. London: Fortune Press, 1946), 16; G. Wilson Knight, *The Mutual Flame: On Shakespeare's "Sonnets" and "The Phoenix and the Turtle"* (London: Methuen, 1955), 9, 11, 114; and G. Wilson Knight, *The Poetry of Pope*, 166.

54. G. Wilson Knight, *The Golden Labyrinth: A Study of British Drama* (London: Phoenix House, 1962), 218.

55. G. Wilson Knight, *Shakespearian Dimensions*, 120.

56. G. Wilson Knight, *Shakespeare's Dramatic Challenge* (New York: Barnes and Noble Books, 1977), 79.

57. G. Wilson Knight, *Sovereign Flower*, 155.

58. G. Wilson Knight, *Shakespearian Dimensions*, 103; see also 54.

59. G. Wilson Knight, *The Christian Renaissance*, 182.

60. Ibid., 184.

61. G. Wilson Knight, *Sovereign Flower*, 226. *Romance*, while not used by the editors of the First Folio, was an accepted term, made famous by Edward Dowden in *Shakespeare Primer* (London: Macmillan, 1877), 57.

62. G. Wilson Knight, *Sovereign Flower*, 281–86, 226, 212

63. G. Wilson Knight, *The Christian Renaissance*, 119–20.

64. Ibid., 121.

65. G. Wilson Knight, *The Shakespearian Tempest*, 5. Knight was somewhat flexible on the subject. In *Shakespeare and Religion*, Knight argued that Fletcher may have had a hand in some plays, but that his influence did not diminish in any way his thesis: "Once you forgot the received academic reasons previously current to account for these strange works—copying Fletcher's romances, trying to please the public, the work of an ageing and wearied man—once you forget all this and let yourself be passive to what actually happens, then the resurrection of Hermione and similar events in other plays hit you, dramatically and inevitably, with an impact of mystic affinities. We do, in fact, thrill to the experience of watching a supposedly dead person come to life, in a chapel, to the sound of music. There is no getting away from it . . . All that the scholars said might be true. These plays might be the work of a tired con copying Fletcher in order to make money; but even so, that had nothing whatsoever to do with the matter under discussion" (G. Wilson Knight, "New Dimensions in Shakespearian Interpretation," in *Shakespeare and Religion*, 197–210; 205). As for *Pericles*, in *The Shakespearian Tempest* Knight, albeit temporarily, allowed that that particular play was best left to one side: "I have no space to enter here the question of authorship. That the play was rejected from the Folio indicates that it is not completely by Shakespeare; and that this was done although so much of it was of Shakespeare's best, and the play itself so popular, shows us how scrupulous were the Folio editors" (218 n.).

66. On Edward Dowden, see Chapter 3.

67. G. Wilson Knight, *The Christian Renaissance*, 175.

68. Ibid., 184.

69. G. Wilson Knight was partially influenced by A. C. Bradley here. See G. Wilson Knight, *Shakespeare's Dramatic Challenge*, 71–72.

70. G. Wilson Knight, *Shakespeare's Dramatic Challenge*, 109.

71. Ibid., 82.

72. G. Wilson Knight, *Christ and Nietzsche: An Essay in Poetic Wisdom* (New York: Staples Press, 1948), 123, 234.

73. G. Wilson Knight, *Shakespeare's Dramatic Challenge*, 100; *Christ and Nietzsche*, 85.

74. G. Wilson Knight, *Wheel of Fire*, 38, 46.

75. G. Wilson Knight, *The Christian Renaissance*, 189.

76. G. Wilson Knight, *The Shakespearian Tempest*, 292; emphasis my own.

77. G. Wilson Knight, *Byron and Shakespeare*, 58.

78. G. Wilson Knight, *The Golden Labyrinth*, 69.

79. G. Wilson Knight, introduction to *Shakespeare and Religion*, 25.

80. G. Wilson Knight, *The Golden Labyrinth*, 68.

81. Ibid., 67.

82. Ibid., 133.

83. G. Wilson Knight, *Byron and Shakespeare*, 58; *The Saturnian Quest*, 57–58, see also 125. Elsewhere, he refers to this same bisexual state as a "supersexual purity" (G. Wilson Knight, *The Dynasty of Stowe*, 42) and a "supersexual understanding" (G. Wilson Knight, *The Mutual Flame*, 31). Knight's sexuality is complex. In Knight's memoir, the unpublished "Road to Kasvin" (composed in 1943 with undated revisions, Special Collection, University of Exeter), he writes that as a teenager, he wrote poetry to a girl whom "he admired," but then adds "Also I wrote many poems for my mother" (7). In the same manuscript, Knight expressed some disgust for homosexual activity. He writes of an Australian doctor with whom he had a "rather intimate conversation on the machinery of sex," and notes that his "intentions were immoral"—read: homosexual (117). In a memoir concerning his years in Canada, he writes of a brief heterosexual attraction (G. Wilson Knight, *Atlantic Crossing: An Autobiographical Design* [1936; repr., London: J. M. Dent and Sons, 1939], 118–27), yet in his poetry collection, he writes that "Most of my stronger lyrics . . . were love-poems impelled by Platonic visions and devotions which we may call 'homosexual' provided that the word be read simply as denoting 'toward the same sex', without further assumptions . . . The experiences, though transient, were for me magical, more magical than passionate, and meant much, though the poetic results themselves, of which the addressees knew nothing, meant less" (G. Wilson Knight, *Gold Dust, with Other Poetry* [London: Routledge and Kegan Paul, 1968], xvi–xvii). Elsewhere, he writes of the "homosexual ideal" versus "heterosexual passion" (G. Wilson Knight, *The Mutual Flame*, 30–36).

84. The Spiritualist belief in bisexuality originates with Swedenborg: "duality . . . [in Swedenborg's writings] does not exist merely in the individual. It is found in even a more marked degree in the human race . . . The name we there [in nature] give it is bisexuality. The male is one half, and the female is the other half, of the divine image . . . They are the two halves of a great whole, one of which was designed to complete and supplement the other" (James Reed, *Swedenborg and the New Church* [Boston: Houghton, Osgood, 1880], 132–33). Swedenborg is mentioned twice in G. Wilson Knight's *The Christian Renaissance*, both times in connection to Spiritualism (316, 327). Knight cited Swedenborg copiously in his penultimate Shakespeare book, *Symbol of Man: On Body-Soul for Stage and Studio* (New York: Regency Press, 1979). More Swedenborgian connections: G. Wilson Knight's March 18, 1949 lecture, "Byron and Europe," was delivered at Swedenborg Hall, Bloomsbury, London, the home of Britain's Swedenborg Society. There may be a hint of Hinduisms here as well. In *Lectures on Hindu Religion, Philosophy and Yoga* (Calcutta: U. C. Shome, 1893), author Kshitish Chandra Chakravarti writes, "Divine love is feminine, the Divine wisdom, the masculine principle in the Divine nature. They are inseparable, coexistent, co-animating, co-operating" (60).

85. G. Wilson Knight, introduction to *Shakespeare and Religion*, 27. That being said, Knight did mix Spiritualism, sexuality, and traditional Christianity

idiosyncratically. In *The Christian Renaissance*, he describes Jesus as "'bisexual,'" or "perhaps supersexual"; and while he claims that bisexuality means that Jesus was *not* sexually active, he also argues that Jesus's disciple John was homo-erotically attracted to the Son of God (316, 302–13). The title, The *Christian Renaissance*, suggests a less controversial polemic. In the unpublished "Road to Kasvin," Knight's assessment of traditional Christianity is particularly harsh: "Christianity . . . its phraseology, its symbolism of the body and blood of Christ, meant little more to me than the head-slashings of the Shiah fanat-ics" (290). In an early memoir he admits that his bisexual reading of Jesus is likely to give offense: "the Church it [Christianity] gave rise to has never yet succeeded in Christianizing the pagan evil magic of sex" (G. Wilson Knight, *Atlantic Crossing*, 111). In *Elysion*, he is more approving: Christianity might be called "superspiritualism" (G. Wilson Knight and W. F. Jackson Knight, *Elysion: On Ancient Greek and Roman Beliefs Concerning a Life after Death* [New York: Barnes and Noble, 1970], 15). Despite invoking Christ often in his essays, he took umbrage with Roland Mushat Frye, who, in 1964, accused him of seeing Shakespeare as nothing more than a symbolic version of the King James Bible. A year later Knight replied that he rejects the premise. He is not interested in "Christian dogma" but in "cosmic laws" (G. Wilson Knight, "Christian Doc-trine," in *Shakespeare and Religion*, 293–303; 295). In *The Golden Labyrinth* he writes that one need not choose between Christianity and mysticism: "Spiritu-alism itself does not leave us in this impasse" (389). Elsewhere, he calls himself a "Christian . . . supplemented naturally by the great Spirit guides" (G. Wilson Knight, *Shakespearian Dimensions*, xx).

86. G. Wilson Knight, *Hiroshima: On Prophecy and the Sun-Bomb* (London: Andrew Dakers, 1946), 22.

87. G. Wilson Knight, *Starlit Dome*, 315.

88. Tom Ogden, *The Complete Idiot's Guide to Ghost and Hauntings* (Indianapolis, IN: Alpha Books, 1999), 81–82; and Joel Martin, Patricia Romanowski, and George P. Anderson, *We Don't Die: George Anderson's Conversations with the Other Side* (New York: G. P. Putnam's Sons, 1988), 286–90.

89. Rose Champion De Crespigny, *Quarterly Transactions of the British College of Psychic Science* 10, no. 1 (April 1931–January 1932): 51–56; 51.

90. Martin Gardner, *The Whys of a Philosophical Scrivener* (New York: St. Martin's Griffin, 1999), 65.

91. G. Wilson Knight, "Jesus and Shakespeare," in *Shakespeare and Religion*, 69–73; 69.

92. G. Wilson Knight, *Starlit Dome*, 316.

93. Jackson Knight was later made a reader at Exeter, but this came with no added income or responsibilities.

94. Although his mother thought him quite a ladies' man, a series of love letters shed light on his closeted affections. See G. Wilson Knight, *Jackson Kinght*, 52. On the other hand, G Wilson Knight's typist Olivia Anderson (née Mordue) remembered Jackson as somewhat flirtatious: "once when J. K. and I had had a slight tiff, I cannot recall its origin, but remember his pulling me back into

the oak panelled tea-room in Caroline House when I said I was going home saying that he never knew anyone so quick to take offence over nothing which prompted me to go, even more quickly! Dick used to do automatic writing, that is a spirit moved his pen. The message was from Caroline saying 'Jack must be kind to Olivia.' He greeted me with this on my next visit. I smiled and asked him what he thought she meant. And much to my delight, 'this' he replied, kissing me!" (Olivia Anderson, e-mail to this author, dated February 7, 2012). As for G. Wilson Knight's sexuality, see note 83, above.

95. Many Cambridge graduates championed gay love, including Goldsworthy— "Goldie"—Lowes Dickinson, who spent all his adult life at Cambridge carving recognition as a historian, pacifist, political activist, mentor, and the author of *The Greek View of Life* (1896), a work which celebrates male love, and Edward Carpenter, whose books included *Love's Coming of Age* (1896) and *The Intermediate Sex* (1908).

96. G. Wilson Knight, *Jackson Knight*, 275.

97. G. Wilson Knight and W. F. Jackson Knight, *Elysion*, 10, 13. G. Wilson Knight's typist Olivia Anderson (née Mordue) recently wrote to me of W. F. Jackson Knight. She describes him as "immaculately dressed" and the "greatest university eccentric. In the university's history he is likely to remain the greatest personality" (Olivia Anderson, e-mail to this author, dated March 28, 2011).

98. W. F. Jackson Knight, *Poetic Inspiration: An Approach to Virgil* (Exmouth: Raleigh Press, 1946), 7, 10.

99. W. F. Jackson Knight, *Accentual Symmetry in Vergil* (1939; repr., Oxford: Basil Blackwell, 1950), 12. See "Spirit Wavelength" in the Glossary of Spiritualist Terms and Techniques.

100. The "College of Psychic Sciences" was originally founded in 1920 but disbanded due to lack of funds in 1947. W. F. Jackson Knight's address was, then, not to a true college but to the vestiges of a once-thriving community of amateurs interested in Spiritualist/psychic phenomena. W. F. Jackson Knight's 1962 speech, "Spiritualism among the Ancients," was published posthumously by the Spiritualist magazine *Light* 85 (Autumn 1965): 113–18. See also G. Wilson Knight's introduction to *Elysion*, 7, 17–18.

101. G. Wilson Knight, *Jackson Knight*, 376; and G. Wilson Knight and W. F. Jackson Knight, *Elysion*, 7, 16, 17.

102. Jackson Knight also sought his brother's opinions. In his *Accentual Symmetry in Vergil*, Jackson Knight admits to an "inestimable debt" owed to his brother for his ideas, transmitted both in writing and in conversation (106); in his edition of *The Aeneid*, W. F. Jackson Knight thanked G. Wilson Knight for having "read and criticized the whole book at every stage of its production" (Virgil, *The Aeneid*, trans. W. F. Jackson Knight [Baltimore, MD: Penguin Books, 1956], 9). Before his death in 1964, Jackson also acknowledged that many of the revisions for his second edition of *Roman Vergil* were undertaken by his brother and by John D. Christie (W. F. Jackson Knight, *Roman Vergil* rev. ed. [1966; New York: Barnes and Noble, 1968], 11).

103. Thoedore Johannes Haarhoff received messages from the dead in dreams. See his communication from South African and British Commonwealth statesman Jan Christian Smuts, a supporter of racial segregation, who died in 1950; Haarhoff communicated with him in a dream that took place in 1970 (Thoedore Johannes Haarhoff, *Smuts the Humanist: A Personal Reminiscence* [Oxford: Basil Blackwell, 1970], 101). G. Wilson Knight makes brief mention of Smuts in G. Wilson Knight, *The Poetry of Pope*, 56; and in G. Wilson Knight, *Neglected Powers*, 107.

104. Quoted in G. Wilson Knight, *Jackson Knight*, 382.

105. The letters are in the manuscript collection of the University of Exeter, but some transcriptions are found in Timothy Peter Wiseman, *Talking to Virgil: A Miscellany* (Exeter: University of Exeter Press, 1992), 191–95.

106. Quoted in G. Wilson Knight, *Jackson Knight*, 383.

107. Ibid., 382.

108. G. Wilson Knight, "Caroline: Life after Death," 104. On November 8, 1950, at a sitting in Leeds with Mrs. Louie Hill, Caroline explained that soon after death G. Wilson Knight "would be the other part of herself, a twin soul" (81).

109. Ibid., 105.

110. Ibid., 82.

111. Ibid., 94.

112. Ibid., 119

113. Ibid., 123, 147.

114. Ibid., 83.

115. Ibid.,149–50.

116. G. Wilson Knight, *Jackson Knight*, 339. See also Keith Keating, "The Human Form as Dramatic Symbol: An Interview with G. Wilson Knight," *Literature in Performance: A Journal of Literary and Performing Art* 82, no. 3 (November 1982): 49–59, in which Knight states that "when they [the photos] were done it was all instinct. I had no particular aim in mind" (56). It was only because of his "effort to understand them" that he began to write about them; in the process he discovered that he was interested in the "sharply physical," the "spiritualistic," and the "psychic" (G. Wilson Knight, *Symbol of Man*, 11–12).

117. G. Wilson Knight, "Caroline: Life after Death," 151.

118. Ibid., 55.

119. Ibid., 57.

120. Ibid., 58.

121. Ibid., 59–60.

122. Ibid., 60.

123. Ibid., 108–9.

124. G. Wilson Knight, "Spirit-Writing," 3.

125. G. Wilson Knight, "Caroline: Life after Death," 110.

126. Ibid., 287.

127. Ibid., 152. In honor of his new collaborators, especially his hitherto unknown brother Bob, he also started calling himself George Wilson Richard Knight (G. Wilson Knight, "Caroline: Life after Death," insert 300–303B). The

additional forename is also mentioned in *Blackwood's Magazine* 325 (1979): 362–68; 362.

128. G. Wilson Knight, "Caroline: Life after Death," insert 154–61B.
129. Ibid., 68.
130. Ibid., insert 86–92A.
131. Ibid., insert 86–92B.
132. Ibid., 97.
133. G. Wilson Knight, "Spirit-Writing," 22; emphasis my own.
134. G. Wilson Knight, "Caroline: Life after Death," 98.
135. Ibid., 99.
136. Ibid., 304–5.
137. Ibid., 305.
138. Ibid., 306.
139. Ibid., 309.
140. Ibid., 311; dated as July 31, 1952 in G. Wilson Knight "Spirit-Writing," 36.
141. G. Wilson Knight, "Caroline: Life after Death," 311. Wrote Knight, "It is really a question of degree" (314). In 1967, G. Wilson Knight returned to a tranquil certainty. As he states emphatically, "Spiritualistic messages give us direct reports of the beyond" (G. Wilson Knight, introduction to *Shakespeare and Religion*, 10).
142. G. Wilson Knight, "Caroline: Life after Death," 192.
143. Ibid., 318,
144. Ibid., 319.
145. Ibid., 319 and insert 320–22A.
146. Ibid., insert 76–79A.
147. Ibid., 71.
148. Ibid., 73–74. A further Shakespeare connection: G. Wilson Knight believed that he was related to Maldred, brother to Shakespeare's King Duncan and cousin to Macbeth (see appendix B, "Chart of Scottish Descent," *Jackson Knight*, following 494).
149. G. Wilson Knight, "Caroline: Life after Death," 72.
150. G. Wilson Knight, "Caroline: Life after Death," 74.
151. Ibid., 172.
152. G. Wilson Knight, "Spirit-Writing," 57. Typical of the messages of 1953: May 22, Caroline explained that she visited children in their sleep to "teach them to say their prayers to the Great Spirit which rules the universe. That is my work, and I love it, and you will love it too when you come, my Dickie"; December 26, Caroline reported that she and her husband George "go for walks," and "watch you and Jack, and the house, and help you to plan it all, for we can see so much more than you can, and we want it to be a great success" (G. Wilson Knight, "Spirit-Writing," 45 and 55).
153. G. Wilson Knight, "Spirit-Writing," 66. In his unpublished manuscript "Caroline: Life after Death," Knight writes, "I am not going to argue that the spirits helped me very greatly in this. They did not," but then adds, "as far as I know" (230).

154. G. Wilson Knight, "Spirit-Writing,"81.

155. G. Wilson Knight, "Caroline: Life after Death," 351.

156. G. Wilson Knight, "Caroline: Life after Death," 406.

157. G. Wilson Knight, *The Poetry of Pope*, 182.

158. G. Wilson Knight, *Neglected Powers*, 27. Knight is quoting Silver-Birch, a Spirit Guide.

159. G. Wilson Knight, "Caroline: Life after Death," 12. Caroline's job guidance continued after her death: On August 21, 1953, Caroline told her son to expect an offer to "lecture in America"; on September 5, 1953, Caroline told him to ready himself for an "excellent offer"; when Knight worried that no offer was at hand, she replied on September 25, 1953: "you must leave the rest to God and the Spirits. They know all about it, and they have it all planned out, so you must be very cheerful and not waste energy worrying" (G. Wilson Knight, "Spirit-Writing," 49–50, 81).

160. G. Wilson Knight, "Caroline: Life after Death," 13.

161. Ibid., 23.

162. Ibid., 6.

163. Ibid., insert 293–96A.

164. G. Wilson Knight, "Spirit-Writing," 60.

165. Ibid., 67.

166. G. Wilson Knight, *Neglected Powers*, 164 n.1. At one séance, Powys also appeared to Knight himself. See his *The Saturnian Quest*, 14. See also Martin Blocksidge, "'Professionally Defunct but Invigorating': G. Wilson Knight and *Timon of Athens*," 143.

167. G. Wilson Knight, *Jackson Knight*, 433.

168. Quoted in G. Wilson Knight, *Jackson Knight*, 436.

169. Ibid., 441.

170. As related by G. Wilson Knight's typist Olivia Anderson (née Mordue), e-mail to this author, dated February 7, 2012.

171. G. Wilson Knight, "Spirit-Writing," 119.

172. G. Wilson Knight, *Jackson Knight*, 444.

173. G. Wilson Knight, "Spirit-Writing,"121.

174. Quoted in G. Wilson Knight, *Jackson Knight*, 460–61.

175. Quoted in ibid., 461. The point of this family reunion was to let George know that "if there was anything at all beyond our earth-bound sight, the past tragedy was a closed book" (G. Wilson Knight, "Caroline: Life after Death," 103). In a "Spirit-Writing" entry for July 16, 1971, Caroline explains that this is a "very active time," for she, George (her husband), and W. F. Jackson are all helping "those who have come over without having experienced life on earth for long, and they are lost in the new life" (123).

176. G. Wilson Knight, *Jackson Knight*, 411.

177. Auto-writing of January 8, 1965, quoted in ibid., 464; emphasis my own. According to Christie, G. Wilson Knight "suggested many solutions of editorial problems and whenever re-writing was needed, he created turns of phrase perfectly in tune with his brother's spirit" (G. Wilson Knight and W. F. Jackson

Knight, *Many-Minded Homer: An Introduction*, ed. John D. Christie [London: George and Unwin, 1968], 12). After G. Wilson Knight's death, Christie edited his *Visions and Vices*. He makes no mention of spiritual aid.

178. Jackson had begun the book in the late 1930s.

179. G. Wilson Knight, *Jackson Knight*, 459; and G. Wilson Knight and W. F. Jackson Knight, *Elysion*, 17–18.

180. G. Wilson Knight and W. F. Jackson Knight, *Elysion*, 21.

181. G. Wilson Knight, *Neglected Powers*, 33. I cite the work as a collaboration. I do the same for their *Many-Minded Homer: An Introduction*.

182. A full list of cities on the tour has not survived, but Knight did perform in both England and America.

183. Other times, just a golden cord wrapped his waist. See images of G. Wilson Knight as Richard III, Romeo, Hamlet, Othello, Macbeth, Lear, Timon, Puck, Caliban, and Ariel in his book *Symbol of Man*. For British audiences, he was "obliged to adopt a flesh-toned jockstrap so as to comply with laws on public decency" (Dobson, "Wilson Knight's *Wheel of Fire*," 241). The acting version of his earlier 1948 performance of *Timon* is housed at Birmingham Central Library, England, but it contains no references to nudity.

184. Frank Kermode, *Shakespeare's Language* (New York: Farrar, Straus, Giroux, 2000), 242.

185. G. Wilson Knight, *Wheel of Fire*, 207.

186. Ibid., 231.

187. G. Wilson Knight, *Shakespearian Dimensions*, 72, 79, 87.

188. G. Wilson Knight, *Symbol of Man*, 169.

189. This according to Charles Sprawson's February 7, 2009 review of Charles Rees's *Stowe: The History of a Public School, 1923–1989* ("The True Stoic," *The Spectator*, February 7, 2009, http://www.spectator.co.uk/books/3322756/part_3/the-true-stoic.thtml). More on Knight's nudism: In G. Wilson Knight, *Principles of Shakespearean Production* (Harmondsworth: Penguin Books, 1949), Knight explained his rationale for a naked Hamlet: the character participates in the "stripping away of accepted values, the hero's very nerves [are] laid bare"; likewise, in *King Lear* "subterranean forces" are revealed and expressed through "physical nakedness"; *Timon*, often seen as unfinished, is "itself bare, almost indecently direct," its essence "presented in naked simplicity" (177–78). Privately, Knight enjoyed wearing a "minimum of clothes in summer" (see G. Wilson Knight and John Cowper Powys, *The Letters of John Cowper Powys to G. R. Wilson Knight*, ed. Robert Blackmore [London: Cecil Woolf, 1983], 28). In an interview with the *Sunday Independent*, Knight stated: "I don't like wearing too many clothes when I'm acting. I'm more at ease without clothes than with" (September 18, 1977). In a discussion with Knight, Keith Keating wondered aloud if a naked Timon might lead to "accusations of voyeurism and exhibitionism"; Knight countered that he was merely "the dramatic symbol of the bare human form" (Keating, "The Human Form as Dramatic Symbol," 49–50). Elsewhere he stated that he would have to outface "obvious decencies" but objected to the very notion that his striptease might titillate. Despite the

nudity of the actor, "we must not be aware of the actor undresses; that is, of a negation, and on which plunges us away from art into that wrong kind of reality . . . the result should not point us away from the world of dramatic art, but rather embed our consciousness even more deeply therein"; "We must . . . always give a definite impression of something carefully created, not something removed"; "The intellectual content of the performance must keep continually ahead, as it were, of the sensuous impact" (G. Wilson Knight, *Principles of Shakespearean Production*, 172–74; see also his essay, "What Are Clothes?," in G. Wilson Knight, *Symbol of Man*, 163–70).

190. *Blackwood's Magazine*, 363. Neil Rhodes has recently dismissed Knight's insufficiently clad Timon as "ridiculous" (Neil Rhodes, "Tarzan of Athens, Dionysus in Africa: Wilson Knight and Wole Soyinka," in *Tragedy in Transition*, ed. Sarah Annes Brown and Catherine Silverstone [Oxford: Blackwell, 2007], 232–48; 237).

191. Dobson, "Wilson Knight's *Wheel of Fire*," 244.

192. Keating, "The Human Form as Dramatic Symbol," 53.

193. G. Wilson Knight, "Caroline: Life after Death," 351; emphasis by Knight.

CHAPTER 6

1. Sir Arthur Conan Doyle, *The Coming of the Fairies* (New York: George H. Doran, 1922), 16–17.

2. Ibid., 37; Paul Smith, "The Cottingley Fairies: The End of a Legend," in *The Good People: New Fairylore Essays*, ed. Peter Narváez (New York: Garland, 1991), 371–405; 379. Mr. Wright, while not a Spiritualist, seems to have been an honest, straightforward, and fairly indulgent man (Edward L. Gardner, *Fairies: The Cottingley Photographs and Their Sequel*, rev. ed. [1966; repr., London: Theosophical Publishing, 1974], 21).

3. Ibid., 33. Earlier in the same study, Gardner states that both Else and Frances were clairvoyant (32).

4. Joe Cooper, *The Case of the Cottingley Fairies* (London: Hale, 1990), 36–38, 32. As Doyle wrote this, he was about to set off for Australia, where he was to give some lectures on the occult. Edward L. Gardner notes that there had been some fairy citings in both New Zealand and Australia, but he is unclear as to whether these occurred before or after the events at Cottingley (Gardner, *Fairies*, 43–44).

5. Cooper, *The Case of the Cottingley Fairies*, 33.

6. Doyle, *Coming of the Fairies*, 169, 142.

7. Sir Arthur Conan Doyle, *Do We Live after Death? The New Revelation* (New York: George H. Doran, 1918), 17. So far as I have ascertained, the new Lady Doyle never bothered to reach out to Doyle's first wife. See also Christopher Redmond, *A Sherlock Holmes Handbook* (Toronto: Simon and Pierre, 1993), 130.

8. Bernard M. L. Ernst and Hereward Carrington, *Houdini and Conan Doyle: The Story of a Strange Friendship* (London: Hutchinson, [1933]), 165.

9. Ibid., 47.

10. The former ophthalmologist was also fooled by "Spirit Photography"—photographs which seemed to reveal the evidence of a spirit's face floating near that of the medium; these floating heads have contemporary hairstyles or, in the case of men, Victorian beards (Arthur Conan Doyle, *The History of Spiritualism* [1926; repr., New York: Arno Press, 1975], 2:128–51). For more on Doyle and the fairies, including his belief that these spiritual manifestations signaled a coming apocalypse, see Ruth Brandon, *The Spiritualists: The Passion for the Occult in the Nineteenth and Twentieth Centuries* (New York: Alfred A. Knopf, 1983), 224–27.

11. Doyle, *Do We Live after Death?*, 39.

12. Cooper, *The Case of the Cottingley Fairies*, 59.

13. Doyle, *Coming of the Fairies*, 186. Other Spiritualists used Doyle to confirm their religious beliefs: L. W. Rogers, in his study *Ghosts in Shakespeare* (Chicago: Theo Book Co., 1925), turns to the topic of the fairies in *A Midsummer Night's Dream*: "Those who have read the *Coming of The Fairies* by A. Conan Doyle, will" know that some of "them [the fairies] were photographed in a glen in the North of England" (145).

14. C. W. Leadbeater, *The Astral Plane* (Adyar, India: Theosophical Society, 1973), 154–55; emphasis my own.

15. C. W. Leadbeater, *The Hidden Side of Things* (1913 repr., Adyar, India: Theosophical Publishing, 1954), 99.

16. Ibid., 89.

17. Leadbeater, *The Astral Plane*, 79.

18. Cooper, *The Case of the Cottingley Fairies*, 121–29.

19. Sir Arthur Conan Doyle, *Edge of the Unknown* (1930; repr., Guildford, England: White Crow Books, 2010), 126–27.

20. Horace Greeley and Robert Dale Owen, *Recollections of a Busy Life* (New York: J. B. Ford, 1868), 241; Luther Calvin Tibbets, *Spirit of the South* (Washington, DC: np., 1869), 41; Eugene Crowell, *The Identity of Primitive Christianity and Modern Spiritualism* (New York: Two Worlds, 1881), 2:73; J. M. Peebles, *Seers of the Ages: Embracing Spiritualism Past and Present* (Chicago: Progressive Thinker, 1903), 235; Moses Hull and William F. Jamieson, *The Greatest Debate within a Half Century upon Modern Spiritualism* (Chicago: Progressive Thinker, 1902), 267; *The Medium and Daybreak* 25 (1884): 220; and *Theosophy* 7 (1919): 163.

21. William Shakespeare, *Hamlet*, in *The Riverside Shakespeare*, ed. G. Blakemore Evans and J. J. M. Tobin, 2nd ed. (New York: Houghton Mifflin, 1997), 5.1.166–67.

22. See John Watkins Holden, otherwise known as the "Bohemian Magician," and author of *Wizard's Wanderings from China to Peru* (London: Dean and Son, 1886), 143.

23. Doyle, *History of Spiritualism* 1:250.

24. Harry Houdini, *A Magician Among the Spirits* (1924; repr., Amsterdam: Fredonia Books, 2002), 161–62; see also 141.

25. Ibid.,, 208.

26. Sir Oliver Lodge, *Science and Immortality* (New York: Moffat, Yard, 1908), 72.

27. Sir Oliver Lodge, *The Survival of Man: A Study in Unrecognized Human Faculty* (New York: Moffat, Yard, 1909), 3.

28. Sir Oliver Lodge, *Past Years: An Autobiography* (New York: Charles Scribner's Sons, 1932), 349.

29. Sir Oliver Lodge, *Phantom Walls* (New York: Charles Scribner's Sons, 1932), 77.

30. For examples, see Barrett Harper Clark, *European Theories of the Drama: An Anthology of Dramatic Theory and Criticism from Aristotle to the Present Day* (Cincinnati, OH: Stewart, 1918), 3, 10, 14, 20.

31. John Milton, *Paradise Lost*, ed. Philip Pullman (New York: Oxford University Press, 2005), 1, no. 26.

32. George Crabbe, *The Library* (London: J. Dodsley, 1781), 5.

33. Lisa Zunshine, *Why We Read Fiction: Theory of Mind and the Novel* (Columbus: Ohio State University Press, 2006), 162.

34. Nicola S. Schutte and John M. Malouff, *Why We Read and How Reading Transforms Us: The Psychology of Engagement With Text* (Lewiston, NY: Edwin Mellen Press, 2006), passim.

35. Samuel Johnson, *Johnson on Shakespeare: Essays and Notes Selected and Set Forth with an Introduction*, ed. Walter Raleigh (London: Henry Frowde, 1908), 20–21.

36. On "unnatural metaphors" in *Macbeth*, Johnson explains that metaphors might be a way of exposing Macbeth's duplicity, but there is no doubt that Johnson finds the trait to be poetically irritating, if dramatically justifiable. See his *Johnson on Shakespeare*, 172

37. See Warburton's commentary in *Love's Labor's Lost*, in *The Plays of William Shakespeare*, ed. Samuel Johnson (London: Printed for J. and R. Tonson, 1765), 2:200. Warburton edited the plays in 1747.

38. On this point, we might remind ourselves that as far back as 1961, Lionel Trilling cautioned against reading literature for "presumably practical relevance to modernity" (Lionel Trilling, "On the Teaching of Modern Literature" [1961], in *The Moral Obligation to Be Intelligent* [New York: Farrar, Straus and Giroux, 2000], 381–401; 382).

39. Ann Thompson and John O. Thompson, introduction to *Shakespeare: Meaning and Metaphor* (Iowa City: University of Iowa Press, 1987), 1–12; 1.

40. Ibid., 3; see also Brian Vickers, "Analogy versus Identity: The Rejection of Occult Symbolism, 1580–1680," in *Occult and Scientific Mentalities in the Renaissance*, ed. Brian Vickers (Cambridge: Cambridge University Press, 1984), 95–164; 95. On this point, E. M. W. Tillyard notes Irving Babbitt and other early twentieth-century literary critics adopted a rigorously scientific, hierarchical approach (E. M. W. Tillyard, *Essays Literary and Educational* [New York: Barnes and Noble, 1962], esp.138–39).

41. James Wood, *The Broken Estate: Essays and Literature and Belief* (New York: Random House/Modern Library, 2000), xii, xi.

42. Wood, *The Broken Estate: Essays and Literature and Belief,* xi.

43. Gerald L. Bruns, *Modern Poetry and the Idea of Language: A Critical and Historical Study* (New Haven, CT: Yale University Press, 1974), 53–54.

44. Vickers, "Analogy versus Identity," 95.

45. Norman Rabkin, *Shakespeare and the Problem of Meaning* (Chicago: University of Chicago Press, 1981), 140.

46. A. D. Nuttall, *A New Mimesis: Shakespeare and the Representation of Reality* (New York: Methuen, 1983), 170.

47. On the crisis of spirituality, the transcendent is now so proscribed that even theological scholars often avoid using the word "God," replacing it with euphemisms that perform the same basic function: "first cause," "fine structure," "cosmic envelope," "ultimate," and so forth. See Sean Creaven, *Against the Spiritual Turn: Marxism, Realism and Critical Theory* (New York: Routledge/Francis and Taylor, 2010), 1, 3. On the critics cited, see Keith Windschuttle, *The Killing of History: How Literary Critics and Social Theorists are Murdering Our Past* (New York: Free Press, 1997); John M. Ellis, *Literature Lost: Social Agendas and the Corruption of the Humanities* (New Haven, CT: Yale University Press, 1997); R. V. Young, *At War with the Word: Literary Theory and Liberal Education* (Wilmington, DE: ISI Books, 1999); Tom McAlindon, *Shakespeare Minus 'Theory'* (Burlington, VT: Ashgate, 2004); and Edward Pechter, *Shakespeare Studies Today: Romanticism Lost* (New York: Palgrave Macmillan, 2011), esp. 73. On the supposedly amateurish quality of his criticism, see Harold Bloom, *The Anatomy of Influence: Literature as a Way of Life* (New Haven, CT: Yale University Press, 2011), 17; on the charge of being old-fashioned, see James Wood, who writes that Bloom's argument "is about as antique as a wing collar" (*The Broken Estate*, 20).

48. Michael D. Bristol, *Big-Time Shakespeare* (New York: Routledge, 1996), 117, 123.

49. Stephen Greenblatt, *Hamlet in Purgatory* (Princeton, NJ: Princeton University Press, 2001), 4.

50. For an overview, see E. K. Chambers, *The Disintegration of Shakespeare: Annual Shakespeare Lecture, 1924* (London: British Academy, [1925]), 5–14.

51. Benjamin De Casseres, *Forty Immortals* (New York: Seven Arts, 1926), 364.

52. Ibid. See also Terence Hawkes, *Meaning by Shakespeare* (New York: Routledge, 1992), 3; and Harold Bloom, *Shakespeare: The Invention of the Human* (New York: Riverhead Books, 1998), passim.

53. De Casseres, *Forty Immortals*, 364.

54. Stephen Greenblatt, *Hamlet in Purgatory*, 3. In his scholarly *Shakespearean Negotiations* (1988), Greenblatt yearns to "speak with the dead." See Stephen Greenblatt, *Shakespearean Negotiations: The Circulation of Social Energy in Renaissance England* (Berkeley: University of California Press, 1988), 1; and Stanley Wells, *Coffee with Shakespeare* (London: Duncan Baird, 2008), passim.

WORKS CITED

Allen, Percy. *The Oxford-Shakespeare Case Corroborated.* London: Cecil Palmer, 1931.
———. *Shakespeare, Jonson, and Wilkins as Borrowers.* London: Cecil Palmer, 1928.
———. *Talks with Elizabethans.* New York: Rider, 1947.
Allen, Percy, and Ernest Allen. *Lord Oxford and Shakespeare: A Reply to John Drinkwater.* London: Dennis Archer, 1933.
Anderson, Olivia. E-mails to the author. Dated March 28, 2011, February 7, 2012, and February 28, 2012.
Arensberg, Walter Conrad. *The Baconian Keys.* Rev. ed. Pittsburgh, PA: self-published, 1928.
———. *Burial of Francis Bacon and His Mother in the Lichfield Chapter House.* Pittsburgh, PA: self-published, 1924.
———. *The Cryptography of Dante.* New York: Alfred A. Knopf, 1921.
———. *The Cryptography of Shakespeare.* 2 vols. Los Angeles: Howard Brown, 1922.
———. Letters. Huntington Library Manuscript Collection.
———. *The Magic Ring of Francis Bacon.* Pittsburgh, PA: self-published, 1930.
———. *The Secret Grave of Francis Bacon at Lichfield.* San Francisco: John Howell, 1923.
———. *The Shakespearean Mystery.* Pittsburgh: self-published, 1927.
Arnold, Matthew. *The Strayed Reveller, and Other Poems.* London: B. Fellowes, 1849.
Asquith, Clare. *Shadowplay: The Hidden Beliefs and Coded Politics of William Shakespeare.* New York: PublicAffairs, 2005.
Aubrey, John. *Brief Lives.* 2 vols. Oxford: Clarendon, 1898.
Auerbach, Nina, *Daphne du Maurier, Haunted Heiress.* Philadelphia: University of Pennsylvania Press, 2000.
Augustine of Hippo [Saint Augustine]. *The City of God.* Translated by Marcus Dods. 2 vols. Edinburgh: T. and T. Clark, 1888.
Bacon, Delia. *The Philosophy of the Plays of Shakspere Unfolded.* Boston: Ticknor and Fields, 1857.
Bacon, Francis, *The Advancement of Learning,* edited by Michael Kiernan. Vol. 4 of *The Oxford Francis Bacon.* Oxford: Clarendon Press, 2000.
———. *The Works of Francis Bacon, Baron of Verulam, Viscount St. Alban, and Lord High Chancellor of England.* 10 vols. London: C. and J. Rivington, etc., 1826.
Baconiana (periodical, various dates embedded in text).
Bacon, Theodore. *Delia Bacon: A Biographical Sketch.* Boston: Houghton, Mifflin, 1888.
Bamber, L. Kelway, *Claude's Book.* London: Methuen, 1918.
———. *Claude's Second Book.* New York: H. Holt, 1919.

Barnum, P. T. *The Humbugs of the World*. New York: Carleton, 1866.

Barrow, Logie. *Independent Spirits: Spiritualism and English Plebeians, 1850–1910*. London: Routledge and Kegan Paul, 1986.

Barsi-Greene, Margaret. *I, Prince Tudor, Wrote Shakespeare: An Autobiography From His Two Ciphers in Poetry and Prose*. Boston: Branden Press, 1973.

Barthes, Roland. *Image—Music—Text*. Translated by Stephen Heath. New York: Noonday Press/Farrar, Straus and Giroux, 1977.

Bauer, Maria. *Foundations Unearthed*. Glendale, CA: Veritas Press, 1944.

———. *Francis Bacon's Great Virginia Vault*. N.p.: self-published, 1939.

Baxter, James Phinney. *The Greatest of Literary Problems: The Authorship of the Works of Shakespeare*. Boston: Houghton Mifflin, 1915.

Beaumont, George. *The Anti-Swedenborg: Or, a Declaration of the Principal Errors Contained in the Theological Writings of E. Swedenborg*. London: Richard Baynes, 1824.

Beckett, Jane W. *The Secret of Shakespeare's Doublet*. Hampton, NH: P. E. Randall, 1977.

Begley, Walter. *Is it Shakespeare? The Great Question of Elizabethan Literature*. New York: E. P. Dutton, 1903.

Belsey, Catherine. *Critical Practice*. New York: Methuen, 1980.

Benedetti, Jean. *David Garrick and the Birth of Modern Theatre*. London: Methuen, 2001.

Bennett, Bridget. *Transatlantic Spiritualism and Nineteenth-Century American Literature*. New York: Palgrave Macmillan, 2007.

Bentley, E. C. *Far Horizon*. London: Rider, 1951.

Benz, Ernst. *Emanuel Swedenborg: Visionary Savant in the Age of Reason*. Translated by Nicholas Goodrick-Clarke. West Chester, PA: Swedenborg Foundation, 2002.

Bernauer, James William, and David M. Rasmussen, eds. *The Final Foucault*. Cambridge, MA: MIT Press, 1987.

Bevington, David. "The Late Romances." *Shakespeare: The Late Romances*. New York: Bantam Books, 1988. xxv–xxxiii.

Björnström, Fredrik Johan. *Hypnotism: Its History and Present Development*. Translated by Baron Nils Posse. New York: Humboldt, 1889.

Blackwood's Magazine (periodical, various dates embedded in text).

Bliss, William. *The Real Shakespeare: A Counterblast to Commentators*. London: Sidwick and Jackson, 1947.

Blocksidge, Martin. "'Professionally Defunct but Invigorating': G. Wilson Knight and *Timon of Athens*." *Use of English* 59 (1998–1999): 132–45.

Bloom, Harold. *The Anatomy of Influence: Literature as a Way of Life*. New Haven, CT: Yale University Press, 2011.

———. *Genius: A Mosaic of One Hundred Exemplary Creative Minds*. New York: Warner Books, 2002.

———. *Kabbalah and Criticism*. New York: Continuum, 1993.

———. *Shakespeare: The Invention of the Human*. New York: Riverhead Books, 1998.

Blum, Deborah. *Ghost Hunters: William James and the Search for Scientific Proof of Life after Death*. New York: Penguin Press, 2006.

Bond, Frederick Bligh. *The Gate of Remembrance: The Story of the Psychological Experiment which Resulted in the Discovery of the Edgar Chapel at Glastonbury.* Oxford: Blackwell, 1918.

———. *The Hill of Vision: A Forecast of the Great War and of Social Revolution With the Coming of the New Race.* London: Constable, 1919.

———. *The Return of Johannes.* London: J. O. Hartes, 1925.

Bond, Frederick Bligh, and Hester Dowden. *The Gospel of Philip the Deacon 1932.* New York: Macoy, 1932.

Bossy, John. *Under the Molehill: An Elizabethan Spy Story.* New Haven, CT: Yale University Press, 2001.

Bradley, A. C. *Shakespearean Tragedy.* 1904. Reprint, New York: St. Martin's Press, 1992.

Bradshaw, Graham. *Misrepresentations: Shakespeare and the Materialists.* Ithaca, NY: Cornell University Press, 1993.

———. *Shakespeare's Skepticism.* Ithaca, NY: Cornell University Press, 1987.

Brandon, Ruth. *The Spiritualists: The Passion for the Occult in the Nineteenth and Twentieth Centuries.* New York: Alfred A. Knopf, 1983.

Braude, Ann. *Radical Spirits: Spiritualism and Women's Rights in Nineteenth-Century America.* Boston: Beacon Press, 1989.

Braude, Stephen E. *The Limits of Influence: Psychokinesis and the Philosophy of Science.* New York: Routledge and Kegan Paul, 1986.

Brewer, David A. *The Afterlife of Character, 1726–1825.* Philadelphia: University of Pennsylvania Press, 2005.

Briggs, John C. "Within Athens' Shadow: The Ghost of Plutarch in Shakespeare's *Timon of Athens.*" *Poetica* 48 (1997): 119–40.

Bristol, Michael D. *Shakespeare's America, America's Shakespeare.* New York: Routledge, 1990.

———. *Big-Time Shakespeare.* New York: Routledge, 1996.

British Journal of Dermatology, The (periodical, various dates embedded in text).

British Medical Journal (periodical, various dates embedded in text).

Britten, Emma Hardinge. *Modern American Spiritualism: A Twenty Years' Record.* New York: self-published, 1870.

Browne, Hugh Junor. *The Holy Truth, or, the Coming Reformation.* London: A. Hall, 1876.

Brown, Terence. *Ireland's Literature: Selected Essays.* Totowa, NJ: Rowman and Littlefield, 1988.

Bruns, Gerald L. *Modern Poetry and the Idea of Language: A Critical and Historical Study.* New Haven, CT: Yale University Press, 1974.

Bucke, Richard Maurice. *Cosmic Consciousness.* Philadelphia: Conservator, 1894.

Buckland, Raymond. *Solitary Séance: How You Can Talk With Spirits on Your Own.* Woodbury, MN: Llewellyn Publications, 2011.

Budiansky, Stephen. *Her Majesty's Spymaster: Elizabeth I, Sir Francis Walsingham, and the Birth of Modern Espionage.* New York: Viking, 2005.

Buranelli, Vincent. *The Wizard From Vienna.* London: Peter Owen, 1975.

Burgess, William. *The Bible in Shakspeare: A Study of the Relation of the Works of William Shakspeare to the Bible*. New York: Thomas Y. Crowell, 1903.

Bush, George. *Mesmer and Swedenborg: Or, the Relation of the Developments of Mesmerism to the Doctrines and Disclosures of Swedenborg*. New York: John Allen, 1847.

Cadwallader, Mary E. *Hydesville in History*. Chicago: Progressive Thinker, 1917.

Calvet, Louis-Jean. *Roland Barthes: A Biography*. Translated by Sarah Wykes. Indianapolis: Indiana University Press, 1995.

Carey, George Saville. *Shakespeare's Jubilee, a Masque*. London: T. Becket and P. A. De Hondt, 1769.

Carlyle, Thomas. *On Heroes, Hero-worship, and the Heroic in History: Six Lectures*. New York: John Wiley, 1849.

Carpenter, Edward. *The Intermediate Sex*. London: Swan Sonnenschein, 1908.

———. *Love's Coming of Age*. London: Labour Press, 1896.

Case and Comment: The Lawyer's Magazine (periodical, various dates embedded in text).

Chakravarti, Kshitish Chandra. *Lectures on Hindu Religion, Philosophy and Yoga*. Calcutta: U. C. Shome, 1893.

Chaloner, John Armstrong. *Robbery Under Law; or The Battle of the Millionaires: A Play in Three Acts and Three Scenes*. 2nd ed. Roanoke Rapids, NC: Palmetto Press, 1915.

Chambers, E. K. *The Disintegration of Shakespeare: Annual Shakespeare Lecture, 1924*. London: British Academy, 1925.

Chambers, John. *Victor Hugo's Conversations with the Spirit World: A Literary Genius's Hidden Life*. Rochester, VT: Destiny Books, 1998.

Champion De Crespigny, Rose. Speech. Quoted in "British College of Psychic Science Annual Dinner." *Quarterly Transactions of the British College of Psychic Science* 10, no. 1 (April 1931): 51–56.

Chapin, Anna Alice. *Greenwich Village*. New York: Dodd, Mead, 1917.

Chaplin, David. *Exploring Other Worlds: Margaret Fox, Elisha Kent Kane and the Antebellum Culture of Curiosity*. Amherst: University of Massachusetts Press, 2004.

Chaucer, Geoffrey [disputed]. *The Equatorie of the Planets*. Edited by Derek J. Price. Cambridge: Cambridge University Press, 1955.

Clare, Janet. "*Hamlet* and Modernism: T. S. Eliot and G. Wilson Knight." In *Shakespeare and European Politics*. Edited by Dirk Delabastita, Jozef de Vos, and Paul Franssen, 234–45. Newark: University of Delaware Press, 2008.

Clark, Barrett Harper. *European Theories of the Drama: An Anthology of Dramatic Theory and Criticism from Aristotle to the Present Day*. Cincinnati, OH: Stewart, 1918.

Clodd, Edward. *The Question: "If a Man Die, Shall He Live Again?": Job XIV 14. A Brief History and Examination of Modern Spiritualism*. New York: E. J. Clode, 1918.

Cooper, Joe. *The Case of the Cottingley Fairies*. Foreword by Colin Wilson. London: Hale, 1990.

Cottom, Daniel. *Abyss of Reason: Cultural Movements, Revelations, and Betrayals*. New York: Oxford University Press, 1991.

Coursen, H. R. *Shakespeare: The Two Traditions*. Teaneck, NJ: Fairleigh Dickinson University Press, 1999.

Cox, Robert S. *Body and Soul: A Sympathetic History of Spiritualism*. Charlottesville: University of Virginia Press, 2003.

Crabbe, George. *The Library*. London: J. Dodsley, 1781.

Creaven, Sean. *Against the Spiritual Turn: Marxism, Realism and Critical Theory*. New York: Routledge/Francis and Taylor, 2010.

Crenshaw, James. *Telephone Between Worlds* 1950. 6th printing. Los Angeles: De Vorss, 1957.

Crookes, William. *Researches in the Phenomena of Spiritualism*. London: J. Burns, 1874.

Crouch, J. H. Review of *Shakespeare's Dramatic Challenge: On the Rise of Shakespeare's Tragic Heroes*, by G. Wilson Knight. *Library Journal* 102 (May 15, 1977): 1188.

Crowell, Eugene. *The Identity of Primitive Christianity and Modern Spiritualism*. 2 vols. New York: Two Worlds, 1881.

Crumey, Andrew. "An Experiment with Time." *Picador* [blog]. March 2008. http://www.crumey.toucansurf.com/an_experiment_with_time.html.

Cummins, Geraldine. *The Fate of Colonel Fawcett: A Narrative of His Last Expedition*. London: Aquarian Press, 1955.

———. *Swan on a Black Sea; A Study in Automatic Writing: The Cummins-Willett Scripts*. Edited by Signe Toksvig. Foreword by C. D. Broad. Rev. ed. New York: S. Weiser, 1970.

———. *Unseen Adventures*. London: Rider, 1951.

Cummins, Geraldine Dorothy (see entries for Cummins, Geraldine).

Cummins v. Bond. 1926. C. 1059. Chancery Division. 1927. 1 Ch 167; hearing dates: 21, 22 July 1926; accessed through LexisNexis database.

Cuningham, Granville C. *Bacon's Secret Disclosed in Contemporary Books*. London: Gay and Hancock, 1911.

Cunningham, Henry. "On 'Vllorxa' in 'Timon of Athens.'" *The Athenæum*, July 13, 1901, 71.

Cunningham, Wallace McCook, ed. *The Tragedy of Sir Francis Bacon Prince of England*. Los Angeles: Philosopher's Press, 1940.

Dallas, Eneas Sweetland, ed. "The Shakespeare Jubilee." *Once a Week* 10 (January 16, 1864): 104–12.

Darnton, Robert. *Mesmerism and the End of the Enlightenment in France*. New York: Schocken Books, 1970.

Davenport, Reuben Briggs. *The Death-Blow to Spiritualism*. New York: G. W. Dillingham, 1888.

Davies, Thomas. *Memoirs of the Life of David Garrick*. 2 vols. London: self-published, 1780.

Davis, Andrew Jackson. *The Magic Staff: An Autobiography*. New York: J. S. Brown, 1857.

———. *The Principles of Nature, Her Divine Revelations*. New York: S. S. Lyon and W. Fishbough, 1851.

Dawson, Anthony B., and Paul Yachnin, eds. Introduction to *Richard II*. New York: Oxford University Press, 2011). 1–117.

De Casseres, Benjamin. *Forty Immortals*. New York: Seven Arts, 1926.

Deelman, Christian. *The Great Shakespeare Jubilee*. New York: Viking Press, 1964.

De Grazia, Margreta, and Peter Stallybrass. "The Materiality of the Shakespearean Text." *Shakespeare Quarterly* 44 (1993): 255–83.

Delacour, Jean-Baptiste. *Glimpses of the Beyond: The Extraordinary Experiences of People Who Have Crossed the Brink of Death and Returned*. Translated by E. B. Garside. New York: Delacorte Press, 1974.

De Man, Paul. *The Resistance to Theory*. Edited by Wlad Godzich. Minneapolis: University of Minnesota Press, 1986.

Derrida, Jacques. *Specters of Marx: The State of the Debt, the Work of Mourning, and New International*. Translated by Peggy Kamuf. New York: Routledge, 1994.

Dickens, Charles. *The Letters of Charles Dickens*. Edited by Georgina Hogarth and Mary Dickens. 2 vols. 2nd ed. London: Chapman and Hall, 1880.

Dickinson, Goldsworthy Lowes. *Greek View of Life*. London: Methuen, 1896.

Dirac, Paul Adrien Maurice. *The Collected Works of P. A. M. Dirac, 1924–1948*. Edited by R. H. Dalitz. Cambridge: Cambridge University Press, 1995.

Dobson, Michael. *The Making of the National Poet: Shakespeare, Adaptation and Authorship, 1660–1769*. New York: Oxford University Press, 1992.

———. "Wilson Knight's *Wheel of Fire*." *Essays in Criticism* 52, no. 3 (July 2002): 235–44.

Dodd, Alfred. *Sir Francis Bacon's Diary*. London: G. Lapworth, 1947.

———. *Francis Bacon's Personal Life-Story*. London: Rider, 1949.

———. *The Immortal Master*. London: Rider, 1943.

———. *The Marriage of Elizabeth Tudor*. London: Rider, 1940.

———. *The Martyrdom of Francis Bacon*. London: Rider, [1945?].

———. *The Secret History of Francis Bacon (Our Shake-speare) The Son of Queen Elizabeth*. 7th ed. London: C. W. Daniel, 1941.

———. *Shakespeare: Creator of Freemasonry*. London: Rider, 1937.

———. *Who Was Shake-speare? Was He Francis Bacon, The Earl of Oxford or William Shaksper?* London: George Lapworth, 1947.

Dodd, William. *The Beauties of Shakespeare*. London: Chiswick Press, 1821.

Döllinger, Johann Joseph Ignaz von. *Addresses on Historical and Literary Subjects*. Translated by Margaret Warre. London: John Murray, 1894.

Donawerth, Jane. "Authorial Ethos, Collaborative Voice, and Rhetorical Theory by Women." In *Rhetorical Women: Roles and Representations*. Edited by Hildy Miller and Lillian Bridwell-Bowles, 107–24. Tuscaloosa: The University of Alabama Press, 2005

Donnelly, Ignatius. *Atlantis: The Antediluvian World*. New York: Harper, 1882.

———. *The Cipher in the Plays and on the Tombstone*. Minneapolis, MN: Verulam, 1899.

———. *The Great Cryptogram: Francis Bacon's Cipher in the So-Called Shakespeare Plays*. New York: R. S. Peale, 1887.

Doten, Lizzie. *Poems From the Inner Life*. 17th ed. Boston: Colby and Rich, 1863.

Dowden, Edward. "The Interpretation of Literature." In *Transcripts and Studies*, 237–68. London: Kegan Paul, Trench, Trübner, 1896.

———. *Introduction to Shakespeare*. Freeport, NY: Books for Libraries Press, 1970.

———. *Letters of Edward Dowden and His Correspondents*. Edited by Elizabeth D. Dowden and Hilda M. Dowden. London: J. M. Dent, 1914.

———. *Shakspere: A Critical Study of His Mind and Art*. London: Henry S. King, 1875.

———. "Shakespeare as Man of Science (Bacon-Shakespeare Controversy)." In *Essays Modern and Elizabethan*, 282–307. New York: E. P. Dutton, 1910.

———. *Shakespeare Primer*. London: Macmillan, 1877.

———. *The Sonnets*. London: Kegan, Paul, Trench, 1881.

Dowden, Hester. *Hero: A Story for Dog Lovers of All Ages*. Andrew Dakers: London, 1943.

———. "How I Received Oscar Wilde's 'Spirit Play,'" *The Graphic*, March 10, 1928, 401.

———. *Oscar Wilde From Purgatory: Psychic Messages*. New ed. Whitefish, MT: Kessinger, 2004.

Doyle, Arthur Conan. *The Coming of the Fairies*. New York: George H. Doran, 1922.

———. *Do We Live after Death? The New Revelation*. New York: George H. Doran, 1918.

———. *Edge of the Unknown*. Guildford, England: White Crow Books, 2010.

———. *The History of Spiritualism*. 2 vols. 1926. Reprint, New York: Arno Press, 1975.

Drabelle, Dennis. "Explorer in a Hurry." *The Pennsylvania Gazette*, March/April 2008, 30–35.

Dubrow, Heather. *Captive Victors: Shakespeare's Narrative Poems and Sonnets*. Ithaca, NY: Cornell University Press, 1987.

During, Simon. *Foucault and Literature: Towards a Genealogy of Writing*. New York: Routledge, 1992.

Dwight, John Sullivan, *Dwight's Journal of Music: A Paper of Art and Literature* (periodical, various dates embedded in text).

Eads, Harvey L. *Shaker Sermons: Scripto-Rational. Containing the Substance of Shaker Theology. Together With Replies and Criticisms Logically and Clearly Set Forth*. 3rd ed. South Union, KY: N. p., 1884.

Easthope, Antony. "Freud's Spectres." In *Evil Spirits: Nihilism and the Fate of Modernity*. Edited by Gary Banham and Charlie Blake, 146–64. New York: Manchester University Press, 2000.

Edmonds, John Worth, George T. Dexter, and Nathaniel Pitcher Tallmadge. *Spiritualism*. 2 vols. New York: Partridge and Brittan, 1853–55.

Edwards, Sarah. "Co-Operation and Co-Authorship: Automatic Writing, Socialism and Gender in Late Victorian and Edwardian Birmingham." *Women's Writing: the Elizabethan to Victorian Period* 15, no. 3 (October 2008): 371–89.

Ehnenn, Jill R. *Women's Literary Collaboration, Queerness, and Late-Victorian Culture*. Burlington, VT: Ashgate, 2008.

Ellis, John M. *Literature Lost: Social Agendas and the Corruption of the Humanities.* New Haven, CT: Yale University Press, 1997.

Elze, Karl. *William Shakespeare: A Literary Biography.* Translated by L. Dora Schmitz. London: G. Bell and Sons, 1888.

Encyclopedia of Occultism and Parapsychology. Edited by Leslie Shepard, Lewis Spence, and Nandor Fodor. 2 vols. 3rd ed. Detroit, MI: Gale Research, 1991.

England, Martha Winburn. *Garrick's Jubilee.* Columbus: Ohio University Press, 1964.

Ernst, Bernard M. L., and Hereward Carrington. *Houdini and Conan Doyle: The Story of a Strange Friendship.* London: Hutchinson, 1933.

Faivre, Antoine. *Access to Western Esotericism.* Albany: State University of New York Press, 1994.

Farrar, Mrs. John [née Elizabeth Rotch]. *Recollections of Seventy Years.* Boston: Ticknor and Field, 1865.

Felperin, Howard. "Bardolatry Then and Now." In *The Appropriation of Shakespeare: Post-Renaissance Reconstructions of the Works of the Myth.* Edited by Jean I. Marsden, 129–44. New York: St. Martin's Press, 1991.

Ferguson, Christine. "Zola in Ghostland: Spiritualist Literary Criticism and Naturalist Supernaturalism." *SEL: Studies in English Literature 1500–1900* 50, no. 4 (Autumn 2010): 877–94.

Fernie, Ewan, ed. Introduction to *Spiritual Shakespeares.* 1–27. New York: Routledge, 2005.

Findlay, Arthur. *On the Edge of the Etheric, or Survival after Death Scientifically Explained.* London: Psychic Books, [1949?].

———. *Looking Back: The Autobiography of a Spiritualist.* 4th ed. London: Psychic News, 1961.

Foakes, R. A. "'Armed at Point Exactly': The Ghost in *Hamlet.*" *Shakespeare Survey* 58 (2005): 34–47.

Fornell, Earl Wesley. *The Unhappy Medium: Spiritualism and the Life of Margaret Fox.* Austin: University of Texas, 1964.

Fortean Times (periodical, various dates embedded in text).

Foster, Donald W. "Commentary: In the Name of the Author." *New Literary History* 33, no. 2 (Spring 2002): 375–96.

Foucault, Michel. *History of Sexuality.* Translated by Robert Hurley. Vol. 1, *An Introduction.* New York: Vintage, 1978.

———. *The Order of Things: An Archaeology of the Human Sciences.* New York: Routledge, 2002.

——— *The Politics of Truth.* Edited by Sylvre Lotringer. Translated by Lysa Hochroth and Catherine Porter. Los Angeles: Semiotext[e], 1997.

——— "What is an Author?" In *The Foucault Reader.* Edited by Paul Rabinow, 101–20. New York: Vintage Books, 2010.

Fox, Kate. *Fox-Taylor Automatic Writing 1869–1892 Unabridged Record.* Edited by Sarah E. L. Taylor. Preface by W. G. Langworthy Taylor. Minneapolis, MN: Tribune-Great West, self-published, 1932.

Fox, Margaret. Letters. Seybert Commission Correspondence. Ms. Coll. 412 Folder 73. Rare Book and Manuscript Library, University of Pennsylvania.

Franklin, Colin. *Shakespeare Domesticated: The Eighteenth-Century Editions.* Brookfield, VT: Scolar Press, 1991.

Franklin, J. Jeffrey. *The Lotus and the Lion: Buddhism and the British Empire.* Ithaca, NY: Cornell University Press, 2008.

Frederick, James M., and Olga A. Tildes. *The Silver Cord: Life Here and Hereafter.* N.p.: self-published, 1946.

Frey, Charles H. *Making Sense of Shakespeare.* Teaneck, NJ: Fairleigh Dickinson University Press, 1999.

Friedman, William F., and Elizabeth S. Friedman, *The Shakespearean Ciphers Examined: An Analysis of Cryptographic Systems Used as Evidence that Some Author Other Than William Shakespeare Wrote the Plays Commonly Attributed to Him.* Cambridge: Cambridge University Press, 1957.

Fripp, Peter. *The Mystic Philosophy of Sant Mat.* London: Neville Spearman, 1964.

Fripp, Peter, and Hester Dowden, *The Book of Johannes.* New York: Rider, [1945?].

Frye, Northrop. *Northrop Frye on Shakespeare.* Bloomington: Indiana University Press, 1976.

———. *Spiritus Mundi: Essays on Literature, Myth, and Society.* Markham, Ontario, Canada: Fitzhenry and Whiteside, 1991.

Funk, Isaac K. *The Widow's Mite and Other Psychic Phenomena.* New York: Funk, 1911.

Furness, Horace Howard. "The Argument for Shakespeare as Shakespeare." In *Shakespeare and His Rivals: A Casebook on the Authorship Controversy.* Edited by George McMichael and Edgar M. Glenn, 225–30. New York: Odyssey Press, 1962.

———. *Letters of Horace Howard Furness.* 2 vols. Boston: Houghton Mifflin, 1922.

———. Letters. Seybert Commission Correspondence. Ms. Coll. 412 Folder 73. Rare Book and Manuscript Library, University of Pennsylvania.

———. *Preliminary Report of the Commission Appointed by the University of Pennsylvania to Investigate Modern Spiritualism.* Philadelphia: J. B. Lippincott, 1887.

———. *On the Text of Shakespeare.* Philadelphia: Poet-Lore, 1891.

———. *The Tempest: A New Variorum Edition of Shakespeare.* Philadelphia: J. B. Lippincott, 1892.

Gallup, Elizabeth Wells. *The Bi-literal Cypher of Sir Francis Bacon, Discovered in His Works.* 3 vols. Detroit, MI: Howard, 1910.

———. *The Tragedy of Anne Boleyn: A Drama in Cipher Found in the Works of Sir Francis Bacon.* Detroit, MI: Howard, 1901.

Galston, David. *Archives and the Event of God: The Impact of Michel Foucault on Philosophical Theology.* Montreal: McGill-Queen's University Press, 2011.

Garber, Marjorie. *Shakespeare's Ghost Writers.* New York: Methuen, 1987.

Gardner, Edward L. *Fairies: The Cottingley Photographs and Their Sequel.* Rev. ed. 1966. Reprint, London: Theosophical Publishing, 1974. First published 1945.

Gardner, Martin. *The Whys of a Philosophical Scrivener.* New York: St. Martin's Griffin, 1999.

Garrett, Clarke. *Origins of the Shakers: From the Old World to the New World.* Baltimore, MD: Johns Hopkins University Press, 1998.

Gibson, James M. "Horace Howard Furness: Book Collector and Library Builder." In *Shakespeare Study Today: The Horace Howard Furness Memorial Lectures*. Edited by Georgianna Zeigler, 169–89. New York: AMS Press, 1986.

———. *The Philadelphia Shakespeare Story: Horace Howard Furness and the New Variorum Shakespeare*. New York: AMS Press, 1990.

Gibson, Marion. *Reading Witchcraft: Stories of Early English Witches*. New York: Routledge, 1999.

Goldsmith, Margaret. *Franz Anton Mesmer: A History of Mesmerism*. Garden City, NY: Doubleday, Doran, 1934.

Goodall, Jane R. *Stage Presence*. New York: Routledge, 2008.

Goodman, William. "Milton, Shakespear, and Potatoes," letter to *Cobbett's Political Register* 30 (January 20, 1816): 82–84.

Goyder, David George. *Swedenborg and His Mission*. London: Fred Pitman, 1853.

Grady, Hugh. *The Modernist Shakespeare: Critical Texts in a Material World*. Oxford: Clarendon Press, 1991.

Gray, John. *The Immortalization Commission: Science and the Strange Quest to Cheat Death*. New York: Farrar, Straus and Giroux, 2011.

Greeley, Horace, and Robert Dale Owen. *Recollections of a Busy Life*. New York: J. B. Ford, 1868.

Greenblatt, Stephen. *Hamlet in Purgatory*. Princeton, NJ: Princeton University Press, 2001.

———. *Shakespearean Negotiations: The Circulation of Social Energy in Renaissance England*. Berkeley: University of California Press, 1988.

———. *Will in the World: How Shakespeare Became Shakespeare*. New York: W. W. Norton, 2004.

Greene, Velma O'Donoghue. "Wild(e) Imaginings in *The Extraordinary Play* (1924) by Geraldine Cummins and Hester Travers Smith (nee Dowden)." Paper presented at the Irish Society for Theatre Research, 2008.

Green, Frances H. *Biography of Mrs. Semantha Mettler, The Clairvoyant*. New York: Harmonial Association, 1853.

G. S. [Hugh Macneile, Dean of Ripon]. *Mesmerism the Gift of God: In Reply to "Satanic Agency and Mesmerism."* London: William Edward Painter, 1843.

Güldenstubbé, Ludwig de. *Pneumatologie Positive et Experimentale: La Realité des Esprits et le Phénomène Merveilleux de leur Ecriture Directe Démontrées*. Paris: Librairie A. Franck, 1857.

Gutierrez, Cathy. *Plato's Ghost: Spiritualism in the American Renaissance*. New York: Oxford University Press, 2009.

Haarhoff, Thoedore Johannes. *Smuts the Humanist: A Personal Reminiscence*. Oxford: Basil Blackwell, 1970.

Halliday, F. E. *The Cult of Shakespeare*. London: Gerald Duckworth, 1957.

Hanegraaff, Wouter J. *New Age Religion and Western Culture: Esotericism in the Mirror of Secular Thought*. Albany: State University of New York Press, 1998.

Hardinge, Emma. *Modern American Spiritualism*. 3rd ed. New York: self-published, 1870.

Hardison, O. B. Jr. "A Tree, a Streamlined Fish, and a Self-Squared Dragon: Science as a Form of Culture." In *Poetics and Praxis, Understanding and Imagination: The Collected Essays of O. B. Hardison Jr.* Edited by Arthur F. Kinney, 328–60. Athens: University of Georgia Press, 1997.

Harvey, John. "The Photographic Medium: Representation, Reconstitution, Consciousness, and Collaboration in Early Twentieth-Century Spiritualism." *Technoetic Arts: A Journal of Speculative Research* 2, no. 2 (2004): 109–23.

Hawkes, Terence. General editor's preface to *Alternative Shakespeares 2*, xi–xii (New York: Routledge, 1996).

———. Introduction to *Alternative Shakespeares 2* (New York: Routledge, 1996). 1–16.

———. *Meaning by Shakespeare.* New York: Routledge, 1992.

———. *Shakespeare in the Present.* Accents on Shakespeare. New York: Routledge, 2002.

Hawthorne, Nathaniel. "Recollections of a Gifted Woman." In *Our Old Home*, 78–105. London: Smith, Elder, 1864.

Hazelgrove, Jenny. *Spiritualism and British Society Between the Wars.* Manchester: Manchester University Press, 2000.

Hemans, Dorothea Browne. *Songs of the Affections with Other Poems*, London: William Blackwood, 1830.

Herman, Daniel. "Whose Knocking? Spiritualism as Entertainment and Therapy in Nineteenth-Century San Francisco." *American Nineteenth Century History* 7, no. 3 (September 2006): 417–42.

Heron, Flodden W. *Who Wrote Shakespeare? Recent Discoveries by Members of the Shakespeare Fellowship.* San Francisco: Literary Anniversary Club, 1943.

Hodgdon, Barbara. *The Shakespeare Trade: Performance and Appropriations.* Philadelphia: University of Pennsylvania Press, 1998.

Hodson, Geoffrey. *The Hidden Wisdom in the Holy Bible.* 3 vols. Wheaton, IL: Theosophical Publishing, 1967.

Hoeveler, Diane Long. *Gothic Riffs: Secularizing the Uncanny in the European Imagery, 1780–1820.* Columbus: Ohio State University Press, 2010.

Holden, John Watkins. *Wizard's Wanderings from China to Peru.* London: Dean and Son, 1886.

Holy Bible. King James Version.

Hopkins, Vivian C. *Prodigal Puritan: A Life of Delia Bacon.* Cambridge, MA: Belknap Press of Harvard University Press, 1959.

Houdini, Harry. *A Magician Among the Spirits.* Amsterdam: Fredonia Books, 2002.

Howard, E. Lee. *My Adventure into Spiritualism.* New York: Macmillan, 1935.

Howard, Jennifer. "A Shakespeare Scholar Takes on a 'Taboo' Subject." *The Chronicle of Higher Education*, March 28, 2010. http://chronicle.com/article/A-Shakespeare-Scholar-Takes-on/64811.

Howard, Joseph Jr. *Life of Henry Ward Beecher, the Eminent Pulpit and Platform Orator.* Philadelphia: Hubbard, 1887).

Hughes, Marilynn. *The Mysteries of the Redemption: A Treatise on Out-of-Body Travel and Mysticism.* Morrisville, NC: Lulu.com, 2003.

Hull, Moses, and William F. Jamieson. *The Greatest Debate within a Half Century upon Modern Spiritualism.* Chicago: Progressive Thinker, 1902.

Hutchinson, Robert. *Elizabeth's Spymaster: Francis Walsingham and the Secret War that Saved England.* New York: Thomas Dunne Books, 2007.

Hyslop, James Hervey. *Contact with the Other World: The Latest Evidence as to Communication with the Dead.* New York: Century, 1919.

———. *Proceedings of the American Society for Psychical Research: A Further Record of Mediumistic Experiments* 19 (1925).

Indiana Commission on Public Records. "Medical Treatment for Insanity." http://www.in.gov/icpr/2704.htm.

Irish Playgoer and Amusement Record, The. (periodical, various dates embedded in text).

Isaacs, Earnest. "The Fox Sisters and American Spiritualism." In *The Occult in America: New Historical Perspectives.* Edited by Howard Ker and Charles L. Crow, 79–110. Chicago: University of Illinois Press, 1986.

Isherwood, Christopher. *Lost Years: A Memoir 1945–1951.* Edited by Katherine Bucknell. New York: HarperCollins, 2000.

Jackson, Herbert G. *The Spirit Rappers.* Garden City, NY: Doubleday, 1972.

James, Henry. *The Altar of the Dead: The Beast in the Jungle; The Birthplace, and Other Tales.* New York: Charles Scribner's Sons, 1909.

Jeffrey, Francis. Review of *The Family Shakespeare*, by Thomas Bowdler. *Edinburgh Review* 71 (1821): 52–54.

J. M. [unknown author]. *Shakespeare Self-Revealed in his "Sonnets" and "Phoenix and Turtle."* London: Sherratt and Hughes, 1904.

Johnson, Edward D. *The First Folio of Shake-speare.* London: C. Palmer, 1932.

Johnson, Gerald W. *The Lunatic Fringe.* Westport, CT: Greenwood Press, 1957.

Johnson, Samuel. *Johnson on Shakespeare: Essays and Notes Selected and Set Forth with an Introduction.* Edited by Walter Raleigh. London: Henry Frowde, 1908.

Joicey, G. "Shakspeariana." *Notes and Queries* 87 (February 1893): 102.

Jones, John. "Shakespeare and Wilson Knight (Revisited)." *Scripsi* 4, no. 1 (July 1986): 51–57.

Kahan, Jeffrey. *The Cult of Kean.* Aldershot: Ashgate, 2006.

———. "Shakespeare and the Forging of Belief." *Critical Quarterly* 43, no. 2 (2001): 19–33.

Kane, Elisha Kent, and Margaret Fox. *The Love-Life of Dr. Kane: Containing the Correspondence, and a History of the Acquaintance, Engagement, and Secret Marriage Between Elisha K. Kane and Margaret Fox.* New York: Carleton, 1866.

Kant, Immanuel. *Critique of Pure Reason.* Translated by Max Müller. 1781. Reprint, Garden City, NY: Anchor Books/Double Day, 1966.

Kaplan, Jeffrey, and Heléne Lööw. Introduction to *The Cultic Milieu: Oppositional Subcultures in an Age of Globalization*, 1–11. Walnut Creek, CA: Altamira Press/Roman and Littlefield, 2002.

Kastan, David Scott. *Shakespeare after Theory.* New York: Routledge, 1999.

Kavanagh, Preston. *Secrets of the Jewish Exile: The Bible's Codes, Messiah, and Suffering Servant.* Tarentum, PA: Word Association, 2005.

Keating, Keith. "The Human Form as Dramatic Symbol: An Interview with G. Wilson Knight." *Literature in Performance: A Journal of Literary and Performing Art* 82, no. 3 (November 1982): 49–59.

Kellner, Leon. *Restoring Shakespeare: A Critical Analysis of the Misreadings in Shakespeare's Works*. New York: Biblo and Tannen, 1969. Kemble, John Philip. *Macbeth, and King Richard the Third: An Essay, in Answer to Remarks on Some of the Characters of Shakspeare*. London: John Murray, 1817.

Kermode, Frank. *Shakespeare's Language*. New York: Farrar, Straus, Giroux, 2000.

Kiddle, Henry. *Spiritual Communications*. New York: Authors' Publishing, 1879.

Kiernan, Victor. *Eight Tragedies of Shakespeare: A Marxist Study*. New York: Verso, 1996.

Kipling, Rudyard. *The Works of Rudyard Kipling*. 12 vols. New York: Doubleday and McClure, 1899.

Knight, Charles. *The English Cyclopaedia: A New Dictionary of Universal Knowledge*. Vol. 5. London: Bradbury and Evans, 1860.

Knight, G. Wilson. *Atlantic Crossing: An Autobiographical Design*. London: J. M. Dent and Sons, 1939.

———. *The Burning Oracle: Studies in the Poetry of Action*. Toronto: Oxford University Press, 1939.

———. *Byron and Shakespeare*. New York: Barnes and Noble, 1966.

———. "Caroline: Life after Death." Manuscript Collection of the University of Exeter.

———. *Christ and Nietzsche: An Essay in Poetic Wisdom*. New York: Staples Press, 1948.

———. *The Christian Renaissance*. London: Methuen, 1962.

———. *The Dynasty of Stowe*. London: Fortune Press, 1946

———. *Gold Dust, with Other Poetry*. London: Routledge and Kegan Paul, 1968.

———. *The Golden Labyrinth*. London: Phoenix House, 1962.

———. *Hiroshima: On Prophecy and the Sun-Bomb*. London: Andrew Dakers, 1946.

———. *The Imperial Theme: Further Interpretations of Shakespeare's Tragedies Including the Roman Plays*. 1931. Reprint, London: Methuen, 1965.

———. Interview with the *Sunday Independent* [Dublin, Ireland] September 18, 1977.

———. *Jackson Knight: A Biography*. Oxford: Alden Press, 1975.

———. *Lord Byron; Christian Virtues*. New York: Oxford University Press, 1952.

———. *The Mutual Flame: On Shakespeare's "Sonnets" and "The Phoenix and the Turtle."* London: Methuen, 1955.

———. *Myth and Miracle: An Essay on the Mystic Symbolism of Shakespeare*. London: Edited by J. Burrow, 1929.

———. *Neglected Powers: Essays in Nineteenth and Twentieth Century Literature*. New York: Barnes and Noble, 1971.

———. *The Poetry of Pope: Laureate of Peace*. New York: Barnes and Noble, 1965.

———. *Principles of Shakespearean Production*. Harmondsworth: Penguin Books, 1949.

————. "Road to Kasvin." Unpublished manuscript. Composed in 1943 with undated revisions. Special Collection, University of Exeter.

————. *The Saturnian Quest: A Chart of the Prose Works of John Cowper Powys.* Sussex: Harvester Press, 1978.

————. *Shakespeare and Religion: Essays of Forty Years.* London, Routledge and K. Paul, 1967.

————. *Shakespearian Dimensions.* Brighton, Sussex: Harvester Press, 1984.

————. *The Shakespearian Tempest.* London: Methuen, 1953.

————. *Shakespeare's Dramatic Challenge: On the Rise of Shakespeare's Tragic Heroes.* New York: Barnes and Noble Books, 1977.

————. *Sovereign Flower.* London: Methuen, 1966.

————. "Spirit-Writing." Manuscript Collection of the University of Exeter.

————. *Starlit Dome: Studies in the Poetry of Vision.* London: Oxford University Press, 1943.

————. *Symbol of Man: On Body-Soul for Stage and Studio.* New York: Regency Press, 1979.

————. *This Sceptered Isle: Shakespeare's Message for England at War.* Folcroft, PA: Folcroft Library Editions, 1969.

————. *Visions and Vices: Essays on John Cowper Powys.* Edited by John D. Christie. London: Cecil Woolf, 1990.

————. *The Wheel of Fire.* London: Methuen, 1949.

Knight, G. Wilson, and John Cowper Powys. *The Letters of John Cowper Powys to G. R. Wilson Knight.* Edited by Robert Blackmore. London: Cecil Woolf, 1983.

Knight, G. Wilson, and W. F. Jackson Knight [Title page only cites W. F. Jackson Knight as author.]. *Elysion: On Ancient Greek and Roman Beliefs Concerning a Life after Death.* New York: Barnes and Noble, 1970.

————. *Many-Minded Homer: An Introduction.* Edited by John D. Christie. London: George and Unwin, 1968.

Knight, Jackson W. F. *Accentual Symmetry in Vergil.* Oxford: Basil Blackwell, 1950

————. *Poetic Inspiration: An Approach to Virgil.* Exmouth: Raleigh Press, 1946.

————. *Roman Vergil.* London: Faber and Faber, [1944].

————. *Roman Vergil.* Rev. ed. New York: Barnes and Noble, 1968. First published 1966.

Kollar, Rene. *Searching for Raymond: Anglicanism, Spiritualism, and Bereavement between the Two World Wars.* Lanham, MD: Lexington Books, 2000.

Kontou, Tatiana. *Spiritualism and Women's Writing: From the Fin de Siècle to the Neo-Victorian.* New York: Palgrave Macmillan, 2009.

Kuhn, Alvin Boyd. *Theosophy: A Modern Revival of Ancient Wisdom.* New York: Henry Holt, 1930.

Kurshan, Ilana. "Mind Reading: Literature in the Discourse of Early Victorian Phrenology and Mesmerism." In *Victorian Literary Mesmerism.* Edited by Martin Willis and Catherine Wynne, 17–38. New York: Rodopi, 2006.

Lagercrantz, Olof, and Anders Hallengren. *Epic of the Afterlife: A Literary Approach to Swedenborg.* West Chester, PA: Swedenborg Foundation, 2002.

Lamb, Charles. *The Complete Works in Prose and Verse of Charles Lamb.* Edited by R. H. Shepherd. London: Chatto and Windus, 1875.

Lancet, The (periodical, various dates embedded in text).

Laporte, Charles. "The Bard, the Bible, and the Victorian Shakespeare Question." *ELH* 74, no. 3 (2007): 609–28.

Lazar [pseudonym]. *The Ghost Epigrams of Oscar Wilde as Taken Down through Automatic Writing.* New York: Covici Friede, 1928.

Leadbeater, C. W. *The Astral Plane.* Adyar, India: Theosophical Society, 1973.

———. *The Hidden Side of Things.* Adyar, India: Theosophical Publishing, 1954.

Leary, Penn. *The Second Cryptographic Shakespeare.* Omaha, NE: Westchester House, 1990.

Leek, Sybil. *Numerology: The Magic of Numbers.* 2nd ed. New York: Macmillan, 1969.

Lehman, Amy. *Victorian Women and the Theatre of Trance: Mediums, Spiritualists and Mesmerists in Performance.* Jefferson, NC: McFarland, 2009.

Lehmann, Courtney. *Shakespeare's Remains: Theater to Film, Early Modern to Postmodern.* Ithaca, NY: Cornell University Press, 2002.

Leonard, Gladys Osborne. *My Life in Two Worlds.* London: Cassell, 1931.

Leonard, Maurice. *People from the Other Side: The Enigmatic Fox Sisters and the History of Victorian Spiritualism.* Stroud, Gloucestershire: History Press, 2008.

Leonard, Todd Jay. *Talking to the Other Side.* New York: iUniverse, 2005.

León-Jones, Karen Silvia de. *Giordano Bruno and the Kabbalah: Prophets, Magicians, and Rabbis.* Lincoln: University of Nebraska Press, 2004.

Lewis, James R., ed. *Odd Gods: New Religions and the Cult Controversy.* Amherst, NY: Prometheus Books, 2001.

Light: A Journal of Psychical, Occult, and Mystical Research (periodical, various dates embedded in text).

Lodge, Oliver. *Past Years: An Autobiography.* New York: Charles Scribner's Sons, 1932.

———. *Phantom Walls.* New York: G. P. Putnam's Sons, 1930.

———. *Science and Immortality.* 1908. Reprint, New York: Moffat, Yard, 1916.

———. *The Survival of Man: A Study in Unrecognized Human Faculty.* New York: George H. Doran, 1909.

London (periodical, various dates embedded in the text).

London, Bette. *Writing Double: Women's Literary Partnerships.* Ithaca, NY: Cornell University Press, 1999.

Lorimer, David. *Survival? Body, Mind and Death in the Light of Psychic Experience.* London: Routledge, 1989.

Los Angeles Times (newspaper, various dates embedded in text).

Lovecraft, H. P. "The Rats in the Walls." In *Tales of H. P. Lovecraft.* Edited by Joyce Carol Oates, 14–29. New York: HarperCollins, 2000.

Loy, David R. *Awareness Bound and Unbound: Buddhist Essays.* Albany: State University of New York, 2009.

Lucas, J. R. *The Future: An Essay on God, Temporality, and Truth.* New York: Blackwell, 1989.

———. *Space, Time and Causality: An Essay in Natural Philosophy.* Oxford: Clarendon Press, 1984.

Lucey, Donna M. *Archie and Amélie: Love and Madness in the Gilded Age.* New York: Three Rivers Press, 2006.

Ludwigson, Kathryn R. *Edward Dowden.* New York: Twayne, 1973.

Lynch, Jack. *Becoming Shakespeare: The Unlikely Afterlife That Turned a Provincial Playwright into the Bard.* New York: Walker, 2007.

Lyte, Henry F. "Abide With Me." Composed 1847. Music added by William H. Monk 1861.

Macey, David. *The Lives of Michel Foucault.* New York: Vintage/Random House, 1993.

MacGregor, S. L. *Kabbala Denudata: The Kabbalah Unveiled, Containing the Following Books of the Zohar.* London: Kegan Paul, Trench, Trubner, 1926.

Macmillan, Hugh. *Two Worlds Are Ours.* London: Macmillan, 1880.

Mallin, Eric S. *Godless Shakespeare.* Shakespeare Now. London: Continuum, 2007.

Malone, Edmond, and James Boswell Jr., eds. *The Plays and Poems of William Shakespeare.* 21 vols. London: J. R. Rivington, etc., 1821.

Marcus, Leah S. *Puzzling Shakespeare: Local Reading and Its Discontents.* Berkeley: University of California Press, 1988.

———. *Unediting the Renaissance: Shakespeare, Marlowe, Milton.* New York: Routledge, 1996.

"Marlowe in Exile? 3. Sonnet 74." The Marlowe Society. http://www.marlowe-society.org/marlowe/life/exile3.html.

Martin, Joel, Patricia Romanowski, and George P. Anderson. *We Don't Die: George Anderson's Conversations with the Other Side.* New York: G. P. Putnam's Sons, 1988.

Martin, Rux. "Truth, Power, Self: An Interview with Michel Foucault October 25, 1982." In *Technologies of the Self: A Seminar With Michel Foucault.* Edited by Luther H. Martin, Huck Gutman, and Patrick H. Hutton, 7–15. Amherst: University of Massachusetts Press, 1988.

Massey, Gerald. *Ancient Egypt: The Light of the World.* London: T. F. Unwin, 1907.

———. *Concerning Spiritualism.* London: J. Burns, [1872].

———. *The Secret Drama of Shakespeare's Sonnets.* N. p.: Richard Clay, 1888.

———. *Shakspeare's Sonnets Never Before Interpreted: His Private Friends Identified: Together with a Recorded Likeness of Himself.* London: Longmans, Green, 1866.

McAlindon, Tom. *Shakespeare Minus 'Theory.'* Burlington, VT: Ashgate, 2004.

McCormack, Jerusha Hull. "Domesticating Delphi: Emily Dickinson and the Electro-Magnetic Telegraph." *American Quarterly* 55, no. 4 (December 2003): 569–601.

McCorristine, Shane. *Spectres of the Self: Thinking About Ghosts and Ghost-seeing in England, 1750–1920.* New York: Cambridge University Press, 2010.

McGarry, Molly. *Ghosts of Futures Past: Spiritualism and the Cultural Politics of Nineteenth-Century America.* Berkeley: University of California Press, 2008.

———. "'The Quick, the Dead, and the Yet Unborn': Untimely Sexualities and Secular Hauntings." In *Secularisms.* Edited by Janet R. Jakobsen and Ann Pellegrini, 249–79. Durham, NC: Duke University Press, 2008.

McMullan, Gordon. *Shakespeare and the Idea of Late Writing: Authorship in the Proximity of Death.* New York: Cambridge University Press, 2007.

McMullin, Stan. *Anatomy of a Seance: A History of Spirit Communication in Central Canada.* Montreal: McGill-Queen's University Press, 2004.

McTaggart, J. M. E. "The Unreality of Time." *Mind: A Quarterly Review of Psychology and Philosophy* 17 (1908): 456–73.

Medium and Daybreak, The (periodical, various dates embedded in text).

Melechi, Antonio. *Servants of the Supernatural: The Night Side of the Victorian Mind.* London: William Heinemann, 2008.

Merrill, James. *Changing Light at Sandover.* New York: Atheneum, 1982.

Mesmer, Franz Anton. *Mesmerism: A Translation of the Original Scientific and Medical Writings of F. A. Mesmer.* Los Altos, CA: Kaufmann, 1980.

Michell, John. *Eccentric Lives and Peculiar Notions.* 2nd ed. New York: Black Dog and Leventhal, 1999.

Milton, John. *Paradise Lost.* Edited by Philip Pullman. New York: Oxford University Press, 2005.

Modern Medicine (periodical, various dates embedded in text).

Monroe, Jack. "Making the Séance 'Serious': *Tables Tournantes* and the Second Empire Bourgeois Culture, 1852–1861." *History of Religions* 38, no. 3 (February 1999): 219–46.

Monroe, John Warne. *Laboratories of Faith: Mesmerism, Spiritism, and Occultism in Modern France.* Ithaca, NY: Cornell University Press, 2008.

Montrose, Louis. *The Purpose of Playing: Shakespeare and the Cultural Politics of the Elizabethan Theatre.* Chicago: University of Chicago Press, 1996.

Moore, R. Laurence. "Spiritualism and Science: Reflections on the First Decade of Spirit Rappings." *American Quarterly* 24, no. 4 (1972): 474–500.

Morning Light: The New-Church Weekly (periodical, various dates embedded in text).

Muir, Kenneth. Review of *Shakespearian Dimensions*, by G. Wilson Knight. *Modern Language Review* 83 (1988): 406–7.

Murphy, Arthur. *The Life of David Garrick.* 2 vols. Dublin: Brett Smith, 1801.

National Spiritualist Association of the United States of America. *Spiritualist Manual.* Rev. ed. Washington, DC: National Spiritualist Association of the United States of America, 1925.

New York Times, The (newspaper, various dates embedded in text).

North American Review, The (periodical, various dates embedded in text).

Nuttall, A. D. *A New Mimesis: Shakespeare and the Representation of Reality.* New York: Methuen, 1983.

O'Donnell, Elliott. *The Menace of Spiritualism.* New York: Frederick A. Stokes, 1920.

O'Farrell, Clare. *Michel Foucault.* London: Sage Publications, 2005.

Ogden, Tom. *The Complete Idiot's Guide to Ghosts and Hauntings.* Indianapolis, IN: Alpha Books, 1999.

Oppenhiem, Janet. *The Other World: Spiritualism and Psychical Research in England, 1850–1914.* Cambridge: Cambridge University Press, 1985.

Ovason, David. *Shakespeare's Secret Booke: Deciphering Magical and Rosicrucian Codes.* Forest Row, East Sussex: Clairview, 2010.

Owen, Alex. *The Darkened Room: Women, Power and Spiritualism in Late Victorian England.* Philadelphia: University of Pennsylvania Press, 1989.

Owen, Orville Ward. *Sir Francis Bacon's Cipher Story.* 5 vols. Detroit, MI: Howard, 1893–1895.

Owen, Robert Dale. *The Debatable Land Between This World and the Next: With Illustrative Narrations.* London: Trübner, 1871.

Palfrey, Simon. *Late Shakespeare: A New World of Words.* Oxford: Clarendon Press, 1997.

Parisious, Roger Nyle. "Occultist Influence on the Authorship Controversy." *The Elizabethan Review* 6, no. 1 (Spring 1998): 9–43.

Patterson, Annabel. *Censorship and Interpretation: The Conditions of Writing and Reading in Early Modern England.* Madison: University of Wisconsin Press, 1984.

Pearsall, Ronald. *The Table-Rappers: The Victorians and the Occult.* 1972. Reprint, Stroud, Gloucestershire: Sutton, 2004.

Pechter, Edward. *Shakespeare Studies Today: Romanticism Lost.* New York: Palgrave Macmillan, 2011.

Peebles, J. M. *Seers of the Ages: Embracing Spiritualism Past and Present.* Chicago: Progressive Thinker, 1903.

Peterson, Larry Richard. *Ignatius Donnelly: A Psychohistorical Study in Moral Development Psychology: Dissertations in American Biography.* PhD Thesis, University of Minnesota, 1977. Reprint, New York: Arno Press, 1982.

Philadelphia Inquirer (periodical, various dates embedded in text).

Phreno-Magnet, and Mirror of Nature, The (periodical, various dates embedded in text).

Pincock, Stephen. *Codebreaker: The History of Codes and Ciphers, from the Ancient Pharaohs to Quantum Cryptography.* New York: Walker, 2006.

Popular Science Monthly, The (periodical, various dates embedded in text).

Potter, Lois. *Secret Rites and Secret Writing: Royalist Literature, 1641–1660.* Cambridge: Cambridge University Press, 1989.

Pressing, R. G. *Rappings That Startled the World: Facts About the Fox Sisters.* Lily Dale, NY: Dale News, [1940?].

Price, G. Ward. *Extra-Special Correspondent.* London: G. Harrap, 1957.

Price, Leah. "From Ghostwriter to Typewriter: Delegating Authority at *Fin de Siècle*." In *The Faces of Anonymity: Anonymous and Pseudonymous Publication from the Sixteenth to the Twentieth Century.* Edited by Robert J. Griffin, 211–31. London: Palgrave Macmillan, 2003.

Proceedings of the Society for Psychical Research (periodical, various dates embedded in text).

Punch (periodical, various dates embedded in text).

Rabkin, Norman. *Shakespeare and the Problem of Meaning.* Chicago: University of Chicago Press, 1981.

Redmond, Christopher. *A Sherlock Holmes Handbook.* Toronto: Simon and Pierre, 1993.

Reed, James. *Swedenborg and the New Church.* Boston: Houghton, Osgood, 1880.

Report on Spiritualism of the Committee of the London Dialectical Society. London: Longmans, Green, Reader and Dyer, 1871.

Rhodes, Neil. "Tarzan of Athens, Dionysus in Africa: Wilson Knight and Wole Soyinka." In *Tragedy in Transition*. Edited by Sarah Annes Brown and Catherine Silverstone, 232–48. Oxford: Blackwell, 2007.

Richet, Charles Robert. *Thirty Years of Psychical Research: Being a Treatise on Metaphysics*. Translated by Stanley De Brath. London: Collins and Sons, 1923.

Riskin, Jessica. *Science in the Age of Sensibility: The Sentimental Empiricists of the French Enlightenment*. Chicago: University of Chicago Press, 2002.

Ritson, Joseph. *Remarks, Critical and Illustrative, on the Text and Notes of the Last Edition of Shakspeare*. London: J. Johnson, 1783.

Roach, Mary. *Spook: Science Tackles the Afterlife*. New York: W. W. Norton, 2005.

Robert-Houdin, Jean-Eugène. *Memoirs of Robert-Houdin: Ambassador, Author, and Conjurer*. Translated by R. Shelton Mackenzie. Philadelphia: G. G. Evan, 1859.

Roberts, Daisy O. *Why in the World?* London: Linden Press, 1961.

Roberts, Daisy O., and Collin E. Woolcock. *Elizabethan Episode Incorporating Shakespeare and Co., Unlimited*. London: Regency Press, 1961.

Roberts, Lewis C. "'The Production of a Female Hand': Professional Writing and the Career of Geraldine Jewsbury." *Women's Writing* 12, no. 3 (2005): 399–418.

Robertson, John Mackinnon. *Pioneer Humanists*. London: Watts, 1907.

Rochelle, Gerald. *Behind Time: The Incoherence of Time and McTaggart's Atemporal Replacement*. Brookfield, VT: Ashgate, 1998.

Rogers, L. W. *Ghosts in Shakespeare*. Chicago: Theo Book Co., 1925.

Rogo, D. Scott. *Parapsychology: A Century of Inquiry*. New York: Taplinger, 1975.

Rosenberg, Marvin. *The Masks of Hamlet*. Newark: University of Delaware Press: Associated University Presses, 1992.

———. *The Masks of Macbeth*. Newark: University of Delaware Press, 1992.

Rosenheim, Shawn James. *The Cryptographic Imagination: Secret Writing from Edgar Poe to the Internet*. Baltimore, MD: Johns Hopkins University Press, 1997.

Routledge, Edmund, ed. *Every Boy's Book: A Complete Encyclopædia of Sports and Amusements*. London: George Routledge and Sons, 1881.

Ruedebusch, Emil F. *The Old and the New Ideal*. Mayville, WI: self-published, 1896.

Ruskin, John. *Sesame and Lilies*. Rev. ed. New York: John Wiley and Son, 1873.

Sage, Lorna, Germaine Greer, and Elaine Showalter, eds. *The Cambridge Guide to Women's Writing in English*. New York: Cambridge University Press, 1999.

Sale, Robert. "G. Wilson Knight." *Modern Language Quarterly* 29 (March 1968): 77–83.

San Jose News (newspaper, various dates embedded in text).

Saunders, J. "Civic Government." *London* 5–6 (1843): 81–96.

Scherzinger, Martin Rudoy. "Music, Spirit Possession and the Copyright Law: Cross-Cultural Comparisons and Strategic Speculations." *Yearbook for Traditional Music* 31 (1999): 102–25.

Schmitt, Kari Anne Rand. *The Authorship of The Equatorie of the Planetis*. Woodbridge: D. S. Brewer/Boydell and Brewer, 1993.

Schneider, Ben Ross Jr., ed., *Index to the London Stage, 1660–1800*. Carbondale: Southern Illinois University Press, 1979.

Schoenbaum, Samuel. *Shakespeare's Lives*. New ed. New York: Oxford University Press, 1993.

Schrage, Michael. "Writing to Collaborate: Collaborating to Write." In *Author-ity and Textuality: Current Views of Collaborative Writing*. Edited by James S. Leonard, Christine E. Wharton, Robert Murray Davis, and Jeanette Harris, 17–22. West Cornwall, CT: Locust Hull Press, 1994.

Schuld, J. Joyce. *Foucault and Augustine: Reconsidering Power and Love*. Notre Dame, IN: University of Notre Dame Press, 2003.

Schutte, Nicola S., and John M. Malouff. *Why We Read and How Reading Transforms Us: The Psychology of Engagement With Text*. Lewiston, NY: Edwin Mellen Press, 2006.

Scott, Walter. *The Journal of Sir Walter Scott, From the Original Manuscript at Abbotsford*. 2 vols. Edinburgh: David Douglas, 1890.

Sewall, May Wright. *Neither Dead Nor Sleeping*. Indianapolis, IN: Bobbs-Merrill, 1920.

Shaaber, M. A. "The Furness Variorum Shakespeare." *Proceedings of the American Philosophical Society* 75 (1935): 281–85.

Shakespeare, William. *The Plays of William Shakespeare*, ed. Samuel Johnson. 8 vols. London: Printed for J. and R. Tonson, 1765,

———. *The Riverside Shakespeare*. Edited by G. Blakemore Evans and J. J. M. Tobin. 2nd ed. New York: Houghton Mifflin, 1997.

Shakespeariana, Shakespeare Society of New York (periodical, various dates embedded in text).

Shapiro, James. *Contested Will: Who Wrote Shakespeare?* New York: Simon and Schuster, 2010.

Sharp, Lynn L. *Secular Spirituality: Reincarnation and Spiritism in Nineteenth-Century France*. Lanham, MD: Lexington Books, 2006.

Shatford, Sarah Taylor. *Shakespeare's Revelations by Shakespeare's Spirit*. New York: Torch Press, 1919.

Shelton, Harriet M. *Abraham Lincoln Returns*. New York: Evans, 1957.

Sherme, Michael. *In Darwin's Shadow: The Life and Science of Alfred Russel Wallace: A Biographical Study on the Psychology of History*. New York: Oxford University Press, 2002.

Silberer, Herbert. *Problems of Mysticism and Its Symbolism*. New York: Moffat, Yard, 1917.

Silver, Alan. *Jews, Myth and History: A Critical Exploration of Contemporary Jewish Belief*. Leicester: Matador/Troubadour, 2008.

Sinfield, Alan. *Cultural Politics—Queer Reading*. Philadelphia: University of Pennsylvania Press, 1994.

Singer, Charles. *From Magic to Science: Essay on the Scientific Twilight*. New York: Dover Publications, 1968.

Smith, Eleanor Touhey. *Psychic People*. New York: William Morrow, 1968.

Smith, Emma. "The Critical Reception of Shakespeare." In *The New Cambridge Companion to Shakespeare*. Edited by Margreta de Grazia and Stanley Wells, 253–67. Cambridge: Cambridge University Press, 2010.

Smith, Hester Travers (see entries for Dowden, Hester).

Smith, Paul. "The Cottingley Fairies: The End of a Legend." In *The Good People: New Fairylore Essays*. Edited by Peter Narváez, 371–405. New York: Garland, 1991.

Snape, Michael. "Civilians, Soldiers and Perceptions of the Afterlife in Britain during the First World War." In *The Church, the Afterlife, and the Fate of the Soul*. Edited by Peter Clarke and Tony Claydon, 371–403. Rochester, NY: Boydell Press, 2009.

Somerville, Margaret J. "Editorial: 'Waiting in the Chaotic Place of Unknowing': Articulating Postmodern Emergence." *International Journal of Qualitative Studies in Education* 21, no. 3 (May–June 2008), 209–20.

Spiritual Magazine, The (periodical, various dates embedded in text).

Spokane Daily Chronicle (newspaper, various dates embedded in text).

Sprawson, Charles. "The True Stoic," review of *Stowe: The History of a Public School, 1923–1989* by Brian Rees. *The Spectator*, February 7, 2009. http://www.spectator.co.uk/books/3322756/part_3/the-true-stoic.thtml

Spurgeon, Caroline. *Shakespeare's Imagery and What It Tells Us*. Cambridge: Cambridge University Press, 1958.

Stanley, William. *The Case of The Fox: Being His Prophecies, Under Hypnotism, of the Period Ending A.D. 1950: A Political Utopia*. London: Truslove and Hanson, 1903.

Steiner, Rudolf. *Spiritualism, Madame Blavatsky, and Theosophy: An Eye Witness View of Occult History*. Edited by Christopher Bamford. Great Barrington, MA: Anthroposophic Press, 2001.

Stewart, Stanley. *"Renaissance" Talk: Ordinary Language and the Mystique of Critical Problems*. Pittsburgh, PA: Duquesne University Press, 1997.

Stillinger, Jack. *Multiple Authorship and the Myth of Solitary Genius*. New York: Oxford University Press, 1991.

Storm, Margaret. *Return of the Dove*. Baltimore, MD: Margaret Storm, 1957.

Strachey, Lytton. "Shakespeare's Final Period." *Books and Characters*. New York Harcourt, Brace, 1922. 49–69.

Stuart, Nancy Rubin. *The Reluctant Spiritualist: The Life of Maggie Fox*. New York: Harcourt, 2005.

Sturgess, Kim C. *Shakespeare and the American Nation*. New York: Cambridge University Press, 2004.

Sunday Independent (newspaper, various dates embedded in text).

Swedenborg, Emmanuel. *True Christian Religion: Containing the Universal Theology of the New Church*. 2 vols. London: J. Phillips, 1781.

Swinburne, Algernon Charles. *A Study of Ben Jonson*. London: Chatto and Windus, 1889.

Sword, Helen. *Ghostwriting Modernism*. Ithaca, NY: Cornell University Press, 2002.

Tafel, Johann Friedrich Immanuel. *Documents Concerning the Life and Character of Emanuel Swedenborg*. Manchester: Joseph Hayward, 1841.

Tannenbaum, Samuel A. "Farewell to 'Vllorxa,'" *Shakespeare Association Bulletin* 11, no. 1 (January 1936): 41–45.

Taylor, Gary. *Reinventing Shakespeare: A Cultural History from the Restoration to the Present*. New York: Oxford University Press, 1989.

Taylor, Thomas. *The Theoretic Arithmetic of the Pythagoreans*. Los Angeles: Phoenix Press, 1934.

Theobald, Lewis. *Shakespeare Restored: Or, a Specimen of Many Errors, As Well Commited, and Unamended, by Mr. Pope in His Late Edition of This Poet*. London: Francklin, J. Woodman and D. Lyon, and C. Davis, 1726.

Theosophy (periodical, various dates embedded in text).

Thompson, Ann, and John O. Thompson. *Shakespeare: Meaning and Metaphor*. Iowa City: University of Iowa Press, 1987.

Tibbets, Luther Calvin. *Spirit of the South*. Washington, DC: np., 1869.

Tillyard, E. M. W. *Essays Literary and Educational*. New York: Barnes and Noble, 1962.

———. *Shakespeare's Last Plays*. London: Chatto and Windus, 1938.

Toksvig, Signe. *Emanuel Swedenborg: Scientist and Mystic*. London: Faber, 1949.

Tran, Jonathan. *Foucault and Theology*. New York: Continuum, 2011.

Triezenberg, Henry J. *Spiritualism: Asking the Dead*. Grand Rapids, MI: Zondervan, 1939.

Trilling, Lionel. "On the Teaching of Modern Literature." *The Moral Obligation to Be Intelligent*. New York: Farrar, Straus and Giroux, 2000. 381–401.

Tromp, Marlene. *Altered States: Sex, Nation, Drugs, and Self-Transformation in Victorian Spiritualism*. Albany: State University of New York Press, 2006.

Tuttle, Hudson, and J. M. Peebles. *The Year-Book of Spiritualism for 1871*. Boston: William White, 1871.

Underhill [née Fox], A. Leah. *The Missing Link in Modern Spiritualism*. New York: Thomas R. Knox, 1885.

Van Domelen, John E. *Tarzan of Athens: A Biographical Study of G. Wilson Knight*. Bristol: Redcliffe, 1987.

Velz, John W. "G. Wilson Knight Revisited: *The Shakespearian Tempest* and the Symbolic Interpretation of Shakespeare." *Symbolism: An International Journal of Critical Aesthetics* 1 (January 2000): 21–40.

———. Review of *Shakespearian Dimensions*, by G. Wilson Knight. *Shakespeare Studies* 18 (1986): 292–94

Venton, W. B. *Analyses of Shake-speares Sonnets Using the Cipher Code*. London: Mitre Press, 1968.

Vickers, Brian. "Analogy versus Identity: The Rejection of Occult Symbolism, 1580–1680." In *Occult and Scientific Mentalities in the Renaissance*. Edited by Brian Vickers, 95–164. Cambridge: Cambridge University Press, 1984.

Vince, Ronald W. *Ancient and Medieval Theatre: A Historiographical Handbook*. Westport, CT: Greenwood Press, 1984.

Vinitsky, Ilya. *Ghostly Paradoxes: Modern Spiritualism and Russian Culture in the Age of Reason*. Toronto: University of Toronto Press, 2009.

Virgil. *The Aeneid*. Translated by W. F. Jackson Knight. Baltimore, MD: Penguin Books, 1956.

Vivian, Joyce Mary (see entries for Dowden, Hester).

Walker, D. P. *Spiritual and Demonic Magic from Ficino to Campanella*. London: Warburg Institute, University of London, 1958.

Walter, James. *Shakespeare's True Life*. London: Longmans, Green, 1890.

Wanganui Chronicle (newspaper, various dates embedded in text).

Warren, Samuel M. *Compendium of the Theological Writings of Emanuel Swedenborg, A*. New York: Board of Publication of the General Convention of the New Jerusalem in the U.S., 1875.

Warton, Thomas. *An Enquiry into the Authenticity of the Poems Attributed to Thomas Rowley*. London: J. Dodsley, 1782.

Washington, Peter. *Madame Blavatsky's Baboon: A History of the Mystics, Mediums, and Misfits Who Brought Spiritualism to America*. 1993. Reprint, New York: Schocken Books, 1995.

Watson, Albert Durrant. *The Twentieth Plane: A Psychic Revelation*. Philadelphia: George W. Jacobs, 1919.

Weisberg, Barbara. *Talking to the Dead: Kate and Maggie Fox and the Rise of Spiritualism*. New York: HarperCollins, 2004.

Welleck, René. *A History of Modern Criticism: 1750–1950*. 8 vols. New Haven, CT: Yale University Press, 1986.

Wells, Stanley. *Coffee with Shakespeare*. London: Duncan Baird; New York: distributed in the USA by Sterling, 2008.

Westfall, Richard S. *The Life of Isaac Newton*. Cambridge: Cambridge University Press, 1994.

West, Robert Hunter. *Shakespeare and the Outer Mystery*. Lexington: University of Kentucky Press, 1968.

White, Michael. *Isaac Newton: The Last Sorcerer*. New York: Basic Books, 1999.

White, R. S. "Where is Shakespeare's Autobiography?" In *Early Modern Autobiography: Theories, Genres, Practices*. Edited by Ronald Bedford, Lloyd Davis, and Philippa Kelly, 174–88. Ann Arbor: University of Michigan, 2006.

Williams, William Carlos. *The Embodiment of Knowledge*. Introduction by Ron Loewinsohn. New York: New Directions, 1977.

Wilson, Derek. *Sir Francis Walsingham: A Courtier in an Age of Terror*. New York: Carroll and Graf, 2007.

Wilson, Ian. *The After Death Experience: The Physics of the Non-Physical*. London: Sidgwick and Jackson, 1987.

Wilson, Richard. *Secret Shakespeare: Studies in Theatre, Religion and Resistance*. New York: Manchester University Press, 2004.

———. *Shakespeare in French Theory: King of Shadows*. New York: Routledge/Francis and Taylor, 2007.

Wimsatt, William Kurtz. *The Verbal Icon: Studies in the Meaning of Poetry*. 1954. Reprint, Lexington: University of Kentucky, 1982.

Windschuttle, Keith. *The Killing of History: How Literary Critics and Social Theorists Are Murdering Our Past*. New York: Free Press, 1997.

Wiseman, Timothy Peter. *Talking to Virgil: A Miscellany*. Exeter: University of Exeter Press, 1992.

Wittgenstein, Ludwig. *On Certainty*. Edited by G. E. M. Anscombe and G. H. von Wright. Translated by Denis Paul and G. E. M. Anscombe. New York: Harper and Row, 1969.

Wood, James. *The Broken Estate: Essays on Literature and Belief.* New York: Random House/Modern Library, 2000.

Wyckoff, James. *Franz Anton Mesmer: Between God and Devil.* Englewood Cliffs, NJ: Prentice-Hall, 1975.

Yale Law Journal (periodical, various dates embedded in text).

Young, R. V. *At War with the Word: Literary Theory and Liberal Education.* Wilmington, DE: ISI Books, 1999.

Žižek, Slavoj. *The Žižek Reader.* Edited by Elizabeth Wright and Edmond Wright. Malden, MA: Blackwell, 1999.

Zoist: A Journal of Cerebral Physiology and Mesmerism, and Their Applications to Human Welfare, The (periodical, various dates embedded in text).

Zöllner, Johann Carl Friedrich. *Transcendental Physics.* Translated by Charles Carleton Massey. New York: W. H. Harrison, 1880.

Zunshine, Lisa. *Why We Read Fiction: Theory of Mind and the Novel.* Columbus: Ohio State University Press, 2006.

Zusne, Leonard, and Warren H. Jones. *Anomalistic Psychology: A Study of Magical Thinking.* Hillsdale, NJ: L. Erlbaum, 1989.

INDEX

Allen, Percy, 1, 77, 79–82, 86–88, 91, 93, 94–95, 130, 138, 139, 159, 161
Anderson, Olivia, 26, 147, 219n94, 219n97
Arensberg, Walter, 50–54, 56, 60, 61, 62, 72
Arnold, Matthew, 11, 26
Asquith, Clare, 68

Bacon, Delia, 39–42, 44, 45, 49, 52, 65, 157
Bacon, Francis, 6, 8, 10, 11, 38, 44, 71, 72, 74, 77–79, 80, 81, 139
  alleged invention of an airship, 48
  alleged murder of Shakespeare, 47
  alleged secret manuscripts, 48, 49–50
  alleged son to Queen Elizabeth, 47, 77, 78 (*see also* Shakespeare, William)
Barnum, P. T., 2, 25, 99
Barsi-Greene, Margaret, 61
Barthes, Roland, 3, 82, 84, 88
Beckett, Jane W., 64
Belsey, Catherine, 68, 69
Benjamin, Louis, 9, 10
Bentley, E. C., 75
Betterton, Thomas, 25
Bloom, Harold, 5, 157, 159
Bond, Frederick Bligh, 89, 92–93
Bowdler, Thomas, 26
Bradley, Andrew Cecil, 128
Bradshaw, Graham, 70
Bristol, Michael D., 4, 5, 104, 157
Browne, Hugh Junor, 17
Bruns, Gerald L., 156

Bucke, Richard Maurice, 12
Burgess, William, 27
Bush, George, 32

Caffray, Joseph, 118
Carlyle, Thomas, 26, 40
Chaloner, John Armstrong, 1–2
Christie, John D., 143, 144
Cook, Florence, 112–13, 153
Cooke, George Frederick, 118
Coursen, H. R., 70
Crabbe, George, 155
cryptogram, 39–67, 69, 72
Cummins, Geraldine, 89–90, 92–93, 128, 138
Cunningham, Wallace McCook, 72

Darnton, Robert, 33
De Casseres, Benjamin, 10, 159
de Vere, Edward (Earl of Oxford), 6, 80, 81–82, 87, 131, 140 (*see also* Shakespeare, William)
Dickens, Charles, 25
Dobson, Michael, 64–65, 147, 184n57
Dodd, Alfred, 10, 11, 54–56, 62–63, 71, 77–79, 80, 81, 82, 91, 136, 159
Dodd, William, 26
Donnelly, Ignatius, 12, 42–45, 47, 52, 54, 56
Doten, Lizzie, 2
Dowden, Edward, 73–77
Dowden, Hester, 74–82, 86–95, 161
Doyle, Arthur Conan, 2, 149–54, 157
Drabelle, Dennis, 102
Duncan, Helen, 78
Dunne, John William, 10, 128

ectoplasm, 11, 13, 78, 100, 101, 103, 112, 128, 149, 163
Edmonds, John Worth, 14
Ehnenn, Jill R., 88
Ellis, John M., 8, 157
Emerson, Ralph Waldo, 12

Foster, Charles Henry, 10, 11, 17, 21
Foucault, Michel, 3, 82–85, 88, 93
Fox, David, 99, 164
Fox sisters, 32, 34, 98–103
    Kate, 32, 34, 97, 98, 99, 101, 113, 121
    Leah, 34, 99, 101, 121, 163
    Margaret or Maggie, 6–7, 34, 110–22
Franklin, Benjamin (ghost of), 32, 101
Franklin, Colin, 105
Frey, Charles H., 4, 5
Friedman, William F. and Elizabeth S., 6
Fripp, Peter, 89, 93, 138
Furness, Horace Howard, 6, 32, 103–22, 135, 136, 161
Furnivall, James Frederick, 76

Gallup, Elizabeth, 48–50, 52, 78
Gardner, Edward, 149–50
Garrick, David, 22–25
Gildon, Charles, 55
Goodall, Jane, 33
Grazia, Margreta de, 4, 5
Grebanier, Bernard, 50
Green, Frances H., 36
Greenblatt, Stephen, 4, 33, 125, 157, 160
Griffiths, Elsie and Frances, 149, 150, 152
Güldenstubbé, Ludwig de, 119–20

Haarhoff, Theodore Johannes, 134, 136, 137, 138, 144
Hawkes, Terence, 4, 5, 66, 69, 125, 159
Hawthorne, Nathaniel, 40, 41
Hemans, Dorothea Browne, 119

Houdini, Harry, 35, 115, 151–52, 153
Howard, E. Lee, 12
Hugo, Victor, 2, 13
Husserl, Edmund, 83
Hyslop, James Hervey, 11

Isherwood, Christopher, 50

Jeffrey, Francis, 26
Johnson, Edward D., 62
Johnson, Samuel, 104, 155
Jones, Kelvin I., 155

Kane, Elisha Kent, 102
Kant, Immanuel, 19, 69
Kardec, Allan (Hippolyte Léon Denizard Rivail), 188n81
Kiddle, Henry, 2, 10
King, Katie. *See* Cook, Florence
Kipling, Rudyard, 55
Knight, Caroline (physical and ghostly), 10, 123–24, 135–36, 140, 141, 142
Knight, George Wilson, 7, 10, 11, 160, 161
    career, 124
    collaborates with dead brother's spirit, 142–44
    communicates with dead father, mother, and brothers, 135–39
    communicates with Shakespeare, 138–39
    critical reception/reputation, 124–25
    key concepts, 128–32
    message for Jeffrey Kahan, 147–48
    Spiritualism and Shakespeare criticism, 125–28
    Spiritualist-infused performances, 144–47
Knight, William Francis Jackson, 123, 124, 126, 135–39, 141, 142, 160,
    career, 132–33
    collaborates with Virgil's ghost, 134–35
    posthumous collaboration, 142–44

Lamb, Charles, 30
Leadbeater, Charles Webster, 152, 154
Lehmann, Courtney, 3, 173n13
Livermore, Charles F., 101
Lodge, Oliver, 51, 154

Mallin, Eric S., 4, 5
Malone, Edmond, 25, 26, 67, 105, 106, 107, 109, 158
Marcus, Leah, 69
Maskeyne, John Nevil, 115
Massey, Gerald, 10, 12
McAlindon, Tom, 157
McMullan, Gordon, 73
McTaggert, John M. E., 10
Merleau-Ponty, Maurice, 83
Merrill, James, 9
Mesmer, Anton, 18, 19, 31–32, 33, 48, 127, 164
Milton, John, 155
Montgomery, Charles Alexander, 61, 72
Montrose, Louis, 68
Mordue, Olivia. *See* Anderson, Olivia

Nuttall, Anthony David, 156

O'Donnell, Elliot, 15
Oppenhiem, Janet, 179nn71–72, 211n68
Ovason, David, 64
Owen, Orville W., 46–48, 49
Owen, Robert Dale, 100

Parisious, Roger Nyle, 79
Patterson, Annabel, 68
Pechter, Edward, 157
Pope, Alexander, 105, 158

Rabkin, Norman, 67, 156
Rackham, Arthur, 153
Raleigh, Walter, 104
Ritson, Joseph, 25
Roberts, Daisy O., 9, 10, 13, 139
Rogers, Evan, 103
Rowe, Nicholas, 25, 55, 105

Schrage, Michael, 88
Schuld, J. Joyce, 83
Scott, Walter, 26
Sewall, May Wright, 35–36
Seybert, Henry, 103, 111
Seybert Commission, 104, 109–13, 120
Shakespeare, William
  authorship (sole, collaborative, posthumous, pseudonymous), 10–11, 88–92, 95, 126, 140, 158–59, 160
  critical mysticism, of 67–72
  cryptographs, riddles, 46, 57, 65–66
  proto-Spiritualist beliefs within plays, 27–30
  Spiritualist-themed messages from beyond, 1–3, 11, 18–19, 46, 81
  superstitious embarrassment, 6, 30–31
Shakespeare Jubilee (and religiosity of), 22–25
Shapiro, James, 66, 67
Shatford, Sarah, 2, 9, 11, 127
Shelton, Harriet M., 12
Sinfield, Alan, 67
Singer, Charles, 56
Sitwell, George, 153, 154
Slade, Henry, 114–16, 117
Soal, Samuel George, 89, 90
Spiritualism, 1–2
  beliefs, common manifestations, techniques, 12–15, 163–68
  connection to Buddhism, Hinduism, Mesmerism, Satanism, Swedenborgism, Theosophy, 22, 31, 32, 120, 149, 153, 164, 168, 177n61, 187n70, 218n84
  fairies, 89, 149–50, 152–53
  publications, 128
  Spirit Photography, 77, 136, 145, 152–53, 154, 167
  Spirit rapping, 34, 97–100, 109–11, 167

Spiritualism (*continued*)
   Spirit Realm, also known as
      Summerland, and amusements,
      1, 2, 6, 9, 11, 13, 17, 21, 22, 32,
      85, 88, 93, 95, 127, 130, 137,
      139, 141, 142, 160, 166, 167
   Spirit's progress, 11, 135, 167–68
   Spirit Wavelength, 9, 127, 133, 144,
      167, 178n67, 187n74
   theatricality, 32–38, 107, 108–9,
      112–13
Stallybrass, Peter, 4, 5
Steevens, George, 25, 107
Stillinger, Jack, 85
Swedenborg, Emmanuel, 18, 19–22,
   32, 81, 127, 168
Sword, Helen, 125

Taylor, Gary, 5, 105
Taylor, George, 101
Thompson, Ann and John O., 155–56
Tillyard, Eustace Mandeville Wetenhall,
   199n1, 227n40
Travers-Smith, Mrs. Richard. *See*
   Dowden, Hester
Triezenberg, Henry J., 14
Tromp, Marlene, 211n69

Underhill, Daniel, 100, 110

Vickers, Brian, 156
Vivian, Gwendolen, 94–95
Vivian, Joyce. *See* Dowden,
   Hester

Walter, James, 27
Warburton, William, 155
Warton, Thomas, 106
Watson, William, 75, 76
Wells, Stanley, 160
West, Elizabeth Dickinson, 75, 76
White, R. S., 9
Wilde, Oscar (ghost of), 89–90,
   95
Williams, William Carlos, 50
Wilson, Richard, 68
Wimsatt, William K., 125
Windschuttle, Keith, 157
Wittgenstein, Ludwig, 67, 70
Woods, James, 156

Young, Robert V., 157

Zenor, Richard, 36–37
Zöllner, Johann, 115–16

CPSIA information can be obtained at www.ICGtesting.com
Printed in the USA
LVOW10*1459021213

363566LV00011B/463/P